POP PAGANS

STUDIES IN CONTEMPORARY AND HISTORICAL PAGANISM
Series Editors: Chas S. Clifton and Nikki Bado

This series examines all aspects of paganism, from historical case studies to burgeoning contemporary practices.

Pop Pagans: Paganism and Popular Music
Edited by Donna Weston and Andy Bennett

Modern Pagan and Native Faith Movements in Central and Eastern Europe
Edited by Kaarina Aitamurto and Scott Simpson

POP PAGANS
Paganism and Popular Music

Edited by
DONNA WESTON AND ANDY BENNETT

Routledge
Taylor & Francis Group

LONDON AND NEW YORK

First published 2013 by Acumen

Published 2014 by Routledge
2 Park Square, Milton Park, Abingdon, Oxon OX14 4RN
711 Third Avenue, New York, NY 10017, USA

Routledge is an imprint of the Taylor & Francis Group, an informa business

ISBN: 978-1-84465-646-2 (hardcover)
       978-1-84465-647-9 (paperback)

British Library Cataloguing-in-Publication Data
A catalogue record for this book is available from the British Library.

Typeset in Warnock Pro by JS Typesetting Ltd, Mid Glamorgan, UK.

CONTENTS

CONTRIBUTORS

Andy Bennett is professor of cultural sociology and director of the Griffith Centre for Cultural Research at Griffith University, Queensland, Australia.

Christopher Chase is a lecturer in the Department of Philosophy and Religious Studies, Iowa State University, USA.

Douglas Ezzy is associate professor and head of school in the School of Sociology and Social Work, University of Tasmania, Australia.

Graham Harvey is a reader in religious studies at the Open University, UK.

Andy Letcher is a lecturer, freelance writer and folk musician based at Oxford Brookes University, Oxford, UK.

Narelle McCoy is a lecturer and PhD candidate at the Queensland Conservatorium, Griffith University, Queensland, Australia.

Alan Nixon is a doctoral candidate in the Religion and Society Research Centre, University of Western Sydney, Australia.

Christopher Partridge is professor of religious studies in the Department of Politics, Philosophy and Religion, Lancaster University, UK.

Jason Pitzl-Waters is an independent Pagan writer, journalist and DJ, who can be contacted at jpitzl@wildhunt.org.

Adam Possamai is associate professor in the School of Sociology and co-director of the Religion and Society Research Centre, University of Western Sydney, Australia.

Graham St John is an independent researcher and executive editor of *Dancecult: Journal of Electronic Dance Music Culture.*

Rupert Till is a senior lecturer the School of Music, Humanities and Media and the Centre for Research in New Music, University of Huddersfield, UK.

Deena Weinstein is professor of sociology, DePaul University, Chicago, IL, United States.

Donna Weston is a senior lecturer in popular music and deputy director at the Queensland Conservatorium, Griffith University, Gold Coast, Australia.

FOREWORD

Graham Harvey

"The isle is full of noises" (Shakespeare, *The Tempest* 3.2.148). It is too good a line not to quote! Rich, resonant and evocative. The whole speech invites us to attend to what enters our ears but largely gets filtered out by our brains: the entire cacophony of sound in which we find ourselves immersed. So much calls out for our attention, far more than Caliban could have dreamed of on his island – well, so much more human noise, anyway. Perhaps there is incrementally less other-than-human noise. Though the wind and the rain may still be sonorously present, there are fewer animals, birds and insects each day. Fewer bees, for instance, "hum about mine ears" (*ibid.*).

Pagans often identify their religion as being "of nature". Whether this really means that it is somehow innate, primordial or natural may be debated (especially if the claim is that *this* religion is more innate, primordial or natural than any other way of acting in this small soundful planet). But the claim may certainly be expected to mean something about Pagan attempts to listen attentively to those noises that swirl around us all, enticing us to follow. Pagans might be people who listen to the "speaking earth", as the title of my book about Paganism claimed (Harvey 2007). Valuation of and attention to what might be called nature, the environment, the larger-than-human world or the weather-world (Ingold 2011: 126–35) varies considerably among Pagans. Indeed, they are encouraged variably by different kinds of Paganism. Nonetheless, within this abundant variety Pagans are typically attentive to the sensual world and make efforts to be positively responsive to what their sensorium indicates is going on.

For some Pagans, again with varying emphases of effort and value, the domains of ancestry, heritage or ethnicity (or some sense of belonging-as-identity) present further opportunities to define Paganism as "natural". The stories and musics of the past can be (treated as) vital (and vitalizing perhaps) calls upon Pagans. So too, however, are contemporary needs and desires. The seemingly incessant noise of consumerist modernity (especially in marketing commercials and in competitive "talent shows") certainly generates a background noise against which all our lives take place. For many, of course, this is a noise worthy of celebration and participation. For others, it is oppressive and discordant – countering the desired sounds of alternative lifeways. Defining natural, popular, alternative and many more of our hard-working words and what they might say about contemporary culture is part of what makes Paganism interesting to many scholars.

In diverse ways, then, sounding out Pagan music is a promising venture. The relationship between Pagans and popular culture is a rich one, especially as it is rarely a neat one. There again, since "popular" can mean everything from "commercially successful" to "arising from among marginalized people rather than elites" (and much more), the scope of this exploration is potentially profligate! In this collection, the editors are to be congratulated for bringing together authors expert on a truly representative range of Pagan engagement with popular music and cognate performance cultures. Thus we get to read about everything from folk to metal, from efforts to express ethnicity to efforts to express psychedelic states of consciousness. Celebratory, incantational, polemical, meditative, mood and dance musics are all included. Scholars of religion and of music are offered a rich field of debate. No easy or too-neat a tune is played here – no single composition. Rather, we are forced to recognize both Paganism and popular music as diverse and conflictual arenas. The coexistence of different forms and expressions, of wildly different sounds and performed cultures/communities, is an exciting provocation of further reflection and research. The refusal to collapse diversity into some allegedly definitive cohering theme in relation to either Paganism or popular music is one of the great virtues of this book.

Paganisms and popular musics are continuously emergent. Their producers, performers, audiences, purchasers, supporters, disseminators, enthusiasts and researchers are continuously in production. Long gone are the days when "folk" could be imagined or presented as a label for a fixed phenomena. Fluid conversation, cross-fertilization and improvisation have become increasingly evident. Other genres (or music or cultural community-building) have rarely suffered the same allegation of static fixity, but have commonly been judged to evidence change and vitality. Thus we might think (again) that neither Paganism nor popular music is expressed in particular forms because there is no stable prior form awaiting expression. There is only ever an always nascent desire emerging. There are only relationships in negotiation. There is only conversation. Or rather, there are only conversations – plural. Paganisms are full of musics – and at last we are offered a vibrant introduction to their study. Popular musics are full of Pagan-like interests – and here, if not for the first time, certainly in a properly polyphonous way, we are offered enticing ways to engage with them.

Finally, celebrating the work of the editors and contributors to this book, I congratulate them on not giving us "the Pagan soundscape" but, with evident reference to Tim Ingold's ever insightful works (especially Ingold 2011), I am grateful for all that they speak of the "ensounding" of Paganism and popular music.

1. TOWARDS A DEFINITION OF PAGAN MUSIC

Donna Weston and Andy Bennett

In 1993, the first international Pagan studies conference was held, bringing together scholars from all over the world in fields as diverse as psychology, theology and ecology. In *Researching Paganisms*, published in 2004, Blain, Ezzy and Harvey cite multiplicity as central to the discipline of Pagan studies, and note that just as contemporary Paganisms are still evolving, so are the methodologies and approaches of those who choose to study them. Popular music studies is one area in which Pagan studies activity is only just emerging, yet – as seen in a Pagan history of celebration and story-telling through music – it is a voice through which Paganism might readily be expressed. Indeed, as this book explores, popular music has already proved a highly effective medium for the articulation of Pagan ideology and aesthetics. A diverse range of genres, from folk through punk and Goth to heavy metal, frequently embodies images and discourses drawn from Paganism. Similarly, a number of popular music artists profess a deep-seated investment in and expression of Paganism and Pagan identity through their music.

Depending on the interpretation, Paganism is a religion, a worldview, a way of life and even a human trait. This multiplicity varies according to modes of perception, reception and dissemination, and is represented in the range of topics discussed in the chapters of this book. This multiplicity is also reflected in the range of readers to whom this book will appeal: in the broad sense, it will be of benefit not only to those with an interest in Paganism and Pagan studies, but it will also raise questions for those engaged in studies of religion, particularly popular religion. As Catherine Albanese notes, "to suggest that religion is somehow implicated in the production of the popular is to nod toward that other thorny growth among academic problems regarding it – the meaning of popular religion" (Albanese 1996: 733). The topic will evidently be of interest to those with an interest in popular music studies in general, however, the subject raises interesting specific questions regarding intent versus interpretation, and of insider/outsider, emic/etic points of view – or any combination of the above along that continuum.

By investigating a group of popular music practices and cultures from a Pagan studies perspective, this book brings the two fields together in original ways that shed new light on both. It is intended that the readership of this book will be drawn from both Pagan studies and popular music studies – indeed, anyone with an interest in music and religion, and how the two connect. Because of the diverse background of that readership, a short discussion of what we mean by Pagan, and where popular music fits into that context, would seem a logical starting point.

PAGANISM

The distinction between Pagan and Neo-Pagan can be problematic, with the former sometimes used to describe pre-Christian Paganism, and the latter reconstructions of that religion. Contemporary Pagans may, however, reject the "Neo-" prefix as disconnecting Paganism from its past. In recognition of personal interpretations of these terms, for the purpose of this book authors have been allowed to choose the descriptor with which they feel most comfortable. Other variations may also arise – Andy Letcher, for example, prefers "pagan" (with a lower case "p") to refer to Pre-Christian paganism, and Pagan (upper case) to refer to contemporary practices, while Neo-Pagan is claimed to be the US equivalent of the latter. York uses the term "geoPaganism" to describe an unstructured, and somewhat unconscious, veneration of nature that is characteristic of what he calls "folk religion" (York 2003). He differentiates this from "recoPaganism", which he describes as more deliberate attempts to reconstruct the rituals of a Pagan past, such as is exemplified by "NeoPaganism" for example; both are subsumed under the broad Paganisms umbrella. Michael York leans towards a fluid definition, noting that what we might recognize as Pagan identities are in fact sharing selectively from a common pool, a list of Pagan characteristics.

Primarily, Pagan identity is constructed as a continuation of a religious tradition that, while having been suppressed – sometimes violently – during its history, can claim a pedigree extending long before the advent of Christianity, and at least to the Classical era. However, the difficulty in studying – and defining – Pagan religions lies partly in the fact that they are not organized systematically on a large scale, but rather consist of smaller local, national and international networks, groups and organizations, and also individual or sole practitioners, often networking through the internet. Paganism is evolving, fluid and non-codified, and has no orthodox form; indeed, Harvey (1997) suggests it is not an "ism" at all, but rather a broad movement. How, then, might a definition of these Paganisms be expressed? York proposes one definition: "Paganism is an affirmation of interactive and polymorphic sacred relationship by individual or community with the tangible, sentient and nonempirical" (York 2003: 161). Harvey (1997) defines it as a "polytheistic Nature religion" and an "ecological spirituality". A theme of interconnectedness links both of these descriptions, to which can be added animistic beliefs, polytheism and anthropomorphism, and a reverence for tradition, antiquity and ancestry. To this definition can also be appended the consistent expression of a veneration of "place". Paganism is rooted in the sacredness of place and, by extension, the divine in nature. York lists as characteristics "polytheism, animism, humanism, magic, organic and numinous qualities, pantheism or at least a quasi-pantheistic immanence of deity" (York 2003: 60).

"Paganism" is a term that encompasses pre-Christian European religions and many contemporary Pagan religions such as Wicca, Heathenism and Druidry. Its revival owes much to the ideologies of the Romantic era, through which nature was idealized, the "peasant" held up as representative of an idyllic lifestyle lived in harmony with nature, and the "noble savage" seen to be the connection to a lost utopia. Rousseau himself theorized an ancient polytheistic, nature-based religion, which he believed could be found again, offering an antidote to the ills of contemporary society. Contemporary Paganism also owes much to the folklore revival of this period, the *volk*, or people seen to have much in common with the idealized peasant. Folklore has informed much Pagan ritual since. Because of its history, modern Paganism is characterized by a blend of old and new practices – mostly Western, but also drawing on indigenous and Eastern belief systems. The Romans used the term *Paganus* to refer to rural dwellers, "people of place", those whose customs and rituals were intrinsically tied to their locality – and hence, to land. In English language usage, and within the context of the Christian hegemony, the term has come to mean anything from non-Christian to non-believer, and has often taken on negative or pejorative connotations. This definition of Paganism is sometimes reflected in the ways in which many Pagans construct their identity as oppositional to dominant Christian belief systems, by which some contemporary Pagans "have crafted a history for themselves that specifically links them to the marginalized and the oppressed" (Magliocco 2004: 187).

These kinds of binaries are, however, not useful ways by which to understand Paganism. This book is based on the concept of Paganism as more of a continuum – not a set of constructed beliefs that refer *to* nature, the earth and so on, but arising from the point of view of the earth manifesting *in* various culturally specific contexts, and which may be *informed by* phenomena held sacred to Pagans such as land, place, and nature. Sabina Magliocco describes how one Pagan community member describes Paganism as "somehow innate or essential, its seeds already present in childhood" (Magliocco 2004: 57), and notes that "the idea of Paganism as something natural or inherent is common in the movement" (*ibid*.: 58). Viewed in this way, Paganism can be seen more as something instinctual – a human condition – and therefore arguably as more mainstream than might immediately be obvious.

Considering Paganism – and Pagan studies – in this way removes the essentializing characteristics that problematize oppositional constructions of Pagan identity. By examining popular music and its practitioners through a Pagan "looking glass", and from a Pagan studies perspective, we can gain an understanding that not only emphasizes commonalities rather than difference, but that offers new insights into the production and consumption of popular music that are not evident in current approaches. This means understanding people through their connections to land or place, the ways in which they interact with it and how it informs their culture, not from an outside point of view but rather from one of mutual understanding. It means understanding "others" through the Pagan lens of "feeling" rather than the more distanced eye of observation and analysis, of being "in" the world of the music studied rather than "outside looking in".

PAGANISM AND MUSIC

As in many cultures, music plays an important role in Pagan practice. It is often the focal point of the many Pagan gatherings and festivals that occur throughout the world, some of which are specific music festivals. It can play a role in many aspects of Pagan ritual and is an important vehicle for the expression of Pagan beliefs. Pagan songs can express solidarity, or reinforce common Pagan beliefs. Magliocco (2004: 93–197) gives the example of "The Burning Times" by Charlie Murphy, the lyrics of which link European witches to Pagan religion, and describe their execution – usually by burning – as a "war against women", specifically by the Catholic Church. That memory of the burning times galvanizes contemporary Pagans is the theme of "We Won't Wait any Longer", by the late Gwydion Pendderwen, in which Pagans are survivors, ready to "rise again and reclaim what is theirs". It would be impossible to describe any one style of music that is specifically Pagan, and the diversity of Pagan music and music employed by Pagans is indeed representative of the range of popular music in general. However, the importance of music to Pagan culture is best evidenced through analysis of its presence in the one place that unites nearly all Pagans: online. The internet provides a vibrant virtual community for Pagan practitioners, and in many ways has contributed to the growth of the religion, connecting like-minded people and offering "Pagan advocacy and support networks operating at both national and international level", such as the Pagan Federation, the Circle Network, the Lady Liberty Network and the World Congress of Ethnic Religions (Strmiska 2005: 45). A survey of Pagan music sites on the internet reveals the diversity of the ways in which music and Paganism intersect. At the time of writing (2011), a YouTube search of the phrase "Pagan music" gave 545 hits, mostly original music from the English-speaking world, although Russia and Lithuania also made an appearance. The search also resulted in some instructional and more explanatory videos. The same search on Google resulted in 178,000 hits, which contained a combination of blogs, forums, online stores and more regular websites, while a search for "Pagan radio" resulted in 151,000 hits. A survey of these sites paints a telling picture of the importance of music to Pagan culture, while the variety of ways in which it is presented demonstrates the diversity of its membership.

Pagan Music and Poetry is one example of the kind of Pagan forum that offers members opportunities to discuss and share Pagan art and music. It is part of the Tribe.net network of websites, where members discuss topics of interest to them – this is part of a collection of "Tribes" dedicated to Pagan culture and is the one dedicated most prominently to music and the arts. It contains reviews, interviews and extensive forum discussions.[1] The *Pagan Dance Pagan Music Forum* is dedicated to a "love of spiritual dance, Paganism, Wicca, drumming, inkubus sukkubus, and all other Pagan music", and describes its target membership as those who are looking to find spirituality through music and dance, with a focus on Pagan music. The majority of the content is available to members of the forum only.[2] *The Pagan Wheel* describes itself as "all about Pagan Music", and is a blog dedicated to Pagan music of all kinds. It contains comprehensive forums and links, as well as CD reviews, and musician and band profiles. It also contains announcements of Pagan music events and gigs.[3] *The Bardic Blog* is the blog of Welsh musician Damh the Bard. It includes entries describing the Pagan music festivals and gigs in the United Kingdom that he attends, as well as Pagan music articles of interest. What he describes as Wiccan and Druidic music is most prominent.[4]

While the above examples show the ways in which Pagan music is discussed, its dissemination relies on sites such as that of Folk Records, a traditional and Slavic Pagan folk record label that offers free downloads of the bands on its roster as well as information on Slavic music and the Pagan culture of pre-Christian Russia, including a description of the different prominent genres of modern Slavic music that uphold traditional Slavic culture and Pagan spirituality.[5] Arula Records is a distribution and record company; its website consists of descriptions of the Pagan music on the label, and the artists who make it, alongside a catalogue and online store.[6] Serpentine Music Productions is a large Pagan music record label and distributor. The website is quite comprehensive, and the Pagan Music Library section contains links to blogs and articles on Pagan music.[7] Independent Pagan Music, Literature and Arts Label UK is an independent label based in Wiltshire in the United Kingdom. The site contains a catalogue of its affiliated artists, and various other information related to the label and its connected companies and artists.[8]

Related to online distributors of Pagan music are other sites that feature lists or collections of songs, which in some cases can be streamed. *The New Oral Tradition* (pagan music collection), for example, "includes new and original Pagan music by Willow Firesong and BarleySinger, along with Pagan music of all kinds collected from the web and other sources."[9] *Pagan Heart Music and Songs* is essentially a collection of streamed Pagan songs (or songs that the site's creator dubs as Pagan).[10] *Bardic Arts* contains an extensive list of "song, chant, poetry and satire for the Pagan community". When each chant or song is clicked on, it brings up the lyrics and information about the song, and contains links to online sources for the song, chant or poem that one is viewing.[11] *Pagan Playlist @ Pagan Space* is a Pagan community site where Pagans post their online playlists. This site contains comments on the playlists and a discussion forum.[12]

Other sites compile lists of links to various Pagan music sites on the web. *Witchvox*, or *Witch's Voice*, for example, promises a "Pagan music ... Celebration!" It is a large web community that is dedicated to all things Wiccan. This site contains a list of links and essays discussing Pagan music, predominantly centred on the United States. It contains a link to *Witch's Voice: Pagan Music on the Net*, which has a large list of links to individual Pagan artists, contains thorough information on all things Pagan and has many sections dedicated to music and art.[13] *The Wicca Folk and Neo-Pagan Folk Directory* is essentially a directory of sites and articles dedicated to music as described in the title. It also has links to sites that are not essentially Pagan or Wicca but are in some way linked to the aesthetic, such as sites dedicated to tribal music and world music.[14]

Pagan music is also available via various online radio stations dedicated to Pagan music. The Pagan Radio Network broadcasts a range of music and spoken Pagan programmes via the internet. The programme list includes *A Darker Shade of Pagan*, hosted by Jason Pitzl-Waters, a contributor to this book, which "looks at modern music from a unique spiritual perspective" across a range of genres.[15] *Pagan FM!* combines talk with music from Pagan artists, while *Night Ritual* "brings together chants from the various Gods and Goddesses from around the world". Many of the various internet radio stations are tagged as Pagan, New Age and world (for example), showing the crossover between these genres.[16]

A survey of these sites reveals themes consistent with Pagan belief, both in lyrical content and website discourse, including but not limited to reclaiming ancient ways, themes and deities as an alternative to the dominant paradigm of contemporary society, acknowledgement of the spirit in plants and animals, the sacredness of the earth, the cycle of nature and the wheel of the year, polytheism, reclaiming the goddesses (especially the "Earth Mother"), ancestor worship, inner divinity, and reclaiming one's own "indigenous" religion/culture or taking on the perspective/mythology of other indigenous peoples.

It would be an impossible task to classify Pagan music, or even what is meant by the term, and the above is meant only to illustrate the diversity of music culture surrounding Paganism. This book does not set out to define

Pagan music – it is not a book about Pagan music from a particular perspective, but rather a book that attempts to both complement existing understandings of Paganism through an exploration of some of the music that may be associated with it, and to propose new understandings of popular music through approaching it from a Pagan studies perspective.

OVERVIEW OF THE BOOK

Histories

While the above has focused on the diversity of music that currently represents Pagans and Pagan practices, the relationship between Paganism and music has a long history, not all of which is immediately obvious. Part I of this book explores three quite different ways in which this relationship has developed.

In Chapter 2, Andy Bennett explores a range of ways in which the 1960s counter-culture paved the way for the broader development and articulation of Pagan beliefs through the medium of popular music. As Bennett observes, though a great deal of highly romanticized rhetoric has been created around the significance of the counter-culture as a medium for socio-political change, it is clear that at one level the counter-culture did serve as a platform for greater awareness and tolerance of alternative forms of ideology, spirituality and aesthetic belief, many of which continue to manifest themselves in current popular music scenes and their associated cultural practices. As Bennett argues, embedded within the counter-culture's oppositional stance were ideas and practices clearly influenced by Paganism. Notable here is the counter-culture's back-to-the-land ethos, as seen in the emergence of the commune movement and the shared-earth philosophy that articulated itself at the greenfield sites of several counter-cultural music festivals.

Moving further back in history, in Chapter 3 Rupert Till explores the relationships between Stonehenge, popular music and Paganisms, and how Stonehenge became associated with popular music in general and "rock music in particular". Till explores archaeo-acoustic research, through which he has looked at how the acoustic qualities of Stonehenge may have impacted on the experience of ritual and music within the circle of the stones, and argues that sound has played, and continues to play, an important role in Stonehenge's ritual history. Both in prehistory and more recently, Stonehenge has been the focal point of gatherings at significant times in the earth's annual planetary cycle, especially the equinoxes and solstices, and Till proposes that music and sound have helped it "to become an iconic representation of Pagan spiritualities". Stonehenge has become linked to popular music culture through its evocation by artists like The Beatles, Ten Years After,

Hawkwind, Spinal Tap and Black Sabbath, and by the music festivals held at the site. Till concludes that such "links between the ancient and the modern, the sacred and secular, are an artefact of the impact of postmodernity upon religion". It continues to be a "signifier of the interaction of popular music and Paganisms in the popular imagination … a site outside of mainstream religious control for experiences that allow individuals to feel connected to past histories, to their embodied present, and to a sense of place".

In Chapter 4, Donna Weston approaches history in a different way, viewing it not as bounded by temporality, but rather as something constructed through memory. Bringing together theories of memory and place, Weston examines how a collective cultural memory of sacredness of place might find its expression in popular music, and argues that attachment to conceptual place is the expression of unconscious "rememberings" of a Pagan past. Through analysis of a range of musical styles and practices – none of which is overtly Pagan – she draws on theories of place and of cultural memory to establish a framework within which references to place, and uses of space in popular music, can be recontextualized as drawing on innate Pagan impulses.

Genres

While much Pagan music is defined by its lyrical focus, and to a lesser extent its intended audience, rather than by style, there are nonetheless a number of genres that are linked explicitly to Paganism. This is the topic of Part II of this book. In Chapter 5, Deena Weinstein looks in detail at the sonic, visual and verbal aspects of several well-known Pagan metal bands from various European regions, drawing conclusions about the importance of localized culture to the Pagan metal scene and its use as a reaction to the perceived hegemonic tendencies of the European Union, a move against post-national deterritorialization (Europeanism) in Scandinavia and a shift towards reterritorialization (post-Communism) in the countries of the former Soviet Bloc. Weinstein classifies Pagan metal according to three "clusters": Neo-Paganism, which she describes as deriving from the same sources that informed Neo-Paganism and Wicca in the United Kingdom and United States – for example, the work of Gerald Gardner; "roots Paganism", which draws on pre-Christian religions – especially those of Northern Europe; and "chauvinistic Paganism", which Weinstein defines as being practised by a group that sets itself consciously in opposition to any other group that may pose a threat to one's roots. Conducting an in-depth musical and paramusical analysis, Weinstein comes to the conclusion that Pagan metal introduces identity politics into the culture of metal.

Jason Pitzl-Waters defines Goth as a post-punk musical subculture originating in Britain, which represented a romantic, decadent and "inward-looking" alternative to the anger and nihilism of the wider punk scene. In Chapter 6, he argues that many Pagans, dissatisfied with the music and culture of the traditional Pagan communities, found a spiritual home in Goth music, eventually coming to constitute a third of the scene's members. By the mid-1990s, this "cross-pollination" of Goth music and Paganism would result in what Pitzl-Waters refers to as a "darker shade of Pagan", distinct enough to identify as a discrete "Pagan Goth" musical sub-genre. Pagan Goths have now been absorbed by, and integrated into, the mainstream of modern Paganism. Pitzl-Waters explores "Pagan Goth", darkwave and other Goth sub-genres through discussing the work of bands such as Inkubus Sukkubus, Sisters of Mercy, Dead Can Dance; "ethno-Gothic" Pagan bands such as Ataraxia and Rhea's Obsession; and "darkwave" bands like Faith and The Muse, Unto Ashes and The Dreamside.

British Pagan folk musician Andy Letcher focuses on the difficulty of truly defining current folk music, as what it has come to stand for is now so closely intertwined with how it sounds. He posits that both the left and the right have tried to claim folk music, with the left utilizing it as the authentic voice of the working class and the right as the voice of the folk, of tradition and of the imagined past. Letcher is concerned primarily with the following questions: If we trace the folk tradition back far enough, don't we come to an "archaeological" layer that predates Christianity? And aren't the origins of folk music ultimately Pagan? In Chapter 7, using examples of traditional song, Letcher broadly examines contemporary British folk music (in particular, three modern Pagan folk music idioms: "Pagan folk", "dark folk" and "traditional folk") in order to describe the three ways in which musicians relate to the "supposed" Pagan origins of their craft and discusses their claim to folk music as a vehicle for the expression of religious identity.

Performance

As anthropologist Sarah Pike observes, "NeoPagan identity is primarily expressed through music and dance" (Pike 2001: 5), and it is the performative relationship between Paganism and music that is the focus of the third section of this book. In Chapter 8, Douglas Ezzy argues that the embodied performed aspects of religion make it "meaningful and transformative". He explores religious transcendence and its importance in leading the individual into relationships, as well as the significance of shared beliefs and symbolic systems in providing frameworks of meaning and morality. Ezzy posits that deities, spirits and ancestors are "significant beings" in relationship with humans and engaged with via ritual, and sees the collective ritual of dance as a site for resistance and defiance as expressed by a seemingly marginalized group. The argument made in this chapter is that for Pagans in Australia, dancing to the music of Pagan bands creates a spiritual community in which individual transformation can occur. Ezzy focuses on dancing's centrality in contemporary Pagan religious practice, generally through giving auto-ethnographic depictions of his own experiences at Pagan festivals and meetings, and through descriptions of common dances such as the spiral dance. He concludes that dancing, as an embodied experience, is one of the primary sources of religious transcendence, secondary to dogma and narrative.

In Chapter 9, Graham St John draws parallels between eclipse (rave) festivals and Neo-Pagan festivals because of the emphasis of both on planetary cycles. He describes what he calls a *cosmic nature spirituality*, which is expressed in these eclipse festivals; he contextualizes this through the three aspects of natural (geological), cosmic (astronomical) and social (festival) embodied by the festival and through mystical states of consciousness that may be experienced. St John describes several "types" of Pagan who are drawn to these festivals – Neo-Pagans, those who actively construct their own kind of Paganism or revive older traditions, and "geoPagans". Describing the eclipse festival experience as a techno-shamanic experience, linking the sensory world of physical sensation through dance to the transcendent experience of self, St John describes a "socio-sensual confluence" through which emerging forms of Paganism can be observed.

Staying in the realm of electronic music and dance, Adam Possamai and Alan Nixon also explore the concepts of techno-shamans and altered states of consciousness in Chapter 10, but do so in the context of what they call primordial religious experiences (PREs), and religious ecstasy in the rave scene. Possamai and Nixon explore the history of different subcultural movements within the rave scene, looking in detail at the history of Goa and the psychedelic dance music that emerged from the hippie communes set up there by Westerners in the 1960s. This particular Goan brand of electronic dance music (EDM), which eventually morphed into the sub-genre of Psytrance, is cited as the root of techno-shamanism. At its core, this chapter argues that three "agents" are providing an interpretation of ecstasy in the field of EDM culture; these agents are the Neo-Pagan, the Christian and the secular (or mainstream), all of which provide "cultural and symbolic capital to this economy of ecstasy". The authors also evoke Mafessoli's theories of neo-tribalism and relate them to rave culture, concluding that over the course of this discussion that each dance music participant – whether Pagan, Christian or secular – sees the primordial religious experience induced in dance culture from a different perspective.

Communities

As seen in the short survey of websites presented earlier in this chapter, music evidently plays an important role in expressing and supporting Pagan belief, and supporting a Pagan network. In Chapter 11, Christopher Chase explores this role in his discussion of the way in which religious communities have employed musical traditions as a medium for the transmission of different types of knowledge. He analyses the lyrics of a number of Pagan songs within the context of what he calls "Pagan theologizing", and describes the central role that music plays in exploring the place and role of humans in the natural and social worlds. Chase frames his discussion within Mary Bednarowski's (1989) concept of the "theological imagination", and focuses specifically on the role of music in exploring polarities that locate the communal sense of relationship in sacred power.

Narelle McCoy explores a different kind of community in Chapter 12 – the one that exists online. Focusing on the music of Irish singer and composer Enya, McCoy argues that the dissemination of Celtic mysticism via New Age websites invites anyone who shares these core beliefs to identify as Celtic. She proposes that this New Age "cyber-diaspora" may be a reason for the popularity of artists such as Enya, who has tapped into this fascination with Celtic Pagan mythology. This chapter explores the music of Enya as well as lesser-known composers and performers who advertise and promote their music on New Age/Pagan websites under the banner of Celtic popular music.

In the final chapter, Christopher Partridge describes a more underground, transgressive community, and through it explores what he refers to as "occulture". He explains that "occulture" is a term probably coined by Genesis P-Orridge, the founder of the experimental ritual magick network Thee Temple ov Psychick Youth (TOPY). P-Orridge, the main subject of Chapter 13, is a musician, artist, occultist and self-styled "cultural engineer", best known for his projects COUM Transmissions, Throbbing Gristle, Psychic TV, Splinter Test and Thee Majesty. Through these projects, Partridge finds that P-Orridge's idiosyncratic experimental art, a blend of the audio and the visual, transgresses societal norms through its exploration of taboo themes such as sexuality, violence and death. Partridge discovers nothing of the typical Pagan in P-Orridge's work, and goes on to explore the dystopian, confrontational, decadent and urban nature of his particular brand of Paganism, one that subverts the hegemony and explores the darker aspects of human existence. P-Orridge is depicted throughout as an artist who is mainly concerned with Paganism as "esoterrorism" – a tool to subvert societal norms and religious hegemony.

CONCLUSION

Paganism expresses itself though popular music in myriad ways, often characteristically nuanced by the specific local socio-cultural circumstances in which popular music is produced and consumed. As such, this book cannot – and does not – profess to offer a definitive account of the intersection between contemporary Paganism and popular music. Rather, the aim is to offer a series of critical insights relating to key examples of the expression of Paganism in popular music as these range across particular genres and/or the work of specific artists. In doing so, the book is also intended to broaden debates about Paganism and popular music that are presently emerging in popular music studies and cognate disciplinary and multidisciplinary fields. As with other modes of contemporary cultural identity that draw on pre-modern beliefs and practices, the study of Paganism and its expression through popular music enriches our understanding of the increasingly plural and postmodern terrain of everyday life and its cultural sphere.

NOTES

1. http://Pagansongs.tribe.net (accessed December 2012).
2. http://dir.groups.yahoo.com/group/PAGANDANCE/?v=1&t=directory&ch=web&pub =groups&sec=dir&slk=13 (accessed January 2012).
3. http://thePaganwheel.com/?p=7 (accessed January 2012).
4. http://damh.wordpress.com (accessed December 2012).
5. http://folkrec.blogspot.com/2008/06/traditional-slavic-folk-and-Pagan-music.html (accessed January 2012).
6. www.arularecords.com (accessed December 2012).
7. http://serpentinemusic.com (accessed January 2013)
8. www.maethelyiah.com (accessed December 2012).
9. http://members.tripod.com/~Willow_Firesong/PagMusic/index.htm (accessed January 2012).
10. www.Pagan-heart.co.uk/music.html (accessed December 2012).
11. www.bardicarts.com (accessed February 2013).
12. www.Paganspace.net/group/Paganplaylist (accessed December 2012).
13. www.witchvox.com/_x.html?c=music (accessed December 2012).
14. http://psychevanhetfolk.homestead.com/WICCA_FOLK_and_NEOPAGAN_FOLK. html (accessed December 2012).
15. www.Paganradio.net/programming/shows/adsop (accessed December 2012).
16. www.Paganfm.com (accessed December 2012).

2. PAGANISM AND THE COUNTER-CULTURE

Andy Bennett

The counter-culture of the late 1960s and early 1970s is typically represented as a global youth cultural phenomenon that casts itself in opposition to the technocracy of Western capitalist society. Central to this oppositional stance was a rejection of mainstream societal values which, in addition to the core ideologies of industrial capitalism itself, also extended to associated institutions – notably marriage, the nuclear family and organized religion. Although, the term "counter-culture" actually encompasses a wide range of quite diverse groups and interests (Clecak 1983), and although the oppositional nature of the counter-culture frequently has been romanticized and misrepresented, there is little doubt that the counter-cultural era brought with it an openness to alternative ideologies, spiritualities and aesthetic beliefs, many of which continue to manifest themselves in current youth cultures and music scenes (A. Bennett 2001).

A key aspect of the counter-culture's oppositional stance was its drawing on ideas and practices associated with pre-modern ideology, including elements of Paganism. Among these was a back-to-the-land ethos exemplified in the rural hippie communes that sprang up across North America and Europe; this was also evident at some counter-cultural rock festivals – notably the 1969 Woodstock Music and Art Fair, which took place at a greenfield site in upper New York state (see A. Bennett 2004). As the example of Woodstock suggests, significant elements of the counter-cultural ideology were communicated through the popular music of the era, and this extended to the traces of Pagan belief evident in the counter-culture. A range of artists, from The Beatles, Canned Heat and Traffic through to emerging hard rock and heavy metal groups such as Black Sabbath and Led Zeppelin, drew on imagery with varying degrees of Pagan influence. This chapter discusses the role of music in articulating aspects of Pagan belief and ideology among members of the counter-culture. As the chapter will illustrate, rather than articulating the full-blown form of Paganism evident in much contemporary Pagan music, counter-cultural music drew loosely on a range of themes and imagery whose Pagan associations were not directly articulated but rather worked at a variety of levels as a means of challenging the dominant technocratic discourse of the time. Pagan overtones were also evident in a variety of objects, images and texts associated with the music of the counter-cultural era. The chapter will argue that this music served as an important impetus for counter-cultural sensibilities, with the latter drawing inspiration and nourishment from pre- and anti-modern customs and practices within which Paganism played a significant, if not specifically explored, role.

THE DAWNING OF THE COUNTER-CULTURE

Historically, the counter-culture emerged at a point in late-twentieth-century history marked by the onset of scepticism towards the rational-scientific basis of progress and development in Western society (Reich 1971). According to Roszak, at that point Western society had become a technocracy, which he describes as "that social form in which an industrial society reaches the peak of its organizational integration. It is the ideal men usually have in mind when they speak of modernizing, up-dating, rationalizing, planning" (Roszak 1969: 5). Critical of the technocratic basis of contemporary everyday life, the counter-culture sought to establish alternative aesthetic sensibilities often characterized by a reinvestment in pre-modern values, notably spiritualism and a focus on the natural world. As Clecak (1983) observes, the basis of this distrust of science was to no small extent grounded in the palpably negative effects it had had on the trajectory of twentieth-century history – notable, for example, in the Holocaust, the development and use of the atomic bomb and the subsequent onset of the Cold War. Race riots across America and widespread socio-economic inequality further fuelled the counter-culture's rejection of the technocracy. Against the backdrop of such acute socio-economic dislocation, and the over-arching spectre of a global nuclear war that could annihilate all life on the planet, the counter-culture provided an alternative vision of the future, one in which values of peace, love and trust would – so it was believed – overturn and supplant the technocracy. Reich (1971) describes this as a shift in consciousness, in which the technological basis of rational understanding in industrial capitalist society is supplanted by a new understanding based on transcendence, spiritualism and respect for the natural world and the human subject's connectedness to it.

The early stirrings of a counter-cultural aesthetic began in the mid-1960s. Inspired by the Beat culture of the 1950s, during the mid-1960s many young people became increasingly critical of the trajectory of mainstream society. In the United States, opposition to the Vietnam War and the drafting of young men into the US Army signalled one key driver of youth opposition that fuelled support and a new form of ideology for which "peace, love, and understanding" became a popular slogan of the time. This striving for a new pathway for society was also supported through the popular music of the day, which – at several levels – contributed to the alternative social awareness and heightened levels of consciousness sought by members of the counter-culture. The music of established groups such as The Beatles became more experimental, with songs such as "Tomorrow Never Knows" (from the *Revolver* album, released in 1966) breaking away from the traditional verse–chorus–middle-eight structure and using studio technology to create sound-scapes that were entirely exotic from the point of view of the audience. The Beatles' follow-up work, *Sergeant Pepper's Lonely Hearts Club Band*, released in 1967, took this musical experimentation to new heights. As the first offer-ing from The Beatles as a "studio band" following their retirement from live performance in 1966, *Sergeant Pepper* utilized state-of-the-art recording techniques in the crafting of a highly varied and richly textured set of songs. The album's references to Eastern mysticism, drugs, carnival and celebration, while simultaneously poking fun at the fears, anxieties and idiosyncrasies of the dominant society, quickly helped to establish *Sergeant Pepper* as a coun-ter-cultural icon. Such musical experimentation also paved the way for a new generation of groups, such as Pink Floyd and the Grateful Dead, whose long improvisational live performances incorporated multimedia installations that began to alter the properties of musical experience – something accen-tuated through the consumption of hallucinogenic drugs, notably the syn-thetically produced lysergic acid diethylamide (LSD). When combined with music listening, such drugs could change the perception of sound, attuning the listener's ears to new tones and textures, and opening up different experi-ential states for understanding and appreciating music (Willis 1978).

Moreover, it was not only the musical properties but also the lyrical con-tent of pop and rock that began to change in the mid-1960s. Inspired by the lyrics of artists such as Bob Dylan and The Beatles, songwriters began to experiment with new themes. At one level, lyrics became increasingly radi-cal in their opposition to mainstream politics and dominant societal institu-tions. At another level, however, song lyrics took on mystical and esoteric qualities, often painting exaggerated images of natural phenomena meshed with references to spiritualism and/or transcendence as pathways to new levels of perception and being. Although spearheaded by rock music and the heightened levels of technological sophistication afforded in its produc-tion by the recording studio, from the late 1960s onwards the more gentle acoustic music of artists such as the Incredible String Band (see A. Bennett 2013) also became an important platform through which counter-cultural ideology could interface with alternative spiritualities linked to the natural world. Although seldom (if ever) referred to as Pagan at this point, counter-cultural music and its associated ideologies established critical pathways for the realization of Pagan beliefs and practices in and through popular music in the late twentieth and early twenty-first centuries.

15

BACK TO THE LAND

An important element of what can be seen as Pagan sensibilities within the counter-culture was its back-to-the-land ethos. References to the countryside and its significance as a place of transgression and retreat from the technocratic city to the world of nature – and peace – form an important part of counter-cultural music's sonic and lyrical repertoire. The Beatles' track "Mother Nature's Son" (from *The White Album*, released in 1968) is one of two sparsely arranged tracks featuring a picked acoustic guitar and solo vocal by Paul McCartney (the other track being "Blackbird"). Although ostensibly focusing on a fictitious individual subject born and raised in the countryside and attuned with nature, the song has clear resonances with a growing sentiment among hippies and other supporters of counter-cultural ideology that a rural, greenfield environment was preferable to life in the city, and the strains and pressures experienced as a result of such an urban existence. References in the song to the personal content garnered from looking over a patch of daisies in a field of grass, or watching the movement of water in a mountain stream are, at an obvious level, attempting to focus the mind of the listener on a rural landscape and the spiritually cleansing qualities this evokes. While in itself this is barely a reference to Paganism, a message about connectedness to Mother Earth emerges in the song, and would undoubtedly have found resonance among a counter-cultural audience.

At the time *The White Album* was released, an increasing number of rural hippie communes were being established across North America and Europe.[1] The commune attempted to position the back-to-the-land aesthetic as a long-term alternative to, and in many ways a rejection of, the urban way of life. In an early academic study of the commune movement, British cultural theorist Webster suggests that it represented a collective rejection of and opting out of a mainstream, dominant, technology-based society and an escape to the natural environment, which is perceived as a haven. Thus, argues Webster:

> The eschatological basis of the rural theme also takes the form of the "end-of-the-world" both *experientially* (the dropout experiences *his* or *her* urban middle-class world ending) and through the imagery of environmental pollution, ecological catastrophe, racial strife, war and the "demonic" technocratic system that supports it. The commune becomes here a "saving remnant" and ritually and practically anticipates the paradise that will come after the demonic reality has passed away.   (Webster 1976: 128)

Although the commune movement had limited success, largely due to the practical organizational issues of establishing rural-based agrarian communities comprising individuals with few or none of the required skills, it did establish a precedent for connection with the natural world among members of the counter-culture. A clear reference to the ideological and aesthetic qualities of the rural hippie commune is heard in US blues-rock group Canned Heat's "Going Up the Country", in which references to the countryside as a green and peaceful alternative to the structures and strictures of city life are clearly expressed. Again, the imagery of the song lyrics – although far more frenetically phrased and delivered than those in "Mother Nature's Son", portray the countryside as a place of purity and revelation, in contrast to the crowdedness and violence of the city. The importance of "Going Up the Country" as a counter-cultural anthem was cemented through its use in the opening sequences of Michael Wadleigh's *Woodstock: The Movie* (1970), which – as the title suggests – documents the 1969 Woodstock Music and Art Fair (see also Bell 1999). Now regarded as the seminal counter-cultural festival, Woodstock has assumed iconic resonance as a site where the back-to-the-land ethos of the counter-culture acquired critical currency as half a million people came together in a greenfield site near the Upper New York state town of Bethel for three days between 15 and 17 August 1969 to watch and listen to some of the biggest rock, folk and blues artists of the era (see A. Bennett 2004). As Wadleigh's film effectively depicts, however, while music was at the core of the event, the rural setting for the festival engendered other articulations of the counter-cultural aesthetic – including wild camping, naked bathing and swimming in lakes situated on or near the festival site, quasi-tribal dancing and meditation. The sense depicted in the movie is of a counter-cultural generation finding its natural home in the greenfield environment of the Woodstock event, with the festival taking on the aura of a ritual homecoming.[2] This message was further embedded in the collective counter-cultural consciousness through Canadian singer-songwriter Joni Mitchell's "Woodstock". Although Mitchell had not performed at the 1969 Woodstock event herself, her song became emblematic of what was quickly to become referred to as "the Woodstock nation" – a structure of feeling shared among followers of the counter-culture throughout the world, irrespective of whether or not they had been physically present at Woodstock. Within that, Woodstock came to symbolize the collective voice of the counter-culture. Mitchell's unusual and slightly ethereal vocal melody combined with lyrics evoking a oneness with nature are punctuated with repeated references to "the garden" as a place of peace, innocence and renewal. While again not directly referencing a Pagan aesthetic, Mitchell's "Woodstock" has clear Pagan overtones in both its topic matter and aspects of delivery.

References to the countryside can also be heard in some of the acoustic music produced by the heavy and progressive rock bands that emerged, primarily from Britain, during the late 1960s and early 1970s. Pink Floyd's "Greatchester Meadows" (from the 1969 *Ummagumma* album) evokes a pastoral atmosphere through its gentle acoustic guitar composition and the

17

use of tape-looped skylark song throughout the track. Another band from this era whose work is inclined to evoke a back-to-the-land ethos on occasion is Led Zeppelin. While Led Zeppelin emerged from the British blues boom of the late 1960s (an influence clearly evident in the band's first two albums), the influence of counter-cultural themes and musical elements became increasingly apparent in their early 1970s work. The group's more acoustically orientated tracks often reflect a more esoteric quality in which either the lyrics and/or the musical arrangements draw on some of the more abstract, quasi-Pagan-inflected sounds of counter-cultural music – including the folk-tinged style of groups such as The Incredible String Band. The track "Bron-Yr-Aur Stomp" from the album *Led Zeppelin III* situates the countryside as a place where a close connection with nature can evoke feelings of peace and rejuvenation, in contrast to the bricks and mortar terrain of the city, which traps and restrains the human spirit. Significantly, the track is named after Bron-Yr-Aur, a small cottage in the Welsh countryside where Led Zeppelin retreated in 1970 to write material for the album that would become *Led Zeppelin III*.

Another track whose arrangement evokes a quasi-Pagan influence is "Gallows Pole" (also from *Led Zeppelin III*). Although credited as a traditional folk song on the album's track listing, Led Zeppelin's treatment of the song, and in particular Jimmy Page's acoustic guitar work (based around a riff that moves between A7, A minor 7 with the A minor 7 chord shape then being lifted up two frets), creates a highly unusual atmosphere in which a typical English folk/pastoral sound is combined with a slightly hypnotic droning effect that evokes a more spiritual, transcendental tone in the music. The later addition of a mandolin (played by John Paul Jones) and a banjo overdub add to the madcap "dark-folk" flavour of the song.

ROCK, PAGANISM AND NORDIC MYTHOLOGY

The *Led Zeppelin III* album also contained a song that, through its topic matter, was to play a major part in establishing an aesthetic link between rock music and Pagan beliefs during the 1970s. "The Immigrant Song", which opens the album, combines a now-signature rock guitar riff with a lyric that evokes memories of Viking warriors crossing the sea in search of new lands to conquer. Through references to the midnight sun, volcanic springs of hot water and snowy wastelands, vocalist Robert Plant creates a rich imagery of an exotic netherworld ruled by heathen deities whose power over nature is equal to their power over man. If the instrumental composition of "The Immigrant Song" is crafted in a blues tradition, Plant's vocal style adds a highly unusual, ethereal and inherently dark tone to the song; his wandering phrasing sounds almost chant-like against the relentless chopping of the synchronized bass–guitar–drums rhythm.

In later Led Zeppelin work, Plant was to revisit and refine the subject-matter explored in "The Immigrant Song", typically in the song "No Quarter" from Led Zeppelin's fifth studio album, *Houses of the Holy*, released in 1973. The lyrics of the song are overlaid with references to Thor (the Nordic god of thunder, lightning and storms) and mythical warriors clad in armour and braving the extremes of a frozen wasteland on an unspecified mission. The mood of the vocal and lyrical subject is effectively complemented by the music. Driven by the sullen tone of a sparse keyboard line (played on a Fender Rhodes electric piano by John Paul Jones and utilizing a flange effect), the guitar and drums are largely confined to the song's chorus. Plant's vocal is thus able to weave in and out of the keyboard line, and the overall effect is of dark ambience highly suited to the subject-matter of the song. Interestingly, when featured in the 1976 concert film *The Song Remains the Same*, "No Quarter" formed the soundtrack for one of five short fantasy film sequences created around the four members of Led Zeppelin and their manager, the late Peter Grant. In this particular sequence, bassist/keyboard player John Paul Jones is depicted as a Lord of the Manor-type character whose evenings are spent leading a horseback gang through the streets of a pre-industrial village in rural England, clad in black clothes, including a long, flowing cape, and a grotesque face mask. Through a combination of back-lit scenes – including a churchyard – and dry ice, the suggestion of a quasi-heathen world wrought with fear and suspicion is suggested – it is an atmosphere similar to that which pre-figured much of the work of nineteenth- and early-twentieth-century English novelist and poet Thomas Hardy. Again, while it would be presumptuous to describe either "The Immigrant Song" or "No Quarter" as Pagan songs, each contains lyrical and musical themes grounded in a darker, more ethereal quality than most of the rock music being produced during the early 1970s.

PAGANISM AND THE OCCULT IN ROCK LYRICS AND IMAGERY

Heavy metal music is another genre to emerge from the counter-culture that has made significant contributions to the infusion of Pagan influences in contemporary popular music. Pagan metal is now an established sub-genre of the contemporary metal scene (D. Weston 2010; see also Chapter 5 of this book). The roots of Pagan metal are largely located in the work of late 1960s/1970s rock bands such as Led Zeppelin (see above) and Black Sabbath. Also emerging from the British blues scene, Black Sabbath underwent a musical and lyrical transformation, largely inspired by occult literature such as Dennis Wheatley's novel *The Devil Rides Out*, which had achieved a new wave of popularity in Britain and elsewhere due to the Hammer Horror movies being made at the time (see A. Bennett 2005).[3] According to Black Sabbath bassist Geezer Butler (who also wrote a number

19

of the group's song lyrics), the initial intention of using occult themes in Black Sabbath songs was to take rock lyrics in a new direction, away from the more blues-based lyrics that prevailed at the time.[4] Butler felt that lyrics with a darker, more sinister edge would find appeal among the rock audience; this was an assumption that was also to fuel the approach of Butler and guitarist Tony Iommi to the melodic composition of Black Sabbath songs. Although the riffs they used were clearly grounded in the blues rock of the time, the Black Sabbath style deviated in part from the blues trope through incorporation of note sequences with minor intervals that created a more menacing feel. Another aspect of the Black Sabbath sound that fostered this quality in the music was the high levels of overdrive (much higher than other rock bands of the time) used on the guitar. As a victim of an industrial accident in the days prior to his professional music career (in which a steel cutter severed the tips of two fingers on his right hand), Iommi, a left-handed player, was forced to play with plastic caps on the two affected fingers. This led him to develop a then-novel style of rhythm guitar playing in which power-chords featuring only two notes (root and harmonic fifth) were used instead of the conventional bar-chord (where the first finger of the fretting-hand is placed across a fret and a chord shape formed with the remaining fingers). Combined with overdrive, and doubled on the bass by Butler, Iommi's new power-chord technique gave Black Sabbath a highly distinctive, bass-heavy sound.

The material featured on Black Sabbath's first two albums, *Black Sabbath* and *Paranoid* (both released in 1970), contained references to witchcraft and black magic. Although both Geezer Butler and original Black Sabbath vocalist Ozzy Osbourne were later to deny any actual connection with occultism among the band members, Black Sabbath's music was quickly latched on to by rock fans and others with an interest in and/or leanings towards the occult. At the same time, this identified trait in Black Sabbath music led on occasion to an over-interpretation among fans of song meanings, an example of this being "N.I.B.", a track from the band's first album. Many fans took this to be an abbreviation for "Nativity in Black", whereas according to the band "N.I.B" referred to the goatee beard being sported by drummer Bill Ward at the time, which was shaped like a pen-nib. Despite such ambiguity, the sound created by Black Sabbath was relatively unique during the early 1970s – indeed, the band has often been credited with pioneering the heavy metal sound and, as noted above, with paving the way for heavier and darker brands of metal in which references to black magic and other occult topics have been articulated more overtly (see A. Bennett 2001). Black Sabbath songs such as the opening track on the band's debut album, "Black Sabbath", "The Wizard" and the intro section to the primarily instrumental "Sleeping Village" all invoke images drawn from a pre-modern, Pagan-infused world. An emphasis on individuals drawing power from, or being at the mercy of, the natural world is a central theme in much of Black

Sabbath's music. Furthermore, it is not just in the band's more characteristically heavy tracks that this trait can be heard. More gentle acoustic songs such as "Planet Caravan" (from the album *Paranoid*) create a transcendental, other-worldly mood. The lyrics vaguely focus on space travel, but in a context of staring down at the wonderment of trees bathed in moonlight and of watching the sunrise on other worlds. The ethereal quality of the song is enhanced through Osbourne's vocal being recorded through a Leslie rotating speaker cabinet (originally designed for use with an electronic organ but used to dramatic effect with vocal and guitar during the late 1960s and early 1970s). Through this effect, the vocal achieves a spirit-like quality, appearing to float gently above the music and giving further credence to the song's intended effect of floating through the universe.

COUNTER-CULTURAL MUSIC AND THE SPIRIT OF NATURE

Pagan imagery is also to be found in "progressive rock", another genre of popular music that finds its roots in the counter-culture (Stump 1997). Jethro Tull, a band formed in the late 1960s during the folk-rock boom in Britain, drew heavily on aspects of British folklore on albums such as *Songs from the Wood*, *Heavy Horses* and *Stormwatch*. The title and opening track of *Songs from the Wood* draws on rustic imagery, emphasizing the healthy and wholesome nature of country life, and pointing to its healing and cleansing qualities. A Pagan quality is also strongly punctuated in the second track on the album "Jack-in-the-Green". Here, the constant renewal of nature through the seasons, and the slow triumph of the natural world over the human-made world are personified into a mythical character-like presence. "Jack" becomes the embodiment of the life force of nature, a ubiquitous presence that commands the plants to grow and brings the green leaves back to the trees and forests after the winter months. Jack also ensures that cities, roads, motorways and other things that impact on the natural world must wage a constant battle with the forces of nature – that is, with Jack himself. The topic and theme of the song keenly resonates with some of the key principles of Pagan ideology explored elsewhere in this book, particularly in relation to the underlying belief among Pagans in the spirit forces that dominate the natural world and the place of human beings within it.

While the work of Jethro Tull connotes one of the more obvious references to Pagan themes in the progressive rock genre, there are numerous instances of such engagement in progressive rock lyrics and associated imagery. Pink Floyd's signature album *Dark Side of the Moon* (1973), although dealing with a range of issues relating to the pressures of contemporary life, offers, in the song "Eclipse", the summary statement that all of this pales into insignificance during a total eclipse of the sun. As one of the more spectacular examples of a natural phenomenon, total eclipses have fuelled human suspicion, doubt and wonderment since the dawn of human existence. The song "Eclipse" uses this premise as a means of pointing to the frailty of human existence and the futility of technocratic obsession, given the over-arching superiority of the natural world. Such a sentiment clearly embeds a quasi-Pagan sensibility that, just as much as the ambient soundscapes in much of Pink Floyd's music, has served to inspire current generations of Pagan musicians.

The early music of Genesis also contains occasional lyrical references to quasi-Pagan imagery. A case in point is the song "Harlequin" from the band's third album, *Nursery Cryme* (1971). Although typical of the abstract rock poetry (A. Bennett 2008) that characterized much rock and progressive rock music during the early 1970s, references to the lingering summer presence in the flames of an autumn fire link to the continual cycle of death and renewal in nature as this is articulated in Pagan ideology. Similarly, images such as children dancing in a glade, their laughter merging with the sound of flowing waters in a stream, are suggestive of a race memory through which the contact with nature allows a spiritual sojourn back through time to a pre-modern state where humans were more connected to the land and to the forces of nature.

Another song in the progressive rock tradition with clear Pagan overtones is Traffic's 1970 reworking of the traditional English folk song "John Barleycorn Must Die" from the band's album of the same name. Accompanied by a minimal backing track comprising acoustic guitar, wood block, flute and acoustic piano, the track is highly distinctive compared with other material featured on the album. At the same time, however, there is a clear continuity between this and material featured on other rock albums of the time, which often featured songs of a more gentle acoustic, folk-orientated leaning (as in the instance of Led Zeppelin's version of another traditional English folk song, "Gallows Pole"). The personification of the cornfield into a character, "John", in the original lyric of the song is given a contemporary furnishing by Traffic, presumably to give the song more relevance for a contemporary rock audience. Having already undergone various adaptations, the vocal melody is reframed into a more contemporary ballad feel. However, Traffic's version of the song retains a distinctly ethereal quality in keeping with much counter-cultural music of the time. In keeping with the era in which the song was recorded, it bespeaks a less complex, pre-modern era of English history, where folklore and superstition still held sway over communities – particularly rural communities whose agrarian livelihood depended on the weather and success of the annual harvest. Through the reworking of a well-established English folk song as part of the counter-culture's general discourse of opposition to technocratic society, in its version of "John Barleycorn Must Die", Traffic communicates an element of the pre-modern, Pagan ideology that has accompanied the song down through generations of folk singers.

CONCLUSION

This chapter has examined the role played by counter-cultural music in communicating elements of Pagan belief, ideology and imagery to a contemporary rock audience, thus contributing to the foundations of today's Pagan music scene. The chapter began by sketching out for the reader the origins and the late 1960s/early 1970s counter-culture, and grounding its emergence in a context of resistance to the dominant technocratic ideology that prevailed in Western late capitalist society at this time. The chapter then went on to explore some key issues associated with the counter-culture that reflected a quasi-Pagan set of concerns. This began with a discussion of the "back-to-the-land" ethos that was strongly articulated among certain sections of the counter-culture and articulated through, for example, rock festivals held at greenfield sites and the rural commune movement. The chapter then went on to consider how counter-cultural music's frequent references to aspects of ancient mythology, specifically from the Nordic countries, and to the occult, through the lyrical themes and issues explored, frequently evoked aspects of a pre-modern, Pagan ideology. Finally, the chapter turned its attention to counter-cultural music's referencing of natural events, such as the seasons and astronomical phenomena, and how such references also articulated quasi-Pagan ideas in opposition to the technocratic basis of society during the late 1960s and early 1970s.

NOTES

1. This aspect of the counter-culture is vividly depicted in the 1969 counter-cultural "road movie" *Easy Rider*. Depicting a motorcycle trek across the United States by Wyatt (Peter Fonda) and Billy (Dennis Hopper), the film quickly acquired a reputation and kudos as *the* "counter-cultural" road movie. Made at a time when the counter-culture was still gathering momentum, the film does indeed take on a quasi-documentary air, its often semi-fictional accounts providing an unrivalled insight into the hippie lifestyle. A large part of the film's distinctiveness relates to its fixation with the land. From the outset, *Easy Rider*'s message relates strongly to the counter-cultural ideology of leaving behind the city and its restricted mode of urban existence for an alternative rural lifestyle. The rural hippie commune featured in *Easy Rider*, replete with accounts of living off the land, although in itself a fictional creation, sought to represent an actual commune movement in the United States.
2. As rock music performance moved beyond the concert hall and the festival emerged as a new space for the enactment of alternative counter-cultural community (Frith 1981), the greenfield sites chosen for many rock festivals assumed their own resonance as liminal spaces for collective spiritual connections to the natural world.
3. The film version of *The Devil Rides Out* was actually an EMI production (released in 1968).
4. The source of this information is the DVD *Classic Albums*, dedicated to the making of Black Sabbath's second album, *Paranoid* (released in 1970).

23

3. PAGANISM, POPULAR MUSIC AND STONEHENGE

Rupert Till

Places associated with ritual activity have a particular ability to connect individuals to each other and to the ecology of the local geography. This certainly seems to be the case at Stonehenge, a megalithic site that has a particular resonance within both popular music and Pagan traditions. For thousands of years, people have gathered at Stonehenge to watch the rising of the sun on the summer solstice or the setting of the sun on the winter solstice. The site is arranged to fit this solar alignment, and in recent years as many as 20,000 people have congregated at this ancient monument on the solstice, trying to connect with what they perceive as ancient Pagan traditions. Such congregations, as well as the many other traditions that have grown up around the site, have sacralized the space, turning it into a place that has complex meanings.

This chapter aims to explore the relationships between Stonehenge, popular music and Paganisms. It begins by exploring attitudes to physical and situated culture within Pagan and popular music cultures, and looking at how this has created oppositional dynamics with Christianity. This is followed by an exploration of how Stonehenge became associated with popular music in general, and rock music in particular. It investigates the field of Stonehenge, including its acoustic field, discussing the importance of sound in Stonehenge's ritual culture throughout history, helping it to become an iconic representation of Pagan spiritualities.

The concept of *axis mundi* is examined in relation to Stonehenge and ritual practice, discussing how archaeological theories of Stonehenge as a place of the dead may interrelate with Jungian psychological terms such as the shadow or the collective unconscious. The chapter explores issues relating to the sense of place in collective experiences, with particular reference to the links between Stonehenge and sound. It explores ritual technologies for the reinsertion of the individual into the group, and the importance to human cultures of what Émile Durkheim called collective effervescence and Victor Turner described as *communitas*. It looks at the importance of place in Pagan and popular music ritual cultures, and suggests Stonehenge as a site of pilgrimage for the postmodern homeless self.

PAGANS, POPULAR MUSIC AND PLACE

It is clear that a key and common feature of Paganisms is a positive relation-ship with place, and with the earth. Some belief systems, such as Christianity, focus on deities and heavenly realms, to which believers will one day escape. In contrast, Paganisms often present a focus on one's relationship with the physical world. This offers the opportunity to relate in particular to the con-cept of place. Whereas one might describe space in terms of geographical location, place adds to position related associations and meanings:

> Place is also a way of seeing, knowing and understanding the world. When we look at the world as a world of places we see different things. We see attachments and connections between people and place. We see worlds of meaning and experience. Sometimes this way of seeing can seem to be an act of resist-ance against rationalization of the world, a way of seeing that has more space than place. To think of an area of the world as a rich and complicated interplay of people and the environment – as a place – is to free us from thinking of it as facts and figures.
>
> (Cresswell 2004: 11)

Place is thus a significant concept within Paganisms: places are often sacral-ized and treated with reverence, whether this refers to human-built monu-ments, such as prehistoric stone circles, or places in the natural landscape, such as mountains, water sources or woodland. Thus Paganisms are often situated belief systems.

Many European Paganisms were (re-)born in the late nineteenth century, often inspired by earlier traditions – in many cases consisting of imagin-ings of what local pre-Christian religious traditions might have been like. They often drew inspiration from literary sources, such as the writings on druids of Aubrey or Stukeley, requiring a level of storytelling, invention and imagination in order to fill gaps in detail of the ritual practices and beliefs of the original religions (Harvey 2005). Druidism is particularly relevant to this subject, as Druids – or Neo-Druids – have made a particular claim to a historical link to Stonehenge.

Paganisms often reincarnate or reconstruct the pre-Christian beliefs of a European region into which Christianity migrated from its original source in the Middle East. The secular and the sacred were indivisible, or very closely linked, within Christian states during much of Europe's history. Christian evangelists aimed to change the beliefs of a region, wiping out and demonizing existing Pagan belief systems in order to indoctrinate the local populace into Christian culture. Thus contemporary Paganisms are often set in opposition to Christianity, an opposition created by early such acts of cultural imperialism.

One key difference between Christian and Pagan religious traditions is their attitudes to the body and the physical. One characteristic of Christianity that has become an ingrained part of its practice in western Europe is a mind–body dualism, which has roots in Zoroastrian apocalyptic writings (Cohn 1995: 222). Zoroastrians were the close neighbours of Biblical Hebrew culture, and a pronounced separation between forces of good and evil, a personification of evil and the creation of a powerful opponent of God became part of Judaism through this local religious competitor, and subsequently also became part of Christianity. The Platonic and Manichaean ideas that influenced St Augustine (Marrou 1957) further developed duality within Christianity. Augustine held Manichaean beliefs before becoming a Christian, and was also influenced by Plotinus and Plato. Within Augustinian theological traditions, the body was seen as a failed, sinful sack of flesh, while the mind was the focus of good and virtue. Augustine was an enormously important influence upon Christianity as Western Christian orthodoxies were being canonized, and his ideas were revived after the reformation – for example, by Calvinists. Augustine and the Zoroastrians are two of the more significant elements that led to Christianity adopting a body–mind duality, and an apocalyptic tradition.

The mystical, apocalyptic Revelation of St John became the last book of the Christian Bible, imagined to be the work of the apostle John, although this is most likely not actually the case (Cohn 1995: 212). Revelation became a key inspiration for Christian demonology, which also drew upon imagery from pre-Christian religious traditions, including those that have also been sources for various Paganisms. The result was a Christian devil whose realm was the earth, a fallen post-Eden sinful zone, full of temptations of the flesh and invitations to sin or stray from God's path. This devil was constructed by demonizing the physical and the local, by combining together the images and characters of local deities or earthy horned gods such as Dionysus and Pan with biblical characters such as Satan, the serpent, Lucifer and Baal (Partridge 2005: 213).

In comparison, many Paganisms adopt a more positive approach to the body and the physical, engaging with the earth, the sensate, sensuality, sexuality and human emotions. Within Paganisms, the earth is often seen as mother, as a source of power and energy, and in the influential Gaia theory (Lovelock 1995) as a God-like living organism. Also common are animistic tendencies, associating animals, plants or places with spirits or spiritual dimensions. Connection with the earth, with the environment and thus the physical, is an important part of many Pagan rituals and beliefs (York 2003). This positive attitude to the physical continues through into approaches to the human body. As a result, physicality is approached in some contemporary Paganisms in a far less restricted manner than within Abrahimic religions. The body is more fully integrated into rituals than in Christianity; women are treated equally, or even given priority; and instinctive bodily responses are more readily trusted or accepted.

Overall, Paganisms are set in opposition to Christianity in particular – and indeed the word "Pagan" has roots that refer to any non-Abrahimic religion. Christianity's oppression of other historical belief systems, which are now associated with contemporary Paganisms; its history of demonization, witch trials and inquisition; and its different approaches to physicality set it specifically in opposition to Paganisms. The positive attitudes of Paganisms to embodiment, to place, to the earthly as opposed (or as well as) to the heavenly, to the material world or to a unified holistic concept of the material and spiritual is a primary method used to differentiate them from Christianity.

Paganisms and popular music have in common that they have both been demonized by Christianity, and that they have a more open attitude to physicality than Christianity. Christianity came into conflict with Paganisms as it tried to replace them as the dominant European religious tradition. Popular music came into conflict with Christianity as it invaded mainstream culture in the West, replacing Christian attitudes to physicality with a more vigorous, sexually charged, cultural tradition – one that is certainly far more compatible with Paganisms than it is with Christianity.

Blues, jazz, rhythm'n'blues, rock'n'roll, soul music, disco, hip hop and house music have all been accused of inspiring a loss of morality among young people, accused of being the devil's music, or of leading young people astray. It was often when such African American popular music forms (Farley 2009: 75) became increasingly popular with a mainstream white audience that this caused a moral panic, driven by a mixture of media frenzy and the repressive and conservative opinions dominant in of some parts of the United States, especially within the so-called "Bible belt". This demonization of black secular music by Christianity is tied up in part with issues in the United States of racism and racial stereotyping, and in part with tensions within African American music between secular traditions such as blues and sacred traditions such as gospel.

Rock'n'roll caused a moral panic when it appeared – television producers showed Elvis Presley from the waist upwards, to ensure teenagers were not sexually enflamed by his gyrating pelvis, moves copied from blues singer Wynonie Harris (T. Collins 1995: 112). The Beatles, inspired by black artists such as Chuck Berry, Little Richard, the Isley Brothers and Bobby Parker, famously courted controversy when John Lennon suggested in 1966 that the Beatles were bigger than Jesus, and that Christianity was reducing in cultural significance. In response, Christians organized public burnings and breakings of Beatles records. The Rolling Stones offended Christian sensibilities with rhythm'n'blues that contained references to Lucifer and the satanic in song lyrics and album titles. Disco, a black and Latin dance music that emerged from gay culture, provoked a "disco sucks" campaign that again featured record burning. Prince's sexually charged lyrics inspired Tipper Gore and others to launch the censorship campaign of the Parents' Music Resource Centre. Again and again, popular music has been accused of being a pernicious and negative force, accelerating moral decay, and tempting the young into sexual depravity and away from the Christian church. Such actions recognized the challenge presented to the Christian mainstream by popular music culture.

Many authors have discussed how popular music has replaced some of the functions previously addressed by religions (see Till 2010a). Popular music cultures have been described as cults, new religious movements, implicit religion or secondary religious institutions. The star cults created by fanatical audiences around individuals such as Madonna, Cliff Richard, Prince and Michael Jackson are very cult-like. Elvis Presley has inspired the formation of the First Presleytarian Church, and some of his followers are called Elvites (Harrison 1992; Mallay & Vaughn 1993; Reece 2006). Electronic dance music culture (EDMC) has been described in religious terms (St John 2004c), sometimes behaving like a form of possession cult (Till 2009), involving all-night, ritualized, drug-fuelled dancing to hypnotic rhythmic music. Extreme metal forms have embraced imagery associated by Christians with Paganisms, as can be seen in the apocalyptic imagery of black and death metal.

Like Paganisms, popular music cultures are often set in opposition to Christianity and embrace the physical, frequently joyfully engaging with dancing and other physical expressions such as jiving, headbanging, moshing, pogoing or stagediving. Popular music often associates itself with an overt sexuality, and is physically embodied. It is also often defined by its locality, as part of a scene. These scenes include grunge in Seattle, disco in New York, hip hop in the Bronx, Baggy in Manchester, metal in Los Angeles, Merseybeat in Liverpool or trip hop in Bristol (A. Bennett & Peterson 2004). Thus popular music also has a close association with the material world – with places, venues and scenes. It is not a music that is appreciated solely or principally in the head, but in the body – with emotions – and in a specific cultural setting or place. In many cases, Paganisms and popular music have developed links forged in their oppositional common ground. Their embracing of the physical world has seen them interact in particular places in very specific ways. As we will see, this is the case at Stonehenge.

STONEHENGE AND ROCK MUSIC

Stonehenge is a megalithic stone circle. It was built over a period of hundreds of years, between 3000 and 1600 BCE (Richards 2007: 30). It has numerous associations with New Age thinking and various Pagan traditions, and in the 1970s and early 1980s the anarchic Stonehenge Free Festival was held there each year, at the time of the summer solstice. There are a huge number of stone circles in the United Kingdom, and Stonehenge is not as large and impressive as Avebury or as well preserved as Callanish. However, archaeologically speaking it is deservedly famous for a number of reasons. The stones at the site are particularly well dressed – that is, they have been carefully worked to make them smooth. The largest are made of very hard local Sarsen stone, and are carefully dressed on the inside – an operation that must have taken an enormous effort using only Stone Age tools. The stone circle is also unusual because there are precisely fitted stone lintels capping the upright stones of the outer circle, as well as huge pairs of stones inside. These latter stones form five stone archways known as trilithons. The area around the stone circle is filled with ritual sites, including the Cursus, Woodenge, Durrington Walls (with its own timber circles) and the recently discovered Bluestone Henge.

The stone circle is orientated towards the mid-winter solstice sunset, and also the mid-summer solstice sunrise, although archaeologists believe there is more evidence for ritual activity in prehistory at the winter event. It is certain, however, that for hundreds or perhaps thousands of years, people in Britain have been collecting at Stonehenge to celebrate the solstice. There are many theories about the original purpose and meaning of the stone circle. One predominant current theory describes Stonehenge as a place of the dead, of the ancestors – perhaps a city for the dead, a place for them, a place to meet them or a place to represent them (see Parker Pearson *et al.* 2006).

It is clear from archaeological evidence that Stonehenge was an important ritual site in prehistory. There were few stone buildings in Britain at the time, and Stonehenge and its surrounding monuments would have made a powerful impression on visitors. The specific positioning of many religious sites in the landscape is important, but this is particularly the case at Stonehenge, as the specific latitude of Stonehenge means that solar and lunar events can happen at right-angles to one another. For example, on the winter solstice of 2010, the full moon set, and very soon afterwards the sun rose 90 degrees around the horizon, past stones placed to mark these alignments. There are a number of similar alignments related to the sun and moon that make Stonehenge a particularly special place at which to watch the solstice.

The sun and moon were important signifiers of light and dark, summer and winter, and life and death in prehistory, as they are in many other religious traditions. Stonehenge was a place where it was traditional for many prehistoric people, including the rich and powerful, to gather to mark the day when the sun was at its weakest, to celebrate the fact that the days would grow longer and warmer, and the sun would grow stronger and more powerful day by day. Western Europe still celebrates this, as New Year or

Christmas, with the latter replacing the return of the Pagan sun with the return of the Christian son. In prehistory, the rich and powerful were buried in this significant place, and perhaps their spirits were thought to rise at the midwinter solstice, the day of darkness, in this home of the ancestors. There are many books providing archaeologically based information and context related to Stonehenge (e.g. Cleal *et al.* 1995; Richards 2007).

In more recent history, Stonehenge has also been a place of pilgrimage on the solstices. From the beginning of the twentieth century, groups calling themselves Druids (sometimes now called Neo-Druids) gathered at Stonehenge to carry out rituals on the solstice (Hutton 2009a). This was a formalization and revival of Pagan traditions and beliefs, and a sign of the increasing power of popular cultural traditions. The site became the epitome of pre-Christian Pagan religious beliefs, an iconic representation of British Paganisms.

Stonehenge therefore remained a popular place for people to collect and celebrate the solstices. As New Age beliefs and different Paganisms became increasingly popular during the 1960s – especially within a nascent counter-culture in which music played a key role – the site also became associated with popular music. Darvill (2009) has discussed in some detail the links between Stonehenge and rock music. The Beatles' film *Help!* (directed by Richard Lester in 1965) had a scene shot at Stonehenge, bringing the site into the view of popular musicians at the beginning of the "swinging sixties". Two acts at the 1969 Woodstock festival, Ten Years After and Richie Havens, released albums with images of Stonehenge on the cover. Ten Years After's album *Stonedhenge* was released in 1969, and features the sun rising through the stones; Richie Havens's 1970 album is entitled *Stonehenge*, and it seems both did much to further popularize the site within the hippie movement.

In the United Kingdom, there had been a long tradition of summer fairs, fayres or festivals, as discussed in detail by George McKay (1996). These began as traditional, free community events, but several of them developed a focus on musical content, following the success of musical festivals such as Newport, Pink Pop, Monterey, Isle of Wight and Woodstock. Some were free festivals, while others such as the Glastonbury Festival in Pilton charged admission fees. The free events were less regulated than ticketed festivals, and the Stonehenge Free Festival in particular became known for its law-less environment, with illegal drugs openly on sale. The tradition of New Agers, hippies, druids and others going to Stonehenge for the summer solstice developed around this free music festival, held across the road from the stone circle from 1972 to 1984. McKay describes how the festival was set up with hippie-inspired ideals to reclaim the site from government authority (*ibid.*: 17–20), although it increasingly became associated with musical rather than political agendas.

British band Hawkwind in particular became associated with the event, and was known for performing at the festival each year. The band's 1976 tour was entitled Atomhenge, as the stage set was based on Stonehenge, and its 1976 album *Astounding Sounds, Amazing Music* was released on the Atomhenge record label. Hawkwind's 1983 album *Zones* featured Stonehenge on the front cover, and a DVD entitled *Hawkwind – The Solstice at Stonehenge* (2004) records a performance at the festival. Attendance at the Stonehenge festival became a badge of underground authenticity for both rock music fans and bands – the antithesis of the increasingly industrialized music business, which had grown away in the 1970s and 1980s from the hippie counter-cultural ideals of the 1960s. The festival was stopped by force in 1984, amid considerable controversy and violence, due to the fears of English Heritage that the archaeological site would be damaged (Worthington 2005). A metal fence was erected around the stones and access to the site was restricted.

There are many other references to Stonehenge in popular music culture in general, and rock music culture in particular. As Darvill puts it, "Stonehenge remains an icon of choice for the perpetrators of rock music and their stooges, a source of inspiration and a rallying point for counter-cultures just as it has been for centuries" (Darvill 2009: 72). In 1983 heavy metal band Black Sabbath made an album, *Born Again*, that featured an instrumental piece called "Stonehenge". Both original singer Ozzy Osbourne and his replacement Ronnie James Dio had left the band, and the new front-man was ex-Deep Purple singer Ian Gillan, creating much media interest and publicity. When the band started to prepare for a tour to promote the album, manager Don Arden (the father of Sharon Osbourne, who later married Ozzy Osbourne) suggested that the band should have a stage set built that would resemble Stonehenge. The plans sent to the makers mistakenly specified the stage set in metres instead of feet, making the end-product more than three times the required size (McIver 2006: 166). As a result, the set dwarfed the band, and was physically too large to fit on stage much of the time. Most of the set was only used once, at the 1983 Reading Rock Festival, as the outdoor setting provided adequate on-stage space.

A year later, this unfortunate event was parodied in spoof rockumentary *This is Spinal Tap*. The film documented a tour by a fictional heavy metal band, and became a cult hit among heavy metal fans and bands, largely because it was actually quite realistic and well researched, many of the comical situations and extreme characters involved having been inspired by real-life events. In the film, the band has a song in its set called "Stonehenge", and decides to create a stage set that looks like the stones, writing the plans on a restaurant napkin. The band's manager takes the drawing and has the scenery made up, but the dimensions are read in inches, when they should be feet, and thus the scenery is comically small. The film was released in the last year of the Stonehenge Free Festival.

This linked Stonehenge further with rock music, helping to permanently embed it within popular music culture in a more widespread context than that of an underground free festival. This is reflected, for example, in the computer game *Guitar Hero*. Players move in this game to increasingly impressive venues, from bars to clubs, theatres, halls and stadiums. If one plays the game to the end, eventually the player gets to perform at Stonehenge, complete with an audience of hooded, robe-wearing, Druid-like figures. Stonehenge is therefore presented as the ultimate performance venue for rock music. If all the game's guitar parts are played correctly, a spaceship arrives overhead, then destroys and takes the place of the lighting rig, and if the encore of "Freebird" is performed adequately, the game climaxes in the lead guitarist character being beamed up into the spaceship, which flies away.

Apart from archaeological interpretations discussing the original purpose of Stonehenge, there have been innumerable popular suggestions and theories put forward. One was that the stone circle was filled with water like a lake (see Gaus212 2009), and another that the encircling ditch was water-filled (Orion 2003); however, both suggestions have been rejected by most archaeologists due to the permeability of the chalk-based ground. Other suggestions include that the site had a roof (Bedlam 2008), that it was the home of Druids (Trull 1998), that it was an intersection of leylines (Huneidi 2006) or that it was a landing pad for UFOs (Thompson 2010). Stonehenge was in use long before Druids existed, leylines are a largely Victorian invention, and there is no secure evidence of either a roof or UFO landing pad, despite the video game reference already mentioned. Stonehenge is certainly a site that is of significance for various reasons to all sorts of fringe religious and special-interest groups, including various Paganisms.

Stonehenge may have numerous public interpretations, but access to the site is now carefully regulated. In general, visitors are only allowed to walk around the outside of the stone circle, and cannot come close enough to touch it. While Neo-Druid groups were sometimes allowed access to hold their ceremonies within the circle, such a restricted level of access was challenged by groups who wanted to be able to worship at the site, especially at both solstices and at each equinox. Various groups had claimed that Stonehenge was a site of religious importance to them, and that English Heritage's approach was overly restrictive. Those who campaigned for more open access included the Neo-Druids, who had worshipped there regularly for over a hundred years at least, and claimed to be inheritors of thousands of years of tradition; and Arthur Pendragon, who claims to embody the historical King Arthur, dressing and acting the part and having changed his name by deed poll (Pendragon & Stone 2003).

Open access to the site was begun in 2000, carefully managed, with the public being allowed free access, including within the stone circle, within certain hours on the solstices and at each equinox. In recent years, between 20,000 and 30,000 people have attended the summer solstice. Planned rituals are not allowed, but impromptu activities take place. Acoustic musical instruments are allowed, and are common, and in some years samba bands and other musical groups have performed. Various groups hold ceremonies that nearly always involve music of some kind, often using drums and wind instruments. The summer solstice activities are the best-attended, although even in mid-winter thousands attend.

English (2002: 4) discusses Foucault's concept of *heterotopia* to describe the "marginal" space of Stonehenge as being something that is appealing to Druid groups and others, while McKay (1996: 8) uses the term "temporary autonomous zone". Whichever conceptual term one adopts, the contesting of access to Stonehenge by authorities, Pagans and festival-goers has made Stonehenge a shrine or holy place in the popular imagination, a liminal site with histories that link Paganisms and popular music.

We can say in conclusion that both in prehistory and more recently Stonehenge has been a place where people have gathered in some numbers to celebrate the solstice, and that such gatherings were and are shrouded in ritual, meaning and significances of various kinds. These traditions have welded together a sense of place, of connection to position, to the planet, to the physical, the body and the material, along with issues of day and night, light and dark, sun and moon, the passing of time, and the marking of years and seasons. They have brought together the uncertain worlds of meaning and significance, religion and ritual, gods and the future, with the physicality and certainty of a set space in the landscape, the marginal liminality of this place contrasting with the immovability of megalithic monumental architecture.

THE ROLE OF RITUAL TECHNOLOGIES

Those participating in events at Stonehenge are often aware of the long history of activities at the site, including both fictional and real elements of Stonehenge's story, and are affected by the numerous agents who have contributed to the overall field of Stonehenge. They are able to draw both consciously and subconsciously on these elements, on the presence of the past, or morphic field (Sheldrake 2009) at the site, perhaps connecting through Jung's collective unconscious (Jung 1996: 43). Whether one describes such associations as a morphic field, using Bourdieu's field (Bourdieu 1993) or Jung's psychological terminology, it is clear that the site holds a powerful sense of meaning far beyond its physical and material presence, especially among those involved in various Paganisms within the United Kingdom. Such a concept of the field of Stonehenge fits in with recent archaeological theories that imply that the stone circle was a domain, home or place of the dead (Parker Pearson *et al.* 2006), built as a place to remember the past, to create a sacred space to mark the cycle of passing of years, and to develop a field that venerates the past.

Recent archaeological studies have also made interesting discoveries regarding another part of the site's field, the acoustic field of Stonehenge. Studies have shown that a number of British megalithic prehistoric sites have interesting acoustic effects that may have enhanced the experiences of those participating in ritual activities (Devereux 2001; Scarre & Lawson 2006). Aaron Watson and David Keating's pilot study of the acoustics of Stonehenge showed that there were interesting patterns of loudness, standing waves and filtering, and that sound would have been perceived differently inside and outside the site, and would have changed when entering the stone circle (A. Watson & Keating 1999). This may have contributed to a perception of otherness, or of the presence of ancestral spirits. Watson and Keating also point out that the stones at Stonehenge are curved in the horizontal plane, something that is very deliberate, and that could imply that Stonehenge was designed purposefully to have specific acoustic properties.

My own studies at Stonehenge, carried out with Bruno Fazenda (Till 2010b, 2011; Fazenda 2010), have confirmed and extended these results, also showing that Stonehenge would have had a noticeable reverberant field as well as unusual echo effects, something that would have been unusual and striking in a prehistoric culture where there were few stone buildings. The acoustic qualities of the space varied in different positions, and we showed that it was possible to make the space resonate, setting up standing waves using only sounds from replicas of prehistoric European hand drums made by archaeologist Simon Wyatt (see Wyatt 2008 for more information). We also showed that the stones at Stonehenge were shaped in a number of interesting ways, being curved vertically as well as horizontally. We showed that the circle's centre would have specific focused acoustic effects, that the very edge of the circle would have been a significant position to make sounds, and that the stones outside the circle – for example, the Heel and Slaughter Stones – would also have caused acoustic effects. We also located evidence that strong winds in the past could have caused the circle to emit a dramatic low-frequency hum at a resonant frequency of around 48Hz.

Whether the acoustics at Stonehenge were deliberate or accidental, we know that prehistory was not a silent place, and that the acoustics would have enhanced music-making at the site. We know from fragments of stones that were worked at the site (Darvill & Wainwright 2011) that there must have been many percussive sounds in and around the space, and we can safely assume that ritual activity was likely to include music- or sound-making of some kind. According to Nettl (2000), most ritual involves music. He underlines "the importance of music in ritual, and, as it were, in addressing the supernatural. This seems to me to be truly a universal, shared by all known societies, however different the sound" (*ibid*.: 469).

Recent studies have discussed music in prehistory, such as Mithen's *The Singing Neanderthals*. Walter Freeman also makes it clear that cultural music-related activities are hard-wired into humanity through biological and evolutionary development:

> Music and dance originated through the biological evolution of brain chemistry, which interacted with the cultural evolution of behaviour. This led to the development of chemical and behavioral technology for inducing altered states of consciousness. The role of trance states was particularly important for breaking down pre-existing habits and beliefs. That meltdown appears to be necessary for personality changes leading to the formation of social groups by cooperative action leading to trust. Bonding is not simply a release of a neurochemical in an altered state. It is the social action of dancing and singing together that induces new forms of behaviour, owing to the malleability that can come due to the altered state. It is reasonable to suppose that musical skills played a major role early in evolution of human intellect, because they made possible formation of human societies as a prerequisite for the transmission of acquired knowledge across generations. (Freeman 2000: 422)

Music played a vital role in early human culture, and is a key human technology for building and maintaining community. Freeman also tells us that a "significant discovery by our remote ancestors may have been the use of music and dance for bonding in groups larger than nuclear families", and that music

> may have accompanied or even preceded the invention of fire, tools and shelter, because the maintenance, development, and transmission across generations of information about techniques for working matter into useful forms must have required existence of channels to support social interactions. (*Ibid.*: 420–21)

Ehrenreich describes the importance of such musical community-building using Durkheim's term "collective effervescence" (Ehrenreich 2006: 14) to describe ecstatic merger with the group, and Turner's term "*communitas*", or "the spontaneous love and solidarity that can arise within a community of equals" (*ibid.*: 10) to describe the result.

In an aural and oral prehistoric culture, music and sound would have been vital elements of human life. Today, we are surrounded by sounds of musical and mechanical activity, and often enveloped by the acoustics of modern buildings. The sounds that were heard in prehistory would have had different significance. Ritual in many human cultures involves music, and it often provides a structure for activities that construct meaning. Music is a key part of human ritual activities. If we think of any such practices –

35

funerals, weddings, Christian church services, Buddhist temple chanting, or even more secular events such as birthday parties – music plays a significant role. It creates mood, it sets scene, and it can also seem to take us out of our usual relationship with time.

We can become temporally lost in music, sometimes time goes by so slowly that it feels like we are out of time altogether, that we are at pause. When one emerges from a musical experience, one can be surprised that more or less time has passed than one thinks. When a number of people participate in a ritual that involves music, they are synchronized to a beat that bonds the group together in terms of temporality as well as communal experience. Music is therefore often something that causes entrainment, the synchronization of a person to an external clock, and entrancement, both of which are capable of having powerful effects within a ritual context. There are various levels of entrainment and entrancement – this does not have to mean being taken over in some kind of possession trance, and indeed there can be subtle effects that may be little-noticed but still significant.

According to Rouget: "The universality of trance indicates that it corresponds to a psychophysiological disposition innate in human nature" (Rouget 1985: 3). Rouget also makes it clear that throughout the world trance is usually associated with religion and ritual as well as music and dance:

> To dance is to inscribe music in space, and this inscription is realised by means of a constant modification of the relations between the various parts of the body. The dancer's awareness of his body is totally transformed by this process. Insofar as it is a spur to dancing, therefore, music does appear to be capable of profoundly modifying the relation of the self with itself, or, in other words, the structure of consciousness. Psychologically music also modifies the experience of being, in space and time simultaneously. (*Ibid.*: 121)

Similarly, Nettl tells us that "another universal is the use of music to provide some kind of fundamental change in an individual's consciousness, or in the ambiance of a gathering" (Nettl 2000: 469). Ehrenreich describes the history of the loss of these traditions in mainstream Western culture. She also makes it clear that this kind of activity is a core part of traditional human activity: "These ingredients of ecstatic rituals and festivities – music, dancing, eating, drinking or indulging in other mind-altering drugs, costuming and/or various forms of self-decoration, such as face and body painting – seem to be universal" (Ehrenreich 2006: 18). Thus we can expect musical activity at Stonehenge, in prehistory and today, that involves some level of change of perception of consciousness within the participants, perhaps involving some level of entrancement, or caused by sonic entrainment of the brain (Will & Berg 2007; Clayton *et al.* 2005). Such behaviour is often associated with altered perception, and rituals at a site of the dead may well have involved such elements. Echoes in the acoustic field of Stonehenge could have built up resonances and standing waves, further enhancing this process.

Tantalizingly, the bluestones present at Stonehenge may have been known as healing stones, with special acoustic properties. In particular, the bluestones – which are thought to have come from the Preseli Hills in Wales – have been associated with healing springs near a Preseli village called Maenclochog, which means "ringing rocks" or "bell stones", named after two standing stones. Paul Devereux's research has shown that a number of stones at Carn Menyn in Preseli, a possible source of the Stonehenge bluestones, are lithophones – that is, when struck they ring (Wozencroft & Devereux 2012).

In summary, we have at Stonehenge bluestones associated with sound and healing; issues of entrainment, entrancement and veneration of the dead; ritual music and sound; and interesting acoustic effects. In addition, we have a number of links to Jung's ideas of the collective unconscious, through links to entrancement and the bridging of the conscious and unconscious minds. Though we may never be able to draw any definite conclusions about sound in prehistory, there is evidence that sonic culture has been significant in pre-history, and is something that should be carefully considered at Stonehenge today.

In addition, modern Pagans and popular music culture have each found their way to engage with the acoustic field of the site and its ancient cul-ture. Although the Stonehenge Free Festival happened across the road from the stone circle, participants certainly crossed that road, and in doing so engaged with Pagans and Paganisms. McKay describes the interaction of the ancient acoustics of the site, festival-goers and Pagans in the diary of his 1984 visit to the festival:

> Eventually we go to see the stones, and the druids (looking remarkably like a bunch of smashed ramshackle hippies) were performing one of their ceremonies. It wasn't very Pagan, though I did get blessed by one chief man with a daub of holy mud on my forehead. Bongos and assorted drums beat out an earth rhythm, which all right did have the hypnotic effect of feeling sort of like mother nature's heartbeat or whatever. We were inside the broken rings, sitting on the stones, right in the middle of any force that might call upon us or forth from us.
>
> (McKay 1996: 20)

Behind such simple interactions lies a complex net of relationships and traditions, of similarities and interactions.

THE SHADOW OF THE *AXIS MUNDI*

A recurrent archetype within religion is the *axis mundi*. This is a place where the human and spiritual worlds meet (Eliade 1964: 269). It is a crossroads of the living and the dead, of the human and the divine, of the real and the imaginary, of experience and belief. Jung's theories of the collective unconscious tell us that archetypes such as this arise as "mythological motifs that are also to be found in legends and fairytales around the world ... *archetypes*: that is, typical modes or forms in which these collective phenomena are experienced" (Jung 1976: 444–57).

Stonehenge can be described as an *axis mundi*, where heaven and earth come together at the solstice, where sun and moon, light and dark interact. This archetype can also be perceived both in the rituals of contemporary Pagans at the site and within popular music cultural references. The *Guitar Hero* computer game mentioned earlier, with its rock music, dancing Druids and spaceship, illustrates Stonehenge's interaction with this archetype well, with the winning game player climbing his stairway to heaven up the light beams of the spaceship.

The *axis mundi* is an interesting archetype because it often relates in part to a dark underworld, a place of the dead. One can travel up the *axis mundi* into the light, or down into the dark. This relates to Jung's concept of the shadow, an element of the collective unconscious "recognising the dark aspects of the personality as present and real" (*ibid*.: 14). Jung suggests that lack of understanding and acceptance of the shadow side of the individual leads to projecting these characteristics on to others, and on to the surrounding environment, and empowers the unconscious to carry out this projection. Christian theology and cosmology demonize the shadow, and in the past have projected the resultant imagery on to Paganisms; in the present, they have also projected it on to popular music cultures. Christianity also projects shadowy imagery on to the planet – as fallen, as the sinful realm of the devil.

Ritual structure can allow healthy exploration of the shadow without becoming lost within it, allowing individuals to go to a psychologically or spiritually dark place, to navigate through the dark archetypes of the collective unconscious, or other realms of the spirits of the dead. Such ritual structures exist within both Paganisms and popular music cultures. Access through an *axis mundi* to explore the shadow is often carried out through the rituals of possession or trance already discussed. Jung made the importance of such practices clear:

> Modern Man does not understand how much his "rationalism" (which has destroyed his capacity to respond to numinous symbols and ideas) has put him at the mercy of the psychic "underworld". He has freed himself from "superstition" (or so

he believes), but in the process, he has lost his spiritual values to a positively dangerous degree. His moral and spiritual tradition has disintegrated, and he is now paying for this break up in world-wide disorientation and dissociation.   (Jung 1964: 94)

Through connection with, and exploration of, the unconscious, Jung suggests that "the release of the unconscious through undoing repression can also lead to psychological transformation and the affirmation of life" (Stein 1995: 4). Such explorations are discussed as important and positive, contrasting with the way that "most major religious systems have actively discouraged direct contact with the numinous, reserving this for selected priests who follow proscribed patterns of worship" (Allen & Sabini 1997: 223). Approaches of this kind are key areas of interest for many Pagan groups, sometimes described as or linked to "shamanic" practices.

Popular cultural participants at Stonehenge are also engaging with this archetype, whether in the past at the free festival or in the present day when attending the solstices in such great numbers. They are also connecting with idealized notions of a prehistoric past, the ancestors and the line drawn through the modern utopian ideals of Woodstock, hippies and the Stonehenge Free Festival to the present day. Discussing the original purposes of founding the Stonehenge Free Festival, McKay quotes organizer Sid Rawle as saying "we come to Stonehenge because in an unstable world it is proper that the people should look for stability to the past in order to learn for the future" (McKay 1996: 17–20). The current musicalized representation of Stonehenge is perhaps a romanticized notion based around a hippie ideal, in which ancient images have been acted upon within contemporary media such as television, film and popular music imagery, but it remains a powerful representation that, in the minds of many, links popular music culture and Paganism.

POSTMODERN PILGRIMAGE

Numerous commentators have described the issues raised by the lack of ritual, meaning and religion in a secularized modern society (Heelas & Woodhead 2001). The increasing popularity of Paganisms is in part a response to this, through their appeal due to perceived links to ancient traditions, and as new forms of religious expression that are free from cultural ossification and the weight of hundreds of years of religious law and dogma. Stonehenge provides a suitable focus for such new forms of belief. We know it had ritual purpose in prehistory and that it ties into romantic historical views of earlier cultures – illustrated, for example, in Stukeley's discussion of Druids at Stonehenge (Piggot 1985), featuring in Thomas Hardy's novel *Tess of the D'Urbervilles* and in paintings by the likes of Turner and Constable.

Its significance, mystery and history have helped to make it a significant site within contemporary Paganisms.

Such links between the ancient and the modern, the sacred and secular, are an artefact of the impact of postmodernity upon religion. In such liquid times (Bauman 1993), morality is individuated, and organized religions, primary institutions (Lynch 2005) that proscribe set dogmatic approaches to behaviour, have tended to decrease in size and significance. Instead, an interest in spirituality and other methods of self-identification and exploration of beliefs has emerged in less formalized situations.

Paganisms can be described as secondary institutions (*ibid*.), as new religious movements (Cowan & Bromley 2008), as having a focus on spirituality rather than religion (Heelas *et al.* 2005) and as fulfilling the functions in society previously met by organized religions, which one might call old religious movements (ORMs). Popular music has also been described in these terms (Till 2010a).

Stonehenge is the best-known and most visited prehistoric site in the United Kingdom, and indeed is well known worldwide. It represents, or signifies, the ancient and the religious. Because Christianity has branded both Paganisms and popular musics that reference non-Christian religion as being linked to the demonic or shadow side of belief, both are perceived as oppositional to Christianity and, for a number of reasons, have become associated with one another. Stonehenge has a particular power to drive such associations, and to present a sacred popular, which includes various new forms of religion that are mixed with popular music culture. Thus an association between music, sound and Stonehenge is entirely understandable. Whether such religious activity is explicit religion, or more likely implicit religion (Bailey 1997, 2001), is perhaps not as important as knowing that it has a role in re-enchanting the world (Partridge 2005) and is of significance to those participating.

Stonehenge acts today for the postmodern homeless self (Heelas & Woodhead 2001: 53) as a site of Pagan pilgrimage, just as it has for thousands of years. It brings together the powers of contemporary Paganisms and popular music culture to create a sense of collective effervescence through elements such as ritual, entrainment and trance, which helps to develop *communitas*, to bond groups of people together using ritual practices that involve music and sound, much as it did in the past. It is hard to know how much the acoustics of the site have influenced these rituals, but it seems that they may have at least played a part. Certainly it seems Stonehenge was likely to have sounded as interesting in prehistory as it does today, and that the acoustic field of the site is an important part of its overall field and its identity today.

The relationship between person and place is important within Paganisms, as the embodied and the relationship with the physical and the planet are more significant than they are within, for example, contemporary Christian culture. In popular music, a sense of place is important, as many popular music cultures have developed from specific scenes and are associated with particular local cultures. Collective ritual experiences are thus situated and localized, giving more significance to the experience of the individual and also to the power and energy of the local, rather than trying to embrace a religious experience rooted in a meta-narrative that is the same everywhere. Many old religious movements are focused on experience of a God that is the same everywhere, of a special revelation reserved, for example, for Christians. Paganisms and popular music culture are set within the context of a more widely focused general revelation, validating an experience of local gods, the power and uniqueness of the singular experience. Thus they work well in context of ritual constructed around a specific setting such as a stone circle or music festival, and within a postmodern or liquid culture. They also have no single over-arching power structure that controls and bureaucratizes belief. They are therefore effective at plugging into the individual field of a specific place, and drawing upon its power and tradition.

As a site of ritual activity, Stonehenge seems to connect individuals to each other, and to the ecology of the local geography. It is has been a principal site of pilgrimage for participation in collective ritual experiences – especially at the solstices – since prehistory. It continues to be a signifier of the interaction of popular music and Paganisms in the popular imagination, and to provide a site outside of mainstream religious control for experiences that allow individuals to feel connected to past histories, to their embodied present and to a sense of place. As Yi-Fu Tuan tells us:

> The ideas "space" and "place" require each other for definition. From within the security and stability of place we are aware of the openness, freedom, and threat of space, and vice-versa. Furthermore, if we think of space as that which allows movement, then place is pause; each pause in movement makes it possible for location to be transformed into place.   (Tuan 1977: 6)

Stonehenge is indeed a place of pause – especially at the solstice, when the sun and even the passing of time seem to stand still, as the shortening or lengthening of the day and the associated march across the horizon of the point of sunrise and sunset pause before changing direction. In the liminal space of Stonehenge, the dead and the living, the past and the present, day and night, light and dark, summer and winter all meet. Stonehenge has for thousands of years been a crossroads, an *axis mundi*, and a place to mark the changes of the seasons. This impressive megalithic monument has created a sense of place that has drawn popular music and Pagan cultures together It is a good example of a ritual site that could be said to have a morphic field, within which the sonic field is an important component. If spirituality can be said to focus on relationships, then Stonehenge's field has developed through the interrelation of participants in collective ritual activities with the place of those activities. Built to venerate the ancestors, Stonehenge shows how the presence of the past charges the fields of cultural memory using the light and shade of the collective unconscious, allowing those who populate the site on the solstices today communion with the ancestors who stood there in the past.

4. REMEMBERINGS OF A PAGAN PAST: POPULAR MUSIC AND SACRED PLACE

Donna Weston

> Aren't we the carriers of the entire history of mankind? ... When
> a man is fifty years old, only one part of his being has existed for
> half a century. The other part, which also lives in his psyche, may
> be millions of years old ... Contemporary man is but the latest
> ripe fruit on the tree of the human race. None of us knows what
> we know.   (Carl G. Jung, in McGuire & Hull 1977)

The Romans used the term *Paganus* to refer to "people of place" – those whose customs and rituals were intrinsically tied to locality, and hence to land (York 2003: 12). In this context, identification with place is not an individual quality, but rather a collective identity in which the significance of the individual is understood by their place in a community and that community's connection with place. Michael York describes Paganism as an inherent human impulse and a collective identity. Bringing together these two concepts of memory and place, this chapter examines how a collective cultural memory of sacredness of place might find its expression in popular music, and argues that attachment to conceptual place is the expression of unconscious "rememberings" of a Pagan past. Theories of place and cultural memory are explored, with the aim of providing a framework within which references to place and uses of space in popular music can be recontextualised. It is proposed that while contemporary Paganism in many ways draws on a Romantic reification of nature, that Enlightenment rationalism forced a rupture between people and nature – and, by extension, place. In reference to Carl Jung's writing on nature, Sabini argues that this "loss of connection with Nature is ... neither a practical nor psychological but a religious one" (Sabini 2002: 2). Within this context, the Pagan impulse has become essentialized, so we have worship of "nature" as a whole (for example, in New Age music) or of "place" as a whole (as in world music), or it may manifest as references to nature and place in popular music that are not overtly Pagan – the inherent Pagan voice.

PAGANISM

Paganism is part of our cultural heritage. Although some might see current Neo-Pagan expressions as a resurgence of "ancient" belief systems, and therefore separated by centuries from their origins, what we know as Paganism has had a sustained existence, although often hidden from mainstream view through its vilification and subjugation by the Christian Church. The current resurgence of Pagan worldviews is sometimes attributed to the 1960s counter-culture, which witnessed a resurgence of interest in Celtic and Norse Pagan religions – the precursor, perhaps, to later revivals of Asatru, an ancient Nordic religion, and Druidism. The counter-cultural revolution itself, with its worldviews encompassing the celebration of life, communing with nature, and exploring alternative consciousnesses and spiritualities, has clear parallels with Pagan worldviews. Christopher Partridge argues that this movement "needs to be understood in the context of a prominent stream of Western Romantic Idealism which has, for over two centuries, expounded an optimistic, evolutionary, detraditionalized, mystical immanentism" (Partridge 2004: 96). From this period onwards, Partridge notes that it would be hard to find someone who was not familiar with at least some of the cultural symbols of alternative spiritualities, contributing to a "spiritual bricolage in which a range of beliefs and practices are reinterpreted in terms of the experience and well-being of the seeking self" (*ibid*.: 104).

However, this interest in alternative spiritualities – especially Paganism – has a much longer, continuous history. A revival of Greco-Roman magic during the Renaissance period, for example, reflected a growing interest in Pagan traditions. In the seventeenth century, scholars began to explore religion as related to ethnic identity, triggering the study of the religions of so-called "primitive" peoples. In the early 1600s, French astronomer and scholar Nicolas Fabri de Peiresc studied African Pagan traditions as a way of understanding the origins of Paganism in classical antiquity. In 1720, philosopher John Toland published *Pantheisticon*, or the Liturgy of the Socratic Fraternity (see Pattison 1987: 23), in which he imagined a British society in which two religions dominated: one was Christianity, which Toland envisaged as the religion of the ignorant masses; the other was pantheistic, conducted in secret for fear of "bewildering the credulous multitude". Within this pantheistic worldview, everything was seen as connected and organic.

The Romantic period witnessed the literary Celtic and Viking revivals, which portrayed these historical Pagans as noble savages. Reconstructions of Pagan mythology from folklore or fairy tales also enjoyed a resurgence at this time, most notably in the tales of the Brothers Grimm. The latter half of the nineteenth century saw the rise of the Spiritualist movement and non-traditional worldviews such as Helena Blavatsky's Theosophy, triggering a renewed interest in the occult. *The Witch Cult in Western Europe* was published in 1921 by Margaret Murray, in which she claimed witchcraft as an ancient fertility religion, following this in 1931 with a controversial book, *The God of the Witches*, in which she described Paganism as a religion with an unbroken line up until that time. In 1951, the last of the old witchcraft laws in England was repealed, followed shortly after by the publication in 1954 of self-claimed "hereditary witch" Gerald Gardner's *Witchcraft Today*, often cited as the catalyst for the rise of Neo-Paganism. While the above does not attempt to represent a conscious continuity of Pagan thought, York notes that "these responses ... tend to spring from deep-rooted collective habits that antedate any self-consciously created theological system. They may be Pagan, but they are Pagan behaviorally rather than Pagan religiously" (York 2003: 149).

Graham Harvey's description of Paganism as an "ecological spirituality" (Harvey 1997: 21) is especially pertinent to this chapter and to this definition can be added the consistent expression of a veneration of "place". Paganism therefore is rooted in the sacredness of place. York uses the terms "geoPaganism" and "recoPaganism" to encapsulate the ways in which this attachment to place is expressed. While recoPaganism refers to deliberate attempts to reconstruct the rituals of a Pagan past, geoPaganism encapsulates a more reflexive, unconscious sense of connectedness to place (York 2003: 60–61). These two terms are useful ways to frame the discussion of the music and musical events that follows, in that they describe the ways in which space is used and place imagined in these contexts. For York, Paganism is understood as "endorsing the relationship between physical and supernatural realities as well as human ... consciousness" (*ibid.*: 162). He understands it as "both a behavior and a religion. As a behavior it is to be seen in the spontaneous and auto-reflexive quality." (York 2000: 31). This is the quality explored here, specifically in musical expression.

MUSIC

Connell and Gibson note that "popular music illuminates place, either directly through lyrics and visuals, metaphorically through heightened perceptions, through sounds that are seen as symbolic of place ... and in performances that create spaces of sentiment" (Connell & Gibson 2003: 88). They describe a conceptual shift in the way musical texts are examined geographically, marked by a move from more objective studies to those that interpret spaces as a form of text and describe how "music nourishes imagined communities, traces links to distant and past places" (*ibid.*: 271). This is precisely the framework that informs the following discussion of a selection of musical expressions: what can we read from the spaces in which this music is produced and consumed, what communities do they imagine, which distant pasts do they draw from, and could these pasts be Pagan ones?

At Australian music festivals such as WOMADelaide, the Woodford Folk Festival and Melbourne's Rainbow Serpent Festival, we witness a focus on indigeneity, cultural identity, connection with nature and place, and an acceptance – indeed celebration – of alternative modes of thinking at odds with the hegemonic monotheistic worldviews that dominate the industrialized world. In other words, when interpreted through a Pagan lens, it is in these festivals and their music that the ideologies of Paganism, and theories of memory and place, coincide. Marketed as a world music festival, WOMADelaide clearly aligns itself with environmental issues, with media releases in 2008 declaring it a carbon-neutral weekend. The focus on stage at festivals like WOMADelaide is cultural and ethnic identity – in other words, on place of origin, as well as an alignment with ideals that convey a sense of deep connection with the earth. These festivals are often themed as a celebration of these ideals, with many non-musical activities promoting a sense of community and connection – even ritual, such as in the nightly lighting of a spectacular candle display at WOMADelaide in 2008.

Although the name of the Woodford Folk Festival highlights its folk origins, many of the artists performing also perform at the various WOMAD (which stands for World of Music, Arts and Dance) and similar music festivals around the world. What is interesting about this cross-fertilization of genres is that while at WOMADelaide the focus is clearly on cultural and ethnic identity, at Woodford it is on the authenticity of the folk musician as the storyteller, the carrier of cultural memory. This was especially evident in the "Folklines" programme of the 2010–11 festival, described as touching "the cultural heart – the heart connected to the sacred, to ritual and celebratory traditions of music and dance … sustained or revived by families and communities immersed in the strengths of their culture". The "traditional folk" programme invites the listener to "connect to the timeless human experience through the legacy of our ancestors … Sing with the session players … as they blend and weave to create a venue that explores the vibrancy of our roots." The importance of cultural memory is highlighted, with the traditional folk programme describing how "at every point in time, we are at a unique juncture between past and present, remembering and embodying the lore passed down by our ancestors, and unravelling the golden thread by which this knowledge travels to our children". Pagan themes are evident from the first pages of the programme booklet, which outlines the focus on ritual and ceremony as a way to "remember and re-create our connection with the physical and non-physical environments". The opening ceremony featured Morris dancers, a burning of the Wickerman, and a puppeteer who led the "BABELbarong, mythological spirit of protection for the forest and land". The "voice of the ancestors" fire event is a highlight of the opening ceremony. Environmental concerns are as prominent at Woodford as they are at WOMADelaide, with the "Greenhouse Programme" highlighting ecological events throughout the duration of the festival.

Another kind of festival that often displays overtly Pagan themes is found in some rave cultures in which a kind of neo-tribalism is evident. Graham St John has written extensively on such festivals, and discusses the topic further in Chapter 9. He has referred to some as "techno-Pagan doofs", which have come to be connected with a strong sense of ecological spirituality (St John 2004c: 43). These festivals are often aligned with eclipses, solstices and full moons, expressing a connection with natural rhythms in what York would identify as recoPaganism. The annual Rainbow Serpent Festival exemplifies this ethos – for example, on its 2008 festival website (http://rainbowserpent. net) it described itself as welcoming us to "the land, honouring the ancestors who walked before us" and creating a "harmonious relationship with the local people, the ancestors and the spirits of the land".

Drawing on a past that stretches back at least four millennia, the Stonehenge Free Festival, which was held between 1974 and 1984, and the Glastonbury Festival, which has been running since 1970 (see McKay 2000) are examples of musical events with connections to specific places in which alternative identities are constructed with strong links to the genius loci of those places. Rupert Till explores the connections between Stonehenge and music in Chapter 3. That these places hold strong cultural memories is perhaps best exemplified through music in Led Zeppelin's "Battle of Evermore" (1971), where Robert Plant refers to the apples of Avalon, a possible reference to the translation of the Celtic word *avalon* as apple; the ancient place of Avalon is often referred to as the "apple isle". Plant goes on to describe how the land there is cared for, and should not be forgotten, describing the debt of gratitude the earth is owed.

These sites have a prominent place in recent and past cultural memory. Archaeologists Jenny Blain and Robert Wallis explore the interactions between modern Pagans and ancient, sacred sites, which occur in ways that align with York's definition of recoPaganism. They describe the context of modern Pagan engagements with these sites as a "new folklore", which centres on the sacredness of such places, where it is claimed that "the spirit/ energy of the land can be felt more strongly" (Blain & Wallis 2003: 310). Arguably, recoPagan practices actively construct myths of place; however, "myth is tested against the emotional needs of the living, not the objective events of the past" (Pattison 1987: x). In other words, the specificities of the past are less relevant than the ways in which they are reconstructed to meet contemporary socio-cultural needs.

Although visually and musically varied, all of these festivals display in various ways a deep reverence for the earth, often overtly expressing alternative worldviews and ways of thinking, focusing especially on themes of connectedness to place. In most, there is a clear connection between Paganism and eco-sensibilities, but rather than a codified Paganism, these festivals represent a set of expressions that draws from a pool of common characteristics. Martin Stokes points to the power of musical events to evoke collective memories and "present experiences of place with an intensity, power and simplicity unmatched by any other social activity" (Stokes 1994: 3). These festivals are evidence of this, and support Connell and Gibson's description of popular music having "the ability to mediate social knowledge [and] reinforce (or challenge) ideological constructions of contemporary (or past) life" (Connell & Gibson 2003: 270).

A genre specific to Paganism is Pagan metal, discussed in depth by Deena Weinstein in Chapter 5 (see also D. Weston 2010); it looks to the ancient past for identity. It is a "global culture", transcending national boundaries, but is what nationalism studies professor Anthony Smith (1990: 179) would describe as "essentially memoryless", and therefore has to be "painfully put together, artificially, out of the many existing folk and national identities into which humanity has been so long divided". Pagan metal constructs meaning from the Pagan commonalities of each of the local genres through which it is represented. It is somewhat different from other sub-genres of rock in that it began as a construction of local identity, and is therefore *a priori* linked with place. Pagan metal venerates the earth differently from the above festivals by actively constructing memory *through* place. Wherever they manifest locally, Pagan metal lyrics and imagery will always refer to the specificity of the local context, with particular emphasis on a sense of historical continuity through landscape. These are just a few examples that lend themselves to exploration in the context of cultural memory, Paganism and place. Reverence for the past is seen in the focus on mythology in progressive rock and the ancient folk themes explored by Rush and Hawkwind, while alternative spiritualities are explored in the occult themes heard in the music of Black Sabbath, and seen in Led Zeppelin's concert film *The Song Remains the Same* (1976), where Jimmy Page's character meets with tarot figure The Hermit; they are also there in Jim Morrison's obsession with native American culture. All are examples of the intersection of place and cultural memory, and all lend themselves to interpretation from a Pagan perspective.

While these are fairly overt expressions of Pagan sensibilities, and provide clear examples of the links between Paganism and place, references to place in lyrics are more ambiguous. Connell and Gibson (2003: 71) note that "not all lyrics seek to convey a sense of place or identity", arguing that most popular music "is subtle, ambivalent or vague in its destinations and descriptions of place and identity", creating an "imaginary identification". They point to the range of possible themes of place, from "classical cartographies of country and western to the metaphysical spaces of ambient and 'new age' genres" (*ibid.*: 73). What follow are examples of the ways in which lyrical themes of connection to place can reflect Pagan beliefs, while offering insights into cultural perceptions and memories of place. These are exemplars, aimed at illustrating a number of ways in which lyrical content can be interpreted from a Pagan perspective, and have been chosen from different decades and countries to illustrate that such examples are not specific to any one socio-cultural context.

The Beatles' "Mother Nature's Son" (1968), for example, invites the listener to sit by a stream in the mountains and, in an overt anthropomorphism, asks us to listen to music as *she* surrounds around us. There we will find Paul McCartney – who refers to himself as Mother Nature's son, as indicated in the title of the song – clearly linking person to place and nature. At "Solsbury Hill" (1977), an eagle offers to take Peter Gabriel "home" while Gabriel is feeling connected to the scenery around him, and disconnected from the mechanical or industrial world. Home here can be read as somewhere away from the urban, a reading supported by his 1982 track "Rhythm of the Heat", in which he sings about the power of the land and invites the listener not only to appreciate the fresh water and air, but to slow down time, or disregard it altogether, through quite literally breaking physical connections to time and space. This can be read as a critique of modernity, industrialization and technology, all of which are described as standing in the way of fulfilment, which can only come from connecting with nature. It is perhaps no surprise that Gabriel later went on to establish the Real World recording label, out of which evolved the WOMAD music festivals.

In Australia, Goanna's "Solid Rock" (1982), while ostensibly describing the wrongs of the Anglo-Celtic invasion of Australia, also notes the sacredness of the land in the lyrics, equating the "solid rock" of the title quite literally with sacred ground. Icehouse tells the same story in "Great Southern Land" – or rather, asks the listener to pay attention to the stories the land is telling to those who care to – or know how to – listen. Reflecting the anthropomorphism of The Beatles, the song invokes the listener to the wind so they can hear it talking like Iva Davies does. While ostensibly a socio-political commentary on the treatment of Indigenous Australians, these songs also clearly recognize the sacredness of place.

American artist Bright Eyes perhaps best sums up ideas of connection to and sacredness of place in the song "I Must Belong Somewhere", from the 2007 album *Cassadaga*, in which he describes his connection to the earth in terms of the forest's ability to hear every sound down to individual blades of grass, emphasizing a sacred interconnectedness inherent in nature from which a sense of belonging is drawn, as hinted at in the title. XTC make direct reference to Pagan beliefs and their links to the earth in the song "Greenman" (1999), a direct reference to a nature god of the Pagan pantheon: the lyrics ask the listener to pay homage to the Greenman. In recognition of the long history of both mythology and of human connection to nature, XTC describe a connection to the Greenman, and by extension to nature, that has endured throughout eternity, and will continue to do so.

All the above examples – whether festival, genre or song – have in common their attachment to even reverence for, place. But these are not specific places that can be identified on a map; even when identified by name, they stand for much more – they are places as concepts, as constructs, idealized places that can be read as cultural texts. Most importantly, they are places where the physicality of the land is more important than its location. That this is consistent across generations and genres is testament to an enduring attachment to the land. George Lipsitz offers one possible contribution to this consistency in his discussion of the effect of electronic media on memory, in which he describes how audiences can now "experience a common heritage with people they have never seen" (Lipsitz 2001: 5), a cultural memory that transcends national, ethnic and cultural boundaries and differentiations. Lipsitz further notes that "all cultural expressions speak to both residual memories of the past and emergent hopes for the future" (*ibid*.: 13), providing a context within which a memory of a past linked to land, and a future in which this land will be revered, can be understood.

Ethnomusicologist Caroline Bithell shows that the pasts expressed through music can coexist, as she explores "alternative worlds … onto which we can project a multitude of meanings and interpretations" (Bithell 2006: 5). The past, then, is a "source of cultural symbols that have a power beyond mere history" (*ibid*.: 32). In the context of these various reflections on the multiplicity of potential manifestations of borderless pasts, the next section seeks to define the ways in which cultural memory brings these cultural symbols into the present.

CULTURAL MEMORY

Memory is classified in various ways – for example, collective, social and cultural – but however classified, Edward Saïd argues that many "people now look to this refashioned memory, especially in its collective form, to give themselves a coherent identity … a place in the world" (Saïd 2000: 179). Cultural memory theories are interdisciplinary, drawing from the fields of cultural studies, historiography and psychology, the last of which is addressed by Halbwachs. In realizing that mental life is not entirely dependent on an individual's psychology, Halbwachs recognizes that psychologists needed to turn to new theory, cultural rather than biological, to explain group manifestations of these mental states. He describes these collective manifestations as a "mental reality which constitutes and at the same time transcends the individual consciousness" (Halbwachs 1939: 814). Collective psychology looks to the social – that which can be seen from the outside, but which each individual carries internally. If we are to understand the motivations behind the various individual expressions of place found in the musical examples, it is to the collective consciousness and experience that we should turn.

Expanding Halbwachs's theories of collective memory, the term "cultural memory" was first developed by historian Jan Assmann, who describes its function as one that "disseminates and reproduces a consciousness of unity … and a sense of belonging to members of a group" (Assmann 2006: 38).

Of particular relevance here are what Assmann describes as narrative linguistic and scenic visual memory (*ibid.*: 2): scenic memory is involuntary, further from consciousness, and deeper embedded in the psyche, but is at some stage transformed into narrative, or voluntary, memory. If popular music reconstructions of place are indeed a manifestation of a cultural memory of past connections to land, as is proposed here, then the concept of scenic memory is especially pertinent in that it relates to referred meanings that are an unconscious yet essential aspect of what it is to be human, and therefore must – and will – be transported to the conscious in narrative form. These expressions, which are "imagined or perceived", "become knowable only when they enter the frame of reference of social thought; but ... they are transformed into collective states with only a fringe of organic consciousness" (Halbwachs 1939: 816). Halbwachs notes that while these memories manifest in "the states of consciousness of a ... number of individuals comprising the group ... it is necessary, in order to reach it and study it, to seek it in the manifestations and expressions of the entire group taken as a whole" (*ibid.*: 819). Therefore, in examining group products within the social framework of popular music production, it should be possible to identify aspects which reflect the cultural memory of the group.

References to place are found throughout popular music events and lyrics, and while in many cases they refer to specific places – the product of individual memory – it is argued here that many such references will fall into the category of Halbwachs' scenic memory: perhaps imagined, and certainly intangible, these places will reflect the cultural memory of the group, but are realized in the consciousness of the individual. Such memories are not pure representations of a collective past, and are "rooted not only in traditions but also in images and ideas derived from the present and in a concrete experiential reality ... these collective memories are not pure recollections but reconstructions" (*ibid.*: 511). For example, while a cultural memory of connection to the land may exist, it will be reconstructed within, and be relevant to, its contemporary cultural context.

Assmann and Czaplicka (1995) identify six characteristics of cultural memory; the second, "its capacity to reconstruct", is pertinent here. Noting that memory on its own is not capable of preserving the past, the remembered past is dependent on "which society in which era can reconstruct within its contemporary frame of reference" (*ibid.*: 130). "Through its cultural heritage a society becomes visible to itself and to others" (*ibid.*: 133). We can therefore learn much about a group and its tendencies through examining the past with which it identifies and which it expresses. Cultural memory theory seeks to understand the conditions surrounding the creation and transmission of texts, focusing on the role of the past, the ways it re-presents itself, and the motives for seeking it (*ibid.*: 1). It is argued here that one past that is remembered is an essentialized Pagan one, motivated by an inherent attachment to nature, and manifested in lyrical references to sacred place and space. As will be explored later, the social and cultural context of recent history is one that lends itself to such memory, with its increasing focus on ecological concerns that value the physicality of natural places, and increasing expressions of those concerns in popular music culture. It is to concepts of place that we now turn.

PLACE

The references to place in the examples above encompass an array of expressions from metaphysical, conceptual and imagined places to specific places whose communicative reach expands limitlessly beyond their physical boundaries. In many ways reflecting the Roman description of the *Paganus* – people of place – for Edward Casey, "taken for granted is the fact that we are emplaced beings to begin with, that place is an *a priori* of our existence on earth" (Casey 1998: x). This concept is supported by French philosopher Gaston Bachelard, who proposed that "the first image of immensity is a terrestrial image", placing the focus of place in its "true place" in the mind, or soul (in *ibid.*: 287). For Bachelard, non-physical spaces were as valid or real as physical places. In this context, place is less about spatial dimensions than an opportunity to gain understanding of the world and the "place" of humans in that world. "Place, at a basic level, is space invested with meaning" (Cresswell 2004: 12).

Humanistic geography is a field that conceptualizes place as a subjective experience, drawing on the philosophies of existentialism and phenomenology, and is associated with leading thinkers in the field such as Yi-Fu Tuan and Edward Relph. "It was not so much places (in the world) that interested the humanists but 'place' as an idea, concept and way of being-in-the-world" (*ibid.*: 20). "Relph's notion of existential insideness – a situation of feeling completely but unselfconsciously at home in place – is especially crucial to study of the vernacular lifeworld since it identifies immersion in its most profoundly unreflective state" (in Seamon 1991: 204). Alan Drengson, editor of environmental journal *The Trumpeter*, argues that phenomenological studies of place show that the more people are rooted in place, "the more their psyches become interwoven with the unique element of those places" (Drengson 1991: 160).

The conceptualization of place of Bachelard, Relph, Tuan and others is important here: it allows for the non-physical, of place as a phenomenon and opens the way for consideration of places that transcend their physical boundaries, while maintaining the physicality inherent in all places. These theories allow for an understanding of place as the subjective expression of those to whom it is attached, which Yi-Fu Tuan develops further, describing an "affective bond between people and place" (in Cresswell 2004: 20), for which he invented the descriptive term "topophilia". But by this he means something greater than an attachment to the dimensionality of a physical location, referring more to the physicality of any-place. Landscape architect Mary-Jo Gordon expands this notion to one of spirituality that draws on attachment to places, understanding it as "the reality of a non-material realm [which] intersects with the material realm of the landscape", seen in "the recognition of places with inherent sacredness as well as places where sacredness is invested by human intuition" (Gordon 1999: 10). She describes a long history of associating natural phenomena with the transcendental experience, and notes its recognition within global indigenous and ancient cultures. It is in the context of this history that we can begin to imagine a sense of place that transcends confined places, and times. It is through the cultural memory of these relationships to place, nourished by a history of transcendent experience associated with nature, that a true topophilia has developed and survived. This "love of place", in all of its musical manifestations, is most clearly seen in the more overt Pagan expressions of the various festivals and genres discussed, especially those that actively promote alternative spiritualities, but is also discernible in the countless lyrical references to place in various ways, which are more prevalent than the small sample presented in this chapter.

SYNTHESIS

In bringing together space, place, memory and culture, a number of problems arise: the questions surrounding border inhabitants, also problematic for ethnic and national identity studies; the possibility for significant cultural differences to exist within the one locality; post-colonial hybrid cultures; and the transformations resulting from the increasing connectedness of places due to globalization and technology (J. Ferguson & Gupta 1992: 7–8). The last of these is especially pertinent to this chapter: that cultural products and practices, as well as the people who produce and consume them, are increasingly mobile can result in "a profound sense of loss of territorial roots" (*ibid.*: 9). But as the places themselves become increasingly nebulous, we see more and more that "imagined communities … come to be attached to imagined places, as displaced peoples cluster around remembered or imagined homelands, places or communities" (*ibid.*: 10).

Some cultural memory theorists approach this issue of displacement by contextualizing collective memory as a result of rupture, absence or a break with the past, a "substitute, surrogate or consolation for something that is missing" (Bardenstein 1999: 148). Exactly what is missing will determine the form and content of the collective memory. Contemporary humanistic and transpersonal psychology addresses this rupture overtly, specifically within a growing branch of the discipline known as "ecopsychology", which "offers a diagnosis for an assumed human estrangement from nature and

offers prescriptions designed to help industrial humans re-connect to earth"
(Taylor 2001a: 237), an approach also promoted by Carl Jung as seen in the
following extract:

> Seeking to control nature isolates itself from her and so robs man
> of his own natural history. He finds himself transplanted into a
> limited present … Hemmed round by rationalistic walls, we are
> cut off from the eternity of nature. Analytical psychology seeks
> to break through these walls by digging up again the fantasy-
> images of the unconscious that our rationalism has rejected.
> These images lie beyond the walls, they are part of the nature in
> us, which lies buried in our past and against which we have bar-
> ricaded ourselves behind walls of reason.
> (Jung 1970, para 739, in Sabini 2002: 199)

At this point, I wish to expand on this idea of displacement, and the idea of
"conceptual processes of placemaking" (J. Ferguson & Gupta 1992: 11). Due
to the rapid sequence of changes symptomatic of the modern world, "people
are looking for a past seemingly removed from the unrelenting … forces that
have come to be called globalization" (Alderman & Hoelscher 2004: 349).
In doing so, they turn to what historian Pierre Nora calls "sites of memory",
both concrete and physical, and non-material, for example rituals which give
a sense of the past (in *ibid.*: 349) or, in the case presented in this chapter, the
"terrestrial" site of cultural memory which all humans hold in common –
the earth. As has been shown, Paganism is one of the sites of this cultural
memory, and has seen a long history of relatively continuous recognition in
one form or another. However, it has also endured a long history of persecution based on political and moralistic motives, which date at least to the
time of the establishment of Christianity as the dominant religion.

It was, however, around the Enlightenment era that more intellectually
derived factors contributed to its positioning at the periphery of mainstream
thought and belief. "Rationalized" out of the West through movements such
as Protestantism and Humanism, the Pagan impulse was pushed back into
the unconscious as somehow primitive and "uncultured". Contributing to
this rupture from nature was the Enlightenment idea of the Noble Savage, a
"creation of a Western minority and coeval with the industrial era, of which
it is the pastoral reflection" (Pattison 1987: 37). The Noble Savage is not
aware that he is noble, or savage; the concept is dependent on the projection of these attributes by the "intellectually superior white man"; the Noble
Savage and his environment are therefore firmly placed at the periphery of
what is perceived as cultivated.

It is proposed here that the rationalism embraced by the Enlightenment
resulted in alienation from the land, exacerbated through urbanization,
and also from place through migration and consequent globalization. Jung

argued that nature, the "primitive" human instinct, animals and creative fantasy had been the most severely repressed aspects of human existence, due to the influence of Judeo-Christian religion (Sabini 2002: 2). Modern Paganism in many ways draws from reactions to this alienation – for example, the Romantic "philosophical celebration of the popular, something of a displaced desire for 'archaic roots'" (Albanese 1996: 41). Rousseau wrote of a polytheistic religion that he argued had its roots in antiquity, and idealized nature and the "savage spirit" as at the heart of what it was to be human, and "saw folklore as the path to nature, and therefore to the sacred" (Magliocco 2004: 38). The dichotomy represented in Romantic (abstracted Pagan) and Enlightenment tensions can be expressed in a number of ways: land as sacred, land as property; getting back to nature, usurping nature; natural cycles, the forward arrow of progress; music as ritual, music for profit.

Turning to the idea of the rural, or nature, as conceptual place, Bauerle-Willert argues that "nature generates culture, which in turn changes or even destroys that very nature … culture becomes something that should close the gap, that should restore an attachment to our natural base … an organic emanation of the genius loci" (Bauerle-Willert 2003: 150). Placing nature as the rupture point, Edward Casey asks "What if nature is the true a priori, that which was there first, that from which we came, that which sustains us even as we cultivate and construct?" (Casey 1993: x). He proposes that this rupture is at least in part the result of an increasing tendency – the result of urbanization – to see nature as something outside of ourselves: "the very idea of edging out from built place into the wild world beyond presumes the primacy of a humanocentric starting point … the very act of putting the non-human world at the periphery of what is cultivated marginalizes nature" (*ibid.*: 186).

Arguably, it marginalizes worldviews that revere nature as well. According to philosopher Ingrid Stefanovic (1991: 196), we tend to see ourselves as managers of the environment, which in turn is seen as something "out there" – at least for urban dwellers.

Casey proposes that "an outright geocentrism – or perhaps better, an engaged eco-centrism – is the most efficacious antidote to centuries of un-self-questioning anthropocentrism" (Casey 1993: 187). This proposal is to a great extent being met by environmental movements, which manifest themselves in a variety of ways, and are often supported by and expressed through music festivals as seen above, but most overtly within radical ecological movements such as bioregionalism. The preamble of the First North American Bioregional Congress in 1984 makes the connections clear: "Bioregionalism recognizes, nurtures, sustains and celebrates our local connections with land … It is taking the time to learn the possibilities of place." (Taylor 2000: 57). Taylor describes bioregionalism as "the conscious manifestation of the unconscious Pagan impulse … a rapidly growing green political philosophy emerging with greatest force from within the "counter-culture" in the United States" (*ibid.*: 49).

Linking Paganism, memory and place are the two main convictions central to bioregionalism: that an ecologically sustainable lifeway is dependent on "being there and learning the land", and that to do so requires a "fundamental reorienting of human consciousness", both based on the clearly Pagan premise that "the land is sacred and all its inhabitants are worthy of reverence" (*ibid.*: 2). Taylor contextualizes bioregionalism and movements like it within Aldous Huxley's "perennial philosophy", "a global religion of primal, ancient lineage, encompassing diverse, nature-beneficent cultures and lifeways" (*ibid.*: 180). "Earth-based spiritualities are based on personal experiences that foster a bonding with nature. These experiences ... are expressed in plural ways ... [through] a creative bricolage assembled from older religious traditions" (Taylor 2001b: 226). This bricolage is only possible through cultural memory; that this memory has links to earth-based spiritualities shows the importance of physical places to the human psyche and offers ways of understanding the importance of place in popular music culture.

CONCLUSION

Through an interdisciplinary exploration of uses of and references to place in popular music, this chapter has explored new ways of understanding the relevance of place to expressions of Paganism in popular culture. It has been shown that Paganism is informed primarily by a reverence for place; its relative continuity in recorded history demonstrates not only its durability, but also its cultural relevance – testimony to the importance of nature, and therefore conceptual place, to the human psyche. That nature and place are inherent needs is evidenced in the continuing growth of movements such as bioregionalism, and it is no coincidence that such movements have significant Pagan involvement. The longevity of various Paganisms has provided a legacy of symbols in the cultural memory from which its recontextualizations can draw, demonstrated in the multiplicity of ways in which Pagan ways of thinking are conceptualized in popular music production, performance and reception.

In presenting this research, I am aware of the subjective nature of the hypothesis, and that it does not address questions of reception and intent. Gordon Lynch, in his article examining the role of popular music in constructing alternative spiritual identities, acknowledges the contributions of Graham St John and Christopher Partridge in demonstrating how alternative spiritual symbols can be encoded in music, but notes that they do not demonstrate how audiences make use of the music and its symbols in constructing their own alternative identities (Lynch 2006: 481). I would argue, however, that while this would be a valuable contribution to the field, given the demographic range of the audiences and the wide range of potential "uses" of the music, the information gleaned from such a study may not be as pertinent as first thought – at best, it would be narrow. Further, it does not take into consideration the implicit, unconscious and involuntary kinds of memory that may be at the core of the music's production and reception. It also does not take into account how audiences may subconsciously be "shaped" rather than how they consciously shape themselves.

George Lipsitz proposes that "popular culture has no fixed forms ... similarly artefacts of popular culture have no fixed meanings ... consumers of popular culture move in and out of subject positions in a way that allows the same message to have widely varying meanings at the point of reception" (Lipsitz 2001: 13). Lynch proposes examining "the role of popular music in stimulating the rise of alternative spiritual identities and ideologies" as potentially a more relevant and fruitful endeavour (Lynch 2006). What he does not suggest, and what is addressed here, is the opposite: the influence of a long history, a cultural memory, of (now) alternative spiritual ideologies, specifically nature-based ones, on popular music texts. Further, this analysis focuses on the implicit rather than explicit use of just symbols, more in keeping with Christopher Partridge's (2004: 40) theory that Western culture is currently experiencing a resacralization, seen in a turn away from orthodox religion to alternative ones. As Partridge argues, "popular culture has a relationship with contemporary alternative religious thought that is both expressive and formative ... [it] is both an expression of the cultural milieu from which it emerges and formative of that culture" (*ibid*.: 123). The cultural milieu from which the musical examples emerge is long and continuous, filled with a wealth of cultural symbols from which a cultural memory can draw. Further, in identifying this milieu as a Pagan one, implicit and explicit connections to place as one of those cultural symbols enables an understanding of musical texts as constructions of an identity strongly linked to a primordial identification with a conceptual place that embodies landscape, nature and the earth.

5. PAGAN METAL

Deena Weinstein

Pagan metal arose from diverse strands of the metal meta-genre, and was initiated by bands spread across Europe's northern tier – from Ireland to Finland – at the start of the last decade of the twentieth century. It is not characterized by a cohesive musical style. Sonically, Pagan metal draws from a wide variety of metal styles, typically incorporating additional features of pre-modern instrumentation, rhythms and melodies. Textual elements, from the specific Pagan references in lyrics to the language in which they are expressed, also diverge widely.

What Pagan metal bands mean by the term "Pagan" varies wildly. The same can be said more generally about practitioners of Paganism today. Pagan metal bands can be grouped into three clusters. One is related to what is often called Neo-Paganism, derived from the work of Gerald Gardner ([1954] 2004) and other nineteenth-century sources that influenced Wiccan groups in the United Kingdom and North America. Gardner "effectively founded modern witchcraft, complete with its magic, tools, festivals, pantheon, and 'skyclad' (i.e., naked) rituals, with his book *Witchcraft Today*" (Sage 2009: 33). Another grouping of Pagan metal bands can be called "roots Paganism", focused on ancestral pre-Christian cultures – particularly warriors and ancient gods, such as the Vikings and the pantheon of Norse gods. A third set of bands is designated here as "chauvinistic Paganism", which scapegoats and demonizes those seen to be, or who have been, a threat to one's ethnic heritage – one's "roots".

In *Pagan Metal: A Documentary* (Zebub 2009), Alan Nemtheanga, lead vocalist of the Irish band Primordial, was asked to define "Pagan". His response was: "Realistically, if you were to get ten different people here from ten different Pagan bands in Europe and ask them 'What is a Pagan?' you'd get ten different answers." He bravely attempted to grasp the core of the sub-genre, saying it was composed of "a bunch of bands from different areas who are trying somehow to go against the grain to preserve some element of their own culture, of their own history, of their own past".

Like Pagan metal, Christian metal – another sub-genre held together not by its music but by its theme – is, as Marcus Moberg states, "as much about religion as it is about music or style" (Moberg 2007). The same could be said about some Pagan metal bands, but many more are as much about politics as they are about music, while others are about all three – music, religion and politics.

To add to the complexity, even the sub-genre designation "Pagan metal" is not used in any consistent manner. Bands, fans and mediators, such as record labels and concert promoters, tend to use the term "folk metal"[1] as a synonym, employing the two interchangeably. Many also use "Pagan/folk metal" or "folk/Pagan metal" (with or without the virgule) as the label for the style. For example, when a member of the Latvian band Skyforger was asked how the band liked its music to be described, he replied: "I guess 'Pagan metal' or 'folk metal' would be more proper … I don't know, we never have put any sticker to our music. That's mostly metal press and their imagination" (Fjordi 2005). Writing about Pagan metal, a frustrated rock journalist concludes that it "is almost more of an idea than a genre" (Wiederhorn 2009: 60). Stéphane François uses the term "discursive syncretism" to describe the Euro-Pagan scene in general (François 2008: 51); it is a most appropriate descriptor for Pagan metal as well.

HISTORY OF PAGAN METAL

Pagan metal is firmly based in heavy metal. And heavy metal is a child of the 1960s counter-culture, with its interests in the occult, shamans, nature and pre-modern modes of living (Roszak 1969). Starting with heavy metal's origins in Black Sabbath and Led Zeppelin, Pagan elements of one sort or another, such as songs about the occult and Viking warriors, have abounded. The genre was also steeped in a medievalism of sorts, the revival of Romanticism's look backwards that privileges muscle over machine, warriors over technocrats, and an interest in rebellious symbols like the devil (Weinstein 1991). Sage argues that:

> Romanticism and Paganism are both counter-movements – counter-Enlightenment and countercultural, respectively. What they counter – for example, the Industrial Revolution, and what is imagined to be the barrenness and loneliness of modern social life – are critical themes at this moment in history.   (Sage 2009: 28)

Both are interested in nature and in heroism, she contends, and "both the Romantic and Pagan movements are diverse and nonhomogenous".

Pagan metal was specifically parented at the start of the 1990s by a handful of northern European bands. They came from the1980s fragmentations of heavy metal – thrash, death, doom and black sub-genres – that collectively have become known as extreme metal. The most notable of these early Pagan metal bands include Skyclad from Britain, Bathory from Sweden, Enslaved from Norway, Primordial from Ireland and Amorphis from Finland. As with all styles of music, bands were playing Pagan metal before their similarities were grasped, and thus before the new style was named.

In Newcastle in the United Kingdom, Martin Walkyier, vocalist for the thrash metal band Sabbat, founded Skyclad. Walkyier's Pagan metal future was foreshadowed in Sabbat's 1989 release, *Dreamweaver*, which dealt with Celtic and Anglo-Saxon mythology. His thrash metal core, coated with Celtic musical elements, was evident in the new project, named by the term for nudity in Wiccan rituals (Sage 2009: 33). The title of Skyclad's 1991 debut, *The Wayward Songs of Mother Earth*, gives evidence of the centrality of "nature" that runs though the band's work. Skyclad was the first band to be described as Pagan metal. That term was used in a major metal magazine, *Kerrang!*, in its review of Skyclad's first release, taking it from the album's first track, "Pagan Man".

At the same time, a different form of Pagan metal was emerging in Scandinavia that eventually would be called Viking metal. It was initiated by the Swedish band Bathory (mainly a project of one person, Quorthon), which had also originated black metal in the latter part of the 1980s. Bathory's fourth release, *Hammerheart*, in 1990, can be cited as the first Pagan metal recording. Its songs are stories of the Viking era. "Shores in Flames", for example, describes the mayhem of the plundering Vikings. "One Rode to Asa Bay" tells of their forced conversion to Christianity; it is a requiem for the loss of a better way of life. *Hammerheart* was an important influence on black metal bands, starting with Enslaved in Norway and Unleashed in Sweden, then spreading to many others, including Einhejer, Borknagar and Ensiferum. It is fitting that Pagan metal began with Viking metal, given that the Vikings were Europe's last Pagans, converted slowly and with reluctance to Christianity.

Early black metal had an anti-Christian/pro-Satanism focus, and on a symbolic level it was not a stretch for some bands to shift to Norse religion and heroic Viking history. Although Norse gods are plentiful, metal bands tend to select those that embody the heroic masculinity that metalheads have always valued. Chief among them is Odin (Wodin), god of War, and his son, Tor (Thor), whose hammer, "the hammer of the gods", defended the Pagans against the Christians.

In addition to their lyrical focus, Viking metal bands tend toward a heavy use of keyboards, often played at a swift, galloping pace. They commonly add some local cultural flourishes – traditional instruments, ethnic melodies and Norwegian, or even old Norse, textual elements. Enslaved's singer Grutle Kjellson "used to sing in Icelandic because of that language's similarity to Old Norse" (Sanneh 2007). Enslaved had a split album with Emperor some months earlier, before the former band's first full-length release. The media storm about murders and church burnings by some members of black metal bands, including Emperor, had helped draw attention to Norwegian black metal. *Frost*, Enslaved's 1994 debut, added some Scandinavian folk melodies to the band's black metal and, to underscore the point, the inner sleeve announced, in big letters, "Viking Metal". Subsequent Enslaved albums were titled with other aspects of Nordic character.

In Sweden, where the key extreme metal style was melodic death metal (the "Gothenberg sound"), Amon Amarth – whose name was taken from Tolkien's *The Lord of the Rings*,[2] also took up the Viking theme. The band's 1993 demo, *Thor Arise*, gave evidence of the group's commitment, which remains unbroken on its seventh album, *With Oden on Our Side*.

Keith Kahn-Harris describes these bands as:

> yearning for a Pagan past … constantly invoking the Vikings. They mourn the arrival of Christianity in the Middle Ages, almost claiming themselves to be colonised people. Pagan society is constructed as lacking the "weakness" that characterises contemporary society. Scandinavian bands are also fascinated by the Scandinavian countryside. Drawing on an ideology of romanticism, the "wildness" of the forests and mountains is contrasted with the effete cosmopolitanism of contemporary cities. These themes have also been incorporated by black metallers from other countries, with varying degrees of success.
>
> (Kahn-Harris 2007: 40–41)

Viking metal has travelled further than any Viking ship. Self-defined Pagan metal bands who describe their music as Viking metal can be found in the United States, Brazil and Uruguay, among other places. The sensationalism of some early Norwegian black metal musicians was a major impetus for the spread of black metal (Moynihan & Søderlind 1998). But Viking metal's greatest influence has been the inspiration that it has given to others to explore their own roots.

The echoes of Viking metal did not have far to go before being heard across the Baltic Sea. Starting in Lithuania – most notably with the band Obtest – the sound was called Baltic War metal. Obtest began in a black metal style with Lithuanian lyrics in 1993, but it was the band's 1997 release, *Tukstantmetis* (Millennium) that "signified the birth of Baltic War metal whose basic framework is based on folk music and is filled with combinations and influences from all possible metal styles" (Saltanaviciute 2002). Contesting the Scandinavian claim to the "last Pagans in Europe title", Michael Strmiska contends that: "A point of particular pride is the knowledge that Lithuania was the last country in all of Europe to officially abandon its native Pagan traditions and convert to Christianity in 1387" (Strmiska 2005: 241).

In neighbouring Latvia, another Baltic War metal band, Skyforger, began singing in Latvian. Skyforger focused on Pagan battles on *Kauja Pie Saules* (1998) then turned towards ancient Latvian religion on *Thunderforge* (2003). "The best way to describe Skyforger's sound," wrote a reviewer of *Kurbads* (AngryMetalguy 2010), "is a blend of 80s thrash, Iron Maiden and Bathory with a healthy dose of folk melodies." Baltic War metal bands sing about their ancestors' victorious battles and mythological encounters, and add folk instruments, such as kankles, whistles and bagpipes to their metal.

Another early Pagan metal band influenced by Viking metal is Graveland, from Poland. In the band's second release, *Thousand Swords*, in 1995, various folk styles were added to the group's black metal, and lyrics about Polish history and Slavic gods were introduced. The band's founder, guitarist and vocalist Rob Darken (b. Robert Fudali), is "considered to be one of the instigators of the National Socialist black metal movement, a controversial Pagan ideology that also frequently promotes racial separatism and anti-Semitism" (Larkin 2006).

Finland, also on the Baltic Sea, is a significant origination point of Pagan metal. Members of Amorphis came out of death metal, but their 1993 debut, *The Karelian Isthmus*, sported keyboards and doom metal riffs. Although the album was named after the site of a major Finnish battleground, it was Amorphis's next release, *Tales from the Thousand Lakes* (1994), whose lyrics firmly rooted the band in their homeland's past. This concept album is based on the Finnish epic of *Kalevala*,[3] which also inspired Johan Sibelius's nineteenth-century *Kullervo Symphony*, composed in support of his country's war of independence from Russia (according to Joseph Campbell, Kalevala means "heroes' land"; Campbell 2008: 256). "There'd be no Paganfest … if it wasn't for Amorphis' early dabbling in folk music and folk culture," exults a metal journalist interviewing the band (Chris D. 2009). Beyond Amorphis, a host of other Finnish Pagan megtal bands emerged at the end of the twentieth century, many of which are currently the most famous groups in the sub-genre. These include Ensiferum and Moonsorrow – both founded in 1995, Turisas and Finntroll – which started in 1997, and Korpiklaani – which began in 1999.

PAGAN METAL TODAY

Starting with those originating bands located in an arc across Northern Europe in the 1990s, and the dozens of others that swelled their ranks later in that decade, Pagan metal came into its own in the twenty-first century. There are now hundreds – or, depending on how one parses the sub-genre, thousands – of Pagan metal bands, found on all continents.

To get some idea of geographic distribution, the listing of the "Pagan metal" sub-genre bands in the online *Encyclopedia Metallicum* was consulted.

There were 1538 bands in the sub-genre. The site has the most extensive listing of metal bands of all types. Each band lists its sub-genre, musical style, lyrical themes, home country and the names of past and present members.

Western Europe, where Pagan metal began, makes up 44.4 per cent of all the bands in this dataset. Another 33.5 per cent of bands are from eastern Europe's former Soviet Bloc. North America has 8.2 per cent, and 11.5 per cent are in Latin America. There are few bands in Asia, Australasia, the Middle East and Africa, together comprising less than 2.4 per cent of all Pagan metal bands in the dataset.

The term "Pagan" has European roots, and this is one reason why there are few bands in areas outside Europe and North America. A number of metal bands exist in Singapore, Taiwan, India, Indonesia and Japan that do not refer to themselves as Pagan metal, nor do their fans or media. Yet these bands have all the Pagan metal features: use of folk instruments mixed into some extreme metal style, songs referencing their ethnic history and/ or old gods (particularly gods of war and nature), and musicians attired in ancient clothing, make-up and props. Chthonic from Taiwan and Rudra from Singapore are the best known among these.

By country, the largest number of Pagan metal bands – 212 – are in Germany, followed by 167 in Poland and 136 in Russia. Obviously, countries with larger populations potentially can have more bands than those with smaller populations. To adjust for this variable, a ratio was made between the number of Pagan metal bands and the country's population. The top ten countries, those with the highest ratio of Pagan metal bands per person, are led by the tiny Faroe Islands, with a population of fewer than 50,000; it is followed, in order, by Estonia, Finland, Iceland, Slovenia, Poland, Norway, Lithuania, Sweden and Greece.

Given that Pagan metal is as much about Paganism as it is about music, it is relevant to note the relative strength of Pagan metal to all metal bands in a given area. Examining those countries with twenty or more metal bands of any style (six of the sixty-eight countries that had any metal bands had fewer than twenty), those with the highest percentage of Pagan metal to all metal bands are Lithuania (12.3 per cent), Ukraine (10.7 per cent), Belarus (9.7 per cent), Estonia (9.2 per cent), Russia (8 per cent), Poland (7.4 per cent), Bulgaria (6.9 per cent), Serbia (5.9 per cent), Slovenia (5.6 per cent), and Latvia (5.3 per cent). It should be noted that *all* of the above are former Soviet Bloc countries. Recent analysis by Shnirelman (2002) and Ivakhiv (2005), among others, indicates that former Soviet Bloc nations, some of whom had groups practising Paganism for decades, have shown a marked increase in the number of such groups since the fall of the Soviet Union.

Today, Pagan metal tours traverse rock venues throughout Europe and North America. There are annual Pagan metal festivals – most notably Ragnarök in Germany, which began in 2004 and attracts thousands of fans each year. The annual festival's name is somewhat ironic, given that it means "the end of the world", or at least "the destruction of the gods" in Scandinavian mythology. In addition, major and less prominent Pagan metal bands tour and play at festivals with metal bands from other sub-genres. Since none of Pagan metal's elements – textual, verbal, instrumental and visual – violate metal's values, Pagan metal bands are appreciated by metal fans who are uninterested in Paganism itself.

Pagan metal bands do have some of their own mediators, but mainly depend upon those for metal in general. All of the major extreme metal record labels – Nuclear Blast, Noise, Spinefarm, and Metal Blade, among others – have Pagan metal bands on their rosters.

A handful of well known Pagan metal bands tour internationally, and receive worldwide coverage in metal media, including Ensiferum, Korpiklaani, Moonsorrow, Finntroll and Turisas, all from Finland. Others are Eluveitie from Switzerland, Týr from the Faroe Islands, Primordial from Ireland, Skyforger from Latvia and Amon Amarth from Sweden.

DESCRIPTION OF PAGAN METAL

Pagan metal can be seen as a deconstruction of globalized metal, which traditionally was transnational. Metal's sound, language (English, whether or not the band spoke it fluently or its audiences understood it at all), themes and look were standard, without national or ethnic distinctions. However, starting in the 1990s, bands in various areas began to localize their work, forming the matrix in which Pagan metal emerged.

Given the diversity of extreme metal sub-genres in the bands initiating Pagan metal, plus the practice of metal bands since the turn of the current century creating their signature sound as an admixture of two sub-genres, it is not surprising that the metal of Pagan metal bands is varied. That variety is seen in the 1538 bands listed in the dataset described above. Some list their style as black metal (34.3 per cent) or death metal (1.2 per cent). Many others report a complex style, describing their music as "Pagan black/death metal", "folk/black metal", "extreme gothic metal" or "electronic black/death metal", among many others. Combining of sub-genres has also been a mark of many extreme metal bands, unrelated to Pagan metal, during the last decade of the twentieth century, and the beginning of the twenty-first. While 2.4 per cent call their style "folk metal", another 10.1 per cent use the word "folk" in addition to other terms. Among the other descriptors used with other styles are "doom" (3.0 per cent), "Viking" (3.5 per cent), "symphonic" (1.8 per cent), "ambient" (4.0 per cent) and "death" (7.4 per cent).

The term "Pagan" as an adjectival descriptor – as in "Pagan black metal", for example – is used by 36.1 per cent of the bands, but none uses it to name a standalone style. Similarly, 12.4 per cent of the bands use "folk" as an adjectival descriptor. The adjectival use of both terms here probably means the incorporation of some folk instruments and/or melodies into the metal. (Since some describe their musical style with terms like "National Socialism", the terms "Pagan" or "folk" may, for some bands, have nothing to do with their sound.)

SOUND

Despite this diversity, Pagan metal bands all play metal, and extreme metal at that. That is, they play loud, with amplified guitars and massive drum kits, often thickened with electronic keyboards; musical diversity enters through the addition, in many Pagan metal bands, of folk instruments.

Primordial, from Ireland, incorporates tin whistles into its sound. The Swiss Eluveitie uses a wide assortment of pre-modern instruments, including tin and low whistles, Uillean pipes, mandola, bodhran, fiddle and hurdy-gurdy. Heidevolk, from the Netherlands, employs mouth harp, violin and horns. While other Pagan metal bands played straight metal before adding folk elements, Korpiklaani started with folk music before turning to metal. The band's members include a fiddler and a squeezebox virtuoso. In their rousing sound, one can also hear the Finnish bowed lyre (*jouhikko*), a zither (*kantele*) and a bagpipe (*säkkipilli*). The *kantele* is also frequently found in nearby Baltic Pagan metal bands like Obtest and Skyforger; Skyforger also makes use of bagpipes.

At times, folk instruments are not fully integrated into the band's sound because they cannot compete with the far louder metal instruments. Turisas compensates by playing solos on an electrified violin. Skyforger saves its folk instruments for the recording studio: "Heavy metal sound is thick and solid, and for such fragile instruments it's hard to break through it. That's why in live concerts we just play those melodies on guitars" (Fjordi 2005).

Folk melodies, played on metal and/or folk instruments, permeate the music of Pagan metal bands. The recurrence of these well-worn tunes is reminiscent of their use by nineteenth-century nationalist symphonic composers such as Tchaikovsky, Smetana and Grieg. Such melodies are double-coded: those who do not recognize them do not feel excluded from appreciating the music; those who are familiar with them receive an added pleasure.

LANGUAGE

The traditional language of metal was English. In part, this was due to the Anglo-American origins of the genre in the 1970s and the global significance of English during that era. Most bands that were well known in their own countries, and all those with strong international exposure sang in English. The hegemony of English began to wane in the 1990s, particularly with bands that would later be classified as Pagan metal.

For their lyrics, album titles, the bands' names and the stage names of their members, Pagan metal bands have indulged in a variety of linguistic choices. Although many use English, for a majority all or some of their words are in their national tongue, a specific dialect or an ancient variant of it. Enslaved's guitarist Roy Kronheim says:

> Viking metal is all about using our mythology as lyrical metaphors concerning our daily lives and doings. We prefer to write our lyrics in our own language (a dialect from Norway's west coast) simply because they sound more powerful when singing them.
> (Pizek 2000: 32)

The popular Týr sing in their native language too, despite coming from the tiny Faroe Islands. Most of the Baltic metal bands write in their own languages. Obtest, Ha Lela and Zpoan Vtenz sing in Lithuanian. Skyforger began in English but explained in an interview:

> Later we decided to keep up a national touch and to sing only in Latvian. Also Peter [who writes the lyrics] is not so good at English poetry; it comes more naturally for him to compose lyrics in Latvian. I just can say that his lyrics in our tongue are pure masterpieces; I could never do it. He is definitely a real poet, and many people have told me that lyrics for "Latvian Riflemen" are so real and alive, so you can feel yourself like being into the battle-pit and the result is tears ... About bands which turn later into English speaking ones as success approaches ... I can say that this is not what we ever will do, this is not possible with Skyforger!
> (Fjordi 2005)

Going local is not merely done because it is easier; there is pride in this choice. The 2008 press release for the Dutch band Heidevolk states: "Since language is the vehicle of the mind, Heidevolk conveys its thoughts in their purest and most authentic way: their native tongue." Finntroll, mixing black and death metal with Finnish folk music called *humppa* (similar to polka), mainly sings in Swedish, Finland's second language. The band's first singer, Katla, was from the Swedish-speaking minority and convinced his bandmates that the sound of that language was better suited to Finntroll's image – or, as he put it, "because Swedish just sounds 'damn trollish'" (de Klepper *et al.* 2007).

A few bands – especially if they reference the old gods – even make use of an ancient tongue. For example, while many of the Swiss band Eluveitie's lyrics are in English, some (all in their 2009 release) are in the ancient, no longer spoken Gaulish (related to Celtic) language. Ásmegin, from Norway, sing in an older version of Norwegian, which draws from both Danish and Norse.

Pagan metal's recurrent reversion to native languages signifies that bands evince a certain "roots" understanding of Paganism that endows them with authenticity and enhances their appeal to their fan-base. Nevertheless, much of extreme metal is, in the main, aurally appreciated for the vocalist's emotion and the sound of the voice, rather than for the communication of verbal meaning. In extreme metal, the rasped scream typical of black metal and the gutter-pipe growls of death metal render even listeners who are fluent in the language of the vocalist incapable of discerning most, if not all, of the words. Serious fans – and in extreme metal fans tend to be serious – read the lyrics enclosed with the CD or online, and you can see them mouthing the words at concerts along with the vocalist. Years ago, when I asked a death metal growler why he had lyrics at all, he insisted that they were crucial in guiding the emotion put into his vocalizations.

Pagan metal band names, band members' "nicknames" and album titles are also likely to be in the local language. For example, Finland's Korpiklaani's name roughly translates as "forest clan"; Heidevolk, from the Dutch province of Gelderland, means "folk of the heath land"; in ancient Gaulish, Eluveite translates as "I am the Helvetian" (de Klepper *et al.* 2007). Turisas takes its moniker from a sea monster that is sometimes considered a god of war in Finnish mythology.

A host of ethnomusicologists have studied the use of local languages in a variety of popular music styles. Meic Llewellyn, concentrating on the use of the Welsh language in popular music in Wales, sees the practice as part of an increasing pattern of worldwide "resistance musics" utilizing local languages that aid in "developing national consciousness". One of the bands he studied asserts that "the struggle for the culture *is* the struggle for the language; as the proverb has it, '*sim iaith, dim calan*' ('no language, no heart')." (Llewellyn 2000: 337)

During the Soviet era, says Edward Larkey:

> East German bands from the independent scene increasingly used English as an oppositional identity-marker in order to subvert censorship aimed at achieving conformity to socialist ideology and as a way to repudiate and actively withdraw from the official institutionalized context and discourse of what the government popularized as "GDR Rock". (Larkey 2000: 6)

Larkey also notes that: "Dialects are used by German pop artists as a way to reinforce a regional identity among members of their immediate target audience and to represent that identity to audiences from the majority culture" (*ibid.*: 15)

In his nuanced analysis of underground rock – including metal – in Indonesia, Jeremy Wallach attempts to understand a decline in English and a concomitant rise in Indonesian lyrics (Wallach 2004: 27–8). He found that non-Indonesian "underground scene members were often more interested in Indonesian underground music that sounded 'Indonesian' in some way than they were in English-language songs". Wallach asks: "Could this then be a case of cultural globalization actually strengthening the hold of the nation state on the imagination of its citizens?" (*ibid.*: 43).

VISUALS

Musicians in Pagan metal maintain that main metal visual trope: males with long, loose hair. As in most metal, Pagan metal musicians are overwhelmingly male; however, a random sampling of pictures in the dataset used here found that 13.7 per cent[4] of Pagan metal bands have at least one female member, a far higher proportion than metal bands during the genre's first quarter-century. Female musicians in Pagan metal either play the traditional instruments or are singers; very rarely do they play electric guitars or drums.

One of the visual characteristics of Pagan metal is the use of face paint. One style is war paint, like the one thick horizontal black line high on each cheek sported by the Finnish Ensiferum, or the numerous red and black stripes adorning the faces of their compatriots, Turisas. Far more Pagan metal bands appear in the traditional black metal corpsepaint. Still others, like Moonsorrow, do not wear any makeup at all.

Pagan metal attire is not uniform either. One option is the jeans, t-shirts and black leather jackets popular in extreme metal since the 1980s. Those working in the Viking or black metal traditions are often clothed in daggerishly studded black leather garments. Then there are those who opt for costumes that Hollywood might design for movies about pre-civilized peoples. They wear long, loose long-sleeved shirts, jackets or hooded capes; some, like those worn by the members of Turisas, are embellished with fur. Pagan metal bands tend to augment their appearance on stage and in their promotional photographs with significant props, foremost among which are swords –not thin fencing blades, but big heavy ones meant to kill indelicately.

Settings for photographs and album covers typically show band members outdoors, ominously at night, near fires, or against unspoiled landscapes – lush, green, rolling mountains or stark snow-covered peaks. These visuals scream "nature".

VERBAL SIGNIFIERS

The verbal features of Pagan metal – band names, comments made by the band, and especially lyrics – are a major defining feature of the subgenre. An analysis of the names – references to specific myths, gods, and ethnicities – provides some hints about the takes bands have on Paganism. A random selection includes: Garmenhord, Wotans Destiny, Skaldenkraft, Mystic Shadows, Folklord, NeverChrist, Dark Wisdom Horde, Horna, Spiritual Origin, Asatru and Slavogorje.

The listing site from which the dataset described above was drawn provides space for bands to briefly indicate their theme(s). A few merely state theirs in a word – "Paganism", "Nature" or "Mythology". Most provide two to four themes, such as "Paganism, Nature", "Paganism, Pride", "Satanism, Paganism", "Armenian Folklore, Mythology, Paganism, Nature", "Nordic Tales, Winter, War, Paganism" or "National Socialist, Paganism".

The most frequent term listed as a theme – by 81.1 per cent of the bands – is "Pagan" (or "Paganism"), although only five offer it as their only selection. In addition to Paganism as a theme, more than a third of the bands – 36.2 per cent – use the adjective "Pagan" to modify their style of metal music. Taken together, almost all of the bands – 96.6 per cent – reference the term Pagan as a theme and/or sound, including all of the twenty-nine bands with the term Pagan in their name, such as Pagan Throne, Pagan Obsession, Pagan Flame, Pagan Poetry and Pagan Blood.

What specific bands mean by the term "Pagan" is, as hinted earlier, up for grabs. In her research on Paganism, anthropologist Venesa Sage concludes that, "while there may be common threads linking current expressions of Paganism, it is important to remember that there is really no single thing that can be accurately termed Paganism" (Sage 2009: 36).

In addition to the term "Pagan", the bands in the dataset list more than 100 different words for their themes. Some terms are related to Paganism – or at least some well-known varieties of it – but are foreign to any sort of metal, such as Wicca or Druid. Others are familiar to metal, but unconnected to any sort of Paganism, such as "hate", "evil" or "alcohol". Many of the terms, however, overlap these two discourses.

The frequency of other terms is far less than that for "Pagan(ism)". The next most popular terms, almost tied, form an odd trio: "war" (14.5 per cent), "nature" (14.4 per cent) and "anti-Christianity" (12.4 per cent). The first two relate to visuals – particularly the backgrounds in photographs of the bands. Swords are the major prop, and the bands are posed in "natural" settings, such as green meadows and snowy mountains.

The term "battle(s)" is listed by 3.6 per cent in the dataset; bands listing that or "war" (or both) comprise 17.3 per cent of the total. If one were only aware of Paganism in its mainly Anglo-American (Neo-)Pagan forms, these allusions to combat would seem misplaced, and would be seen to be merely a metal theme. However, much European Paganism is based on history and myths with a focus on warfare.

Nature is not a theme typically found in any style of metal. Given that the emergence of Pagan metal coincided with the rise of interest in ecological issues, one might think that "nature" is a theme of the times, and new bands would focus on it too. However, nature is far too related to Paganism to give much credence to this idea. Bands mentioning "nature" (including the themes "mountains" or "forests") in the dataset comprise 15.6 per cent of the total.[5] At least as problematic as the concept of Pagan is the concept of nature – "perhaps the most complex word in the [English] language" according to Raymond Williams (1985: 219). Adrian Ivakhiv argues that the word functions "as a boundary term demarcating a primary realm ... from a secondary realm of the 'human', 'cultural', or 'unnatural'. It is a term that denotes value and that, as Mary Douglas puts it, has often been used as a kind of discursive 'trump card'" (Ivakhiv 2005: 196–7). For some, nature has ecological significance; for many others, it is a reference to the soil – the territory – of their ethnic group.

To the third most popular theme term, "anti-Christianity" (12.4 per cent), should be added "Satan(ism)" (6.2 per cent) and "Lucifer" (0.3 per cent). Those using one or more of those terms comprise 17.5 per cent of all bands.

Before the rise of Pagan metal, anti-Christian thematics were familiar in metal music. There still are hundreds of extreme metal bands that focus on satanism. Yet these bands – especially in death metal – have no relation to Pagan metal. Within the context of Pagan metal, anti-Christianity is a response to an alien religion (including those foes adhering to it), whereas in extreme metal it signifies theological opposition in the name of the Christian devil.

Within Paganism and Pagan metal, anti-Christianity takes several forms. In some cases, it appears as a religious opposition to favoured pre-Christian, Pagan gods. Another focus is the historical grievance against those Christian groups that defeated ancestors, changing or replacing their original culture. Among Pagan metal bands focused on a particular ethnic group, opposition can also be based on Christianity's universalism. Yet another tendency espouses anti-Christianity as an ecological position standing against Christianity's elevation of humans above the rest of nature. "The adversary, according to the neoPagans, is therefore the anthropocentrism stemming from the Bible, which considers humanity as qualitatively superior to the other forms of nature" (François 2008: 46).

Clearly some of the bands take their brand of Paganism in a religious sense – such as the members of Týr, who said in an interview: "We are not Christians. We are Pagans" (Twilightheart & OhLi 2007). In the dataset, ten bands list the theme "spirituality". Other Pagan metal bands do not seem to see Paganism in a religious sense. For example, 9.6 per cent of the dataset's bands name "myths" (or "mythology") as a theme; religious believers do not use such terms for their gods. Kronheim, from Enslaved, exemplifies this stance when he states: "Viking metal is all about using our mythology as lyrical metaphors concerning our daily lives and doings" (Pizek 2000).

The specific meanings of various themes listed by Pagan metal bands need to be understood within two discourses: Paganism and metal. Further, terms may well be polysemic, interpreted in one way by some and in another by others – and even perhaps as both, as undecidable in a Derridian sense. Examined in terms of both the contexts of the extensive literature on contemporary Paganism and the features of Pagan metal bands described above, one can discern three core themes of Pagan metal. One is Neo-Paganism, which relates to the revival of the nineteenth-century Neo-Pagan movement in the1960s. Although most popular in the United Kingdom and United States, this is a universalist, rather than an ethnically specific, position. Skyclad is the best-known band adopting this view, which is shared by the smallest number of Pagan metal bands.[6]

A second theme-cluster, called here "roots Paganism", references some specific ancient (pre-modern/pre-Christian) ethnic culture – particularly its gods, folklore, military history and music. This is the position of the largest portion of Pagan metal bands in the dataset,[7] and almost all of the well-known Pagan metal bands. An analyst of Baltic War metal, a retro-Pagan grouping, concludes that they "tend to glorify the ancient prosperity of their nations and the victories in wars by their ancestors, using vivid battle images and mythological encounters" (Saltanaviciute 2002). Amorphis, an early example, continues to mine the epic Finnish folktale, the *Kalevala*. The band's 2009 release is about one of its characters,

> an ancient blacksmith [Ilmarinen]. He's the forger of the skies. That's why the album title is Skyforger. He's a powerful guy ... It's an exotic thing for people outside Finland. We have folk melodies and sad melodies, which are very Finnish. They fit the stories.
> (Chris D. 2009)

Sage indicates that:

> The survival of an ancient Pagan religion is a major theme in contemporary Pagan beliefs and practices. The past provides a source of legitimation, strength and comfort even as it becomes a storehouse to be pillaged. The past here suggests a place where you can walk in the same footsteps as the ancestors (a much-used idea in Pagan circles), and pay homage to them so that the dead, in a sense, return to life. (Sage 2009: 32–3)

A third core thematic – one that overlaps with roots Paganism – is termed chauvinistic Paganism. Rather than laud some features of ancient culture, chauvinistic Paganism rails against ethnic or religious others. More than 10 per cent of the dataset's bands espouse this view, using terms including "national socialism" (or its abbreviation, "NS"), "fascism," "zog" and "aryanism". Paganist themes permeate Hitler's construction of Nazism: ancestors and nature, blood and soil. Kahn-Harris observes: "The apparently uncritical celebration of Pagan pasts, the obsession with the 'unpolluted' countryside and the distrust of the cosmopolitan city are common features in 19th- and 20th-century fascist and racist movements" (2007: 40).[8]

For the most part, bands with professional ambitions do not pursue chauvinistic Paganism, because in Europe – and most particularly in Germany (which is the largest market for metal in general, including Pagan metal recordings and concerts) – such a stance is outlawed. Indeed, some bands with elements that might be interpreted as having affinities to Nazism have been at pains to deny those links. One instance is the statement issued by Moonsorrow:

> Recently there have been claims about Moonsorrow being a fascistic-oriented Nazi band. We would hereby like to declare that Moonsorrow is not affiliated or fascinated with the Nazi movement in any way. We apologise if drawing one letter in such a way makes the logo look national socialistic – it is and has not been our or Moonsorrow's intention to sympathise with the Nazis by drawing the S in such a way. Changing the letter's appearance would make the whole logo look inconsistent and incomplete – hence we have not even considered changing it nor do we intend to … Some have said that the lyrics to the bands [sic] song "Blood of an Apostate" are close to an old Nazi song which is against Jews. We have to say first that the members of Moonsorrow have not to this date heard of such a song … Secondly we have to say that the lyrics come from a wholly different, easily recognisable Finnish source … from an old Finnish legend – the murder of the Bishop Henrik committed by the peasant Lalli … a very common Finnish folk tale.   (Blabbermouth 2008)

Whether or not the band intended this confusion, fans are certainly able to read Moonsorrow in different ways. With other bands, the intention is obvious; however, as the former editor of the extreme metal magazine *Terrorizer* wrote: "What makes it hard for us is distinguishing between those borrowings which play on the symbolism for the artistic effect and those which are truly politically charged" (Terry 1998: 66).

PAGAN METAL IS POSTMODERN

For the metal meta-genre, Pagan metal poses no problems; by now metal's diversity of styles and themes is well established, and as long as bands conform to broadly construed sonic codes they will be welcomed into the fold. Drawing upon metal sub-genres that already exist, Pagan metal is not a gatecrasher, but rather another example of how metal mutates into new forms and hybrids. In keeping with metal's current tendency to bend and blend,

Pagan metal's sonic eclecticism is in tune with the times. Its themes, for the most part, are consistent with metal's traditional heroic romanticism. Indeed, Pagan metal is another addition to metal's ever-growing menu, providing the long-in-the-tooth meta-genre with some new, revitalizing tastes.

Pagan metal's most significant new wrinkle is roots Pagan metal's form of romantic reaction – its assertion of particular ethnic identities in what had grown to be, from its origins in the United Kingdom, a transnational-universalistic music-based subculture. In one sense, the eruption of the particular does not oppose metal's transnationalism – the example of going back to one's own roots can be taken up by anyone or any group. Indeed, most roots Pagan metal groups share the perspective of nineteenth-century liberal nationalism – each nationality should strengthen its own identity and welcome others to do the same, as long as they are not chauvinistic. As part of the metal meta-genre, Pagan metal never leaves the transnational cultural flows and deterritorialization; its bands travel well and willingly from their origins, gaining fans and appreciators outside their identity base.

Nonetheless, Pagan metal is rooted in time and space – in the arc of northern Europe extending from Great Britain, through Scandinavia, Germany and the Baltic states to the Slavic states of the former Soviet Union. Its origins and continued concentration in the Northern European arc indicates that Pagan metal is a response to specific historical and social circumstances.

It is most indicative – and initially surprising – that the dominant "roots" form of Pagan metal has appeared in two of the most contrasting regions of Europe: Scandinavia, which is the most culturally modernized, socially egalitarian and technologically sophisticated region in Europe (and indeed the world); and the former Soviet Bloc states, which lag behind the rest of Europe in economic development and cultural modernization. That a turn towards Paganism should become manifest in such contrasting social contexts becomes explicable through understanding that in both cases national identity is perceived by certain individuals and groups as being or having been threatened.

For the Scandinavians, national identity is perceived as being under attack from the supra-national European Union; particularized Paganism is an act of reactionary resistance. For example, a member of Finntroll said: "The only part of the Finnish culture I hate is how everyone is concerned with how they'll look to the rest of Europe." His compatriot in Korpiklaani complained:

> everything is supposed to be European Union and everybody is supposed to be European. But no one really wants that, and people are much more interested in getting to their own heart, their own history. People don't want to be European; they still want to be Finnish, or German, or whoever.   (Zebub 2009)

For nationalities in the former Soviet Bloc, national identity was not only threatened, but severely damaged, by communism's universalism and the communist regimes' repressive indoctrination. Here particularized Paganism is an act of recovery. For example, in a 2005 interview, a member of Skyforger stated:

> Latvia is [a] small Baltic country ... we parted from USSR ... it was a terrible time, our nation was almost close to obliteration, our language was out of use and in all places Russian was the main language. Latvians were repressed by all means; some were deported to distant districts into Siberia, where there's no daylight and where it's eternal coldness. [It] was totalitarian regime and secret agents were everywhere. Skyforger could not be possible in that time.   (Fjordi 2005)

With its musical origins in extreme metal sub-genres, Pagan metal has appeared at the extremes of (post)modern European society, as a move against post-national deterritorialization (Europeanism) in Scandinavia, and a move towards reterritorialization (post-communism) in the countries of the former Soviet Bloc. Polysemic to begin with, Paganism also performs different functions that respond to different circumstances. Pagan metal introduces identity politics – itself a complex phenomenon – into the metal meta-genre.

The connection between contemporary metal as a Pagan metal form and the appearance of Pagan metal's nationalism is the emphasis on particularistic, rather than universalistic, identity in Pagan metal as a social phenomenon. In its opposition to all pretensions to essentialism and the use of essentialism in the elaboration of globalist discourses, Pagan metal gathered under its umbrella marginalized identity groups of all kinds – racial, class, gender and now national. On a cultural level, Pagan metal has encouraged a proliferation of belief systems, none of which has a claim to essential truth, among them Paganism of various types. Pagan nationalism in metal is one of the eruptions on the Pagan metal polyglot scene of resistance/affirmation identity.

NOTES

1. One of several reasons for the conflation of these two labels is that there are some Nazi-identified Pagan metal bands, so other bands who for a variety reasons do not want to be identified with them, refer to their style as folk metal. Also, folk metal tends to be used, but not exclusively so, when the band's music is not derived from black metal and also uses pre-modern instruments.
2. Tolkien's novels were like a gateway drug to Pagan themes for so many Scandinavian bands whose members were avid readers of his fictionalized heroic Paganism. Of course, the irony is that Tolkien intended his books to enhance Christianity.

3. For an analysis of the *Kalevala* in Finnish music – including metal – see Tolvanen (2007).
4. In a random survey of fifty-eight band pictures (of seventy-one, thirteen had no photos), only seven had at least one women musician.
5. There are thirty-one bands (2.0 per cent) that mention both battles/war and nature as themes.
6. The smallest, if we count all those in the dataset that mention Wicca (0.1 per cent), witchcraft (0.5 per cent), magic (0.4 per cent), spirits (0.9 per cent), the occult (4.2 per cent), heathen (27 per cent), nature (14.4 per cent), or some form of nature (mountain or forest, 1.2 per cent). Those mentioning one or more of these comprise 23 per cent of the bands, but since so many bands in the other two positions also reference some of these, especially nature, the proportion of Neo-Pagan metal bands is far less than 23 per cent.
7. A total of 45.6 per cent of all bands have some reference to one or more of the themes abstracted into this cluster: they are "myths" or "mythology" (9.6 per cent), "gods" (4.1 per cent), "folk" or "folklore" (3.6 per cent), "history" (4.2 per cent), "battle" (3.6 per cent), or "war" (14.5 per cent), "heritage" (0.8 per cent) or the specific culture ethnic group of the band (17.8 per cent).
8. For the relationship between Paganism and Nazism, see Goodrick-Clarke (1992).

6. THE DARKER SHADE OF PAGAN: THE EMERGENCE OF GOTH

Jason Pitzl-Waters

The late 1970s and early 1980s spawned an insular and self-consciously Pagan folk music scene, centred around festivals and conventions, but that wasn't the only expression of a modern Pagan music to emerge. "Goth", a unique musical subculture that developed during the post-punk era in Britain, provided a parallel creative environment.

Following the punk rock explosion of the late 1970s, Gothic music presented a romantic, decadent and inward-looking alternative to anger and nihilism; Byronic moods largely replaced political posturing (Reynolds 2006), and black became the clothing colour of choice (Hodkinson 2002). Goth subculture in both fashion and art appropriated religious iconography from a variety of sources – Catholic, Anglican, Buddhist, Pagan and occult, but there were "no established norms for the interpretation of such signifiers" (Powell 2007: 361). Due to this broadly secular tolerance, many modern Pagan and occult practitioners found a comfortable sanctuary within Goth. According to a survey conducted by Nancy Kilpatrick for her book *The Goth Bible* (2004), up to 33 per cent of respondents who self-identified as Goths held allegiance to some form of Pagan belief system – by far the largest theistic grouping within Goth.

The convergence of contemporary Pagan religions and the Goth subculture is not surprising. Goth's inherent romanticism valued "medieval superstitions and primordial longings" (Reynolds 2006), while religions like Wicca promised a link to a pre-Christian past hidden within Britain's folklore (Hutton 1999). Prominent British Wiccans like Alex Sanders and cult films like *The Wicker Man* (1973) previously had forged a connection between Pagan religion and folk music (R. Young 2010), and by the 1990s links between adherents to Pagan faiths and the Goth subculture would be strong enough to warrant regular mention in a seminal resource guide (Mercer 1997).

Throughout this chapter, there will be references to the modern Pagan community or subculture. Paganism (also called Neo-Paganism) is a broadly based but still largely counter-cultural religious movement that revives,

re-envisions or reconstructs pre-Christian religions. Some examples of contemporary Pagan religions are Wicca, Druidry and Asatru. Though very
diverse, adherents to these faiths often congregate, form communities and
create a shared identity in festival settings (Pike 2001). It was within those
settings that the idea of a "Pagan" music was formed, influenced in part by
British ideas of pre-Christian survivals within folk songs (R. Young 2010).
While Pagan musical culture has thrived since emerging in the 1960s, it
has also tended to favour the preferences of the Baby Boom generation that
helped build its events and institutions. This created a generational discon-
nect that found many Pagans and occultists in subsequent generations looking elsewhere for a musical component to their spirituality.

We will examine the cross-pollination between Goth music and culture
and modern Pagan belief systems, and how by the mid-1990s this "darker
shade of Pagan" became prevalent enough that some would identify a discrete "Pagan Goth" musical sub-genre. In addition, the chapter will explore
how the Goth scene provided an alternative aesthetic for younger Pagans
who were dissatisfied with the musical and cultural offerings of traditional
Pagan or occult communities. Finally, it will touch on how Pagan Goths have
slowly been absorbed by and integrated into the mainstream of modern
Paganism.[1]

FERTILE GROUND: LIFE FROM DEATH AND DEATH INTO LIFE

> To understand why we chose the name, think of the transforma-
> tion of inanimacy to animacy. Think of the processes concern-
> ing life from death and death into life. So many people missed
> the inherent symbolism, and assumed that we must be "morbid
> Gothic types", a mistake we deplored and deplore ...
> (Brendan Perry, of the band Dead Can Dance, 1984)

The high-water mark in the intertwining relationship between the Goth
subculture and the modern Pagan community was most likely the publication of the book *Goth Craft* by Raven Digitalis in 2007. While hardly breaking new ground in terms of content or intent, the book signalled that Goth
– long on the margins of Pagan culture – had gained a place at the table. If
Llewellyn Publications, the largest publisher of books aimed at a Pagan audience (and generally known for their "lighter", more positive fare), was willing
to directly market to self-identified Pagan-Goths (or Goth-Pagans), it could
only mean there was a large potential audience for the work. This assumption was borne out, as the book has since enjoyed multiple printings, and
Digitalis joined a growing stable of "dark Pagans" at the publishing house.

The current cosy relationship between the Goth subculture and modern
Pagan religion is one that has been gestating almost from Goth's beginnings

as a darkly romantic subcultural offshoot of post-punk in the late 1970s. Resisting the increasingly strident politicization of punk, and the faceless and high-minded anti-mystique of the post-punkers, Goths embraced a ritualism and mystery that spoke of a yearning for "atavistic pre-Christian urges" (Reynolds 2006). Goth also presented a different and far more androgynous gender presentation than the hyper-masculine punk rockers (Goodlad & Bibby 2007), making it far more friendly to the full participation and leadership of women, a trait that would make it especially attractive to the predominantly female Pagan religions (Davy 2007).

Still, due to its punk roots, Goth was in no hurry to express fondness for any religious tradition. Rebellion against religiously based oppression and playful displays of blasphemy were far more common. But even within those constraints, certain themes and subject-matters would start to pop up within Goth that would presage the coming influx of modern Pagans. The band Bauhaus, famous for the 1979 Goth anthem "Bela Lugosi's Dead", would plunge into mythical themes with songs like "Hollow Hills" (1981), a song dealing with faerie mounds in Ireland, later covered by the Pagan-friendly band Faith and The Muse, and "A God in An Alcove" (1980), a meditation on the forgotten bust of a pagan god. Meanwhile, the band Killing Joke (who enjoy a large Goth following) became quite interested in the works of the notorious occultist Aleister Crowley, culminating in several members moving to Iceland in order to avoid the Apocalypse. Although the Apocalypse never occurred, some band members went on to collaborate with the influential Icelandic new-wave band Theyr, also deeply interested in occult and pre-Christian themes.

But while these early manifestations were rare (and in the case of Bauhaus, hardly a sign of any serious allegiance to pre-Christian belief), they did point to a fertile ground for later expansion and growth that by the mid-1980s would start to develop into a noticeable disposition towards occult practices and modern Paganism.

FROM GOTHIC ROCK TO PAGAN ROCK WITH INKUBUS SUKKUBUS

> To some of you the added elements of the Fetish, Pagan and Vampire contents, none of which interest me, may seem like a strange mixture, but these are all relevant now. A lot of people have made it quite clear they want to know more, so they're in. If you hate the idea, that's your problem.   (Mercer 1997: 7)

By the time music journalist Mick Mercer published *Hex Files: The Goth Bible* in 1997, an update on previous works exploring and cataloguing the Goth subculture, modern Paganism was beginning to be seen as a vital influence and identity within the community. According to UK music promoter and journalist Michael "Uncle Nemesis" Johnson, by the mid-1990s "Pagan" and "Goth" were synonyms and could be used interchangeably by promoters.

The band most often invoked as starting this self-conscious interplay between Goth and Pagan was Inkubus Sukkubus. This UK band took the Gothic rock style that had dominated the Goth scene in the mid- to late 1980s, and pared it down to its most basic components. Turning the resulting relentless (some would say almost monotonous) sound into a spiritual megaphone, the band transmitted its ferociously proud Pagan message to as many people as they could. If any band pointed to the growing popularity of Pagan and occult themes within the large Goth subculture, it was this one.

Before we detail Inkubus Sukkubus's birth and evolution into one of the most popular Pagan-identified bands in the world, we should first take a quick trip through what is called "Gothic rock" (also known as second-wave Goth) to see how occult and Pagan themes in this stylistic evolution of the Goth sound helped pave the way. As discussed briefly at the beginning of this chapter, the first wave was influenced largely by the highly creative and arty post-punk movements, and that experimental vision defined the sound of the first six years of the genre (1979–85). The second wave, which would run from 1985 until 1995 (and would gain the most mainstream attention), was much more rock-oriented, and in some ways simplistic, with drummers often being replaced by drum machines.

The two biggest bands that helped define the second wave were the Sisters of Mercy and Fields of the Nephilim, both from the United Kingdom. The Sisters of Mercy, led by Andrew Eldritch, was one of the biggest "dark rock" bands during the late 1980s and early 1990s. (Eldritch has long fought against the "Goth" label, to the point where many in the Goth scene now disavow his inclusion.) The Sisters of Mercy solidified the loud guitars/deep vocals/drum machine template that would come to dominate the "Gothic rock" sound.

While the Sisters were never directly involved in occult or pagan themes, the band's guitarist from the band's first full-length album, Wayne Hussey, did dabble in occult themes with his own band The Mission. Mission albums over the years would reference Aleister Crowley ("Severina"), romantic visions of a pagan past ("Deliverance") and songs decrying the religious establishment ("Sacrilege"). Hussey would also be instrumental in launching the career of Julianne Regan's band, All About Eve, which dabbled in similar lyrical themes and would create a unique sonic link between Gothic rock and the folk rock of the late 1960s.

But while the Sisters of Mercy steered away from any definite religious point of view (other than perhaps a post-apocalyptic one), and The Mission referenced the occult and pagan themes occasionally in its lyrics, Fields of the Nephilim was a completely different animal. Led by frontman Carl McCoy, Fields of the Nephilim was perhaps the heaviest of the Gothic rock bands, incorporating elements of hard rock into its early sound, with stage shows that invoked Spaghetti Westerns as well as the post-apocalyptic *Mad Max* films. McCoy had a very public admiration for the occult, and referenced Aleister Crowley, magician/artist Austin Spare, Sumerian mythology and the fictional Cthulhu mythos in the band's songs. While the full band only released four proper albums, their influence has been impressive. Many claim that the band was highly influential on the Goth and black metal scenes, and they still have a large and loyal audience of fans, including such luminaries as fantasy author Storm Constantine.

It was within this atmosphere that the formation in 1989 of the band Inkubus Sukkubus (originally Incubus Succubus), featuring Candia Ridley on vocals and Tony McKormack on guitars, took place. (There have been other members, but for the bulk of their history Ridley and McKormack have been the key players.) Unlike other bands that emerged during the reign of Gothic rock, they had a clear spiritual mandate to spread a Pagan message to as many people as possible:

> More than being a Goth band, we are essentially a Pagan band, and we feel that this is the forefront of our musical direction. We tend to think of ourselves as a Pagan rock band, which is obviously less specific musically and allows us to hopefully appeal to as many people as possible without alienating anyone who feels they are not part of any particular musical subgenre.
>
> (Candia Ridley, quoted in Pitzl-Waters & Enstrom-Waters 2003)

While the early 1990s saw the launch of several bands who typified the sort of musical adventurousness and Romantic spirit that made Goth so appealing to so many – what music critic and author Simon Reynolds called the "studio-savvy post-Goth" of record labels like 4AD, Projekt and Tess – the scene itself was experiencing a fallow period according to journalist Michael "Uncle Nemesis" Johnson:

> The UK Goth scene was at a low ebb in the early-mid 90s – it was essentially the province of rather underwhelming two-men-and-a-drum-machine "bedroom Goth" outfits, diligently trying to reproduce a sub-Sisters sound on a 10p budget to steadily dwindling audiences. Incubus Succubus were exactly the kind of full-on, dynamic rock band that was needed to enliven everything.
>
> (Personal communication, 14 April 2010)

Inkubus Sukkubus toured in the United Kingdom, and received airplay on BBC radio for its debut self-released single "Beltaine" (released in 1989), but it wasn't until the early 1990s, when the band's first full-length commercial release, *Belladonna and Aconite* (the title track of which would go on to become a Goth-club favourite), came out, that Inkubus Sukkubus attracted a larger following. Around this time, a music journalist dubbed the group "Britain's Premier Pagan Rock Band" (a title Inkubus Sukkubus still proudly display on its website). Since the 1993 release of *Belladonna and Aconite*, Inkubus Sukkubus has put out a release of some sort almost every year, and has built up a considerable following on the internet (where the band frequently puts up free songs for download).

What made Inkubus Sukkubus unique was that it would not only play in clubs and bars (and later large Goth festivals), but would also do performances at Pagan festivals in the United Kingdom and Europe (and eventually in America). This exposed the band to a much larger audience than would be typical for a group of its size, and accounts for the fact that many Pagans still name Inkubus Sukkubus as the only Pagan "rock" or "Goth" band they know of. In that sense, Inkubus Sukkubus has become the default "Pagan rock" band, and is often one of the only rock bands (and certainly the only "Goth" band) included in otherwise folk- and chant-dominated Pagan music catalogues.

While in some ways Inkubus Sukkubus may have seemed a bit musically unsophisticated, the band's forthright adoption of a decidedly Pagan message opened doors for other bands, like Legend, Die Laughing and Cries of Tammuz, to do the same, enlivening a temporarily moribund Goth scene in the United Kingdom and creating the possibility of a Pagan-Goth identity that quickly spread to North America, thanks to the emerging ubiquity of the internet.

TEACHING THE DEAD TO DANCE

> In the beginning we were berated for being Gothic two years too late, today we are applauded for being at the vanguard of World Music. Whoever you believe we have always endeavoured to remain true to our convictions, in the belief that our music would eventually find its audience on its own merits and not by way of slavishly pandering to the whims of an industry that continually lacks imagination and is subservient to formula and greed.   (Brendan Perry, Dead Can Dance,
> *Spiritchaser* World Tour Programme, 1996)

Outside of Inkubus Sukkubus, one of the most important bands at the intersection of Pagan and Goth is Dead Can Dance. Formed in 1981 by Brendan Perry and Lisa Gerrard, Dead Can Dance would evolve from a solidly Goth beginning to incorporate world music, ancient musics from the Medieval and Renaissance periods, and stunning vocal work from both members. During its existence, Dead Can Dance has influenced several other bands, spawned multiple tribute records and become a touchstone for music lovers from a variety of scenes, backgrounds and faiths. Neither member has expressed any allegiance to modern Paganism; by most accounts, Lisa Gerrard follows a sort of mystical Christianity and Brendan Perry has never clearly stated a preference, though he seems quite sympathetic to indigenous religions and classical philosophy. Nevertheless, Dead Can Dance has been widely adopted as a "Pagan band", and several other bands directly influenced by Dead Can Dance are forthright in their sympathies for pre/post-Christian religion.

The reasons for the adoption of Dead Can Dance as a "Pagan band" are not too hard to imagine. Several songs in the band's history invoke ancient paganism ("Persephone", "Summoning of the Muse", "Song of the Sibyl"); the band has incorporated lyrics and themes from indigenous African and Native American cultures, as exhibited throughout its album *Spiritchaser*, and Lisa Gerrard's unique form of singing (a type of language-less glossolalia) invites an emotional interpretation by the listener. This connection has grown stronger as Pagan bands that cite Dead Can Dance as an influence have emerged over the past twenty years. These openly Pagan bands, along with a host of other artists directly influenced by Dead Can Dance, formed a sort of spiritual music current within the Goth subculture, which would in turn spill into modern Pagan culture.

> When someone says there is soul in the work, it means that through the music they have allowed themselves to unlock doors within their own unconscious, that through their confidence they have allowed themselves to surrender, so that they can look inside.   (Lisa Gerrard in Ehrlich 1997: 166)

Most of the bands influenced by Dead Can Dance would incorporate strong female vocals (from singers who often adopted elements of Gerrard's unique singing style), world music or folk elements, and electronic or guitar-based effects to provide a modern edge to the music. Dead Can Dance has created a sort of template (which some people call "ethno-Gothic") within a nebulously larger "dark" subculture. Dead Can Dance, and the bands that would emerge in its wake, would garner an audience much wider than their humble Goth roots. Fans could be found in world music circles, New Age enclaves, the chill-out rooms of dance clubs blasting electronic music and in Hollywood, where Gerrard's compositions and siren-like singing have become a popular addition to blockbuster films, including *Gladiator*, *Whale Rider*, *King Arthur* and many others.

There are several openly Pagan and occult-oriented bands, such as Seventh Harmonic, Atrium Animae, Daemonia Nymphe and Íon, that have been influenced by Dead Can Dance and adhere to the ethno-Gothic formula. In fact, so many have appeared since the 1990s that some have (wrongfully) assumed that most Pagan music is automatically "Goth" (and vice versa). This misapprehension evolved partly from the fact that many younger Pagans, witches and occultists preferred the more youth-oriented environments associated with these bands. In fact, a sort of "dark" Pagan underground has sprung up in the wider modern Paganism community, with adherents rejecting what they see as an increasingly shallow and one-sided religious culture that often refuses to acknowledge the more unpleasant aspects of nature or of the world around them:

> Unless this imbalance is corrected, the true mysteries that Paganism offers are lost. Pagan traditions are becoming empty shells of what they once were and the sense of community is becoming shattered by "witch wars" and silly politics. Before we can salvage our beliefs we must first reclaim "darkness" and encourage this reclamation from within. The road ahead will not be an easy one, but with effort those serious about the Craft can slowly pull itself out of the pit of ignorance and again embrace the true teachings and mysteries that Paganism offers   (Coughlin 2002)

Thus, for many, Dead Can Dance, the Pagan and occult bands that followed them and other Pagan Goth musicians like Inkubus Sukkubus define modern "Pagan music" every bit as much as singer-songwriter Gwydion Pendderwen did for Pagans in the mid-1970s. These "ethno-Gothic" and "Pagan-Goth" artists need to be understood as part of a larger continuum in which Pagan music continually reinvents itself to remain relevant.

PAGAN AND OCCULT ETHNO-GOTHIC BANDS

The "ethno-Gothic" formula of Dead Can Dance has spawned several different independent musical scenes throughout Europe. From the "faerie" and "fantasy" music of Hexperos and Narsilion to the "Pagan folk" of bands like Faun and Omnia, ethno-gothic bands are regularly featured at high-profile European festivals like Wave Gotik Treffen in Leipzig, Germany or Castlefest in the Netherlands, with sounds ranging from neo-classical to neo-tribal. Some of the most prominent examples of "ethno-Gothic" Pagan bands would be the Italian band Ataraxia, the Canadian band Rhea's Obsession and the Australian artist Louisa John-Krol. These three artists typify the diversity of sound found within this musical sub-genre, and showcase different approaches to incorporating Pagan and occult themes into this musical context.

The first, Ataraxia, formed in Italy in the late 1980s, and positioned itself as a spiritual continuation of an ancient oral tradition from the Greco-Roman and Celtic cultures. Lead singer Francesca Nicoli, whose powerfully unique voice guides the band, lists "history and time" as the band's "mother and father", and portrays the project as a whole (which incorporates elements of theatre and visual art) as channelled from nature:

> We have a medianic attitude towards art and creation. This is an unconscious gift. Creation is the way to express the divine part of the human being. In the ancient Dionisiac rituals the musician was possessed by the God of Nature who spoke through him/her. We have what you could define a mystic attitude towards life, we are unconscious channels that can vibrate expressing, translating the energy around us. (Ataraxia undated)

Of all the Pagan ethno-Gothic bands, Ataraxia is by far the most productive. This Italian band has created over twenty releases in a variety of formats, both self-released and through a series of smaller indie labels. Having been around for over twenty years, Atarazia – like Dead Can Dance – has spawned other artists inspired by the band's vision, including Chirleison (also from Italy), Arkane and Daemonia Nymphe (both from Greece).

Another frequent theme in ethno-Gothic music is the fusion between Eastern and Western forms of music and religion – perhaps best typified by the now-defunct Canadian band Rhea's Obsession. Sue Hutton, the amazingly versatile lead singer of and lyricist for the band, incorporated Indian, Tibetan, Celtic and Bulgarian folk styles into her vocal performance, which when paired with Jim Field's waves of guitar sound, created a highly innovative and energetic atmosphere. Rhea's Obsession very quickly became a standard-bearer for the mixture of Goth and Pagan sensibilities. Hutton voiced a clear interest in pre-Christian paganism, non-Christian cultures, occultism and embracing death as a part of life:

> It goes back to when I was in India, hanging around these Tibetan people. They told me about how you really have to address death before you can live, how death is really about destroying the old and negative to create the positive and new. And death is, in a sense, positive: to the Tibetans, it's all about celebrating every moment of your existence, because the more you acknowledge death, the more amazing the state of being alive becomes.
> (Sue Hutton, interview in *Eye Weekly*, 20 August 1998)

A good number of Rhea's Obsession's songs touch on occult or Pagan themes, including the band's version of Aleister Crowley's "Hymn to Pan" and "Between Earth and Sky", in which the Hermes Trismegistus's axiom "as above, so below" (commonly encountered in modern Pagan and occult circles) is worked into the chorus. Rhea's Obsession only released two proper albums before breaking up, but each made a big impact on Goths and Pagans.

If Ataraxia's version of the ethno-Gothic sound represented an eclectic and experimental occultism, and Rhea's Obsession a sort of darker world fusion (with loud guitars), then a third artist, Louisa John-Krol, represents a light-hearted and playful spirituality that stands apart. John-Krol, an Australian-born artist who has been releasing CDs since the mid-1990s, has taken the ethno-Gothic template and parlayed it into a new stylistic thread of "faerie music". Generally speaking, faerie music takes a lighter approach than its ethno-Gothic ancestors, emphasizing ethereal vocals or atmospheres and folk elements. The music will often (though not always) focus on Celtic and European folktales and mythology concerning faerie-folk:

> The Craft for me is quite homely and solitary: tending trees, herbs and other plants; collecting stones, shells, feathers, wood; learning faerielore and mythology; or contemplating parallel lives, reincarnation, shamanism and animism. I'm curious about Feng Shui, colour chakras, aromatherapy, astrology, tarot and numerology. Philosophically, I'm more interested in questions than conclusions.
>
> (Louisa John-Krol, *Gothtronic* interview, January 2006)

John-Krol is the biggest star of this musical style, which taps into a somewhat larger Pagan subculture focused around faeries, elves and other related lore. Other faerie-focused artists include Priscilla Hernández, the band Narsilion from Spain, Keltia from Belgium and the Russian artist Caprice. There is even a European music label called Prikosnovénie (based in France), which bills itself as the "fairy world label".

If anything, these three musical projects show just how elastic the concept of "ethno-Gothic" music is. Some would argue that the musical form has long since evolved beyond its humble roots during the early days of Goth, but they remain linked by their thousands of fans within the larger worldwide scene. Additionally, these bands have reinvigorated folk music inside and outside the Pagan or esoteric context. They are now part of a truly global musical movement. Today it is apparent that ethno-Gothic music had an impact on the somewhat insular Pagan musical scene as well. Self-consciously contemporary Pagan music, which emerged in the late 1970s thanks to the work of songwriter Gwydion Pendderwen, had an emphasis on traditional folk and singer-songwriter material. Starting in the late 1990s Pagan bands like The Moors, Pandemonaeon, Lasher Keen and Incus were able to break into a festival circuit that was dominated by a familial, "highly communal, and informal" atmosphere (Jim Alan, personal communication, 2007). Major events that regularly book Pagan-themed artists – like Faerieworlds in Oregon and PantheaCon in San Jose, California – now regularly feature ethno-Gothic influenced artists alongside, and melded with, traditional folk styles.

THE PAGAN AND OCCULT DARKWAVE

One somewhat amorphous category remains: Pagan and occult music within the genre known as "darkwave". Often heard in tandem with the word "Goth", darkwave has encompassed many different sounds and meanings. Originally, it referred to artists and bands (like Gary Numan and Fad Gadget) who explored darker lyrical and musical themes within the electronic pop of the New Wave/New Pop scene of the early 1980s – a "darker wave" to balance out the "squeaky-clean, overground brightness" (Reynolds 2006: 352). By the early 1990s in Europe, it was used to collectively describe a group of bands that incorporated industrial, rock and ethereal sounds into electronic music, while at around the same time in North America, Projekt Records started using the term to describe its stable of ethereal and moody bands. In some sense, the term provided an alternative to the descriptor "Goth" to describe bands with a darker aesthetic – an alternative badly needed during this creatively fallow period for older, explicitly "Goth" bands.

Because the category is rather amorphous, it is hard to track a clear evolution of occult and Pagan-influenced bands within darkwave. At the same time, darkwave contains some of the most influential and creative artists within the scope of this book. What binds them together musically is an iconoclastic outlook and a willingness to incorporate different sonic elements to create something unique and challenging:

> The first time I saw them [The Legendary Pink Dots], Edward Ka-spell cast a circle around the club in the middle of a song … It was a dark, smoky hole in the wall bar full of people in black leather; and it was important to me because of that circle-casting – I'd never seen anyone do it so casually, nor felt the energy move around in such a public venue before, and I thought it was darn cool. It had a big impact on my spiritual/magical aesthetic.
> (Stacey Lawless, Pagan Music Questionnaire, personal correspondence, 2007)

A key reference point, when discussing occult and Pagan influences within the boundaries of darkwave, is the Legendary Pink Dots. Formed in the late 1970s and led by the enigmatic Edward Ka-Spel, this band has encompassed so many musical directions that it is claimed as an influence by several musical genres and sub-genres. Just as we can delineate the band's influence here, we can also place its sound squarely within the post-industrial sounds of neofolk, or even discuss its contributions to what would come to be called "freak folk" – and that wouldn't even get close to the musical ground covered by the Legendary Pink Dots. The band has often touched on occult, mythological and Pagan themes within its records, and its influence can be felt through several occult-tinged bands found today, like Unto Ashes and Skinny Puppy.

Ka-Spel has often discussed his belief in magical forces and entities, and has presented Legendary Pink Dots shows as a ritualistic configuration, a "Mass" with Ka-Spel acting as a sort of "priest" directing the energies raised at the show. Legendary Pink Dots albums have deconstructed organized religion, pondered spiritual transcendence, referenced ancient mythologies and even explored hope and sadness in the wake of September 11. These themes are also explored in Edward Ka-Spel's side projects, including The Tear Garden, a collaboration with Cevin Key of the influential industrial band Skinny Puppy, and his own solo releases. The Legendary Pink Dots has a large cult following (which the band enjoys and nurtures), with an impressive discography of over 40 releases; the band still tours today.

In addition to the Legendary Pink Dots, it is worth briefly discussing one of the most popular darkwave bands currently active, The Cruxshadows. Formed in the early 1990s, the band has toured extensively in the United States and thirty other countries, releasing several albums of dark electro-pop in the process. The Cruzshadows has been listed on the mainstream Billboard singles chart, and enjoys a large following. The band's work (thanks to lead singer and songwriter Rogue) is full of esoteric, mythic and religious symbolism. Mixing angels with Egyptian deities and tragic characters from myth like Eurydice (doomed wife of the poet Orpheus), The Cruxshadows has established a lyrical and musical framework for more self-consciously Pagan and occult bands.

From the early 1990s to today, in terms of influence and importance within a Pagan/occult context, three bands under the "darkwave" banner stand out in terms of their lyrical vision: Faith and The Muse, Unto Ashes, and The Dreamside. All three share a significant crossover audience with more mainstream Pagan/occult communities, and while only one of these bands (The Dreamside) explicitly identifies as a "Pagan" band, all have written or performed songs that resonate deeply with modern Pagans and occultists.

Faith and The Muse, an American band formed in 1993 by William Faith (a former guitarist for seminal Gothic bands Christian Death and Shadow Project) and Monica Richards (former singer for the dark punk-influenced band Strange Boutique), is perhaps one of the most popular Goth/darkwave bands that are currently active. The band won fans within the Goth scene immediately with its first album, *Elyria*, and while nods to pre-Christian inspiration were apparent from the start with songs like "Caesura", it was the group's second album, *Annwyn Beneath the Waves*, that solidified Faith and The Muse's position as a prominently Pagan-friendly band.

Anwyn was a song-cycle based on Welsh mythology, and combined songs dedicated to Celtic pagan gods like Cernunnos and Arianhod with lush, mythologically themed original artwork painted by Monica Richards. From that point on, the band – especially lead singer Richards – was associated with modern Paganism, even though neither member has ever declared any outright allegiance to any form of modern Pagan belief. (This may be changing, as evidenced by Richards's heavily Pagan and Goddess-oriented solo album *InfraWarrior*, released in May 2007.) Faith and The Muse's employment of mythological themes and references to pre-Christian deities has continued with subsequent releases, and the band has appeared on the cover of leading Pagan magazine *newWitch*, further strengthening its connections with the modern Pagan subculture.

While Faith and The Muse has remained consciously on the outside of any allegiance with modern Paganism (or occult practices), Dutch band The Dreamside (formed in the same year as Faith and The Muse) associated themselves from the beginning with a forthright Pagan identity, with songs like "Goddesses", in which lead singer Kemi Vita asks pre-Christian deities to return to save us from an unhealthily patriarchal world. The band's focus on faeries, the supernatural and Pagan spirituality, not to mention its unique mixture of electronic, ethereal and metal elements, earned it a substantial European following, but it wasn't until nearly ten years later that The Dreamside broke through to a larger North American audience with a 2002 retrospective release entitled *Faery Child*. Since then, the band has started doing US shows, and has quickly attained a robust Pagan audience, strongly drawing younger Pagans already involved in the Goth subculture. More recently, the band has incorporated metal elements into its sound, and collaborated with darkwave superstars The Cruxshadows.

The third band mentioned, Unto Ashes, is perhaps one of the most talented within the confines of "darkwave", and often defies easy categorization. The band's music and ideology owe something to occultic strains within the post-industrial "neo-folk" genre, while incorporating elements from the more ethereal strains of Goth and avant-garde experimentalism. Formed in 1997 in New York by Michael Liard, the band has had a rotating cast of players, with singer/keyboardist Natalia Lincoln the only other artist to appear on every album.

From the beginning, Unto Ashes' music had an esoteric bent. On the band's first full-length album, *Moon Oppose Moon*, the song "Conjuration to Lilith" summons the ancient goddess as the "first sorceress" and ends with "Merry meet", a common expression in esoteric and Pagan rituals. From that point on, Unto Ashes' music has often featured songs that touch on magic, ritual, mythology or Pagan practices.

While the band has never labelled itself as "pagan" or "occult", singer Natalia Lincoln has described herself as aligned with religious witchcraft, and Michael Liard describes himself as a "seeker of knowledge" interested in the "occult sciences". It is due to the exploration of these themes that Unto Ashes has found an enthusiastic audience with modern Pagans and occultists. They have been favourably reviewed and interviewed by Pagan and occult publications such as *newWitch* and *Heathen Harvest*. The band has even paid tribute to its philosophical influences by performing poems by occultist Aleister Crowley ("Hymn to Pan") and Wiccan liturgist Doreen

Valiente ("Witches' Rune"). Yet, despite these influences, Unto Ashes remains largely unknown to many within the Pagan/occult subculture, most likely due to a musical generation gap that tends to tune out music from outside the Pagan festival culture.

Several other darkly inclined bands internationally are exploring Pagan and occult themes and worldviews, including Sopor Aeturnus (who has created his own mythology from whole cloth), ethereal drone artist Dark Muse, the esoteric rock band Sumerland and Italian ritualistic bands like Chirleison and Arkane. Those examples represent the tip of the iceberg in terms of the cross-influences between modern Pagan and occult movements and dark musical sub-genres.

SYNTHESIS

The cross-pollination of Goth music and subculture into modern Paganism, and vice versa, is now an all but accepted norm within both communities. Just as "Goth Paganism" (or "dark Paganism") has become a niche market for businesses that cater to modern Pagans, so too have Goth-focused events and festivals, like Wave Gotik Treffen in Germany – with its "Pagan Village" – explicitly welcomed a Pagan audience. The Pagan festival circuit in the United States, once completely insular in its musical choices, has slowly been opening up to acts with more daring and alternative fare, and over the last decade, Europe has spawned a veritable Renaissance of explicitly Pagan-identified bands who clearly have a lineage going back to 1990s Darkwave and Goth music.

In 2009 and 2010, I attended PantheaCon, the largest indoor Pagan-oriented convention in the United States. It was in this context that I was able to witness at first hand how intertwined Goth has become with the mainstream of the modern Pagan movement. While there were still many traditional folk-oriented acts on display, there were also bands like Pandemonaeon and Lasher Keen, who took inspiration from Dead Can Dance's Ethno-Gothic template, or the eclectic darkwave of bands like Unto Ashes. In addition, other outsider genres like metal were starting to find a space within this context. Even some of the artists who mainly operated within a folk context – like the singer-songwriter SJ Tucker – proudly displayed an admiration for non-folk musical styles; Tucker has partially integrated herself within the Faerie subculture.

Within my own personal experience, I have seen my own small contributions to this phenomenon blossom. Many of the bands I played on my internet radio show and podcast are now seen as part of a larger continuum of Pagan music. The band list at the "Pagan rock" entry on Wikipedia sports a new ecosystem of sound that includes many of the bands discussed here, traditional folk performers, symphonic metal projects and more. For these fans, there is no real separation between Dead Can Dance and 1970s Pagan music legend Gwydion Pendderwen, between Thorn Coyle's albums of creative ritual chants and Faun's European "Pagan folk". Increasingly, the idea of Pagan music has grown to absorb and include the bands that younger Pagans once turned to when self-described Pagan music seemed limited and stagnant.

In a certain sense, the Gothic and darkwave subcultures absorbed and nurtured a wholly alternate idea of what "Pagan" or "occult" music can be. In turn, this was reabsorbed back into the contemporary Pagan movement. While much of the modern Pagan world is still very much culturally dominated by the Baby Boomer generation and its musical preferences, one look at a majority of Pagan festival lineups and events shows that changes are taking place. Until now, "dark" music has been ignored or overlooked by scholars and commentators writing about modern Paganism, but these bands inhabit an important place in the history of music made by and for modern Pagans and occultists, one that points to a need for expressions that couldn't be fulfilled within modern Pagan culture – a "shadow" music that lends balance to the sounds emanating from the Pagan mainstream.

NOTE

1. A note on capitalization: in this chapter and in Chapter 7, "Pagan" has been capitalized when referring to the modern religious movement, but it has been left in lower case when referencing religions and individuals that existed in pre-Christian eras. This is the standard used by *The Pomegranate*, the international journal of Pagan studies, and other well-known Pagan studies books.

7. PAGANISM AND THE BRITISH FOLK REVIVAL

Andy Letcher

Folk music in Britain has never been more popular. A nationwide calendar of folk festivals and a thriving scene of folk clubs, pub sessions and ceilidhs support a body of professional and semi-professional artists and a groundswell of amateur players. Newcastle University runs a popular folk music degree course, the mainstream media review the major folk releases and artistic accomplishment is recognized through the BBC Radio 2 Folk Awards. In 2006, BBC 4 produced an acclaimed three-part documentary about the history of the folk revival, *Folk Britannia*, and in 2010 the editor of *The Wire* magazine, Rob Young, published his monumental and even broader history, *Electric Eden: Unearthing Britain's Visionary Music*, to plaudits from both the literary and musical worlds.

In spite of this success, "folk" remains a contested term. It is not easy to say with any great precision what does or does not count as folk music (added to this, the term has rather different connotations within the different Anglophone nations). Because folk music is, by definition, so bound up with notions of tradition and authenticity, what it *signifies* has come to be every bit as important as what it sounds like and how it is played. Consequently, its borders are continually being negotiated.

Part of folk's appeal is that it confers alterity through identification with tradition and the past. That past tends for the most part to be heavily romanticized – typically as a rustic, pre-industrial or prelapsarian golden age, a simpler time of honest labour and straightforward pleasures, and as something lost to us or very nearly forgotten. Georgina Boyes beautifully captures the object of folk's yearning with her memorable phrase "the imagined village" (Boyes 1993). Both left and right wings subsequently have tried to claim folk music, and the past it signifies, as their own, regarding it as the authentic voice of the working class, or as a pure expression of the people – or folk – from a lost age of modesty, tradition and deference respectively (Blake 1997; Boyes 1993; MacKinnon 1994; R. Young 2010).[1]

However, it is another aspect of the past that concerns me here, for if we trace the folk tradition back far enough, do we not come to an "archaeological" layer that predates Christianity? In other words, are not the origins of folk music ultimately pagan? This assumption, which is widely accepted in popular culture, forms a kind of lodestone about which modern folk musicians orientate themselves. Some celebrate it or regard it as the quiddity of folk. Others maintain a healthy distance from what they regard as a troubling episode in their music's history.

In this chapter, I want to examine contemporary British folk music, in its widest sense, to describe the three broad ways in which musicians relate to the supposed pagan origins of their craft. Modern Pagans[2] have seized upon the relationship to claim folk music as theirs, and to use it as a vehicle for the expression of religious identity, "Pagan folk". Others, making so-called "dark folk" – and who may not necessarily be practising Pagan religionists – are drawn to the alterity of identifying with an uncanny pagan past, one supposed to have involved not only a close and magical connection with nature but also sexual licence and, occasionally, heinous ritual. Finally, there are those mainstream or "traditional folk" musicians who might invoke the pagan past occasionally for rhetorical ends but mostly regard it as problematic in some way.

I want to begin by challenging the very idea that British traditional music has pagan origins. I want to demonstrate that this notion derives ultimately from the wishful thinking of Edwardian scholars, who in turn were influenced by a popular misunderstanding of Darwinian evolution. Traditional music in Britain is categorically not of pagan provenance, but the indelible assumption that it is – and the need for that assumption to be true – tell us much about the popularity of folk and Paganism today.

Before I do this, I must declare an interest. Though I am writing as an academic, a scholar of religion who specializes in Paganism, psychedelic spiritualities and the impact of Darwinism on Western thought, I am also writing as a Pagan and a folk musician. I am an unusual Pagan, partly because I do not currently belong to any group or identify with any tradition, but mostly because I am engaged in a continuing process of reflexive negotiation between – put simply – my heart and my head. As a relatively new religion, Paganism has yet to adopt a "hermeneutics of suspicion" towards its tenets (except within some rarefied academic circles). My own academically driven "suspicion" led me to abandon much of what I once held to be foundational Pagan beliefs and practices. Nevertheless, my Pagan identity remains, and my ongoing "project" is to find a robust Pagan theology that will satisfy heart *and* head.

Similarly, as a songwriter and instrumentalist – fronting "post-folk" band Telling the Bees and playing English bagpipes for the French/Breton/Swedish dancing that is currently popular in the south of England – I am necessarily positioned in the ongoing debate about what folk music is, is not or ought to be. What follows, therefore, is the world as I see it from my situated and nuanced perspective; this chapter is offered as part of an ongoing dialogical process of narrative inquiry (see Flood 1999).

CONSTRUCTING THE "FOLK", CONSTRUCTING "THE PAGAN"

In 1903, Cecil Sharp, one-time bank clerk and Oxford-educated musician, overheard a Somerset labourer singing a traditional song while at work, mowing the grass. Sharp was so moved by (the appropriately named) John England's rendition of "The Seeds of Love" that he rushed to get his notebook to transcribe it. Thus began Sharp's love affair with English folk music, which later expanded to include folk dance. Along with other contemporaries – the Reverend Sabine Baring Gould, Francis J. Child, George Butterworth, Ralph Vaughan Williams, Lucy Broadwood and Ernest J. Moeran, to name a few – Sharp began collecting, notating and publishing folk songs (albeit in a somewhat sanitized form) and proselytizing for their dissemination in the classroom and beyond as a kind of "national music".

The word "folk" itself has German origins, and is particularly associated with the Romantic philosopher Johann Gottfried Herder (1744–1803). Herder, writing before German unification, drew attention to the importance of the German language, which was widely disparaged by German intellectuals at the time, and the significance of ordinary people, the *volk*. The *volk*, he argued, were not an illiterate rabble of pitchfork-waving peasants, but the very soil from which language, culture and ultimately nationhood itself sprang. Left to flourish, each distinct *volk* – shaped by climate and terrain – would be predisposed to evolve a unique form of political organization tailored to its character. We should therefore delineate and arrange nations on the basis of these "organic communities", which would easily be picked out by commonalities of language, custom and culture (Barnard 1965; W. A. Wilson 2005). Such was his vision for a united Germany – a vision that, in the light of subsequent events, now seems highly problematic.

Prior to the rise of National Socialism (inspired in part by Herder's nationalism), Herder's influence was regarded in a more benign light, however, and we can see the traces of his ideas at work in Sharp's understanding of folk music. Sharp defined the folk song as "the unaided composition of the [musically] unskilled" (Sharp 1907: 7). Handed down and changed by many generations, it is nevertheless a "spontaneous utterance" (*ibid.*: 1), "a communal and racial product, the expression in musical idiom of aims and ideals that are primarily national in character" (*ibid.*: x). By recording and preserving folk music, Sharp and his contemporaries believed they were saving something quintessentially English, something that modernity was in danger of stripping away. (As we shall see, this idea that the tradition needs to be protected from the times remains central to folk.)

Sharp was less concerned about the question of origins than many of his contemporaries, who argued about whether folk songs had originally been composed by individuals or collectively in groups. For Sharp, every folk song was made anew each time it was performed. Songs were like "the acorns which fell last autumn from an oak. The tree is, perhaps, an old one and has its roots in the past, but the acorns are the products of a season's growth" (Sharp 1907: 125). The search for origins was therefore a rather futile exercise. He did, however, concede that "Wassail songs, and carols associated with the May-day festival, are pagan survivals" (*ibid.*: 101). That he could make such an adamant yet unsupported assertion was due to another related and widely-held discourse of the time: the idea that all manner of folk customs, rites, dances, legends and even children's rhymes and games were relics of an ancient fertility cult centred on an annually dying and reborn vegetation god. This discourse, likewise, can be traced in part to German romanticism.

Herder's nationalistic writings famously inspired the brothers Jacob and Wilhelm Grimm to begin collecting *Märchen*, or fairytales. The brothers worked under the assumption that these stories were expressions of what Herder had termed the *Volksgeist*, the spirit of the folk, and therefore that the tales captured and encapsulated some unique German-ness (see Arvidsson 1999). Jacob Grimm (1785–1863) was similarly inspired by Herder to produce his monumental philological study of the German language, *Geschichte der Deutschen Sprache*, published in 1848. Like fellow philologists of the time, Grimm had discovered that languages not only change through time (for the worse, he thought) but they also split and divide, giving birth to new tongues (Deutscher 2006). This had two implications.

First, working backwards, there must have been an original language from which all others sprang, an *Ursprache* (literally, the language of Ur, the Babylonian city where according to Biblical mythology the tower of Babel was built).[3]

Second, if language degenerates through time – Grimm thought the High Gothic of the Middle Ages the pinnacle of German expression – then so would any remnants of pre-Christian mythology, preserved (as they had to have been) in the amber of language. Fairytales, for Grimm, were the vestigial and decrepit remains of a once much greater, but now lost, epic cycle of Germanic pagan mythology. As he thought the traces of paganism also lingered in customs, folklore, legends, Gothic architecture and laws, he reasoned that just as it was possible to work backwards to reconstruct the original *Ursprache*, so it would be possible to work backwards and reconstruct a picture of the original ur-religion from which these pagan remnants must have come.

Scholars agree now that Grimm's premise was flawed. Fairytales are not degenerate myths (see Dundes 2005); the idea of pagan survivals in customs, folklore and architecture has been scotched (Hutton 1991, 1999); and the traces of paganism preserved in language (such as our "Wednesday" – Woden's Day) are wholly insufficient to reconstruct original practices (Dowden 2000). But Grimm made the attempt in his four-volume *Deutsche Mythologie* (1835–78). Regarding Teutonic paganism as a pure, if occasionally misguided, expression of the German *Volksgeist*, he wrote of it in rather fond terms as a happy, sensual, honourable and law-abiding faith:

> I liken Heathenism to a strange plant whose brilliant fragrant blossom we regard with wonder; Christianity to the crop of nourishing grain that covers wide expanses. To the Heathen too was germinating the true God, who to the Christians had matured into fruit ...   (Grimm [1880] 1999: 7)

The same cannot be said of Grimm's student, Willhelm Mannhardt (1831–80), for whom paganism, and the idea of its persistence, proved altogether more troubling. Mannhardt pioneered folklore research through the use of questionnaires, sent out to willing priests and pastors across the German-speaking principalities. This new method consequently generated vast quantities of data based on eyewitness accounts (Tybjerg 2005). Influenced both by his mentor and by E. B. Tylor's theories of animism and the "doctrine of survivals" – the notion that earlier ritual practices survived in folk customs like "living fossils" – Mannhardt concluded that there was a direct link between the rituals of Classical antiquity and the contemporary harvest customs of German peasants, the latter being the lingering and degenerate remnant of the former.

In his *Wald und Feldkulte* (1875–77), Mannhardt noted that in rural areas the cutting of the last sheaf of corn was often accompanied by strange and rather barbaric rituals. The man who made the last stroke of the scythe was, for example, tied up or ridiculed or humiliated in some way. These rites were, Mannhardt concluded, the remnants of more heinous rituals, where the vegetation spirit (thought to be caught up in the last sheaf) had to be propitiated with the sacrifice of a human representative to ensure a good harvest the following year.

Mannhardt's Gothic reading of harvest customs was contested in 1934 by the Danish folklorist C. W. von Sydow, who pointed out that human representatives of plants amongst the peasantry were rare; that harvest customs had more to do with rivalry, ribaldry and festivity at the end of a gruelling season of labour than with any concern for fertility or propitiation; and that the "spirits" of folklore were more often than not pedagogical fictions, designed to warn or scare children away from dangerous pursuits. The peasants did not literally believe in vegetation spirits any more than we believe in the bogeyman at the end of the garden (von Sydow 1934).

Following such trenchant criticism, Mannhardt's ideas ought not to have had the influence they did, for to the best of my knowledge, his voluminous books have never been translated into English. But they came to have a huge impact on the Anglophone world – and subsequently upon folk music – when they were adopted wholesale by Sir James Frazer (1854–1941).

Frazer's magnum opus, *The Golden Bough*, published in three editions between 1890 and 1915, and eventually reaching twelve volumes, is arguably one of the most influential works of the twentieth century. Drawing upon Mannhardt, Tylor and the work of his mentor, William Robertson Smith (1846–94), Frazer constructed a thesis in which he argued that the origins of *all* religions lie in the same, primitive vegetation cult. A dying and reborn vegetation god – named differently as Osiris, Attis, Adonis and Baldur – was represented on earth by a succession of divine kings and magical priests. These embodied the god and, through seasonal and typically licentious rituals (of which Frazer included countless examples) ensured his annual return and the fertility of the crops. But when these king/priests grew old and infirm, they had to be sacrificed and replaced with younger, more virile representatives lest the harvest fail.

Though Frazer's thesis and methods were roundly criticized by fellow anthropologist Andrew Lang (and others – see Ackerman 1987; Hutton 1991, 1999), even before his death, the influence of *The Golden Bough* upon twentieth-century thought proved immense. Jessie Weston reinterpreted Arthurian legend and the Grail myth through the Frazerian lens (J. L. Weston [1919] 1993). Jane Ellen Harrison and the so-called Cambridge Ritualists were inspired to look for the ancient origins of Greek religion and Greek theatre. Lady Raglan famously named the array of foliate head carvings found in churches from the late Middle Ages onwards "green men", and supposed them to be depictions of Frazer's vegetation spirit. Anthropologist Margaret Murray reinvented the victims of the early modern witch-hunts as the last remnants of Frazer's fertility cult. The poet Robert Graves developed Frazer's ideas, mixing them feverishly with his own fanciful notions in *The White Goddess* (Graves 1961). In turn, Murray and Graves helped inspire the creation of modern Wicca (Hutton 1999): Frazer's mythology of the dying and reborn god remains the core upon which modern Pagan theology is constructed. And *The Golden Bough* directly influenced T. S. Eliot's *The Waste Land*, Francis Ford Coppola's *Apocalypse Now*, Tom Robbins's *Jitterbug Perfume* and Robin Hardy's cult horror classic *The Wicker Man*, to which we shall return shortly.

Most importantly for our subject here, Frazer managed to instil into popular culture a very clear idea of "the pagan", ensuring that it was everywhere associated with "fertility", and claiming that its attenuated vestiges persisted pretty much everywhere – at least once you started to look for them. What's more, he branded paganism as a troubling, atavistic impulse that, like the vegetation god it was supposed to revere, could spring back to life at any moment:

Yet we should deceive ourselves if we imagined that the belief in witchcraft is even now dead in the mass of people; on the contrary there is ample evidence to show that it only hibernates under the chilling influence of rationalism, and that it would start into active life if that influence were ever seriously relaxed. The truth seems to be that to this day the peasant remains a pagan at heart; his civilization is merely a thin veneer which the hard knocks of life soon abrade, exposing the solid core of paganism and savagery below. (Frazer 1913: viii–ix)

Frazer was adamantly an intellectualist, in that he thought "primitive man" arrived at paganism *rationally*, albeit through the misapplication of scientific reasoning and a mistaken view of causality. But as the above passage illustrates, he repeatedly gives the impression of being an *emotionalist*, implying that paganism is instinctual and therefore a throwback to an earlier stage of human evolution.

Writing in the aftermath of the publication of Charles Darwin's *On the Origin of Species* (1859), Frazer – like most of his contemporaries – adhered to a misunderstanding of Darwinian natural selection as so-called "cultural evolution". This purports that human cultures evolve just like species, from the simple to the complex – or, rather, from the savage to the civilized (G. Bennett 1994). Cultural evolution moves at different rates in different places, so to study a primitive tribe or a peasant ritual is therefore to step back into our evolutionary past, to see *our* culture as once it was before the currents of progress propelled us forwards and away to a superior stage of development:

Victorians who were swallowing the idea that they were descended from apes had no trouble in accepting the concept that savages had been the next stage in human development, especially as the sequence turned the modern Western world into the end product of a triumphal story of increasing technological, cultural, and intellectual progress. (Hutton 1999: 8)

To an extent, Frazer's ideas proved popular because of their apparently universal explanatory power: almost any aspect of prehistory or folklore, from stone circles to folk dances, can be explained in terms of "fertility rites". But the notion that paganism was something inside all of us, lurking like an inner Mr Hyde behind the outward persona of Dr Jekyll, generated a strong emotional reaction. It is this, I think, that explains quite why his ideas have endured in the way that they have in the face of such trenchant academic criticism. To use Freud's terminology, the "quality of feeling" they elicited was one of *ambivalence* (Freud [1913] 2001, [1919] 2003). On the one hand, paganism was abhorrent, an affront to decency and an insult to intelligence;

on the other, paganism was *fascinating* – titillating even – with the word "fertility" suggesting all manner of delights behind its euphemistic veil. The idea that, say, a children's playground game or a May song might have pagan origins was at once unsettling *and* thrilling – or, to use another Freudian term, it instilled a sense of *das Unheimliche*: the weird, eerie or uncanny or literally the *unhomely* (Freud [1919] 2003).

Returning now to Cecil Sharp, we have a much clearer picture of the intellectual environment within which he was operating. His assertion that folk music bubbled up through the peasantry as "a purely natural instinct" (Sharp 1907: 1) makes sense in the light of Herder, Grimm, Mannhardt and Frazer, as does his claim that certain folk songs have pagan origins. Indeed, Sharp's contemporary folklorists and folk song collectors were working within a broadly Frazerian paradigm, convinced that through their investigations they were uncovering the indigenous remnants of the pan-European vegetation cult. Sharp's caution regarding the origin of folk songs was rarely heeded by others, and by the time of the second great folk revival, in the aftermath of World War II, a discourse that entwined folk music with paganism had become bound into the popular imagination. Its features are as follows.

Folk song is related to paganism in that both originated as an instinctive, albeit locally contingent, response to the vicissitudes of the natural world and, more specifically, the agricultural year; the rituals and mythology of paganism are preserved in a fragmentary and attenuated way in certain folk songs; those rituals took many forms, though they were always enacted (presumably with the songs to accompany them) to ensure fertility and a good harvest, and they required licentious and occasionally heinous acts (human sacrifice). Finally, paganism, lying just beneath the surface of the modern world, could return at any time. Burdened with such ambivalent connotations, it is unsurprising that, for many, folk music acquired an almost magical ability to evoke feelings of *das Unheimliche* (see R. Young 2010).

"JOHN BARLEYCORN" AND *THE WICKER MAN*

A perfect illustration of this pagan reading of folk music is provided by the traditional song, "John Barleycorn". The song is perhaps one of the most popular and well known from the British canon, and has been performed by pretty much every professional folk artist of the last forty years. It was brought to the attention of the wider public when it was released by rock band Traffic on the album *John Barleycorn Must Die* in 1970.

The song exists in several historical versions, but all concern the fate of the eponymous hero, the anthropomorphic representative of barley, and each consists of the same three structural parts: "Part A concerns the growth, harvesting, and processing of the plant, Part B the brewing process, and part C the effects of beer upon people." (Wood 2004: 439). The song is unambiguously a drinking song and, with the earliest version appearing in a Scottish manuscript in 1568, was composed a good eight centuries after the formal end of paganism in Britain.

Nevertheless, the trials of John Barleycorn, with his apparent death and triumphant rebirth – proving him "the strongest man at last" – have rendered the song open to a popular and unshakeable Frazerian reading: it is now universally regarded as alluding to a dying and reborn vegetation god.

Thus when dynastic folk band The Watersons recorded it on their seminal 1965 album, *Frost and Fire: A Calendar of Ritual and Magical Songs*, they described it as "an unusually coherent figuration of the old myth of the Corn-king cut down and rising again" (The Watersons 1965). Traffic dismissed the drinking song thesis with the enigmatic but portentous statement that "there are many other interpretations" (Traffic 1970). In 2005, Folk Award winner Chris Wood wrote that playing the song had drawn him "deeper into *the passion* of the corn" (Chris Wood 2005; emphasis added). When in 2007, Cold Spring Records released a double CD compilation of contemporary "dark folk" (of which more later), they titled it *John Barleycorn Reborn: Dark Britannica*, explaining in the sleeve notes that "the song tells of the seasonal cycle and the vitality of the fields renewed each year by the gods (embodied by some traditions as the sun) through the symbolic sacrifice of the corn king, John Barleycorn" (Cold Spring 2007). I have heard the song played many times during modern Pagan rituals, most notably at Lughnasadh celebrations. It has become totemic.

Another totemic cultural artefact, which bound "folk" and "the pagan" tighter still, was Robin Hardy's 1973 horror movie *The Wicker Man*. When an upright Presbyterian policeman, Sergeant Howie, is called to the remote Scottish island of Summerisle to investigate the disappearance of a missing girl, he discovers that the islanders have abandoned Christianity for a permissive paganism. Gradually, he comes to suspect that the girl is to be sacrificed. It is a trick, and Howie himself becomes the unwitting victim, immolated in the wicker man of the title – a human sacrifice to propitiate the gods against repeated harvest failures.

The film is Frazerian through and through, not only in its plot but in the way it depicts all manner of actual folk customs (such as the use of a toad to cure a sore throat) as pagan practices: the late Anthony Schaffer, who wrote the screenplay, was explicit about his debt to *The Golden Bough* (Brown 2000). Lord Summerisle, ostensibly the film's villain, played with gusto by Christopher Lee, is Frazerian man incarnate, arriving at paganism through rational choice. He admits to Howie that he is a "heathen, conceivably, but not, I hope, an unenlightened one" (cited in *ibid.*: 222). The islanders, however, are Frazerian in the unintended, emotionalist sense of having reverted to type. "The tradition of the arcane and the mysterious cleaves to the people of this island with a tenacity which makes it seem an inherent and inalienable possession" (Lord Summerisle to Howie, cited in *ibid.*: 217).

The Frazerian backdrop also explains the horror of the film's denouement. It is not so much that we identify with Howie, with his futile cries for mercy drowned by the roar of the inferno and the music of the assembled crowd. Rather, it is that we identify more with the *islanders* – for, however much we are attracted to their licentious freedoms, the idea that it could so easily be us, singing merrily while the sacrifice burns, is what makes the film so chilling. It evokes a profound feeling of *das Unheimliche* by drawing on the now deeply instilled Frazerian fear that paganism is something within us all.

Significantly, the film intensified that feeling through the cunning deployment of folk music. Composed by Paul Giovanni, the score made full use of folk's pagan and uncanny semiotic associations – and, importantly, as the film gained cult status in the years subsequent to its release, reinforced those associations in the popular imagination. "The songs", said Christopher Lee, interviewed in 2002, "sum up the atmosphere of the scenes perfectly". As we shall see, folk musicians would only have to reference the music of *The Wicker Man* to be sure of evoking exactly the same atmosphere.

Having established the provenance of folk's association with paganism – and the emotional potency of the paganism it is supposed to preserve – it is time to examine the ways in which contemporary musicians exploit that association. I identify three sub-genres – traditional folk, Pagan folk and dark folk – that must be regarded as tendencies only, and not as clearly delineated types. Folk artists may express more than one tendency at once, or none, or move between positions at different times. What the three tendencies share is that they all express alterity. Sharp set "the folk" in opposition to modernity; Frazer "the pagan" to "the civilized". To identify with either subjugated term is automatically to embrace otherness. Alterity needs to be proclaimed for it to acquire any potency, and the historical intertwining of folk music and paganism means that folk is the perfect vehicle for doing so (Letcher 2001).

TRADITIONAL FOLK

Though the folk revival instigated by Cecil Sharp was hampered somewhat by the two world wars, it continued in earnest during the second half of the twentieth century. In the 1950s, folk was reinvented as a vehicle of socialism by Ewan MacColl (1915–89), Peggy Seeger, Alan Lomax (1915–2002), Shirley Collins and others; in the 1960s, Davey Graham (1940–2008), Bert Jansch, John Renbourn, Martin Carthy, Roy Harper and others produced a distinctive British guitar-based folk-blues, largely under the all-pervasive influence of Bob Dylan; in the 1970s, folk was fused with rock by Fairport

Convention and Steeleye Span; in the 1980s, a wave of anti-Thatcher sentiment made folk political again, producing figures like Billy Bragg and bands like The Pogues and The Levellers; and from the late 1990s onwards, folk became increasingly professionalized, bootstrapping itself into the wider British music industry (R. Young 2010). Now an agglomeration of agents, festival organizers, record, TV and radio producers, CD distributors, journalists and artists together comprise a "folk industry", while at the same time pub sessions, ceilidhs and folk clubs cater for an important ground layer of amateur players. Yet much traditional folk has adapted itself to the market, and as the name suggests, it remains profoundly concerned with the correct and proper maintenance of "tradition".

Ostensibly, traditional folk musicians play traditional folk music – which is to say the corpus of songs, ballads and carols collected by Sharp and his contemporaries, and a body of English, Welsh, Scottish and Irish instrumental tunes, some of which date back to collections from the seventeenth century or even earlier, using traditional acoustic instruments: fiddle, flute, whistle, melodeon, concertina, guitar, mandolin, bagpipes and so on. However, the ways in which traditional material is played, and the contexts in which it is performed, have changed so much – and so radically – that they share little in common with the music of "source singers" like John England.

So, while John England and others of his ilk sung unaccompanied and unpaid, modern traditional folk musicians support songs with backing and the harmonic know-how of classical music and jazz. Far from being the products of an oral tradition, many professional folk musicians have undergone classical training, often to a high degree, and learn their material from written sources or recordings. Musicians do not just play traditional material, but compose new songs and tunes in a traditional style. And today, folk musicians form bands, record albums, play concerts to paying audiences and expect to make a living from their music – all of which would have astounded John England.

There is therefore a contradiction that runs through the contemporary traditional music scene. On the one hand, traditional folk is as beholden to the market expectations of novelty and innovation as any other aspect of the British popular music industry, and as such has continually been influenced by contemporaneous musical trends. (Thus, for example, the guitar – the iconic instrument of "the folk singer" – was actually imported into British folk music from America during the 1950s.) On the other hand, the scene has taken upon itself the self-appointed task of upholding, maintaining and protecting the "tradition" – "that great act of faith which is our indigenous musical inheritance" (Wood 2005) – from exactly the kinds of innovations that market forces and contemporaneous trends would impress upon it. These tensions – between innovation and tradition, between the individual and "the folk" – have an important bearing upon traditional folk's relationship with the supposed pagan origins of its music.

Within traditional folk, paganism (as laid out in the Frazerian paradigm) is regarded ambivalently. In 2006, Norma Waterson and her husband Martin Carthy released an album of seasonal songs, a homage to the seminal *Frost and Fire* of 1965, titled *Holy Heathens and the Old Green Man*. Unlike its predecessor, and apart from the obvious implications of the title, there were no direct references to paganism in the sleeve notes (Waterson: Carthy 2006). Instead, attention and due deference were given to the tradition – that is, the sources from which the duo acquired the material.

On his 2005 album *The Lark Descending*, Chris Wood – a torchbearer like Carthy and Waterson – recorded the results of his collaboration with storyteller Hugh Lupton. Two of the songs, "Bleary Winter" and "Walk this World", make distinctly Frazerian references, evoking the (supposed) pagan origins of folk customs. In 2006, Wood and Lupton were commissioned by BBC Radio 3 to make a "radio ballad" about the traditional midwinter mummers' plays. The programme, *England in Ribbons*, mixed music, song and storytelling with archive recordings.[4] A version of one of its songs, a setting of a traditional mummers' play to music, also called "England in Ribbons", appeared on Wood's 2007 album *Trespasser*. Wood took a Frazerian reading of the drama, calling it an "enduring midwinter ritual" of death and resurrection, and "English Voodoo at its finest!" (Wood 2007). However, all Wood's Frazerian allusions appear to be for poetic or rhetorical purposes only, for he is an avowed and vocal atheist. On *Trespasser*, he recorded what must count as the first (and probably only) atheist "spiritual", "Come Down Jehovah".

Leaving personal religious orientation to one side, a clue to traditional folk's ambivalence towards paganism can be found right back on The Watersons's 1965 *Frost and Fire*. Ostensibly at least, it appeared as if this band of unaccompanied singers was openly acknowledging folk's debt to the pagan past. The sleeve notes, however, reveal an almost Marxist distaste for it:

> So much is talked of myth and sun worship and such, that it's necessary to recall that behind most of these calendar customs and the songs attached to them lies nothing more mysterious, nothing less realistic, than the yearly round of work carried out in the fields ... it's due to their relation with economic life, not to any mystical connection, that the song-customs have persisted right up to our own time. (The Watersons 1965)

Here, then, is the problem. People come to folk music for many reasons, but serious and committed folk enthusiasts (nicknamed "folkies") are attracted to it not just because they like the way it sounds or what it says, but because of the powerful sense of identity that belonging to the tradition confers. Being a folkie is to feel at one with the "common man", an identification that confers stability, continuity, community and respectability. But the lingering Frazerian orthodoxy, which states that the tradition is founded on heinous rituals and irrational superstition, does not sit well with this preferred notion of the "folk" as producers and holders of a kind of canny, earthy, Herderian wisdom or common sense – or, as Chris Wood puts it, "*the* common sense" (Wood, personal communication). The Frazerian paradigm undermines that sense of stability and respectability, is upsetting or dangerous, and needs to be made safe (as it is by The Watersons). In traditional folk, therefore, pagan associations tend to be employed as lyrical or poetic devices, and typically in the service of an implicit working-class discourse: that folk songs are the songs of the working people, born out of the seasonal round of hard, physical labour.

PAGAN FOLK

Modern Pagans do not have such qualms: given that folk music is supposed to have pagan origins, it is unsurprising that modern Pagan religionists should want to play folk music and to use it to express religious identities. In my doctoral investigation of music within contemporary Paganism (Letcher 2001), I found that performers mostly adapted the kind of music they ordinarily played outside Pagan contexts – be it blues, rock or folk – to Pagan themes. That said, because many performance settings require that players play acoustically – at camps and festivals, say – and necessarily because of folk's pagan associations, there is a gravitational pull towards playing traditional songs and tunes. But currently lacking a distinct musical style, Pagan identity music is best defined by its lyrical content and subject-matter.

Perhaps the most famous Pagan musician in Britain today, and the closest that Paganism has to a star, is Damh the Bard (pronounced "Dave the Bard"). Damh is a Druid, an active member of Druidry's largest order, the Order of Bards, Ovates and Druids (OBOD), and a regular performer at Pagan moots, camps and conferences. He has released six albums to date, as well as a book of his most popular songs; he keeps a regular blog and produces a monthly "Druidcast" of Pagan music and interviews.[5]

Live, Damh accompanies himself on acoustic guitar and often constructs his songs around rock chord progressions (he began his musical life as a drummer in a metal band), adding big, anthemic choruses. Folkier elements are more apparent on his albums, where mandolin, whistle and harp add melodic lines. The songs are almost always expressly about Pagan themes, and he intersperses his compositions with traditional folk songs that lend themselves to Pagan readings, such as the Cornish May song "Hal an Tow".

The chorus of his "Spirit of Albion", from the 2006 album of the same name, provides a good example of his work.

> The Crane, the wolf,
> the bear and the boar,

No longer dwell upon these shores,
You say that the Goddess and God
have gone,
Well I tell you they live on!
For in the cities and hills,
And in circles of stone,
The voices of the Old Ways,
The Spirit of Albion is calling you home!
(Damh the Bard 2006, lyrics printed with author's permission)

The song, a fast minor waltz, presents the pagan past as a time when wild animals were still extant, and hence the land was in some sense more vital. As a Pagan, Damh has regained a magical connection to the land, its God and Goddess, and the "Old Ways". To be a Pagan is necessarily to reawaken to the "Spirit of Albion", to heal the sense of alienation between ourselves and nature caused by modernity, and thus to come "home".

The figure of the Bard is central to Druidry, as is the quest for *awen*, or inspiration, a kind of divine afflatus that supposedly can be channelled into creative acts (Letcher 2012). Druid groups have established public Bardic competitions in Bath, Glastonbury, Exeter, Winchester and other UK towns and cities. The winner, who is judged to have composed the best poem or song on a given theme, holds the "Bardic Chair" for a year, and is expected to undertake public performances and workshops to promote the Bardic arts (*ibid.*; Manwaring 2006). As with Damh's material, Bardic songs tend not to be devotional, or hymns, but refer to insider Pagan themes, and therefore serve to proclaim a religious identity.

Another, less well-known genre of Pagan folk flourished during the 1990s, emerging out of radical environmental protest culture, a genre I term tribe-delica (Letcher 2001). The 1990s saw a range of protests against airport expansion, car culture, GM crops, live animal exports and, most famously, road-building, which produced a lively counter-culture that was broadly (though not exclusively) Pagan in outlook. Eco-Paganism spoke the lan-guage of Paganism – often marking full moons and the eight festivals of the wheel of the year – but eschewed formal group affiliation and choreo-graphed ritual. Eco-Paganism was something to be *celebrated*, and the best way to express any religious sentiment one might feel towards the natural world was to do something active to protect it. The slogan "Gaia told me to do it" was the nearest thing to an eco-Pagan manifesto (Letcher 2003, 2005).

Eco-Paganism acquired its own mythology: the belief that protesters were some prehistoric tribe, returned to save the land from the ravages of modernity and to usher back an "archaic revival" (McKenna 1991), an ecstatic and psychedelic form of paganism that would reconnect culture and nature. "Pok" – aka Simon Miller, lead singer of tribedelic band, Space Goats (and who in fact coined the term tribedelica) – called that feeling of ecstatic connection with the land "enhurument": the band's mantra and mission statement was "get thee enhurued" (Miller personal comment). The Dongas Tribe – the original road-protesters from Twyford Down, near Winchester – actually lived for a while as an itinerant tribe, travelling the droves of southern England with hand-carts, goats, chickens and musical instruments.

As a musical genre, tribedelica was a kind of upbeat psychedelic folk that mixed medieval-style tunes and drones with the rhythms of techno to produce a self-consciously acoustic "organic trance". Favoured instruments included fiddle, whistle, hammered dulcimer, mandolin, bouzouki, saz, djembe, didgeridoo, hurdy-gurdy and bagpipes, instruments that were unusual and exotic, and themselves signs of otherness and alterity. As well as the Space Goats and the Dongas Tribe, bands included Heathens All and my own Jabberwocky. A much greater range of individual songwriters and performers were captured on a series of cassette releases, "Tribal Voices", recorded around the country at various protest sites.[6]

Songs were almost exclusively about eco-Pagan themes: about protecting the earth and the re-enchanted sense of belonging that would result for those who did. The Space Goats' first album, *Inamorata*, told the story of an eponymous heroine, travelling to Avebury stone circle to raise up a slumbering dragon – a symbol for the mysterious earth energy, supposedly channelled by prehistoric megalithic builders (Letcher 2004) – and thereby to save the land (Space Goats 1993).

The typical tribedelic performance (when not actually providing a soundtrack for actual protests) was the participatory fireside jam. When, in the mid-1990s, various protesters started travelling to the annual Rencontres Internationales des Luthiers et Maîtres Sonneurs (the International Meeting of Instrument Makers and Master Pipers) at Saint Chartier in central France, they started to incorporate French and Breton bagpipe tunes, with accompanying dances, into their music. This led to protracted sessions in which these austere and superficially simple tunes were played repeatedly for twenty minutes or more as vehicles of enhurument. Tribedelica effectively ended with the hiatus in road-building in Britain at the end of the 1990s, but many of its leading figures have gone on to become professional or semi-professional folk musicians, playing for French and Breton dance in Britain and Europe.

Finally, brief mention must be made of the growth in explicitly Pagan Morris sides. Frazer thought Morris dancing the relic of a fertility rite, and though this fancy has long been disproved (it originated as a Tudor Court dance – see Hutton 1996), it is a stubborn myth that persists in popular culture: if Morris dancing is pagan, then it stands to reason that modern Pagans should Morris dance. Border Morris is the favoured style. Less precise than Cotswold Morris, Border Morris uses sticks rather than handkerchiefs; dancers wear be-feathered top hats and elaborately tattered costumes; and the rowdy dances are performed with considerable verve and gusto to the accompaniment of melodeons, drums and occasionally bagpipes. The Wild Hunt, Armaleggan and Vixen Morris are just three Pagan sides (the last of these comprising women), and most are Wiccan in orientation. They dance publicly, but regard what they do as a covert but necessary form of seasonal worship.

DARK FOLK

I have already mentioned Cold Spring's 2007 compilation, *John Barleycorn Reborn* (which, as I write, has just been followed by a successor, *We Bring you a King with a Head of Gold* – see Cold Spring 2010b). That an underground label specializing in "dark industrial", "black ambient", "doom" and "power electronics" (Cold Spring 2010a) saw fit to release an album of folk music is perhaps surprising (though not in the light of the connections that the present volume illuminates), although Cold Spring's definition of folk is rather different from that of the traditionalists described above. The sleeve notes state:

> There has been a growing seam of alternative folk music emerging since the folk revival of the 1950s moving beyond concerns about popular music and exploring the original traditions whilst incorporating a range of progressive or experimental styles. This is largely unacknowledged within the area of [traditional] folk music but is equally sincere in its aims.   (Cold Spring 2007)

That those "original traditions" were pagan (and hence Frazerian) is suggested in the name Cold Spring supplied for the genre: "dark folk" (though elsewhere it is known as strange folk, wyrd folk, twisted folk, nu-folk, alt-folk, prog folk, psych folk, folkedelia, acid folk or post-folk).

Unlike Pagan folk, dark folk is more obviously a defined musical genre. It consists of folk songs performed in a "progressive", "experimental" or psychedelic manner – that is, through the mixing of traditional and electric instruments with overt use of digital processing and textures – or new songs about pagan, Frazerian themes. It makes extensive use of minor modes (dorian, aeolian and to a lesser extent, phrygian); drones (played using synths, looped samples or instruments such as bagpipes, hurdy-gurdies, Indian *tampuras* and *shruti* boxes); sparse or austere harmonies; and bells, chimes and other percussion. The tempo is typically slow or downbeat and the music is self-consciously uncanny.

Dark folk makes implicit and explicit reference to bands such as mordant ethno-Goth minimalists Dead Can Dance, and to the array of prog, psychedelic and underground folk and folk-rock bands that flourished during the late 1960s and early 1970s, the so-called "progressive moment": The Incredible String Band, Pentangle, Comus, Fairport Convention, The Young Tradition, and C.O.B., to name a few (on the progressive moment, see Blake 1997; for a more exhaustive discussion of music from this period, see R. Young 2010). Dark folk repeatedly references the most totemic music of all: the soundtrack to *The Wicker Man*. Semiotically complex, dark folk is knowingly referential. It both evokes the imagined pagan past *and* a period of recent musical and cultural history that has, for artists who were mostly children at the time, become something of a golden age.

Dark folk gained popularity and came to prominence during the 2000s thanks to a number of factors: the release of a series of compilations of underground or acid folk from the 1960s and 1970s – *Fuzzy Felt Folk* (Various Artists 2006c), *Gather in the Mushrooms: The British Acid Folk Underground 1968–1974* (Various Artists 2004), *Early Morning Hush: Notes From the UK Folk Underground 1969–1976* (Various Artists 2006a); the first, complete stereo release of *The Wicker Man* soundtrack (*The Wicker Man* 2002); the release of similar compilations of contemporary dark folk – *John Barleycorn Reborn, Strange Folk* (Various Artists 2006d) and *Folk Off!* (Various Artists 2006b), the latter compiled by DJ Rob da Bank; popular and carefully marketed festivals that catered expressly for this music – The Green Man and Moseley Folk festivals; interest from magazines and webzines – *Shindig* magazine, *Magpie* magazine, the *Ptolomaic Terrascope* and *Spiral Earth*; and media interest from the then rock critic of *The Times*, Pete Paphides, and *The Guardian*'s Will Hodgkinson.[7] Paphides appeared in an article about "new folk" on BBC 2's *The Culture Show*, broadcast on 3 February 2007, while Hodgkinson wrote a series of articles for *The Guardian* about his efforts to set up a record label, "Big Bertha", and to promote the Cornish dark folk band Thistletown (whose album *Rosemarie* was released on Big Bertha in 2007).

Other dark folk acts include cod-medievalists Circulus, Tunng, The Eighteenth Day of May, The Owl Service, Sieben, Pantalaimon, Mary Hampton, Tinkerscuss, Vashti Bunyan (who began her career in the 1960s), Drohne, English Heretic and my own band, Telling the Bees.

These three tendencies – traditional folk, Pagan folk and dark folk – are, of course, exactly that – tendencies – and the messy world is more complicated than my typology would suggest. For example, Sharron Kraus is a folk singer with an underground, cult following in Britain and the United States. She is openly a Pagan and an occultist, and has released her own round of Frazerian-themed seasonal songs, *Right Wantonly a-Mumming* (Kraus 2006). By rights, she "belongs" in Pagan folk; however, her songs – which employ drones, chimes, liberal use of minor seconds and unsettling lyrics, all performed with her idiosyncratic spidery voice – evoke a profound feeling of *das Unheimliche*, and so typify dark folk. Yet she is also a traditional singer and player, a stalwart of folk clubs and sessions. She belongs to all categories and none, striking her own path through the contested realm of folk.

FOLK, PAGANISM AND *DAS UNHEIMLICHE*

Our notions of "folk music" and "the pagan" are historically intertwined, sharing roots that go back to German romanticism and the idealism of Herder and Grimm. This odd symbiosis has bequeathed to us the idea that folk music is something old and other, at odds with modernity and urban living. Most of us now live in towns or cities, but folk music typically expresses a desire for the supposed rooted certainties of the countryside and a lost bucolic golden age (Boyes 1993; R. Young 2010). Clearly the popularity of both folk and Paganism says much about our contemporary and oft-commented yearning for an imagined, enchanted past (see Hume & McPhillips 2006; Letcher 2006).

Though the fortunes of folk music wax and wane in cycles far less predictable than those that drive the agricultural year, its renewed fecundity has much to do with the wealth of pagan connotations it has accrued, and as a result its power to invoke *das Unheimliche*. For traditional folk musicians, it is the *homeliness* afforded by tradition that matters, so "the pagan" can only be brought inside occasionally, like a dangerous guest, before being sent firmly on its way again. By contrast, those magical and uncanny connotations are exactly what attract modern Pagans to folk music. They too are looking for a sense of home, only this time a re-enchanted one, imbued with what Damh the Bard calls the "Spirit of Albion". The risk, of course, is that in doing so, by making *das Unheimliche, heimliche* – the unhomely, homely – they strip folk music of the very thing that gave it its attractive power in the first place.

But when the pagan past is alluded to, hinted at, touched upon, or evoked such that the imagination can fill in the gaps with all its ambivalent relish – as dark folk self-consciously attempts to do – then folk's ability to unsettle us, to upset the ordered certainties of urban life and to make us feel anything but at home, finds full expression. Folk was never pagan, but the twentieth century made it so. Now, for many, it embodies or is synonymous with the idea of the pagan, a pervasive – if mistaken – myth of our origins. Consequently, it provides modern musicians with a fecund source of inspiration, one that will undoubtedly provide a rich harvest for years to come – or, as The Watersons put it back in 1965, "to our toiling ancestors ... [folk songs] ... meant everything, and in a queer irrational way they can still mean much to us" (The Watersons 1965).

NOTES

1. This struggle is ongoing. When the far right British National Party attempted to use contemporary folk recordings in its campaign leading up to the 2010 general election, it elicited a swift and angry response from folk musicians and the formation of the pressure group Folk Against Fascism.

2. Following British convention, I refer to pre-Christian religions as "pagan", lower case, and modern revived or reconstructed religions – known in the United States as Neo-Paganism – as "Pagan", upper case.

3. Today linguists refer to this tongue as proto Indo-European (Deutscher 2006).

4. Available at www.bbc.co.uk/radio3/worldmusic/feature_mummers.shtml (accessed December 2012).

5. See www.Paganmusic.co.uk (accessed December 2012).

6. See www.tribalvoices.org.uk (accessed December 2012).

7. The influence of American nu-folk artists such as Devendra Banhart, Joanna Newsom and Espers was also significant, but a full discussion is beyond the scope of this chapter.

8. DANCING PAGANISM: MUSIC, DANCE AND PAGAN IDENTITY

Douglas Ezzy

You are how you move. (Roth 1997: xxiii)

In the video of a Faithless live performance of the song "God is a DJ", the camera pans out over a mass of dancing humanity and Maxi Jazz sings: "This is my church, this is where I heal my hurts" (Faithless 2010). The argument of this chapter is that, for Pagans in Australia, dancing to the music of Pagan bands creates both a sense of individual transformation (hurts are healed), and a spiritual community (perhaps not a church, but a collective with church-like functions nonetheless). Pike makes the same two points in her comment about Pagan festivals: "Festivals are an arena for self-creation as well as a space for making community" (Pike 2001: 155).

The chapter begins with a short introduction to contemporary Paganism in Australia. Dancing to Pagan music is a central part of contemporary Pagan religious practice. It is a key practice that contributes to personal transformation – one that is valued by many Pagans. The latter half of the chapter argues that dancing is also central to the creation of Pagan community and to the collective experience of the sacred. Pagan identities are hybrid and eclectic in nature; they do not cohere around centrally defined beliefs. Dancing at Pagan rituals – particularly to Pagan music – is a key practice that facilitates the identification of oneself as "Pagan". It represents an experiential, embodied and emoted, as well as a cognitive sense of Pagan identity. While some of the academic studies of contemporary Paganisms that inform this chapter come from the United States (Pike 2001) and the United Kingdom (Greenwood 2000), most of the empirical material in the chapter focuses on Australian Paganism. Throughout this chapter I draw on my own experiences as a participant in Pagan rituals to illustrate the central role of dancing to Pagan music. I use these experiences to illustrate the more formal academic research and accounts that mainly inform the chapter.

Music transforms emotions and creates community because when people dance to music, it changes their embodied performed sense of self. Helen

Thomas argues that: "In dancing ... individual embodied subjects/subjectivities enact and 'comment' on a variety of taken-for-granted social and cultural bodily relationalities: gender and sexuality, identity and difference, individual and community, mind and body and so on" (H. Thomas 2003: 215). She goes on to note that "close attention to dancing can provide the social and cultural analyst with layers of insights into culturally contingent relations and practices which have hitherto gone largely unnoticed or unexamined" (*ibid.*).

Applying Thomas's argument to Pagan religion, I argue that dancing is one of the central practices that make contemporary Pagan religion meaningful and transformative. From this perspective, religion is defined by shared ritual practice that shapes the etiquette of relationships (Harvey 2000). In this definition, "transcendence", "beliefs" and "deities" are of secondary consideration. Religious transcendence – vertical or horizontal – may be important in leading the individual out of themselves into relationships with both other people and religious identities. Shared beliefs and symbolic systems may also play significant roles in providing frameworks of meaning and moral justifications for actions (Hanegraaff 1998). Deities, spirits and ancestors are often significant beings that religious actions engage in relationship with humans. However, it is the collective ritual – often experienced in the informally constructed dance – that is the most significant factor in fashioning the commitment of many Pagans. As Roth argues in the opening quote above, dancing changes the way people move, and hence changes their sense of being in the world.

The chorus of the signature track of the first album of Australia's premiere Pagan band Spiral Dance invites listeners to walk and dance with the old Pagan gods. I have often danced to this song – both the recording and live performances by Spiral Dance. I have also heard it sung as a collective chant at several Pagan gatherings. Pike observes that Pagan myths "create the impression of a tradition rooted deeply in time and history, yet with a contemporary focus on self-knowledge and personal experience" (Pike 2004: 12). The chorus certainly alludes to the idea that contemporary Paganism is part of a long tradition of the earth-honouring religious practice. However, this belief is secondary to the "dance and music" (*ibid.*: 12) that creates the experience and blends the old and new practices in personal and collective transformation.

DANCE IN CONTEMPORARY PAGANISM

Contemporary Paganism is defined primarily by shared practice, with shared belief a secondary consideration (Harvey 1997; Hume 1997; Greenwood 2000). This is demonstrated by the centrality of the shared ritual practices of the "wheel of the year" and circle casting to contemporary Pagans. The rituals of the wheel of the year include eight festivals roughly six weeks apart that celebrate the changing of the seasons, including solstices, equinoxes and the cross-quarter festivals. The festival of Beltane that celebrates the season of spring, for example, is typically celebrated on 1 May in the Northern Hemisphere and 30 October in the Southern Hemisphere. Paganism is an umbrella term similar to "Christian". Paganism includes a wide range of traditions such as witchcraft, Wicca (a specific sub-tradition within witchcraft), Druids, Heathens (who follow the Norse myths and deities) and others (Harvey 1997). Even though many Pagans have their own seasonal festivals, defined by their own traditions, most Pagans are familiar with the sacred calendar of the wheel of the year, and larger gatherings traditionally take place on these dates.

The Pagan community typically is a decentralized network, particularly in Australia. There are no centralized authorities that define belief or practice, and most practitioners are "solitaries" – which means that the majority of their practice is performed on their own. There are smaller groups of organized covens (witches and Wiccans), groves (Druids) and hearths (Heathens), typically consisting of a dozen or so members who may meet weekly or fortnightly for ritual and discussion. These events may be inside or out of doors, depending on the climate and preference. Larger festivals take place less regularly, with perhaps one or two such events in each state every year. These larger events may involve up to 150 people and be held at a campground or at venues with a hall and dormitory-style accommodation (Hume 1997).

The ritual of circle casting through which sacred space is created is familiar to most Pagans. The classical circle-casting rite was developed in Wicca, and even though many Pagans may have their own rituals for creating sacred space, most will happily join in the practice of whoever is leading the ritual, and most know the appropriate moves and responses of the Wiccan circle casting rite. A typical circle casting commences with all participants standing in a circle. From the altar, which is typically in the north, but may be at any of the cardinal directions, the priest and priestess take salt, water, incense and a candle, and carry them around the circle, representing earth, water, air and fire respectively. The priestess will then walk around the circle with a sacred knife, or *athame*, and declare the circle to be a sacred space "between the worlds". Four people standing in each of the cardinal directions will then "call the quarters", which involves saying something like: "I call on you spirits of air, guardians of the East, to watch over our rite and guard our circle. Hail and welcome." Everyone typically responds to this with "Hail and welcome" (Harvey 1997; Hume 1997). The central part of the ritual typically involves a ritual drama of some sort in which classical Pagan myths are acted out. At Beltane, for example, someone may be dressed up and crowned the "Spring Queen"; she then chooses a consort from among those in the circle. This is followed by singing, circle dancing (as described below), the sharing of bread and wine, and a circle closing, in which the quarters are farewelled and the rite is declared over. The end of the formal ritual often marks the commencement of a less formal feast, party or dance.

The majority of Pagans share a set of beliefs about the world: that this world is sacred; that sexuality is to be celebrated; that deities are female and male; that individual experience is the ultimate authority; and that ritual changes things. There are, of course, exceptions to these broad orienting ideas, with some groups having a more hierarchical structure and others focusing on a goddess or god to the exclusion of the other. There are also significant differences in theology, varying from atheist Pagans, through agnostics, to others who assert with certainty the reality of deities and other spiritual beings and realms. These divergent theologies can be found even within the one practising group. It is the commitment to a tradition of shared practice that brings most Pagans together.

Dancing, in association with Pagan chants and music, often plays a key role in Pagan ritual. Pagan musicians and bands often have a schedule of gigs or concerts. For example, Spiral Dance – who play music that is folk- and rock-inspired – perform at folk festivals and events. Wendy Rule, whose music is more ambient Goth in style, plays at various venues on her frequent tours around Australia and overseas. While these performances may have ritual elements, they are framed as concerts or gigs, not sacred events. In contrast, the schedule of ritual events defined by the sacred calendar of the wheel of the year provides a routine context in which Pagan dance often plays a central role in shared ritual and the building of Pagan identity and community. The music of Pagan bands is often played at such events after the main ritual is completed. In this context, dancing to their music is transformed into a sacred practice.

Dancing also typically plays a key role in most Pagan ritual. Greenwood, for example, describes a witchcraft ritual involving an invocation to the "Maiden, Mother and Crone aspects of the Goddess" (Greenwood 2000: 87). After the circle casting and chanted invocations accompanied by drumming, "we started dancing and drumming and shaking our rattles around the Triple Goddess in the centre as power was raised" (*ibid.*: 87). "Raising power" typically involves a "spiral dance" and a "cone of power". One of the most common forms of dance in Pagan ritual is the "spiral dance". Salomonsen describes the spiral dance as a focused form of singing and dancing (Salomonsen 2002: 207). Typically, it involves participants holding hands and dancing in a circle that may turn into a line which weaves inwards and then outwards in a spiral. When this dance is focused on "building up energy around a concrete image, [it] is called 'raising a cone of power'". Salomonsen claims that "raising a cone of power is regarded as *the* magical work of witchcraft" (*ibid.*). Sometimes this dance may be short and formalized. In the Reclaiming tradition studied by Salomonsen, non-Western possession and shamanic trance techniques are borrowed to "create room for ecstatic experiences" (*ibid.*).

Circle dancing also often occurs among young, self-taught witches. Ruth is a nineteen-year-old Australian witch. After studying some books and with the encouragement of her mother, she invited some friends to her house to join in a witchcraft ritual:

> And we ended up raising power. And I think that the chant was [the one that] lists all the Goddesses. And we were all holding hands, dancing around the circle. And when we raised enough power and we stopped, the fire actually spiralled upwards and went out and it was [laughs] pretty cool. (Berger & Ezzy 2007: 18)

Such experiences are often transformative for Pagans. Ritual changes people because embodied performances transform their emotional self-understandings. Dancing, often in association with Pagan chants and music, is typically a central aspect of emotionally engaging ritual as it is practised by contemporary Pagans in Australia.

Dancing is also often part of larger Pagan festivals. I was in the crater of an extinct volcano about two hours' drive from a large Australian city. Approximately 150 Pagans camped among the trees around the large central grassy area to celebrate the festival of Beltane. I stood in the evening ritual, part of one huge circle around a massive central bonfire. Led by some Wiccans, the circle was cast, quarters called and the bonfire lit. There was chanting, incense, drinking and singing. At one point, the circle began to turn as we all held hands and danced around the bonfire. As I danced around the circle, I watched a five-year-old boy sitting outside the circle, eyes wide with fascination as he absorbed the heady mixture that saturated the senses.

MUSIC, DANCE AND THE DECENTRING EXPERIENCE OF "FLOW"

When I dance, it always starts with my feet. My feet begin to move to the rhythm of the music, back and forth, up and down. Next, my upper body joins in the swaying, gently, slowly feeling my way into the dance. Next my hands emerge from my pockets and my whole body joins the dance. Finally, my eyes and my voice find their place. I meet the gaze of other dancers and onlookers, bringing them into the presence of the dance. I laugh with the pleasure of being, here, now, in the dance and the song.

Something profound changes in the way I feel about myself as I move from non-dance to dance. When I am standing and watching, I am acutely self-conscious. My self-awareness is, spatially, in my head. I am aware, *thinking* about others in the venue, wondering what they are thinking about me, making judgements and thinking through possible responses to anticipated comments I imagine they might make to me. In contrast, when I dance I *feel* myself in relation to the other people in the venue. I feel the other dancers, and celebrate the pleasure of our jointly moving bodies. There is a sense of relational connectedness, of openness and trust, of constant embodied negotiation of the path of our moving bodies through shared space. My self-awareness is, spatially, in my whole body, head, heart and abdomen. Initially, I find it embarrassing to dance in front of other people. Embarrassment refers to precisely a hypersensitivity to what other people may be thinking about me. As I ease myself into the dance, I lose this sense of hyper-awareness of what other people are thinking.

Dancing also changes the temporality of my self-awareness. When I stand and reflect, I am often conscious of what happened in the past, or of what might happen in the future. Giddens refers to this future-oriented nature of contemporary reflexivity as "colonizing the future" (Giddens 1991). Life-planning, Giddens argues, has become central to individual self-understandings in response to the continuous pressure to calculate risks and manage uncertainty. However, when I dance my self-awareness is focused on the present, on the movement of my body, on my spatial relationships with other dancers in the here and now. A similar form of temporal sensitivity to the present is often found in Animist cultures (Harvey 2005). In comparison to Western obsession with the future, they are more concerned with engaging with the issues of the present day.

Dancing expands my sense of self. The concept of an isolated ego, a thinking *cogito*, an independent hero, and a calculating, strategizing humanity is a central myth of modern Western societies. It is bound up with the idea of our bodies as machines, serving our minds, separated off from the physical earth and the rest of humanity (Plumwood 2002). Dancing undoes this myth. As Roth puts it: "I feel my soul in my body when I dance" (Roth 1997: xxvii).

Academics are becoming increasingly aware of the significance of this form of somatic awareness. In her insightful ethnography of the role of samba in Brazil, Browning observes: "There are things I learned in Brazil with my body, and some of these things have taken me years to learn to articulate in writing" (Browning 1995: xi). Daniel similarly describes the centrality of "embodied knowledge" in Haitian Vodou, Cuban Yoruba and Bahian Candomble (Daniel 2005). Mendoza emphasizes that the dancing at the heart of Peruvian community performances powerfully shapes local people's sense of their place in the world (Mendoza 2000). At the centre of these approaches is the idea that cognitive knowing is not the only way in which people understand the world and learn how to respond to it. Browning summarizes this approach aptly:

> For a time, while I lived in Brazil, I stopped writing. I learned to dance. I also learned to pray and fight – two things I had never before felt called upon to do. I did them with my body. I began to think with my body. That is possible and, in the case of Brazilian

> dance, necessary. What I write here, in words, cannot contain
> the significance of the dances. I only mean to indicate the ground
> of their meaningfulness.   (Browning 1995: xxii)

Csikszentmihalyi's concept of flow points to another aspect of this experience. Csikszentmihalyi describes the state of *flow* as "the state in which people are so involved in an activity that nothing else seems to matter; the experience itself is so enjoyable that people will do it even at great cost, for the sheer sake of doing it" (Csikszentmihalyi 1990: 4). Further: "Listening to music … when seriously attended to, can induce flow experiences" (*ibid.*: 109). Music organizes the mind that attends to it and focuses the listener's attention on "patterns appropriate to a desired mood". Live performances of music, Csikszentmihalyi argues, help to focus people's attention on the music, generating shared thoughts and emotions that can produce a Durkheimian "collective effervescence". Many Pagans experience such an experience of "flow" when dancing to live Pagan music, and to a lesser extent when listening to recorded Pagan music.

The Western tradition's valorization of rationalist understandings of the world is more suspicious of experiences of "flow" or intersubjective recognition. Benjamin suggests that this stems from the long-standing opposition between "rationalism and romanticism, Apollo and Dionysus" (Benjamin 1998: 147). In the Western model of humanity, separation brings maturity and individuation, and the siren call of "undifferentiated infantile bliss" is thought of as a dangerous threat. In contrast, and following Benjamin, I argue that the experience of flow can lead into an expanded sense of self that is profoundly aware of its intersubjective nature.

Music is the medium that makes personal transformation through dancing possible. Music flows. Music changes us. In his insightful ethnography of clubbing, Jackson describes this relationship between the music of club cultures and an experience of flow (Jackson 2004). Jackson argues that: "Music's sensual potential is embodied through the writhing dynamism of the crowd. The sheer power of music to bring people together and radically shift the social and emotional timbre of clubs is truly awesome." (*ibid.*: 25). Music can be understood as a form of subcultural capital, reduced to signs and symbols that are part of clubbers' knowledge. But, Jackson argues, music is more than this: it is central to the "sensual landscape" of clubbing. Music is experienced corporeally, the beat shaping emotions, embodied in the movement of the crowd. The sheer volume of the music in clubs makes them an "intense sensory environment": "The glorious combination of amplification, sub-bass and accelerated beats charges the club environment with a palpable surge of sonic adrenaline, which has the power to unleash the Dionysian reflex in all but the most jaded of souls" (*ibid.*: 27). It is the corporeal experience of music – most commonly expressed in the act of dancing – that produces a similar experience of flow when Pagans dance to music.

116

Pagan festivals and rituals emphasize embodied experience. This is achieved in various ways: unusual dress and holiday locations, late nights, bonfires, breathing techniques, and dancing to drums and music (Bado-Fralick 2005). These techniques are, of course, similar to those used in other forms of dance culture such as raves (St John 2004c) and doofs (Tramacchi 2000). The festivals that I have attended in Australia do not usually have a DJ, but rely on both pre-determined playlists of recorded music and live drumming – typically with a bodhran or djembe. Sarah Pike observes that at Pagan festivals, people who dance around the fire "construct their identities ... by moving back and forth between verbal and somatic ways of knowing" (Pike 2001: 189). I observed a similar experience at an Australian Pagan festival.

I studied a Pagan festival in 2005, interviewing participants both before and after the festival (Ezzy 2011). It lasted five days, from Thursday night until Monday afternoon. The Friday and Saturday night rituals lasted through the night. Eighty people were present at the festival; they participated in long, theatrically complex rituals and danced – often naked – around a huge bonfire under pale moonlight. The festival eased out of this intensity on the last night with a relaxed dance party. There were four different areas, with different types of music. One such area was a disco in the gym with a dozen or so people, where the music was loudish rock'n'roll. It was relatively empty, dark and luscious. In the centre was a methylated spirits-fuelled fire in a cauldron (they look amazing).

The music to which we danced that night was not particularly spiritual – it was classic rock: Led Zeppelin, the Stones, Kate Bush, to name a few. Perhaps the music was meaningful to us because it reminded many of us in the room, who were in our thirties and forties, of our youth. What made it spiritual was the context: the final night of long days and nights of ritual excavation of our souls. I danced with "Wheelchair Dave". I'd never dreamed that you could dance with someone in a wheelchair, but dance we did. In the interview afterwards, Dave recalled his experience:

> Even though the other two rites were extraordinary, in a strange way for me the disco was probably the most powerful. I felt safe enough to just be who I was at that point in time. And found myself spending a lot of time dancing. I felt that I could be there without my armour and feel safe. And not just feel safe, but feel really vibrant and "big". And to be able to dance with beings, with yourself, with your shadow, with your past, with others that you felt a bond to or an attraction.
>
> There was maybe a dozen of us in the gym. And the floor was flat so I could get around easily. I remember going into the gym space because I was attracted to some of the seriously old music to start with. But I just actually felt pretty good and pretty safe.

117

And the environment gave me the option of finding a way to be myself, but also be with someone else. And I think by then people were okay with [me being in a wheelchair] – there was nothing that was particularly odd by then. We were all, in our own way, finding ways to allow each other to be more of themselves in that environment. And that was just brilliant. It just worked.

It's funny because it's the one part of the event that I've probably not talked about to anybody else because I don't really know how to explain it, that sense of being able to dance. And it's something that I don't do. The last time I've done anything like that is probably twenty, thirty years ago. And I thought, well, what made me do that? Where did that come from? And, I think it's the safety that is enabling that physicality of your being to work in unison with your spirituality. And, not have a disjointed relationship there.

Dave describes the sacred dance of the disco night as a safe space that enabled his "physicality" to work "in unison with" his "spirituality". That is the heart of the argument of this chapter. Dancing in the context of Pagan ritual enables an embodied sense of religious experience. Ritual – good ritual – dissolves the sense of self into a collective effervescence (Grimes 2000). It feels like the layers of self – the "armour" of our soul, to use Dave's word – has been stripped away and discarded. Not everyone is nice; we are still human and make mistakes. However, the rituals create a radical openness, and powerful sense of "being with"; they create a sense of openness and trust with each other. The experience Dave describes underlines a deep sense of both the embodied and the intersubjective sources of the self. He was immersed in the flow of the moment with an embodied and decentred sense of self.

The rituals, the music and the dancing were the frame for that experience. There were no drugs or alcohol involved. The organizers explicitly encouraged participants to avoid these, and most people willingly followed their advice. Ritual and dancing to music are enough to provide some profoundly transformative experiences. Further, if the participants did it again, they would experience similar things. It is a way of being that music, ritual and dance make possible. A combination of chemistry, performance and practice creates a sensuous, embodied, dispersed experience of being human.

Dancing doesn't always make me happy; it isn't just about pleasure. I have cried and shed tears in the dance; dancing changes the way I experience these emotions. The words of songs provide a moral vocabulary that shapes the understanding of emotional experiences. Helen Collins has observed that while classical church hymns contain many accounts of God's presence amidst grief and suffering, the songs of contemporary Christian Pentecostals seem to only have space for happy people in the presence of the Christian deity (H. Collins 2010). Contemporary Pagan music has a moral complexity equal to that of classical Christian hymns. Many of Spiral Dance's songs bring me into the presence of sadness, loss and suffering. "Boys of Bedlam" describes the suffering and delusions of men and women with mental illness in the Middle Ages. "The Rape of Maude Bowen" recounts the terror and suffering caused by sexual abuse.

It is always a somewhat conflicted experience dancing to "Boys of Bedlam" or "The Rape of Maude Bowen". Shouldn't I cry in the presence of such suffering? Perhaps. But there is also a sense in which dancing allows me to embrace the pain and suffering these songs describe, and to still celebrate life. Nussbaum (1986) makes a similar argument about the nature of Greek tragedy. Tragedy is not a product of a "fatal flaw" as much as an inevitable consequence of living in a world where "the good" is not unitary. Doing good "here" will have bad consequences "there". The drama and pleasure of Greek tragedy both lie in their representation of precisely this tension. The moment of tragedy in the Greek tragic poets, and the moment of dancing to songs of suffering, share this sense of presence with the inevitability of pain and loss.

Self-consciousness separates me from others and from my emotions of pleasure and pain. I think about what others think of me; I worry, I plan and I remember. All these take my awareness away from the moment, from being conscious of what is happening now. Music and dancing to music do the opposite. My awareness focuses in on the very moment of my movement to the music. I am aware of my body, my felt emotions and the spatial relationships with others who also dance. It is almost as if my sense of self expands beyond my body to the relationships that make up the dance and the music. Pike captures the experience when she says: "My memories of the festival are not simply of the events I saw and conversations I shared with other participants; they are sensual memories embedded in my body as well as written in my field notes" (Pike 2001: 187). One way of talking about this is to say that I am "present" with myself.

In the dance, the "present" self can still plan, still remember, still understand the self as separate from others, but these aspects of the self are balanced by a strong sense of what is happening now and a strong sense of the interrelated nature of the self with all that is happening around me. Being "present" means that when I am sad, for example, I do not fear the sadness; rather, the sadness flows through me. It simply "is". Similarly, when I am happy, being "present" doesn't mean that I attempt to hold on to that happiness, or feel anything right or wrong about it. "Happy" is simply what I am at that moment. Ahmed puts it this way: "the subject does not always know how she feels: the subject is not self-present and emotions are an effect of this splitting of experience. From Freud onwards, this lack of self-presence

119

is articulated as 'the unconscious'" (Ahmed 2004: 11). Following Benjamin (1998), I suggest that this lack of self-presence can also be understood as a loss of awareness of the "intersubjective" sources of the self.

To be human is to find ourselves in relationships. According to Benjamin, much of psychology conceives of the self as developing *out of* relationships. The psychological concept of individuation suggests the need to separate from others in order to mature. In contrast an intersubjective conception of the self sees maturation and growth as a process of "becoming more active and sovereign" within relationships (*ibid*.: 18). The person is not a discrete, separate unit; rather, the self is part of a complex network of relationships.

The need for "mutual recognition" is central to the intersubjective processes described by Benjamin: "Recognition is the essential response, the constant companion of assertion. The subject declares, 'I am, I do', and then waits for the response, 'You are, you have done'" (*ibid*: 21). Erotic union is the experience on which Benjamin focuses as a key moment of mutual recognition: "In erotic union we can experience that form of mutual recognition in which both partners lose themselves in each other without loss of self; they lose self-consciousness without loss of awareness" (*ibid:* 29). I suggest that the experience of collective dancing can also produce a similar experience of mutual recognition – although with a different tone of intimacy, because it is more dispersed, and with a different structure of intensity. This experience is not unique to Pagan dance and Benjamin's work, and it is well described in a variety of other studies of embodiment and intersubjectivity, such as Richard Bradley's (1992) account of rock'n'roll dance styles. The argument of this chapter is that this experience plays a key role in the formation of Pagan identity and community.

Physical movement, such as dancing or "the caress" (Irigaray 2001), provides an embodied experience of mutual recognition. Benjamin suggests that this spatial expression of the desire for recognition is more important than symbolic representation: "The 'dance' becomes the mediating element between the two subjects, the movement in the space between them" (Benjamin 1998: 127). The reference to the "dance" in this quote is intended metaphorically; nonetheless, it is relevant because it provides a spatial metaphor that emphasizes the quality of intersubjectivity that exists between individuals in relationship. It is precisely this quality that exists in the dance.

Dancing, I argue, decentres the subject. Dancing also re-embodies the subject. Knowledge is located both in thought, and in embodied, felt performance (Nussbaum 2001). Browning reports that when teaching the Samba she often says to her students: "Stop thinking and dance". This doesn't mean that you can't think about the dance. Rather: "It's to say that the body is capable of understanding more things at once than can be articulated in language. One has no choice but to *think with the body*" (Browning 1995: 13).

MUSIC, DANCE AND PAGAN COMMUNITY

Ritual functions to create community for Wiccan covens, Druid groves, Heathen hearths and similar small Pagan groups. Ritual also plays a key role in creating community among the larger, more dispersed "collective" of Pagans, who meet more intermittently and virtually. Music and dancing to music form a key part of many of the formal and informal rituals that create Pagan community. Dancing is a "collective way of making meaning" (Grimes 2000: 3). Much of contemporary Pagan practice is solitary (Berger & Ezzy 2007). When people dance as a group they develop a sense of shared purpose that reinforces each individual's sense of the validity of their own religious or spiritual self-understanding. This significance of dance and music to Pagan community parallels the politics of self-identification among some youth cultural groups. Andy Bennett, for example, demonstrates that "the ready availability of new youth commodities, notably fashion items, magazines, films and popular music, during the post-[Second World] war period, was instrumental in youth's realization of itself as a 'culture'" (A. Bennett 2001: 22).

There are three main organizational structures in Paganism in Australia (Hume 1997). First, there are the ties of locally practising groups that might meet weekly or monthly. These are typically small groups, numbering less than a dozen members. Second, there are the looser ties of various traditions, such as Alexandrian Wicca, and various Druid and Heathen traditions. These can number in the hundreds, but the ties are loose, members are spread nationally and internationally, and relationships are mediated by virtual networks. Finally, there are the umbrella organizations that function like union movements for Pagans, fielding media inquiries, assisting with legal advice, and organizing information sessions and networking opportunities. The two main umbrella organizations in Australia are the Pagan Awareness Network and the Pagan Alliance.

There is a close relationship between music and the Pagan community. Australia has five cities in Australia with populations of more than one million. The largest, most active and best organized Pagan community is in Adelaide in South Australia, the home of Australia's premiere Pagan band Spiral Dance. I suggest that the presence of Spiral Dance in Adelaide is one of the main reasons that Pagans in South Australia have formed a larger and better organized community. Spiral Dance has released several CDs, the band's music is well known to Australian Pagans and the group routinely performs at signature Pagan events. The South Australian Pagan Alliance has a large membership, is well organized and conducts regular events and meetings.

Each year, on the Spring Equinox in late September, there is a national Australian "Wiccan Conference" attended by approximately 100 to 150 Pagans from around Australia. The conference commences on Friday night and ends on the following Sunday afternoon. There are workshops, rituals and other events. The key event of this weekend is usually a group ritual on the Saturday evening, followed by a feast and dancing, often to the music of Spiral Dance. The conference moves around Australia, depending on who is prepared to organize it. I still vividly remember the Wiccan conference I attended in the late 1990s. There are two key memories that stand out in my mind. The first is the ritual, which was particularly well organized and a lot of fun. The second memory is of dancing to the music of Spiral Dance.

For the Spiral Dance concert, the hall was completely cleared – all the chairs and tables were pushed up against the walls after the meal. Nearly everyone was in the room, and there was little choice but to dance. At one stage we all held hands as someone led a long line of dancers weaving in and out in a spiral circle. At another moment, my dancing became almost a marshal art as I sparred with a friend.

I can still feel the memory of that moment: the movement of my body; my outstretched arms; the huge grin that displayed the deep joy I was feeling; the intoxication of the pleasure of simply being wholly in the moment. I'd had a few drinks, but not that many. It was the music and the dance into which my body was drawn, and the sense of "being with", of performed community, that transformed me and those with me. At the end of a typical Wiccan conference, people hug new and old friends goodbye. Like other liminal events of this nature, this emotional intimacy is created by the rituals, the shared accommodation and meals, and the group workshops. Dancing to live music is also a critical factor. While Pagans from Australia might meet annually at a Wiccan conference or similar event and dance to Spiral Dance, the Pagans of South Australia meet much more regularly at local performances, and as a consequence the Pagan community in South Australia is much stronger.

Dancing to Pagan music is a part of a politics of resistance for Pagans. Given the fluidity and complexity of the "neo-tribal" (Maffesoli 1996) nature of contemporary Paganisms, it would be a mistake to consider this a defining characteristic (Hall & Jefferson 2007). Nonetheless, it is the case that the experience of belonging to a Pagan community has a political edge. This is perhaps most clearly illustrated in the umbrella organizations such as Pagan Alliance and the Pagan Awareness Network, which play important advocacy roles: supporting Pagans involved in legal cases, providing commentary in the media and supplying advice to various levels of government. Browning's (1995) account of the Samba in Brazil similarly emphasizes both its politics and eroticism. To dance is a form of resistance for both African and indigenous Brazilians. It binds together resistance to slavery, sexual discovery and cultural identity. In a similar way, dancing for Pagans affirms the value of a Pagan identity in contrast to secular and Christian cultures that often devalue Paganism.

Pagan religions such as witchcraft, Druidry and Heathenry continue to be heavily stigmatized religions (Harvey 1997). Christian and political leaders often warn about the dangers of witchcraft and Paganism (Berger & Ezzy

2007). This is despite the presence of positively portrayed Pagan characters in popular culture, and the fact that introductions to witchcraft and
Druidry can be found in mainstream bookshops; no other new religious
movements are represented on their shelves in such numbers (Ezzy 2001).
In a similar way to gays and lesbians, Pagans often keep their religious identity in the "broom closet" out of fear of religious discrimination and persecution. In contrast, at Pagan rituals and festivals one's Pagan identity is
affirmed in a public space. Similarly, the lyrics of Pagan music affirm a Pagan
way of understanding the world. Many of Spiral Dance's songs, for example, are based on myths associated with the festivals of the wheel of the
year. Dancing to that music is a shared bodily celebration and affirmation of
Pagan religion.

Reverend Garry Deverell emphasizes the role of music in creating experienced ritual community. He attended a "massive dance party" organized by
the gay community in Melbourne. The evening unfolded as a ritual, beginning with preparations, including shaving, applying tanning-lotion and
donning appropriate "vestments – loose jeans and a muscle-shirt". This was
followed by a lengthy meal with intimate conversations ("the Liturgy of the
Word"): "Very spiritual it was, very spiritual indeed" (Deverell 2008a: 1).
While he declined to participate in the Sacrament, "a half-tab of ecstasy",
Deverell went on to attend the party:

> People were excited, very excited. From all around, from every
> angle, bodies were pouring into this huge cathedral-like ware-
> house where the heady concoction of electronic rhythms, daz-
> zling lights, and writhing bodies was beginning to work its magic
> – the magic, that is, of turning 9000 individuals into a commun-
> ion of bodies which moved as one. In there, you see, it was too
> loud for talk or conversation. Here the words shared earlier in
> the evening had to take on other forms, mainly the form of the
> Dance. In the Dance, everyone communicated with everyone else
> through the presence of another, the presence of music. Music
> became the great mediator and host. Everyone moved together,
> at once initiating and responding to the impulses of the bodies
> which were nearest. As the night went on, I drank deeply of that
> music, at times even feeling that the Music and I had merged to
> become the same entity, and that, in the same movement, a genu-
> ine communion with these other human beings (usually very dif-
> ferent to me) had become possible as well. I was intoxicated …
> Dancing, I suggest to you tonight, is therefore a potent symbol of
> the gospel covenant as we experience it in our worship. (*Ibid.*: 1)

"In the Dance, everyone communicated with everyone else through the
presence of another, the presence of music". This is precisely my experience

123

of dancing to Pagan music at Pagan festivals. At Pagan festivals and rituals, people do not simply attend a Pagan concert and depart. They meet
beforehand, eat and drink together, chat with friends who haven't been seen
for some time, discussing Pagan theology and the politics of community.
Then they move on to listening to the music, to dancing and to communion. Gabrielle Roth makes a similar point, describing her experience of non-
denominational dance: "I danced till I disappeared inside the dance, till there
was nothing left of me but the rhythm of my breath. And in the rhythm of
my breath I felt totally connected, body and soul. I finally realized what holy
communion was all about" (Roth 1997: xxiii).

Durkheim's account of an Australian Aboriginal corroboree emphasizes
the emotional intensity of the experience: dancing, singing, sex and ritual
excitement (Durkheim [1912] 1976: 217). He argues that the religious idea
of a sacred extraordinary power that develops out of this effervescent collective social environment is a delusion, and that the reality is the experience of the social collective. I am not convinced by Durkheim's sociological
reductionism. As Edith Turner argues: "It's true that I once had an experience of religion, after which I didn't see the point of disbelieving other people's experiences" (E. Turner 1992: xiii). Nonetheless, I think Durkheim is
correct to emphasize the close relationship between emotionally engaging
collective embodied performances and sacred experiences. Deverell puts it
this way: "the human body is a primary site for the constant negotiation
between personal desire and the desire of a divine other" (Deverell 2008b:
2). For Deverell, who is a Christian, that divine other is God or Jesus. For
Pagans, the divine other is more complex, and often symbolic of the sacrality of the earth.

Spiral Dance's signature song "Woman of the Earth" speaks of the link
between the self and the earth. It describes the experienced intimacy
between the earth, Pagan deities and the Pagan practitioner. The point I
want to make here is not simply about Pagan cosmology, which sees this
world as sacred, but that the experience of singing and dancing brings
people into a performed relationship with the earth. Harrod (2000) makes
a similar argument about the role of ritual and dance in forming the relationships between the Native American Plains Indians and the animals with
which they shared their lives.

The experience of sacred community is made possible by dancing. Dancing brings participants into relationships with each other, forming community; dancing also brings participants into relationship with a sacred "other".
Pan draws on the work of the German art theorist Carl Einstein to emphasize the role of bodily experience and aesthetics in shaping religious experience (Pan 2001). Religion, Einstein argues, is less about belief and dogma
and more about aesthetics: "Religious transcendence, and with it a collective
understanding of reality, is not founded on the belief of the viewer but is the
result of aesthetic experience" (*ibid.*: 135).

CONCLUSION

The contemporary Pagan revival is held together by shared ritual, music and performance. It is characterized by a great diversity of theologies, and by a strong emphasis on individual authority. Most contemporary Pagan traditions lack any centralized governing body, and most do not have texts that are considered scripture. Shared ritual forms, and collective experiences of dancing to Pagan music and popular music during Pagan ritual play a key role in creating and maintaining community.

The central role of dancing and music in contemporary Pagan religion parallels that of many other religious traditions. For example, Browning describes the Candomble religion of the West African people of Yoruba as practised in Brazil as "an ancient, complex, and powerfully beautiful belief system in which spirituality is expressed through sophisticated rhythmic structures and divinity makes itself present in the bodies of dancers" (1995: 23). Similarly for Pagans, divinity is experienced in the movement of the ritual and the dance.

Embodied experiences such as dancing are the primary source of experiences of religious transcendence. Religious narratives, including formal dogmas, play a secondary supporting role. It is the Dionysian experience of openness and transformation that is primary: "But carnival can never serve for narrative closure, because it is the place where all boundaries – including narrative – explode" (Browning 1995: xxiv).

ACKNOWLEDGEMENTS

Thanks to Andy Bennett and Donna Weston for their thoughtful comments on an earlier draft of this chapter.

9. TOTAL SOLAR ECLIPSE FESTIVALS, COSMIC PILGRIMS AND PLANETARY CULTURE

Graham St John

"Once I saw people applaud the sky" (Weil 1980). It was 7 March 1970, and later maven of integrative medicine Andrew Weil had become an eyewitness to an extraordinary life-changing event. Under a clear Saturday morning sky, Weil had observed a diversity of villagers crowding into the market town of Miahuatlán, Oaxaca, Mexico, where they were exposed to a total solar eclipse. Marvelling at the sky, the locals are reported to have broken into a "spontaneous ovation of the heavens". Weil describes the excitement: "With great drama, a nebulous darkness grew out of the west – the edge of the umbra, or cone of shadow, whose swift passage over the globe traces the path of the total eclipse." The unearthly light endured for over three minutes, a temporality expanding into a prolonged present. Weil explained that there was

> a quality to those minutes within the umbra that must be like the feeling in the eye of a hurricane. After all the dramatic changes of accelerating intensity, everything stopped: There was an improbable sense of peace and equilibrium. Time did not flow.
>
> (*Ibid.*: 222)

Indeed, it was three and a half minutes of clock-time incomparable to any duration he'd previously known. "Then, all at once, a spot of blinding yellow light appeared, the corona vanished in the glare, shadow bands raced across the landscape once more, and the dome of shadow melted away to the east" (*ibid.*: 223). It was then that all of Miahuatlán broke into applause.

Weil explained that in Mexico he met "eclipse freaks" – people who had followed total solar eclipses around the Earth all of their lives, "getting high on the strangeness and beauty of the event" (*ibid.*: 224). Becoming such a freak himself, Weil committed to transporting himself into the path of subsequent umbras.

Forty years after this transfiguration in Miahuatlán, festivals are staged on the relatively narrow band (up to 250 kilometres wide) of the path of the

Moon's umbra in locations around the planet to magnify the rapture.[1] At the alternative edge of an "eclipse" industry, thousands of pilgrim-like travellers, or "eclipse chasers", camp in close quarters in remote festivals, arriving from a multitude of countries to seek the perfect alignment of Earth, Moon and Sun with their own (ecstatic) bodies. Commonly known as "totality", this superliminal circumstance is measured in precise clock-time, but is an immeasurable experience.

As explained in this chapter, the experience of totality is enabled within the psychedelic festival, a product of the Goa/psychedelic trance (psytrance) movement, which provides the socio-sonic aesthetic animating participants in various global locations. In the path of the eclipse within the context of these festivals, a *cosmic nature spirituality* is cultivated. With the mystical states of consciousness associated with this natural (geological), cosmic (astrological) and social (festival) experience, the eclipse has become a phenomenon adapted to the cause of a progressive planetary millenarianism. The chapter investigates how *trance dance* is integral to this development, since it contextualizes the simultaneous return to "archaic" or "tribal" sensibilities and relationships (associated with ecstatic dance embodiment) and the transcendence of mind (associated with meditation, yoga and trance states). Trance dance festivals are the context for the convergence and alignment of pagan/gnostic and primal/cosmic frameworks and practices in this ostensibly planetary culture. As part of a larger project investigating the music and culture of psytrance and techno-visionary arts, and the first cultural research conducted on the eclipse (through the study of total solar eclipse festivals), this chapter offers a preliminary study of a mutating contemporary spiritual culture.

COSMIC PILGRIMS: CHASING THE MYSTICAL EXPERIENCE

Who are these freaks? Although attracting citizens of the host country – especially those living in the region of the eclipse – in most cases the majority of participants at eclipse festivals hail from countries outside the region, often from other continents. Indeed, eclipse festivals typically attract travellers holding passports from a multitude of countries, and it is not uncommon when attending these events to be in the presence of native speakers from all across Europe, Israel, Japan, Brazil, the United States, Australia and other countries. Exemplifying the conflation of religious and leisure experience in the contemporary, the eclipse festival occasions behaviour not far removed from extreme and experimental recreational industries like skydiving, motorcycle riding and surfing, where voluntary "edgework" involves psycho-somatic risk-taking as "a means of freeing oneself from social conditions that deaden or deform the human spirit through overwhelming social regulation and control" (Lyng 2005: 9). But at the eclipse festival, exhilarating praxis is the province of "expressive expatriates" such as those undergoing simultaneous transnational and transpersonal journeys in Goa and Ibiza (D'Andrea 2007), whose expatriation is rendered with a liminal permanence. In the path of the total solar eclipse, in the person of the "eclipse chaser" and inside the precincts of the eclipse festival, "edgework" is that which is performed by "edgemen" (V. Turner 1969: 128) – bohemians, artists and esotericists who pursue marginal vocations, queer practice and precarious trades, who embrace incongruities only to become transmuted in novel art-forms. For the eclipse freak, the physical "trip" to foreign regions, in which one becomes exposed to the adversities of travel (e.g. theft, loss of passports, illness, and other misfortunes and misadventures), is undertaken in simul-taneity with the psychological "trip" in which one is exposed to uncertain mind-states (associated with foreign language and culture and alternative states of consciousness), risks, whose successful negotiation potentiates lib-eration, fulfilment and transition.[2] Risking the adversities of travel, event-management mishaps and an occluded totality, those who "chase" the cosmic theophany may be rewarded by the perfect alignment of their bodies with the primary celestial spheres. The circumstance is reminiscent of the activities of surf-riders: those liminal participants in an "aquatic nature reli-gion" whose psychedelicized quest for the perfect wave is recognized to have constituted a mystical experience (Taylor 2010: 104, 110). The effect of the "magical" alignment of one's body riding the surf poised upon a board may approximate the singularity of an eclipse in which one stands within the umbra, with the growing realization of the rider's interrelatedness with the world a comparable consequence.

Symptomatic of the conflation of religion and leisure, the mystical expe-rience and the vacation, the eclipse festival is host to a cross-section of pilgrimage and traveller-tourism behaviours. Eclipse festivals attract back-packers and those arriving in self-owned motor-homes and refurbished buses; these people are "neo-nomads", those who D'Andrea sees manifesting in two ways: "one as a stabilized form of self-cultivation (*nomadic spiritu-ality*), the other as a temporary condition of acute self-derailment (*psychic deterritorialization*)" (D'Andrea 2007: 6). The eclipse festival is the setting for both the metamorphosis and apocalypse of subjectivity, which is indeed the complex landscape of the psychedelic festival in which it is rooted (see St John 2010a). The techno-pagans, punk esotericists, amateur astronomers and feral activists who populate these events are like those hypermobile and fissiparous "spiritual virtuosi" identified by Steven Sutcliffe (2000), or "new age travellers" (Hetherington 2000), as well as others among contemporary alternative, disenchanted and questing populations who transform marginal and peripheral sites into "elective centres" (Cohen 1992). Eclipse chasers are among this population whose commitments to travel to the path of totality signify a unique pilgrimage experience in the contemporary world. But the umbric-centres at the edge to which these freaks migrate are temporary and irregular; their sacrality is evanescent and impermanent. They are no less sacred to those "umbraphiles" drawn, and even though the "center out there" (see V. Turner 1973) – unlike those shrines, temples, stone circles and other sites sacred to participants in religious communities where believers migrate toward the divine source of their faith – is a fleeting cosmic synchronicity witnessed in different geo-locations on each incidence, the eclipse becomes itself a sacred centre.[3]

Since the planetary alignment is a destination and a point of departure, eclipse festivals bear some resemblance to Neo-Pagan festivals. As Sarah Pike explains quoting Loretta Orion, at festivals like Lothlorien in Indiana: "Nature is not the setting for the pilgrimage but the destination and object of the pilgrim's quest" (in Pike 2001: 27). At these events, which often celebrate the solstices and equinoxes, "the land itself, the trees, and the earth are invested with the desires and dreams of festival goers and become 'sacred' destinations" (ibid.). In Neo-Pagan gatherings, "nature" is the "event" in which those gathered are immersed, the intimate participation in which potentiates transformative experience in the company of co-liminars inside a social space set apart from the outside world. Neo-Pagan festivals are thus enchanting gateways to nature religions, an effect also of eclipse festivals, although the "ritual" is less formalized and the natural "object" of the pilgrim's quest is a rare cosmic event. Not seasonal/periodic – like the Kumb Mela or Neo-Pagan solstice/equinox festivals held at specific sites or in a circuit of events on privileged days of the calendar – the eclipse festival will rarely if ever transpire in the same location again. While the sense of family and community may be strong within seasonal events that are spatially recurrent year after year, or in regular "travelling festivals" like Rainbow Gatherings (Niman 1997), participants in the irregular eclipse event imagine themselves to be at "home" proximate to "totality" and in the company of those with whom they share the experience, regardless of where and when the festival is held. Moreover, as an occasion for the performance of planetary consciousness, the eclipse festival has become integral to the reproduction of a self-identified "global tribe".

If cosmic nature spirituality has diverse roots, total solar eclipse festivals appear to be its heterotopic expression. Adrian Ivakhiv assists our understanding of this experience and these events in his study of the contested "culture of enchantment" flourishing at Glastonbury and Sedona in which habitués participate in "a new planetary culture" that seeks to "dwell in harmony with the spirit of the Earth" (Ivakhiv 2001). In the study of "Gaian pilgrims" and their harmonic "power spots", Ivakhiv explores a mixed alternative milieu of Earthen and New Age spiritualities. In this "transepistemic cultural arena", eco-spiritual immanentism and off-planetary ascensionism are "two sides of a loosely unified spiritual-cultural movement: one seeks to rekindle the connection with Earth's power directly, while the other looks for wisdom beyond our planet's weakened frame" (ibid.: 8). Those with similarly diverse perspectives are drawn to eclipse festivals that are temporary, albeit advanced, sites for the expression of Pagan and gnostic esotericisms found within alternative spiritual networks (see York 1995; Hanegraaff 1998). In this milieu, one can identify the variable expression of an eco-spirituality expressed through the adoption of "entheogens" (compounds such as psilocybin and DMT or dimethyltriptamine that are said to "awaken the divine within"), commitment towards an ecological consciousness and the appeal of pantheistic beliefs. Events attract participants who may identify as Neo-Pagan (that is, who identify with Wicca or Goddess traditions and practise ritual magic), while others reconstruct or revive traditions both real and imagined, such as that associated with the Festival at Eleusis and other mystery cults in the Ancient Greek or Hellenic traditions (see St John & Baldini 2012), thereby loosely approximating what Michael York refers to as "recopagans" (York 2003: 60). Others – perhaps closer to what York called "geopagans" – will express veneration towards the natural world in folk discourse and ritual practice. But in the context of the eclipse festival, such veneration is deployed in the service of transition, where the eclipse is perceived as a shamanic ritual of transformation. Fresh from the 2006 Soulclipse Festival in Turkey, event production manager and founder of Britain's The Glade Festival, Nick Ladd, imagines that "throughout shamanic history" a total eclipse is "thought of as a spiritual time, a powerful time, and transformational time, when light turns to dark and then returns to light".[4] Recognizing the eclipse as a time for "focused meditation", and an opportunity to "achieve a transitional shift in one's life", he added that "I'm certainly no shaman, but I've felt the transformational power of the total eclipses. Whenever I've exposed myself to one there's always been a shift in my life, a fairly major one." Such a view might be subject to question given that most shamans and other religious specialists throughout history will not have enjoyed the luxury of a calendar-predicted eclipse. Yet, the transition of the Moon across the face of the Sun, and the subsequent renewal of the latter, is commonly recognized to effect a corresponding outcome for the self that is revelatory and potentially positive. Here, "traditions" such as shamanism may be assessed and indeed invented according to the imperatives of the self commonly associated with "individuated self spirituality" (Heelas 2008), and perhaps more pointedly in a critical and revelatory neo-gnostic climate. Within the holistic, ecological and evolutionary perspectives and techniques showcased at these events, "sustainable" techniques of the self are undertaken with increased attention to minimizing "traces", reducing "footprints" and ultimately recognizing that, in relationship to nature, one's self is irreducible. The pinnacle achievement of the psychedelic and visionary arts movement more widely, eclipse events accommodate an experimental confluence of the unaligned pagan sensibilities that are felt to be revived and the new consciousness that is felt to be evolving.

TRANCE DANCE CULTS AND ECLIPSE RAVES

The social contexts that facilitate trance within the domain of dance possess cultic characteristics, the fomentation of group *ekstasis* long associated with seasonal transitions marked by convulsive celebrations animated by rhythmic percussion. This expenditure of physical energy and a corresponding accumulation of metaphysical energy characterize the "psychedelic trance" dance, which animates the total eclipse festival. Those who organize and attend these festivals are not unlike their 1960s counter-cultural forebears, imagining – sometimes in specious terms, at other times assiduously – their descent, heritage and continuity with shamanic and nature religion cults (for example, Dionysian, Shaivite, Indigenous). An electronic dance music culture whose "cosmic" symphonies obtained crescendo during a short few years in the mid-1990s with the output of the likes of The Infinity Project, Astral Projection, Hallucinogen, Total Eclipse, Pleiadians and Cosmosis among others providing the soundtracks to ascension, Goatrance is perceived to be implicated in this lineage.[5] Having experienced its embryonic phase in mid-1980s Goa, India, and evolving into the "Goa" sound a decade later, psychedelic trance had, by the end of that decade, become recognized as "psytrance", with the music and scenes associated with its culture translated in cosmopolitan centres and regions worldwide (St John 2010b; Rom & Querner 2010). The first "eclipse rave" was held near the coastal city of Arica at the edge of the Atacama, Chile on 2–3 November 1994. The pioneering event was organized chiefly through a Chilean–German partnership, and was held in the immediate years of transition from Pinochet's regime. With no more than 300 people gathering, the occasion featured Derrick May, John Aquaviva and, for the first time in his homeland, Ricardo Villalobos, but it was also a convergence of Goa freaks, Japanese techno-hipsters and some dynamic meditation-practising Osho *sannyasins*. Buoyed by a bohemian eclecticism, the event was held in the year the sound labelled Goa Trance made its appearance on the global stage – and one can imagine Black Sun's (Martin Glover) majestic "Sorcerers Apprentice" (Various Artists 1994), which repeats the lines, "I've never seen anything like it", backgrounding the ascension, or Electric Universe's (Boris Blenn) enchanting "Cosmic Symphony" (from the band's debut EP *Solar Energy*, 1994) animating the union of the primary spheres at this time. Over the subsequent fifteen years, eclipse events evolved in time with psychedelic music.

The eclipse festival occasions the goal of the cosmic pilgrim: *experience*. For those in search of transpersonal, transnational and transformative knowledge, the socio-cosmic event potentiates the simultaneous loss of ego and the gaining of the world. It is a context for knowing what it is to be inside the moment, outside time, beyond separation, at a juncture where the "veils have thinned". Most of the iconic figures in the tradition of psychonautical investigations, such as Aldous Huxley, Timothy Leary and Terence

McKenna,[6] knew such moments of singularity, and subsequently have been inducted into psychedelic symphonies by way of their sampled sound bites. These idealists were travellers of mind and body, who undertook experiments of consciousness and returned with visionary insights concerning "Mind at Large" or the "Gaian supermind". McKenna has been integral to the Goa/psytrance development, the mystic and prolific storyteller becoming – following his death in 2000 – the most sampled figure in the meta-genre, arguing that with the "dissolution of boundaries" triggered by tryptamines such as *psilocybin*-containing mushrooms and DMT,[7] "one cannot continue to close one's eyes to the ruination of the earth, the poisoning of the seas, and the consequences of two thousand years of unchallenged dominator culture, based on monotheism, hatred of nature, suppression of the female, and so forth and so on". Beseeching listeners skilled in contemporary techniques of ecstasy to adopt the exemplary way of the shaman by "making this cosmic journey to the domain of the Gaian ideas, and then bringing them back in the form of art in the struggle to save the world",[8] a great many visionary artists took up the challenge by interweaving a piecemeal Pagan revivalism with a progressive millenarianism, the odd bedfellows in McKenna's "re/volutionary" thesis. Influenced by William Blake, Marija Gimbutas and Joseph Campbell, among others, and demonstrating his support for Pagan gatherings and nascent psychedelic dance festivals as sites for collective boundary dissolution and the "respiritualization of matter" (McKenna 1991: 77), for McKenna, "direct communication with the planetary other" undertaken with the primary assistance of tryptamines (McKenna 1991: 218) held promise for a planetary consciousness. From Philadelphia's Gaian Mind Festival to Portugal's Boom Festival, an entire music culture has surfed in the wake of these insights (see St John 2012).

COSMIC DANCERS AT EARTHRISE

Seasonal transitions, planetary alignments, and solar and lunar phases are integral to the cosmic dance experience. Among these peak celestial events, purposeful and removed from routine space and time, the full moon has exerted strong appeal within the psychedelic counter-culture. In popular and folk theories, the "fullness" of the Moon is recognized to incite crazed conditions – a phase ruled by "lunacy". Gatherings marking this transitional period in the synodic month and other celestial occurrences are commonly celebrated by the performance of ecstatic dance in which participants become unrecognizable to themselves, and in which one's rational consciousness may become eclipsed. It is an outcome typical to many dance music events, regardless of their cosmic significance, and in fact it might be argued that a total eclipse of the mind is integral to their "cosmic" significance. That dance gatherings are typically occasioned in "wild" nature is also significant. Whether at Australian "bush doofs", Scandinavian "forest parties", Moontribe gatherings in California's Mojave Desert, or panoramic mountain festivals in Switzerland or Nepal, remote natural locations have been sought by city-dwelling cosmopolitans and suburban habitués as primary sites for the kind of ecstatic experience unachievable inside closed buildings (clubs) within city precincts obstructing a clear view of the night sky. As echoed in the folk-tradition inherited by psytrance and other "visionary arts" scenes, one's connection with wilderness is felt to influence a "wild" other-than-human sociality. It is this entrancing aesthetic that offers the grounds for the mystical experience, and psytrance music producers and DJs – working together with VJs, stage and décor designers, installation artists and event promoters – are motivated to incite these conditions. In music productions, artists sometimes narrate – not unproblematically – the wisdom of "the ancients" as preternatural, primordial, found deep in the wilderness, and at other times the otherness endogenous to this psychedelic sonic fiction is to be located beyond the Earth's exosphere. The music then becomes a critical media of temporal and spatial transportation in the imaginary of the participant. From telescopic excursions into outer space to microscopic journeys within the brain and to folk archaeologies uncovering answers among fictionalized ancients, the cosmos/nature is amplified in this music culture as a source of wonder, mystery and re/enchantment (see St John forthcoming).

The "pagan" characteristics of this dance movement are complicated. Ecstatic dance of the kind practised by enthusiasts within psytrance is sometimes associated with a suppressed "paganism", in which one is called to remember and relive persecuted practice, a theme pursued by some elements of the UK rave movement after dance grew in significance when unpermitted raves were outlawed under the Criminal Justice and Public Order Act in 1994. For instance, liner notes on the compilation album *Return to the Source: Deep Trance and Ritual Beats* (Various Artists 1995), denounce the Bill, which amounted to a "Papal Decree" forbidding dance "rituals", stating that this was consistent with the historical "suppression" of "great rites of community empowerment" in which "our sacred sites where we once danced all night into ecstatic trance had been taken over by a new order of worship".

In many cases, it is not ritual magic but the cachet of an outlaw status for those involved in the ostensible revival of persecuted pre-Christian traditions that attracts revellers to "Paganism". There is also considerable variation in the way ecstatic dance is received – from the unswerving commitment of those for whom trance dance is embraced as a style of life to the blunt reactions of moralists and near-hygienists for whom the raving masses represent an "anti-social" danger.[9]

In his study of popular "occulture", Christopher Partridge (2006) has recognized the connection between the late 1980s and early 1990s UK rave explosion and the earlier "free festival" movement in which Stonehenge and other megalithic sites were visited by modern travellers. Like their forebears, those embracing techno music and neo-nomadic lifestyles, such as Spiral Tribe, sought to convene at ancient sites as a means of reinventing and revivifying their identities in response to the maladies of modern life (St John 2009a: 36–55). With the popularizing of the ecstatic experience in the context of raves perceived, not as a legitimate source of panic, but embraced as effective countermands to the separation from "Mother Nature", "techno-shaman" emerged to promote, harness and repurpose an assemblage of digital, cyber and chemical technologies to fashion ecstatic rituals and form "tribes" that were transnational in their membership. Prominent was Fraser Clark, who used the word "zippy" (sometimes identified as a "zen-inspired pagan professionals") to describe the coming movement (see Rushkoff 1994: 185; St John 2009b: 179–84). For Clark, who had a theophany at an acid house mega-rave outside London in 1988, the "zippy" repurposed technics in the pursuit of ecstatic experience, ecological consciousness and life re-evaluations. Staged in locations affording exposure to the stars, rain and the rising sun, these events occasion communion not only with fellow participants, but with the cosmos, in the place in which one's animated feet caress the earth in dance – circumstances prompting inspired commentators to embrace a heritage to which they now feel indelibly connected, and to which they are actively returning:

> Like the old pagan festivals, we're all in this together. This is our planet. She is indescribably beautiful, gigantic. We are the atoms of that Living Goddess. Personally I can't think of a better way to help people learn a love, respect, reverence for Nature than the classical open-air all night Rave. Can you imagine what it felt like with 20,000 people going for it and actually feeling together, and the power of a people together, and then dancing the Sun up?! It is awesome, it is religious, and it is life-changing.
>
> (Various Artists 1998c)

Raving is by no means synonymous with Pagan practice, but in this text accompanying the cover art of the compilation album *Trip to Cyberspace (Vol. 2)*, Clark was describing a classical mystical experience, with the public secret of the outdoor rave party inciting new entries into the archives of the "perennial philosophy". He might have imagined his connection with the "old pagan festivals", but the "planet" that Clark knew as "indescribably beautiful, gigantic" is a realization that was doubtlessly assisted by the visualization of the Earth from space by NASA astronauts whose missions of the late 1960s and early 1970s bore photographic fruit: especially the *Earthrise* image taken on board the 1968 Apollo 8 craft, whose crew members – the first humans to witness the Earth "rising" – were struck by the awesome sight of the Earth over the lunar horizon. The story was taken up in 1996 on Astral Projection's "Black and White", with retrospective commentary from mission Commander Frank Borman: "And the view of the Earth, it was the only place in the universe that had any color. Everything else was black and white" (Various Artists 1996b). The revelatory image of a blue turning globe, small and vulnerable in the vastness of space, *Earthrise* would become one of the most significant photographs ever taken. Providing what has been referred to as the "overview effect", *Earthrise* and the later *Whole Earth* image would confirm ideas associated with "Spaceship Earth" – a phrase coined by Buckminster Fuller – as well as providing the stimulus for the "Gaia hypothesis" and inspiring the popular expression of ecological and humanitarian concerns, illustrating for the first time "Earth's agency as an autonomous, self-regulating biosphere" (Henry & Taylor 2009: 191).[10] Since the mid-1990s, psychedelic trance has become a vehicle for the expression of the "overview effect". From Shakta's dub-influenced chillout track "Earthrise" (on *Silicon Trip*, 1997), released at the peak of Goa Trance, to Filteria's neo-Goa effort at reproducing that moment of speechless ascension on a track with the same name (*Daze of Our Lives*, 2009), Goa producers have sampled astronauts with the lofty purpose of exposing dancefloor habitués to the revelatory *satori* of those space travellers.

Goa/psytrance music reverberates with timbral elicitations of a planetary consciousness to which participants gravitate like mesmerized voyagers,[11] with those pulled into the path of totality participating in this "global" romance. Among them are those who have gravitated to global "power spots" and events celebrating planetary alignments, or who employ "ancient rites using modern day technology, hoping to reaffirm the bonds of connectedness with each other, the planet, and the spiralling galaxies" (see St John 2004c: 226). The formative event was the Harmonic Convergence of 16–17 August 1987, an act of prayer, meditation and ceremony that simultaneously was coordinated simultaneously at numerous sacred sites and power spots throughout the world to "launch the 25 year transition into a New Age of peace and harmony". Called by founder of the Planet Art Network José Argüelles, in the service of "planetary healing", and held on a date in which seven planets were in close alignment, that event marked the commencement of the final twenty-six-year period of the Maya calendar's 5200-year "Great Cycle" (see Ivakhiv 2003: 97). It thus also marked the beginning of a period to culminate in the galactic alignment of the Earth and the Sun with the equatorial plane of the Milky Way galaxy on 12 December 2012: the end date of the Maya calendar, which is invested with considerable significance by Argüelles and McKenna, and has been recognized as a major transitional juncture within the visionary arts community (see St John 2011a). Such planetary healing events have become integral to a progressive millenarianism that, while expressing a "meta-narrative" of spiritual evolutionism (M. Ferguson 1982) flourishing since the 1960s/1970s, can be traced to "New Age" utopianism that had emerged between the world wars (Sutcliffe 2007: 71).

Around the time Clark knew continuity with his Pagan heritage in a very modern context and imagination, and Argüelles called seekers to the "Harmonic Convergence", Ray Castle began holding his "world beat trance dance" Pagan Production parties in Holland and elsewhere in Europe. Castle, an astrologer and documentary filmmaker as well as a DJ/producer, had at that time returned from an inspired season in Goa where travellers were exchanging their frozen Northern Hemisphere winters for temperate Goa (between October and April). On the beach paradise facing the Arabian Sea, the transition to daylight became the optimized threshold for dance conflagrations, with the Sun's rising greeted like an old friend on Anjuna, Vagator and other beaches in Goa. For the likes of Castle, who has identified as a "psychic surgeon", the light of dawn and the rising of the Sun signifies an awakening from conditions of fear and separation associated with the night, with trance dance events orchestrated like cosmic passage rites whose initiates, enduring the apocalypse of subjectivity native to dark psychedelic trance ("darkpsy") or "night music" (see St John 2011b), may experience transformed subjectivities:

> In the morning, there is a sense of oneness and unity, being together on the dancefloor. A feeling of inseparable timelessness. A kind of ancient rite of passage back to the source with the first sun rise. As the blooming rays of dawn hit your body there is a resurgence of energy and a renewed flight occurs. This is augmented by ascending, angelic-like, reverential, morning music. As opposed to the more deeper, chaotic, hektec-night-atmospheres, in the music. (Castle, in Rich & Dawn 1997).

In his recollections of Goa parties, Castle indicates that the morning sun was "sacramental" and, evoking Joseph Campbell, he states that

> the birth of light is timeless, archetypal, eternal. So it really conjures up mystical experiences, and deep primordial memories, and when you share that with a group of people, boundaries dissolve, and people do have very melting transpersonal experiences. And, he added, such could not be achieved "with a rock band at a rock concert".[12]

Light lifting from the morning horizon is an archetypal theme for the trance dance and visionary arts milieu, signifying an illumination – or rebirth – of consciousness, a period of awakening from darkness, an optimism pressed into the earliest Goa releases. For instance, Electric Universe kicked off a long career with the timeless "Solar Energy" (*Solar Energy*, 1994), capturing the sound of the Sun at the dawn of the Goa sound. While by no means a solar cult resembling Amaterasu-O-Mi-Kami in Japanese Shinto, or any of the historical Sun-worshipping traditions as found among the ancient Egyptians or the Vedic Indians, the popular greeting of the Sun at daybreak following all-night dance parties "suggests", ponders Michael York, "the possibility of a convergence between traditional religious practice and spontaneous sun-worship developments in the Western world" (York 2005: 1607). With the popularity of books like Gregory Sams's *Sun of gOd* (2009) within the psytrance movement, and since many "doofs", forest parties and trance festivals do indeed mark the solstices and equinoxes, the possibility can be seriously entertained. According to techno-Pagans like Castle, there is no better time for a dance party than the equinoxes. As he relates on the fold-out of *Strong Sun Moon* (Various Artists 1998b): "Equinox means the time of equal day and night … It is the relationship between the Earth and Sun in an orbit around the evolving galactic centre of the Universe. The *Anima Mundi*". In the same discourse, Japan's Equinox festival is singled out as being an especially "celestial electro communion – a participation mystique".

ECLIPSE FESTIVALS AND UNIVERSAL TRANCE GATHERINGS

Historically, eclipses of the Sun – whether total or partial – have been received with varying responses. A sign of hope or a cause for alarm, they have been interpreted according to the cosmological hermeneutics of those through whose domains the umbra has passed. Given that these unpredicted events have arrived unheralded in most regions for most of history, the reception has been less than warm. Though scientists have demonstrated great interest in eclipses since the 1700s, we can trace the history of "eclipse chasing" to 1836, when solar physicist Francis Bailey generated popular interest in solar physics (see Littmann *et al.* 2008). From the mid-nineteenth century, populations are known to have travelled from locations outside the line of totality to observe the spectacle, with multinational scientific expeditions mounted over the next century. In a discussion of one of the earliest cases of eclipse tourism, historian of alternative Albion, Andy Worthington, documents "the biggest ever recorded movement of people by train in one day in the UK" (Worthington 2004: 20) when, on 29 June 1927, three million people travelled to north-west England and Wales to observe a total solar eclipse (occluded by clouds). Worthington suggests that the rambling movement of the late nineteenth century, itself influenced by the desire for direct contact with nature expressed by the Romantic poets, partly explains this massive migration. Eclipse chasing eventually grew into a recreational pursuit via the work of the Pedas-Sigler family of educators (including astronomer and founding member of the International Planetarium Society, Ted Pedas) who, from the early 1970s, initiated eclipse tourism on cruise ships. Their first eclipse cruise was the 1972 "Voyage to Darkness" off the North Atlantic coast of Canada. These entrepreneurs had attempted to stage a rock festival ("Eclipse '70" in March 1970 – at the time Weil had experienced his epiphanies in Mexico), in the path of the Moon's umbra in a tiny fishing village in Suffolk, Virginia called Eclipse (named after a total eclipse there in 1900). However, the proposed event was opposed by the townsfolk, who condemned the proposed "freak-out" on their turf only months after Woodstock.

While the 100-mile-wide shadow has drawn multitudes into its path since the early 1970s, it would not be until the mid-1990s that the eclipse – with the aid of cheaper travel, digitization and the internet – was drawn into the orbit of an alternate culture. By the late 1990s, a cavalcade of spiritualists, astrologers and freaks converged in spatio-temporal contexts planned according to the alignment of celestial spheres at sites anticipated as optimum observation points on the path of totality. In this period, a whole new social event came into being as a highly specialized traveller phenomenon. The eclipse festival would become a recurrent – albeit irregular – vehicle for an emerging visionary arts community. Subsequent to the "eclipse rave" in Chile, solar seekers travelled to events mounted in Siberia/Mongolia, South Asia and Venezuela, where an epic twelve-day party, "Total Eclipse '98", was held near the town of Patanemo, attracting 1,000 people. In 1999, the momentous Solipse Festival transpired in Ozora, Hungary, attracting 15,000 people, and this has been the subsequent site of annual festivals. Another Solipse Festival was held in Zambia over ten days in June 2001. This was the first of the larger-scale remote operations. Organisers trucked a sound system 3,500 kilometres to a remote region of the African bush, and as production manager Nick Ladd informed me, introduced electricity to the local town, dug bore holes for water and catered for 4,000 people.[13] In early December the following year, simultaneous festivals were held on the path of totality in South Africa and in the desert near Lindhurst, South Australia. The latter event, Outback Eclipse, was my first eclipse festival, and although I had known various music, dance and alternative arts festivals in Australia by that time, including events mounted in that desert region, little could have prepared me for the cosmic symphony ahead. In the late afternoon of the fourth day, wearing my special "eclipse glasses", I stood on a long elevated earth platform with thousands of others facing west, the direction of the setting Sun, to observe a drama emblazoned across the heavens. It was as if the twin discs of the Moon and the Sun were mixed seamlessly by a divine DJ, and I and my companions back on Earth were dancing in the "sweet spot".[14] Towards the end of March four years later, now living in the United Kingdom and having rendezvous-ed with compatriots in Istanbul, I travelled overnight south to the Mediterranean city of Antalya in Turkey, the nearest city to Soulclipse, billed as a "Universal Trance Gathering". Attended by between 7,000 and 8,000 people, Soulclipse was held from 27 March until 2 April 2006 in Paradise Canyon on the fast-flowing Koprulu Canyon River. The guide issued to festival entrants stated the collective mission of organizers Indigo Kids:

> To unite the tribe in Turkey for this festive occasion. This goal
> comes out of love, harmony with nature, and understand-
> ing towards each other's differences and similarities as human
> beings. The trace festivals have always been where we have found
> our greatest opportunities to learn to grow, to celebrate, to be
> one with our fellow being and our Mother Earth, to serve, to
> pray, to play.

At mid-afternoon on the day of the main event, all present became engulfed
by the dome of shadow as the Sun was occulted and Venus burned high
in the mid-afternoon sky. It was a three-minute cosmic snapshot whose
dark flash left an imprint on the multitude of naked retinas belonging to
the howling massive. Smaller and more exclusive events were mounted over
the remainder of the decade in the mountains of Khan Altay, Siberia, Russia
(Planet Art Festival, July/August 2008), on Amami Island, Japan (2009) and
on the path of totality crossing the Southern Pacific (Honu Eclipse Festival,
Easter Island, and the Black Pearl Eclipse Adventure, Cook Islands, July
2010). Most recently, in November 2012, a week-long festival, Eclipse2012,
was staged near Cairns, Australia.

The total solar eclipse has inspired a great many artists in the psychedelic
trance diaspora, obvious among them being the French act Total Eclipse.
While one of the band's first tracks, the amateurish yet enthusiastic New
Beat-styled "Total Eclipse", released on the first Goa Trance album *Project
II Trance* (1993), battered listeners with the object of reverence by several
times repeating the spoken sample "eclipse", and finally "total eclipse", the
act later provided the soundtrack to the sublime on "Space Clinic" (*Violent
Relaxation*, 1996), a divine departure from standard consciousness and an
exposure to otherness psychotherapeutically applied via the Roland TB-303
bassline synthesizer. Probably the most seminal act inspired by the eclipse
is Shpongle, whose founders, Simon Posford and Raja Ram, produced their
ethnodelic "… And the Day Turned to Night" (the closing epic on their 1998
debut album *Are You Shpongled?*) subsequent to witnessing an eclipse in
India in 1995. Also in 1998, Twisted Records, founded by Posford, released
the compilation *Eclipse – A Journey Of Permanence and Impermanence* in
advance of a "Total Eclipse '98". The album included a few Goa and ethnodelic anthems such as that produced by Nomads of Dub (Simon Posford
and Nick Barber), whose revelation in deep space, "Spirals", sampled a
radio communiqué from a remote observer reporting "vivid colours, different colours, glittering colours … colours that are really indescribable, I've
never seen colours like that". The same album featured Doof's "Balashwaar
Baksheesh", which attempts to sonify the unheralded awe associated with
something akin to a collective birth. A woman announces that "I've never
ever seen anything like it before in my life, the energy that everybody felt,
they were grabbing onto something for the first time … It was amazing, the

139

happiness that everyone felt." Around midway, the track ascends in waves of *ekstasis* with everybody screaming like it's 1966 and they're being exposed to The Beatles live. But the styles of music performed at these events have been as diverse as those accommodated within the shifting soundscapes of psychedelia. Over ten years later, the compilation released by Rockdenashi Productionz, *Black Sun – Eclipse in Japan*, for the July 2009 eclipse on Amami Island, featured local darkpsy artists who, according to the liner notes, expressed their "understanding of the world in creative darkness".

TOTAL MYSTERY CULT

Transporting himself into the path of the umbra in the company of 5,000 mostly Japanese on tropical Myojinzaki beach for the nine-day Amami Island Festival in July 2010, some twenty years after he first set foot in Goa, Ray Castle positioned the festival downstream from the Goa sensibility. "It followed on from the sunrise and cosmic cycles," he stated, "and being sensitive to a universal metaphysical bigger picture in our role on the planet":

> It comes down to people wanting peak experience. They want to feel a cosmic rush. The intensity of eclipses and gathering together is like a collective meltdown. It's a very moving phenomenon, and sharing that with others, I felt I was like in a womb, with 5,000 people gathered; with 3,500 on the beach. And with all the screams and the emotion. It was very animal, very primordial. Deeply moving. I can see why eclipse fanatics travel all around the world to align themselves with these events. On a deeper level, I think they're quite heavy experiences, eclipses, it's not easy-going stuff. They really effect your emotions.[15]

Castle here offers a description of an exceptional experience, one that is numinous and primal, with the "womb" analogy evoking a birthing theme. Enthused by the eclipse in 1970 in Mexico, Weil explains why the eclipse event seems to place those who enter its path in a "natural high". The transfigurement, he conjectures, is a result of one's exquisite alignment with this comic synchronicity (Weil 1980). According to Weil, "to participate in that moment of uncanny equilibrium is to have one's faith strengthened in the possibility of equilibrium and to experience the paradox that balance and stillness are to be found at the heart of all change" (*ibid.*: 232). Furthermore, the alchemical union of the Sun and the Moon is recurrent in philosophies and myths worldwide that are "symbolic of the union of conscious and unconscious forces within the human psyche that must take place if one is to become whole" (*ibid.*). Typically accessed via meditation, drugs, hypnosis, trance and other techniques, those hidden realms of consciousness occulted to us in our daily lives are said to be perfectly represented by the corona of the Sun in union with the Moon – a kind of cosmic mandala that is also recognized as a union of masculine and feminine energies. Thus, according to this interpretation, a total solar eclipse signifies an alchemical exchange of solar and lunar phases of consciousness, with totality contextualizing something of a peak psychocultural experience.

Regardless of the validity of these comments, there exists a mystical ambiance to these events that, following the logic internal to mysteries, is known only to those who are directly exposed. Being inside the umbra, where the demarcation from the routine is amplified by the liminal time–space of the festival, is like being bathed in the strange twilight of a reverse full moon, the Earth's only natural orbiting satellite framed perfectly in those moments of totality by the Sun's corona which most observers recognize is a miraculous cosmic circumstance, given its astonishingly improbable occurrence.[16] If the full moon's periodic illumination of unconscious energies fires crazed states and charges events in which people may become temporary "lunatics", animal-like ravers, the fullness of the Sun-Moon during an eclipse magnifies the experience of numinosity and synchronicity identified by both Castle and Weil. The cosmic drama occasions something of a passage rite for participants, as those who travel to liminalized events mounted within its path will undertake pre-eclipse preparations (which will have begun weeks, months or years prior), enter the superliminality of totality and, in their post-eclipse life, debrief and share interpretations among their fellow travellers – a process that will continue on their return sojourns, and among their friends and families thereafter.

As one approaches the liminal phase of totality, there is an undeniable atmosphere of excitement, smiles, upward gazes and expressions of relief if the weather conditions are clear. These irruptions of anticipation are accompanied by the wearing of special "eclipse glasses" that are issued to all festival-goers, and that are essential for viewing the eclipse as well as preventing damage to one's Sun-gazing eyes. At this juncture, amplified sound is typically turned off, dancing ceases and a reverential attitude takes hold. As the Moon begins its journey across the face of the Sun, what is known as "first contact" – a kind of lycanthropic howling – commences. It takes about an hour or so for the Sun to become completely engulfed by the Moon, but in this period, it is unmistakeable that one has entered a duration in which time itself has been eclipsed as shadow bands race across the surface of the Earth, and as the phenomenon known as "Bailey's Beads" – sunlight shining through valleys on the Moon's surface (or "second contact") – occurs. The delirium is deafening upon the moment when the brilliance of the photosphere finally disappears behind the moon, which now appears as a vast portal in the sky. This colossal synchronicity has become animated under various interpretations. As was earlier suggested, the event has been harnessed according to intentions implicit to a self-transformative gnosis

141

implicit to the New Age, the power of which can be accounted for by way of Weil's Jungian-influenced explanations – that is, the alchemical union of opposites potentiating wholeness, which is also implicit to the work of mystic and "ChaOrder Magician" Orryelle Defenestrate-Bascule.[17]

In this period, which can last up to seven minutes (though it normally takes about three minutes), while one's rational en-light-ened self may be said to become occulted, the umbra affords an exquisite illumination for liminars. Take the lines sampled on Tristan and Lucas's "Magic Umbra" (*Lucas Presents Tales of Heads*, 2010):

> What I love is the fact that I'm watching the mechanics in the solar system at work. I'm standing here watching the Moon pass across the Sun bringing the umbral shadow across the Earth. And for those fleeting moments I'm standing in the magic of the umbra.

But this is not all, since in a rare elliptic "rise", the Sun re-emerges minutes later with the appearance of the "diamond ring effect" ("third contact"). The reception of the Sun post-totality is not dissimilar to that of its "rising" in the tradition of the Goa trance rave, its first light greeted by the raving masses. As the Sun rises from the Moon within those moments of "third contact", it is as if participants are resplendent in reverse equivalence to those astronauts who first witnessed the Earth emerging from the dark side of the Moon, their wonder not dissimilar to the epiphanies experienced by space voyagers. While these Earth-bound voyagers are precisely geo-positioned, a recognition of their irreducible relationship with the cosmos may be visited upon them with a remarkably equivalent clarity. This third and final phase of passage, in which the condition of those on the edge of the umbra is thought to hold correspondence with the positioning of the spheres, appears to have been sonified in work such as that consistently produced by Vibrasphere, basking the habitués of the dance floor in dreamy waves of electronic sunshine, or Solar Fields, whose anthem "Third Time (T-version)" (*V.A. First Impression*, 2002) offers a soundtrack to the "diamond ring effect" and the concurrent rebirth of the self.

While Castle and Weil point to moments of singularity associated with cosmic alignments, synchronicity and planetary "rises", and connote a gnostic sensibility associated with the personal transcendence experienced at this juncture, these are explosive social events. In his memoirs, Bailey wrote of his total eclipse experience in 1842 when he mounted a telescope inside a building at the University in Pavia, Italy: "All I wanted was to be left alone during the whole time of the eclipse," he wrote, "being fully persuaded that nothing is so injurious to the making of accurate observations as the intrusion of unnecessary company" (in Littmann *et al.* 2008: 88). Bailey was expressing a concern common to the singular research scientist, yet remote from the

142

experience of the eclipse festival. For while the presence of people may dis-rupt the scientific experiment, in the immeasurable, mystical landscape of the vibe, "company" is paramount. Furthermore, the eclipse experience – as occasioned by the eclipse festival – is not exclusively or even predominantly ocular; it is a sensual encounter involving one's close proximity to others in an intentional geo-social space from which participants draw personal, primal and cosmic significance. This unique techno-shamanic experience is reliant upon chemical, digital and cyber technologies to potentiate sensory continuity with the physical world in dance, while at the same time ena-bling participants to become familiar with transpersonal states of conscious-ness in trance. Introducing total solar eclipse festivals as exemplary social, astronomical and geophysical events in a *cosmic nature spirituality*, this chapter has shown that these planetary events are the context for a dance music aesthetic potentiating a mystical experience not incomparable with conventional Neo-Pagan festivals. In the path of totality, and in the direct line of astonishing music, this socio-sensual confluence of dancing bodies and transcendent selves should be of interest to scholars of contemporary, transnational and mutating forms of Paganism.

NOTES

1. The path of totality is chased and championed by diverse parties for diverse causes. Included among these are scientists and spiritualists, tourists and travellers, pilgrims and party-makers. This chapter offers an exclusive account of the total solar eclipse festivals and their patrons.
2. Outcomes are also dependent on a successfully executed festival, which is notoriously vulnerable to a unique combination of vicissitudes: the difficulties of staging an event in remote regions of the planet, the high chances of cloud-cover preventing visibility of the eclipse itself, and other factors typically affecting outdoor events. These include extreme weather events like the freak storm that demolished the main stage at Soul-clipse in Turkey in 2006 only minutes before the opening ceremony, and official interventions – especially raids conducted by police.
3. Although on one occasion (Solipse 1999 at Ozora in Hungary), an eclipse has inspired an annual festival (Ozora) held on the original site, which is considered significant to the festival's participants.
4. Nick Ladd, interview with the author, Glastonbury, 3 June 2006.
5. Note on terminology. In this chapter I use "Goa Trance" specifically for the marketed music genre, and "Goatrance" for the associated cultural movement and its various scenes. Also, "psytrance" refers to both the music style and cultural movement.
6. Via different approaches, all three figures championed the use of psychedelics in the expansion of human consciousness.
7. DMT (*N,N*-dimethyltryptamine) is a naturally occurring tryptamine found in many plants worldwide, and is created in small amounts by the human body during metabolism.
8. From "Re: Evolution": www.deoxy.org/t_re-evo.htm (accessed March 2011).
9. The ambivalence with which the Goa DJ is received is not dissimilar to the ambivalent reception of Dionysian cults, as Chiara Baldini (2010) observes in her study of a psytrance party she co-organized in Tuscany, Italy.

10. The *Whole Earth* image would become the logo for Earth Day, and was depicted inside a pair of caring hands by Friends of the Earth. A 1967 satellite photo of the Earth was obtained from NASA by Stewart Brand and famously reproduced on the cover of the Fall 1968 issue of the *Whole Earth Catalog.*

11. Among events that have emerged from psychedelic and New Age roots, Earthdance International is an exemplary manifestation of the conscientious quest for planetary consciousness; see www.earthdance.org (accessed March 2011).

12. Ray Castle, interview with the author (on Skype), February 2010.

13. Nick Ladd, interview with the author, Glastonbury, 3 June 2006.

14. A documentary film featuring dramatic vox-pops of awe-animated eclipse viewers immediately post-event offers excellent insight on the experience (*The Outback Eclipse Story* 2003).

15. Ray Castle, interview with the author (via Skype), 7 February 2010.

16. The sun's distance from the earth is about 400 times the moon's distance, and the sun's diameter is about 400 times the moon's diameter. Because these ratios are approximately the same, the sun and the moon as seen from earth appear to be approximately the same size. As the blurb on *Caribbean Eclipse* (1999) points out, that we can make perfect observation of the sun's corona is a "rare spatial synchronicity" in our solar system.

17. See www.crossroads.wild.net.au/index.html, accessed 17 March 2011.

10. TECHNO-SHAMANISM AND THE ECONOMY OF ECSTASY AS A RELIGIOUS EXPERIENCE

Alan Nixon and Adam Possamai

Raves, or events revolving around electronic dance music (EDM), consist of people dancing and socializing to an electronic form of music with an accompanying light show and visual effects (Jordan 1995; Martin 1999). Raves range in size from small house parties with thirty or so people in attendance up to massive music festivals attracting crowds of more than thirty thousand (Martin 1999; St John 2009a; Sylvan 2005). These events may occur in urban or rural locations, in clubs or abandoned warehouses, or in outdoor settings on public and private land (Sylvan 2005: 33). Events revolving around EDM became one of the most extensive popular youth movements at the end of the twentieth century, and continue to be popular today on a global scale (Fritz, cited in St John 2009a).

EDM is a genre loosely defined by the use of synthetic electronic instruments in its creation, often in ways that do not sound like traditional musical instruments at all (Gibson & Pagan 2006; Rietveld 2004; St John 2004a). In traditional hardware form, these instruments may include sequencers, synthesizers, drum machines and samplers, all of which are used to make the artificial sounds that comprise most EDM. However, the array of music-making technologies has increased significantly over the last twenty years due to the advent of the personal computer (Rietveld 2004). Many of these innovations consist of cheaper software versions of the previously mentioned hardware music-making tools. Sequencers are replaced by software-based digital audio workstations (DAW) such as Cubase, Logic Audio and FLstudio, and a large variety of software plugins (which are inserted into and sequenced by such DAWs) replace synthesizers, drum machines and samplers. It is now also possible to acquire cheap hardware adapters and microphones that allow the easy recording of acoustic or live instruments into the DAW, expanding the possibilities even further. With this integration and a proliferation of hardware control devices for software packages (now including devices such as touch screen phones and hand held game machines like the Nintendo DSI), live electronic music has also become cheaper and easier to perform. This digitization of music-making technologies has had the effect of partially democratizing music production by making do-it-yourself music possible at home relatively cheaply (Rietveld 2004). This democratization has made way for what Rietveld describes as "music by the people for the people, in effect a type of electronic folk music" (*ibid.*: 50).

The EDM scene as a whole can be described as a loose association of groups (including Neo-Pagan sub-groups as explored below) attracted to EDM for the purpose of dancing and socializing (St John 2004a). Though there are many types of EDM events, they share common features and can loosely be grouped together. Electronic music is normally mixed/performed by a DJ/producer in a space with a relaxed social structure, which is designed to disrupt normal sensory perceptions (*ibid.*). Like the New Age scene, rave culture has been portrayed as a free-floating scene in which anything and everything goes. In what appears to be an unlimited world of eclectic choice, people can be inspired by philosophy, religion, popular science and popular and counter-culture to create their subjective myth (Possamai 2007) and enjoy themselves in rave culture. According to much of the theoretical literature, there is a "free floating" of meanings and network affiliations in rave culture. At the extreme, some studies of EDM culture claim that the culture offers little or no explicit ontology, and thus does not offer pre-packaged meaning for consumption (Landau 2004; St John 2006). From this perspective, EDM events are argued to be a multi-narrative space in which participants can experiment with subjectivity (St John 2004a). The experimentation is facilitated by the relaxed social structure provided by EDM events (Olaveson 2004). This allows EDM participants to experiment with new ways of interacting with others, and thus with new aspects of their own identity (St John 2009a). However, recent scholarship has noted that this solidarity has ephemeral, fleeting, negative and exclusive aspects, and these environments might not be completely unstructured (Gavanas 2008; Kavanaugh & Anderson 2008).

This chapter explores whether or not such social structure exists in this supposedly free-floating field by analysing people's interpretation of ecstasy, the very core of the religious experience in rave culture. Hay (1990) has discussed music as a trigger for spiritual or religious experiences. In fact, in Hay's studies music has been found to be the most important trigger to ecstasy, even above attending religious services and prayer. These experiences are linked in the literature (e.g. Tramacchi 2000, 2004) to the archaic techniques of ecstasy used by traditional shamans (techno being the beat of the electronic shaman), but no clear neo- or techno-shamanic tradition or shared interpretation seems to be used in the rave scene. Taking this argument further using Bourdieu's theoretical approach to the "field" (Bourdieu 1971), this chapter argues that three agents are providing differing interpretations of ecstasy, and thus shaping the field of rave and ecstasy. These agents are the Neo-Pagan techno-shaman (a term used as an ideal-type to reflect a sub-group of Paganism that is highly eclectic in its spiritual approach to life, but that has a dominant focus on nature and the spiritual power of technology/music), the Christian (connected to the "Emerging Church" phenomenon) and the secular types ("mainstream" clubbers/ravers). Each group of agents interprets this musical/spiritual experience through their particular cultural lens, and therefore they are all providing cultural and symbolic capital to this economy of ecstasy. In this way, we will attempt to distinguish Neo-Pagan interpretations of popular music-induced ecstasy by contrasting them with competing interpretations within this cultural economy of ecstasy.

RAVE STUDIES AND THE ECONOMY OF ECSTASY

The field of rave studies has inherited the use of postmodernist and post-structuralist philosophies as ways to formulate its objects of inquiry and to evaluate rave as a subversive phenomenon. Generally speaking, this evaluation has been positive, concentrating on the resistance that these sites can pose to categorical social structures, and thus on the transcendence of social difference achieved by this scene. In this discourse, rave contains absolute novelty and exteriority to systems of domination in everyday life (Saldanha 2004). Postmodernism and poststructuralism are easily adopted by those undertaking rave studies because both rave and poststructuralism/post-modernism engage with the anarchistic leanings present in the philosophies of Baudrillard, Foucault, Lyotard, and especially Deleuze and Guattari, who also draw on older types of anarchism such as that of Bey (Bey 1991, cited in Saldanha 2004). Green (2010) and many other theorists see rave or EDM festivals as heterotopias, allowing new forms of sociality, spirituality and politics to develop.

Maffesoli's theories of neo-tribalism (Maffesoli 1996) have also been used in the study of rave culture to portray this culture as a type of free-floating scene that links its participants via a "community of feeling" (Malbon 1999; St John 2004a). Maffesoli's theories also point towards communities "structured" around taste and aesthetics, however fleeting these connections may be. However, would not a true heterotopia contain both unpopular/forbidden "conservative" ideas *and* "progressive" ideas? As Jordan warns, "there is nothing in ... raving that would prevent rave events from incorporating, for example, sexism and racism" (Jordan 1995: 139).

This gives us a hint about the possibility of finding a sense of structure in this field. To understand this issue more extensively, we have decided to focus on a specific angle (or a transversal cut, in terms of a Foucauldian archaeology of knowledge) by using the work of a theorist who has ana-lysed the middle ground between a determinist and an agentic approach. For Bourdieu, society is not a unified and integrated system; it is rather a multidimensional space in which agents possess and defend various forms of capital within specific sub-societal space, which he calls fields. Part of his sociology is to study the positions of key agents in these fields, and understand what economic, cultural, symbolic and social position they hold, as well as the conflicts they have with other agents. Such fields can be education, religion, political parties or the arts, in which we find various types of agent with different forms of capital and logics of action, who are involved in struggles of various types. In the field of religion, for example, Bourdieu analyses the various interactions between priests, prophets, sorcerers and laypeople, and the way the economy of the religious is distributed and contested – especially when competing for religious legitimacy and compensation (Bourdieu 1971). As noted by many theorists, there is less formal hierarchy in the distributed networks of EDM culture (a trait common to many postmodern social groups; (St John 2009a; B. S. Turner 2008). Due to this, the conflicts in the field of ecstasy will be analysed as being between abstract groups of key agents that hold an interpretation of ecstasy, rather than as individual "key agents" in Bourdieu's style.

This chapter studies one sub-field of the religious field, specifically that of religious ecstasy within the rave scene. It focuses on the different actors who invest their cultural and symbolic resources into this economy of ecstasy when competing for cultural legitimacy. It is demonstrated that the Neo-Pagan interpretation of ecstasy is the dominant religious discourse by which to explain this phenomenon, while the Christian interpretation of ecstasy has come to this sub-field at a later stage, in connection with the "emerging church" phenomenon (discussed later in this chapter), and is slowly providing a contested view within the religious/spiritual side of the sub-field. Outside of this religious system, ravers desire secular rather than religious forms of cultural capital from their rave experience. Before coming back to Bourdieu's theory of fields and capitals at the end of the chapter, we will contrast the three techno-shamanic agents after quickly exploring their common history.

EDM developed in the United States from black and Latino gay disco culture, from which elements of Christianity (black/gospel church culture), African trance culture (African American secular music culture) and 1960s psychedelia were transmitted into mainstream EDM (Till 2009). European origins can also be found in the influence that the works of 1970s electronic band Kraftwerk had on the Detroit techno scene (Sylvan 2005) and the influence of European electronic "New Wave" and industrial bands on hippie artists in Goa, India (such as Goa Gil – see Davis 2004; Partridge 2005). Like its African American dance music predecessors (blues, jazz, swing, rock'n'roll, rhythm'n'blues, soul, funk, hip hop and ska), EDM has crossed over into mainstream British culture (Till 2009: 174) and is now global (St John 2009b). In all cases, a secular version of the culture has existed from the onset of the scene. At the same time, the Goa dance scene and the Pagan psychedelic scene associated with it have seen an expansion in the religious part of the EDM. Psychedelic dance has had a large influence on Western dance culture, and should not be underestimated. Without Goa, massive secular dance spaces like Ibiza, British superclubs and commercial dance festivals, along with the trance music that made them famous, would be unlikely to exist (Catchlove 2002; Davis 2004; Saldanha 2004). Later in time, Christian interpretations of this experience have evolved and added to the interpretations available (Lau 2006; Till 2006).

SHAMANISM, NEO-SHAMANISM AND TECHNO-SHAMANISM

> Shamanism was, a generation ago, considered to be either a psychopathic phenomenon or a primitive healing practice and archaic type of black magic, but contemporary scholarship has convincingly demonstrated the complexity, the rigour, and the rich spiritual meaning of shamanic initiation and practices.
>
> (Eliade 1976: 56)

Given its obvious etymological roots, a key to understanding techno-shamanic ecstasy is its complex relationship with traditional shamanism (Green 2010; Rietveld 2004; Tramacchi 2004). The shaman utilizes a trance state, in which his or her soul is said to leave his body and ascend to the sky or descend to the underworld (Eliade 1976). The shaman enters these spirit realms through accessing altered states of consciousness (St John 2009a; Harner [1980] 1990). There are numerous ways to access these states, but the most common include hallucinogenic drug use, dancing and music (Harner [1980] 1990; Takahashi 2004). However, despite the common use of the term "shamanism" in contemporary literature, it does not represent a homogeneous group (Eliade 1964). It has been suggested that it is more appropriate to talk about "shamanisms" rather than a monolithic shaman-ism (Harvey 1997). Despite this, there is a link – all pre-modern shamanic activities involve a connection to the realms of spirits. Outside of this, a shaman could be "psychopomp, priest, healer, therapist, spiritual-warrior, spirit-controller, medium and/or powerful communal leader" (*ibid.*: 108).

Takahashi discusses the dance party environment and the altered state of consciousness (ASC) inducing nature of both environment and drugs (Takahashi 2004), and Tramacchi argues that "[p]sychedelic dance parties share many elements with other ethnogenic dance rituals" (Tramacchi 2004: 140). Likewise, comparing quotes from traditional shamans and ravers, Green has argued that "it appears that traditional shamanic and Techno-shamanic experiences are in some ways related" (Green 2010: 207)·

> Technoshamanism has, for example, digitised tribal beats, chants and sounds from the rainforests; replaced psychotropic "teacher plants" with synthesised highs in the form of amphetamines, LSD

> and Ecstasy; substituted the dances of the Whirling Dervishes with raves; and, swapped ritual bonfires with the strobe, and internet images and computer-generated fractals which are projected onto the walls of the venue. (*Ibid.*: 209)

Green suggests that techno-shamanism is about mutual exploration of ontology and the psyche (*ibid.*), citing Erik Davis, who conceptualizes premodern shamans as "the social and ecological psychiatrists of their societies", suggesting that shamans use "language, costumes, gestures, song, and stagecraft" to apply "*techne* to the social imagination, actively tweaking the images, desires, and stories that partly structure the collective psyche" (Davis 1999: 173). Following William Gibson (see Gibson 1984), Davis terms this psychic process *neuromancy*. In other words, for Green, techno-shamanism – like traditional shamanism – induces the dissolution of the boundaries between performers and audience (Green 2010). Rave participants often talk of processes of dissolution where they feel "at one" with their surroundings, the music and others. These quotes have been compared to the explanations of shamans and a strong correlation of experience has been identified (Takahashi 2004; Tramacchi 2004, 2000; Green 2010). McKenna – a popular figure in the psychedelic scene – describes this dissolution as a change in consciousness from an ordinary state to an altered, collective one. Harvey claims that for McKenna, rave participants actually "change neurological states, and large groups of people getting together in the presence of this kind of music are creating a telepathic community, a bonding" (Harvey, cited in Green 2010: 210). As will be demonstrated, this change can be viewed as the awakening of "relational consciousness" (see Hay 2007) as a physiological form of primordial religious experience, which has multiple interpretations via the worldview of a participant. This becomes particularly clear when contrasting the secular rave scene with the two religious types. Though the traits of the shamanistic experience are implicitly present in the secular rave scene via the technologies employed, they are not necessarily seen as connected to the realm of the spirits, as is the case in traditional shamanism. Thus, as will be discussed later, the secular interpretation of and link to shamanism differ from the experience in the other two agent groups (Pagan and Christian) due to the general lack of spiritual orientation/interpretation in the secular group.

PSYTRANCE AND NEO-PAGAN ECSTASY

Neo-Paganism covers an array of eclectic sub-groups, such as those interested in particular ethnic mythology (e.g. Celtic, Nordic or Egyptian mythology), Goddess worshipping, Druidism, specific types of covens (for example, Alexandrian ones) or indigenous beliefs. Another collection of sub-groups comprises shamanism (sometimes connected to indigenous beliefs), neo-shamanism and techno-shamanism. It is worth noticing that not all Neo-Pagans are techno-shamans.

Before beginning our exploration of the links between Neo-Pagan and rave cultures, it must be noted that not all Pagans are involved with the rave scene, and that Neo-Pagan ravers represent a sub-set of the entire Neo-Pagan "community". Green suggests that techno-shamanism specifically represents a Pagan meeting of "rave" culture and neo-shamanism (Green 2010). This will become clearer as we discuss the history of the psychedelic/Neo-Pagan rave scene. Thus, in order to discover the link between Paganism and techno-shamanism, it is useful to explore the history of one such psychedelic/Neo-Pagan based group: the psytrance scene.

As a particular part of the rave and Pagan scenes, psychedelic raves are EDM parties with an explicitly psychedelic focus that explore the transformational possibilities of shamanic practices. In this (mostly) outdoor psychedelic dance culture, we have seen a revival of Pagan and tribal cultures in which – sometimes – the DJ becomes a shaman or a techno-shaman (Partridge 2006). Such events generally have an explicit connection to 1960s counter-culture through psychedelic spokespersons such as the techno-shamans Terence McKenna and Goa Gil (St John 2009a, 2004a; Tramacchi 2000, 2004). Thus it can be illustrative to look at the history of rave and the development of Pagan techno-shamanism for one possible interpretation of ecstasy.

In the late 1960s, figures such as Gil began to make their way from the West to the beaches of Goa (India) to continue the hippie lifestyle that, according to Goa Gil, was slowly disintegrating in places such as San Francisco. A community was formed in Anjuna, a small village on the island of Goa (Lobo 2007; Saldanha 2004). Throughout the 1970s, Anjuna remained a type of hippie commune with no electricity and most music was acoustically performed; the "music house" was set up as an experimental space for Indian and Western musicians (Catchlove 2002). In the early 1980s, on trips out of Goa to the United States and Europe, Gil discovered the electronically based "New Wave" and Electronic Body Music (EBM) being produced there. These new types of music fascinated him, and he began to use tapes to loop the most psychedelic and vocal-free sections of the music in an early form of sampling, creating the Goa Trance style. The style caught on and began to be reproduced by other DJs and musicians (Catchlove 2002; Saldanha 2004). As the trance phenomenon travelled from Goa to the West, it became increasingly earth-centred and Pagan/shamanic, often placing emphasis on the indigenous religious traditions of the current geographical location (e.g. Celtic in the United Kingdom, Native American in the United States and Aboriginal in Australia; Partridge 2006: 48). An overlap between techno and New Age ritual symbolism places these digital dance events within a framework of neo-shamanic experiences (D'Andrea 2004). Reappropriated from their demonization by Christian culture, Pagan figures like Pan, Bacchus and

Dionysus are celebrated as positive icons in this culture. Partridge, for example, also sees the Pagan connection in this culture in festivals such as those at Glastonbury and Goa (Partridge 2006). Partridge observes how the mystical music was first inspired by Indian religions, and then acquired a more Pagan focus. This movement travelled back to San Francisco in the early 1990s in the form of the intentional party movement (Sylvan 2005), which also claims strong connections to 1960s counter-culture and expresses Pagan themes in its interpretation of rave – "We are the Planet's Future" is a slogan used by the Come Unity Crew (St John 2004a; Sylvan 2005).

Green argues that rave culture and techno-shamanism also became strongly connected to the British conservative politics of the 1980s and 1990s after rave culture travelled across the Atlantic to the United Kingdom (Green 2010). He suggests that this was a result of the moral agenda of that period, and the suppression of particular "folk devils" (for example, trade unions, the underclass, single mothers, travellers (gypsies) and ravers). In his view, these events created an innovative and novel nexus of politics and spiritual belief which has had a lasting impact upon personal and environmental politics (*ibid.*). In this framework, the Glastonbury Festival of 1989 was arguably the start of techno-shamanism. It was the event where the rave and traveller communities first came together. The travellers provided a nomadic lifestyle and a concern with spirituality and psychedelic experimentation. The ravers brought the sound systems, music and technological expertise (Green 2010; St John 2009a). As they travelled, they became increasingly influenced by the New Age psychedelia of traveller communities and by the Pagan folklore of southern England (Green 2010). Free festivals often took place at or near Neolithic sacred sites, and knowledge of these places began to influence the Tribe with a Pagan and environmental ethic.

Green points to techno-shamanism as a catalyst in the do-it-yourself (DIY) politicization of Pagan forms of environmental action in the 1990s and beyond. Indeed, contemporary Paganism is suffused with stories of Pagan environmentalism, sometimes termed "sacred ecology" (*ibid.*). While Pagans had a visible presence at female peace camps at Greenham Common in the 1980s, it was techno-shamanic DIY politics that inspired Pagan politics (McKay 1998). The legislation that was to become the Criminal Justice and Public Order Act of 1994 was passing through Parliament as the Criminal Justice Bill (CJB) (*ibid.*: 159–81). The Tribe became public opponents of the CJB, organizing protests and using the sound systems as a form of propaganda against the Bill. These experiences led the Tribe to an anarchist politics that was both anti-conservative and anti-capitalist (Green 2010). This can be linked to anarchist writers such as Hakim Bey, who was also aware of the connection – though not happy with the techno side of the culture, as he comments: "The ravers were among my biggest readers, I wish they would rethink all this techno stuff … they didn't get that part of my writing" (Bey, cited in Bleyer 2004).

In the late 1980s, music and fashion cultures took inspiration from the late 1960s, with psychedelic-inspired guitar and dance music becoming attached to a neo-psychedelic Flower Power style. A nostalgia for and mimicry of the late 1960s drug culture was also present in this movement. Methylenedioxymethamphetamine (MDMA), better known as the hedonistic love drug ecstasy, aided in breaking down social boundaries, allowing for individuals' more fluid interactions with others and the world. However, as Pagan techno-shamanism developed out of rave, the drug of choice became LSD due to its reputation as a drug of shamanistic insight, and its popularization by figures such as Terence McKenna (Green 2010). This is in contrast to the secular scene, where drug ecstasy has remained dominant, and the Christian scene, which is supposedly drug free (Lynch & Badger 2006; Till 2006).

It is claimed that psytrance exhibits a range of aesthetics, genres and scenes, and that it is a worldwide phenomenon. However, as has been argued, psytrance had its beginnings in the post-1960s psychedelic counter-culture and the EDM developments of the 1980s and 1990s. Psytrance includes the visionary (reflexive–utilitarian) and ecstatic (expressive–Dionysian) aspects of 1960s counter-culture that Musgrove has discussed as the "dialectics of Utopia" (Musgrove 1974, cited in St John 2009a). Psytrance can be seen as a cultural and musical movement that takes on principal aspects of the 1960s-inspired new spirituality and is moulded by them (St John 2009a).

Within psytrance, the symbolic representations of pre-modern tribal groups are mixed with cyborgian and sci-fi narratives and symbolism. The movement derives from the holistic human potential movement, and sees multiple techniques as a way "to augment personal growth, enlightenment status and credibility" (St John 2009a: 43). It is formed out of the group of meanings and experience D'Andrea calls New Age and techno (D'Andrea 2007). According to D'Andrea, identity is formed at the intersection of these two "styles of subjectivity formation, under flexible capitalism" (St John 2009a: 44). The spiritual actors in psytrance culture consume popular culture (for example, as music, aesthetic, lifestyle and philosophy) and add it to a kind of religious bricolage. Psytrance event dance floors are often placed in outdoor locations, in the natural environment, and participants may celebrate celestial events or hold parties to mark the change of seasons (St John 2009a; Sylvan 2005; Tramacchi 2000). According to a participant in the psytrance scene: "The Psy Trance scene is very concerned about ecology and nature, and hence it's very usual to find a lot of workshops with educational activities against racism, and promoting love and care for Our Mother Nature" (DJ Tundra 2007).

St John even describes some dance parties dedicated to healing the planet by mixing ancient rites and the technologies of today in order to gain stronger connectedness with Mother Earth (St John 2009b). Explicitly spiritual scenes such as psytrance are "a repository for those experimenting with alternative spiritual dispositions" (St John 2009a: 49), including Neo-Pagan ones. Thus psytrance participants define themselves *against* dominant modes of thought and practice and psytrance culture becomes a niche for experimental knowledge, heretical religion, unorthodox science and progressive movements. While this sub-field is quite eclectic, as it mixes Buddhist, Hindu and esoteric traditions, the Western version of psytrance is nevertheless more explicitly Pagan (Partridge 2005). This change happened as trance moved from Goa to the West; Eastern sounds in the music were supplemented by indigenous sounds and voices (*ibid.*). Partridge suggests that as this move occurred, the scene became "more Pagan/Shamanic and Earth centered, often focusing on indigenous religious traditions of the area" (*ibid.*: 169).

St John notes that the focus of the psytrance scene is on human/spiritual boundaries *outside* mainstream religion and faith. This is a cultural restriction plausibly derived from the history of the psytrance tradition. As an example of the accentuation of difference with the mainstream, Till observes that when religion and spirituality are used in psychedelic EDM, Christianity can be seen in a negative light, as the history of Christianity (especially the Puritan and Lutheran histories) contains repressed traditions of ecstatic dancing (Till 2009). This helps distinguish the psytrance and Christian scenes from one another, as neither would be willing to accept the interpretations of the other due to cultural history and beliefs. The psytrance raver's Pagan and earth-centred focus contrasts with the Christ- and God-centred focus of the Christian ravers, as highlighted in the next section.

CHRISTIAN ECSTASY AND SHAMANISM

In the first contrasting example, it is poignant to discuss a player that competes on an explicitly religious level with Pagan interpretations. This is because the field of rave ecstasy has changed over the years and the monopoly of interpretation is no longer in the hands of the Neo-Pagans and secular types. A new type of agent has come on board in this field: the Christian raver. In his study of Pentecostalism, Jennings discovers a milieu specialized in the ecstatic trance experience (Jennings 2010). His article demonstrates how Pentecostal music and popular music exhibit elements of shamanic ecstatic trance practices. Through his fieldwork, he observes how hierophantic music leads church attendees on a ritual journey. The music team is there to assist the church members to connect with the sacred. Jennings tells us that once these people have reached the trance state, they claim to experience indescribable bliss, peace, joy and healing. Though Jennings's observations are not situated within the rave culture specifically, in his research we can see a link to the adaptation of the character of the shaman in a Pentecostal context.

154

The link between Christian music and shamanism becomes even stronger when EDM is used in a specifically Christian context. The Nine O'clock Service (NOS) epitomized this mix (Till 2006). This experimental Anglican church started in Sheffield in the United Kingdom, and mixed club culture with postmodern Christianity. In an analysis of the NOS, Till discovered that it was difficult for the church generally to compete with the "visual and aural impact that multimedia experiences in nightclubs and on television have upon young people" (*ibid.*: 91), and that there were more people clubbing each weekend than attending church services. Thus we can witness direct feelings of competition between Christian and other rave interpretations because raves were perceived to be poaching clientele from these churches. To deal with the competition, the NOS took place in a local church at 9.00 pm, after the last conventional service, and was strongly influenced in its liturgies by the clubbing culture and electronic pop music. Its first service took place in 1986, and it quickly became popular. At one stage, it had more staff and more attendees than the Sheffield Cathedral. Although the service stopped because of one of the biggest sex scandals in which the Anglican Church had ever been involved (*ibid.*: 102), it was influential in the development of alternative types of worship in churches:

> The liturgy was rewritten to reflect interests in creation spiritu-
> ality and pre-enlightenment mysticism, with words such as God
> and Christ (seen by the NOS as too deconstructed by overuse
> and misuse) replaced by "Eternal Father" and "Primal Force". Even
> the creed and the Lord's prayer were rewritten. Sometimes two
> dancers wearing masks would spin like whirling dervishes, robes
> billowing out, heads watching a revolving hand.   (*Ibid.*: 102–3)

Till concludes:

> [The Nine O'clock Service] saw itself as an alternative solution
> and it learnt from secular culture how to use music and the arts
> to reach and inspire people. In club culture it found new forms of
> communal expression developed by secular DJs, clubbers, musi-
> cians, and promoters. It took what was useful from club culture
> while disapproving of and expressively forbidding the use of
> drugs and other aspects of excessive hedonism (ironically also
> forbidding any sexual activity outside of marriage).   (*Ibid.*: 105)

The NOS group was influenced by Matthew Fox's "Techno Mass" from California, and Till also makes reference to a Christian group in the United States that held communion with the drug "ecstasy" as the host.

Moving on from this specific case study, Lau studied an evangelical group at Ibiza, the 24–7 Mission team, and interviewed some Christian DJs who viewed their job as a calling from God (Lau 2006). One of Lau's informants states that: "If DJs can tune into the Holy Spirit, that's very powerful! You can direct people to God" (*ibid*.: 83). Lau's interviewees view dance music as a vehicle for the Holy Spirit and as a way to reach out to non-Christians. They also understand the enjoyment of music as an act of worship in itself.

This new Christian phenomenon would fit with what are termed emerging churches (also called Next Wave, New Paradigm and Liquid Churches; De Groot 2006), which have developed recently in Western societies. These churches ask questions about the nature of the church and its engagement in the world, and want to make the Gospel accessible to unchurched people via a new type of ambiance not found in conventional church settings. Other sub-types of emerging churches include café churches where people sit at tables and chairs, drinking and/or eating and chatting; churches in pubs; cyber churches; fifteen-minute commuter churches designed for busy twenty-first century commuters on their way to work with no time to spare for a more conventional church services; and skate churches with ramps inside or outside the church halls where skating is mixed with Bible readings.

By using a style of sociation more appropriate to a society dominated by consumer and popular culture rather than preaching at people from a pulpit, emerging churches hope to increase church attendance and to have the gospel reach a larger audience. Drane defines this complex new cross-continental phenomenon:

> On the one hand, "emerging church" is being used as a short-hand way of describing a genuine concern among leaders of tra-ditional denominations to engage in a meaningful missional way with the changing culture, and as part of that engagement to ask fundamental questions about the nature of the Church as well as about an appropriate contextualization of Christian faith that will honour the tradition while also making the Gospel accessible to otherwise unchurched people ... There is, however, another image of "emerging church", consisting of Christians who have become angry and disillusioned with their previous experience of church (predominantly at the conservative evangelical, fun-damentalist and sometimes charismatic end of the spectrum), and who have established their own faith communities that – far from being accountable to any larger tradition – are fiercely inde-pendent, and often highly critical of those who remain within what they regard as the spiritually bankrupt Establishment ... [T]his second type is more typical of "emerging churches" in North America, while the first is more typical of the English scene (and to a lesser extent of Australia and New Zealand).
>
> (Drane 2006: 4)

The astute observer of this new phenomenon will realize that, as Bader-Saye points out, there are two types of adaptation by these churches to the post-modern world (Bader-Saye 2006). One type is concerned with a cultural and stylistic change only, and not with a change in theology or ecclesiasticism. By being "hip" or "cool" in their engagement with the changes of today, these churches are simply packaging the gospel for a new generation. This type of new church can fall under the label of "Evangelical Pragmatists". Bader-Saye also refers to another type, the "Post-Evangelical Emergents" (*ibid.*), wherein both methodology and theology, *and* form and content, have been adapted to today's concerns.

Within this new phenomenon, it is worth mentioning that some main-stream evangelicals do object to the Christian raves (Lau 2006). However, we can observe that some sub-groups are offering an interpretation of the Pagan shamanic experience of ecstasy within a Christian framework.

RAVE AND SECULAR ECSTASY

> For the majority of young people ... clubbing takes place in the context of a highly commercialised entertainment industry that incorporates clubs, magazines, national radio shows, recording companies and even travel agencies to arrange clubbing-based holidays. (Lynch & Badger 2006: 28)

In our last example, it is pertinent to contrast the Pagan and Christian techno-shamans with a group of agents that interpret their "techno-shamanic" experiences without serious consideration of spiritual/religious concepts and discourse. Through this contrast, we hope to give further clarification to the unique aspects of the Pagan interpretation and to further explain the field of ecstasy interpretation in general.

Lynch and Badger suggest that in order to understand the religious sig-nificance of raving, we need to conduct "more detailed and critical stud-ies of "mainstream" events and networks" (*ibid.*: 30). This is because, for some – perhaps even for the majority – raving is not a spiritual experience but rather a "rush of chemicals" (Jackson 2004; Malbon 1999; Nixon 2009), which can be natural or induced. Lynch and Badger also suggest that the dis-courses of "rave imaginary" discussed by St John as present in the psytrance/neo-trance scene (St John 2004b), and alternative spiritualities in general, have not had much impact on the secular "mainstream" scene (Lynch & Badger 2006). In resonance with this idea, Gavanas notes the lack of studies on mainstream EDM communities that are *not* explicitly defined as "spirit-ual" by their participants (Gavanas 2008). Thus mainstream EDM spaces can be defined by their lack of explicit religious iconography or intentions, and therefore contrasted with the explicitly religious/spiritual interpretations of the Neo-Pagan and Christian agents. Even when religious icons are used in mainstream scenes, they are usually used in an "ironic way, to convey the importance of a dance event but without any sense of commitment to particular metaphysical beliefs" (Lynch & Badger 2006: 29). Some of the literature on EDM discusses the mainstream EDM scene as a degraded form of the underground rave experience, due to its lack of religio-spiritual orientation (Sylvan 2005; Tramacchi 2000). However, it could be suggested that promoting EDM events as an exclusively religious experience could alienate those not interested in religious/spiritual experiences, instead of drawing them in to such events (Lynch & Badger 2006). Lynch and Badger argue that despite this perception, the mainstream scene does offer a type of "religious experience" – albeit one that is not attached to explicit religious ideas: a "secular religious experience" (Bullivant 2008: 8). The transformational experience of raves has been reported in all forms of EDM events, although in different ways.

Lynch and Badger suggest that the mainstream scene offers a form of self-actualization rather than traditional religious enlightenment (Lynch & Badger 2006). They summarize the shared interpretive framework as consisting of: a welcoming and accepting community; an association of clubbing with personal autonomy, authenticity, self-expression and tolerance; and the promotion of self-development. In the Australian clubbing environment, Nixon observes a similar framework (Nixon 2009), in which participants were attracted to EDM events by the type of music/DJs, a friendly and tolerant social network and "relational consciousness" (Hay 2007, discussed later in this chapter) or primordial (ir)religious experience (PRE). The PRE is an altered state of consciousness (ASC) described by participants and induced by environment, drugs and dancing. The descriptions of ecstasy from these secular spaces sounds remarkably like the states described in most of the neo-shamanic and shamanic literature as ASCs (Gauthier 2004; Green 2010; Insane Events 2009; Nixon 2009). It is described in the interviews from Nixon's research as a "perfect moment" or "peak experience" (Nixon 2009). However, it must be noted that these participants often do not interpret the PRE experience within a spiritual framework, choosing to see it instead as a by-product of the EDM experience, such as being "all neurons and chemicals" or as "the vibe and the electricity [being] off the hook" (*ibid.*: 59) – for example, in Nixon's research one participant stated when asked about the connection between raves and spirituality:

> *Mr X:* There is an element of spiritualness to it, without bringing any religious content or context into the word spirituality, and I think it's only because of that experience you're sharing with others that can seem a little unexplainable, a little more than human, a connection or something, you may have a connection

with the music and therefore with the people around you sharing
that music, but I'd say that that's as far as it goes.   (Nixon 2009)

Lynch and Badger also found that "mainstream" clubbers in England considered religious or spiritual talk in relation to clubbing as "naïve", the "consequence of overuse of recreational drugs or the expression of an over-idealised
view of club culture" (Lynch & Badger 2006: 33). This has been supported
further by interviews conducted by Nixon, wherein participants were reluc-
tant to see their clubbing activities in a religious framework (Nixon 2009).
From these participants' perspective, the DJ would be seen as a type of secular techno-shaman who, by his or her choice of music and sound/light-
ing system, creates an ambiance conducive to certain secular experiences of
dancing, drugs, music and socializing. For these agents, the ecstatic experience does not have to – and often should not – be viewed as a religious phenomenon. Thus these actors directly contrast and contradict the (neo)Pagan
actors that are the focus of this book. This is because their raving and peak
experiences are not given spiritual/religious meaning and do not necessarily
provide these participants with connection to spirits, nature and the earth.

THE PRIMORDIAL (IR)RELIGIOUS EXPERIENCE (PRE) AND
THE CULTURAL LENS

All EDM scholars seem to have noted the indescribable nature of this peak
EDM experience, referred to as "ephemeral" or "beyond words" (Gauthier
2004: 77–8). It has even been suggested by some EDM scholars that this
experience is *the* reason for the existence of EDM culture (*ibid.*). According
to Gauthier, the peak rave experience amounts to losing oneself in connection with others; it is the seeking of what Bastide (cited in *ibid.*) calls
"instituant" religion, out of which institutionalized forms of religion emerge.
The instituant is discussed as the catalyst for an individual's participation in
the EDM scene and their transformation through meaning (re)construction
(*ibid.*).

Following these accounts, the altered states described by the various
techno-shamans in this chapter can be seen as primordial religious experiences (PREs), when viewed according to the "relational consciousness" concept discussed by David Hay, who describes the PRE as an awakening to
relational consciousness: the understanding that we are all intricately connected to the universe (Hay 2007). This realization can be understood as a
physiological, psychological, anthropological/sociological and/or historical
fact (Eliade 1964; Hay 1990, 2007; St John 2004a; 2006).

Hay discusses the cross-cultural, cross-denominational findings of
D'Aquili and Newberg (see D'Aquili & Newberg 1999) that suggest a
physiological basis for transcendent experience (Hay 2007). D'Aquili and

159

Newberg's studies were conducted with Tibetan Buddhists and subsequently with Franciscan nuns. In both groups, similar physiological changes were detected by CT scans during the acts of meditation (Buddhists) and prayer (Franciscans). Hay suggests that certain physiological effects occur when someone is in the midst of a PRE or meditative state (or ASC) (*ibid.*). The most dramatic are the changes in blood flow to the parietal lobes and the frontal lobes. Part of the function of the parietal lobes is to position the individual in space by creating a three-dimensional image of their surroundings. Thus, when the blood flow to the parietal lobe is restricted, the effect is a loss of distinction between the self and the rest of reality. This effect is enhanced by increased blood flow to the frontal lobe, which causes a heightened level of awareness. There are also changes in the thalamus, which controls the flow of sensory information. Hay suggests that the end result is the "experience that the isolated self is replaced by the sense that all is One, combined with an intensely enhanced experience of reality – the conviction of being in touch with ultimate reality" (*ibid.*: 79).

Interestingly, in D'Aquili and Newberg's research (as discussed in Hay 2007), the main difference between the Christian nuns and the Buddhist monks studied seems to lie in their systems of belief. The Christians were found to have a focus on language and the Buddhists on vision. This was reflected in increased blood flow to the respective areas of the brain in each group of practitioners. Prior expectation or conscious intentions appeared to play a part in the specifics of the altered state entered into (*ibid.*).

Following this point, while there is a strong link between the use of psychedelics, ASC-inducing technologies and the experience of mystic-religious experiences for many people, Partridge reminds us that presuppositions, worldviews, settings and upbringing shape how a person will understand or interpret such an experience (Partridge 2005). Partridge makes reference to Bowker, who argues that LSD does not necessarily induce religious experience, but primarily initiates a state of excitation and arousal that is interpreted by one's social-cultural background (*ibid.*: 132).

Although not found directly in the field of secular rave culture, it is worth pointing out that one's social-cultural background can lead to the interpretation of these experiences as "irreligious". As Bullivant explains, these are experiences of deconversion in which people can feel an awareness of the absence of God and/or a feeling of loneliness and/or solitude in the world (Bullivant 2008). Although poorly studied, this experience of the irreligious demonstrates how varied and extreme the interpretations of the experience of ecstasy can be when filtered through individual cultural lenses.

CONCLUSION: BACK TO BOURDIEU

In terms of Bourdieu's theories of the field and of social capital, we will focus on the notions of accumulated cultural capital (such as knowledge of the arts, educational attainment, vocal accent) and symbolic capital (status attached to a person because of his or her moral qualities, charisma or type of job). Although some authors have tried to adapt Bourdieu's theory of cultural capital (Bourdieu 1993) to different settings (religious capital: Innaccone 1990; spiritual capital: Verter 2003), this chapter, for the purpose of this analysis, focuses on the religious field as operating across his four defined forms of capital, rather than being a form of religious or spiritual capital itself.

In this sub-field of rave ecstasy, people who experience such phenomena gain a certain type of symbolic capital for having accessed the mysterious/numina. The trigger appears to be the same for the three agents (that is, the Neo-Pagan, the Christian and the secular) analysed in this chapter: the combination of a specific type of music beat, a sense of togetherness, a type of dance and, for some, the consumption of hallucinogenic or other substances. However, the types of cultural capital (linked to this symbolic capital of ecstasy) promoted by each of these agents differ. Although the cultural capital of each type of agent is quite eclectic, we find the differential dominance of a Neo-Pagan, of a Christian and of a secular cultural capital. As Dianteill reminds us, "for Bourdieu, the religious field must not be conceived as an immutable reality: a structural genesis exists for it in relation to transformations of social structure" (Dianteill 2003: 544).

Over the course of this discussion, we have described three interpretations of ecstasy induced by the EDM experience. Pagan, Christian and secular dance music enthusiasts all see the primordial religious experiences induced by this environment through different lenses. Using Bourdieu's theory in this supposedly eclectic field, we have been able to observe a type of economy of ecstasy in which the cultural capital of three agents is in competition in the sub-field of rave culture and the (ir)religious experience. In other words, these cultural transactions of the meaning behind these (ir)religious experiences are in conflict, and thus structure this sub-field of (ir)religion into largely separate scenes with competing interpretations of ecstasy. Thus we have been able to distinguish Neo-Pagan interpretations of ecstasy from those of two other competing agents within the sub-field of rave ecstasy.

11. SACRAMENTAL SONG: THEOLOGICAL IMAGINATION IN THE RELIGIOUS MUSIC OF AMERICAN PAGANS

Christopher Chase

There can be no doubt that the cultural study of music is experiencing something of a renaissance. Over the past decade, works by Stephen Marini, Miriam Ghazza, Michael D. McNally, Tricia Rose, David W. Stowe, Mark Slobin, Susan McClary and Michael D. Largey have largely redefined the way that scholars talk and write about the roles played by music in people's lives. No longer the sole province of formal analysis, this "new musicology" incorporates insights from sociology, economics, aesthetics, gender studies, psychoanalysis and theology (for some important and representative works in this field relating to theology, see Largey 2006; Marini 2003; Stowe 2004).

This last point – theology – is the focus of this chapter. But already I have hit a snag, because among Pagans the term "theology" is often viewed rather sceptically. There are good reasons for this, for – whether in a bookstore, a catalogue or an online site – the term "theology" tends to have an unspoken word in front of it. And it is not just any word. It is the word "Christian", a term to which Pagans often react defensively. But theology itself is much broader than the Christian tradition alone. While there have been scholarly works on topics as broad as Hindu and Jewish theology, academics have also begun to take some of the first systematic assessments of "Pagan theologizing" (for examples, see York 2003; Paper 2005; Harvey 2005). Pagans, like followers of other religions, invoke what Mary F. Bednarowski calls the "theological imagination" (Bednarowski 1989): they engage in questions about the place of human beings in the world, especially relative to other beings – gods, goddesses, nature spirits and/or ancestors; and they make claims and inquiries about death, suffering, morality and the right way to live in the world. These questions are part of what many scholars of religion have come to call the *theoretical* dimension of religion, alongside the *socio-historical* and the *practical* or ritual dimension.[1]

This is where music comes so forcefully into play. For those used to thinking about religion as the study of revealed texts, it may not be immediately apparent that music plays such a central role in religion. But, as David Stowe contends, music is a carrier, a transmitter and a powerful means of inculcating religious doctrines (Stowe 2004: 3). It is also highly contested and contestable; the presence and type of music used in a service can give a student of religion invaluable insight into the power relationships behind different bodies of believers and why they separate from some or congregate with others.

In the umbrella community of Paganism within the United States, this is certainly no less true than for other traditions (Clifton & Harvey 2004: 1). Certain songs have become shorthand for concepts of divinity and gender, for organizational identity and for criticizing other non-Pagan traditions (especially Christianity). It is precisely these forms of discursive "coding" to which I wish to turn, for Pagan music itself openly articulates theological identities and boundaries. To understand the role of popular music in Paganism, we need a sense of the religious claims for truth (and thus claims for power) being made. Obviously, music and its typologies constitute an enormous topic, so we need more clarification as to the subject-matter of this chapter.

The word "Pagan" has also been identified with at least four sets of separate discourses in Western intellectual history, and continues to be used in all these ways by a variety of sources (e.g. Hutton 1999: 4) – some of which occasionally intersect with self-identified contemporary Pagans, among whom Paganism is also an internally contested term. For the sake of simplicity, clarity and consistency, I will focus on those sets of communities that identify themselves as contemporary religious Pagans in the geographical and cultural context of the United States, with the understanding that they participate in an extended set of discourses that is more expansive and extensive than the twentieth century or even the United States itself. Of course, even using this limited scope, I could not begin to analyse in detail the immense scope of Pagan theological discourse. Yet I hope to generate some insight of general thematics and processes to Pagan ideas of "nature religion", its attendant dialectic of opposition and embrace, and the socio-sacred spaces such as the Otherworld and Ocean Mother.[2] These are the concepts I see most at work in American Pagan music today.

By "Pagan music", I mean the broad scope of rhythmic audial culture that members of these Pagan communities either appropriate from outside their own cultural bounds or produce themselves for any number of purposes. In terms of the goals of this specific volume, we also need to characterize the meaning of the word "popular". In talking about Pagan popular music, this chapter will be not be concerned with music primarily produced for ritual use – although the protean inventiveness of Paganism makes such boundaries semi-permeable at best. The "popular-ness" of Pagan popular music derives from its primary production and consumption at the vernacular level of entertainment and instruction, inscribed within or outside large-scale commercial distribution networks.

Just as contemporary Paganisms are working out their own social, economic, political and other purposes in their cultural contexts, so too do they work through their own theological and doctrinal problematics. Whereas larger institutionally focused traditions such as Judaism, Christianity and Buddhism have had centuries to develop their own forums and vehicles for such debates and contentions, most contemporary Pagan traditions are comparatively new, and few have achieved a geo-specific critical social mass to build such institutions. Where they exist, they are often embryonic in scope. Music – especially popular music outside of ritual – has formed one of these spaces for conceiving and articulating what Benedict Anderson calls "imagined community" (Anderson 1983: 7). As musicologist Christopher Small points out, music, broadly conceived, is inherently social and communicative, involving an ever-widening web of kinship related by production and consumption (Small 1998). As others demonstrate, music and its meanings are also negotiated in the process of reception, and cannot simply be defined as a "homology" of the community from which the music came (Frith 2007: 294). As a means of constructing community, it necessarily posits and argues over socio-historical and theological boundaries. In a religious context such as Paganism, this takes on even more importance, since Pagan religions can be very different from one another despite sharing a number of family resemblances.

NATURE WORSHIP AND OPPOSITIONAL POLITICS AS THEOLOGICAL COMMITMENTS

In the United States, the general Pagan focus on living and practising collectively (and ideally) alongside and in the midst of the natural world (both as a physical church structure and as an environmental partner) has provided a uniquely appropriate vehicle and a habitat for cultivation of religious experience, especially in terms of music. While the Abrahamic traditions generally have focused on word and text as the centre for revelation and contact with sacred power, contact points with "Nature" (as culturally inherited and constructed) is often much more the focus and generating engine for theological engagement. In the United States, Paganism quickly became engrained in an artistic, literary (and, I would contend, religious) impulse that has come to be called "Nature Religion" (Clifton 2006: 42–5).

Rather than a resurrection of ancient historical or ethnic traditions, the American transformation of Paganism found its grounding in the hierophanies of Ralph Waldo Emerson, Henry David Thoreau and John Muir, and aspects of the mid-twentieth-century counter-cultural movement, especially environmental politics and second-wave feminism (see Albanese 1990: 83–105; Fuller 2001: 87–98). The ideological power and influence of the Transcendentalists and their focus on "Nature" has, of course, been well covered elsewhere, and needs no explication here. But it deserves to be mentioned that American landscape, identified with the legacy of Amerindian peoples' alleged stewardship, became a rallying symbol for the counter-culture's Cold War protest against the possibility of nuclear annihilation and technocratic dominance (see Roszak 1969). It also became a sacramental nexus point for American Pagans who began to understand their primary kinship as to the earth, rather than capitalism, militarism and Establishment-religiosity that enabled the domination of "Nature".

Songs from counter-cultural artists thus often reflected a diffused spiritual dimension cloaked in a political critique of the dominant culture. Witness 1971's "Earth Mother" from Grace Slick and Paul Kantner's *Sunfighter* album. Jack Traylor's closely miced acoustic guitar belts out folk-rock steeped in Fairport Convention-like riffs while a loose chorus sings:

> Once there was a garden
> It gave us all we need
> Then it grew so barren
> All because of greed
> …
> Its not your fault you're ill now
> It's the men who went before
> Your children are at your side now
> Don't worry anymore.
>   (Kantner & Slick 1971)[3]

While the counter-culture itself changed, transformed and mainstreamed throughout the decade in the United States, ten years later these same concerns would be channelled in a record album alongside powerful statements of gay pride, solidarity with Amerindians and strident anti-nuclear activism. Charlie Murphy's *Catch the Fire* practically became a legend in the grassroots American progressive community. Incorporating ritual chant, Murphy wrote "Burning Times", which tells a traditional narrative of medieval witchcraft persecution by Christians, and links this mythico-historical event to ongoing environmental devastation and pollution of the earth. The song is ubiquitous in the American Pagan community, and has been referenced or covered by many artists. In using Deena Metzger's Goddess Chant ("Isis, Astarte, Diana, Hecate, Demeter, Kali, Inanna") as the refrain for his song, Murphy played an integral role in the fusing of Wiccan fertility cults and historical representations of specific goddesses with a unified model of divine feminine power (the "Mother Goddess") and American "nature religion", giving voice to several discursive impulses at once. Introduced by a short mournful cello vamp and hand-drums beating out an insistent pulse for each beat, Murphy's descending guitar line accompanies his description of a ritual gathering of witches, and their eventual suppression of the "nature people" at the hands of those worshiping "a dead man on a cross".

165

The song not only reinforces the fusion of witchcraft and nature worship already at work in American Paganism, but also accuses the Catholic Church of killing nine million women as part of the Inquisition. Moreover, Murphy says the harm done to the witches still continues today in the form of environmental damage and exploitation against the earth, which Murphy refers to lyrically as a "witch" and healer, giving today's witches energy and courage.[4] Through constant cover versions from different Pagan musicians and performances at American festivals, Murphy's song has attained the status of common cultural currency. The theological co-identification of the earth and the Pagan community as engaged in a common struggle along religious, gender and environmental trajectories continues today among American pagans. This is not to say impulses towards social accommodation are not also present, but it does mark familiarity with, and performance of, oppositional resistance politics as a core element of Pagan culture in the United States.

POLARITY: FROM OPPOSITION TO LOVE, FROM DIVISION TO UNITY

In their embrace of the earth's body as witch, healer and Mother Goddess, American Pagans continued to develop a theme articulated in the deepest heart of its canonical literature. No less an American poet than Walt Whitman foreshadowed much of the same loving devotion to the divine power manifesting in and within the wonders of the natural world that can be seen among contemporary Pagans. In "Starting at Paumanok", he wrote: "was somebody asking to see the soul? ... behold the body includes and is the meaning, the main concern, and includes the soul; Whoever you are, how superb and how divine is your body, or any part of it!" (Whitman 1921: 19).

Indeed, Whitman constructs a song of ecstatic love that would be familiar to most any contemporary devotee of Pagan spirituality:

> Lover divine and perfect Comrade
> Waiting content, invisible yet, but certain,
> Be thou my God.
> ...
> Or Time and Space
> Or shape of Earth divine and wondrous,
> Or some fair shape I viewing, worship,
> Or lustrous orb of sun or star by night,
> Be ye my Gods.
> (Whitman 1904: 213)

From Whitman's pen, the cosmic frontier becomes a heavenly space where the constituents – even the dimensional possibilities of temporality and extension are invited to take their place in a royal ontology of Being – create

166

a romantic metaphysics inclusive of both human identity and worshipful submission of the gods. Decades later, in positioning themselves at the vanguard of ecological religiosity and prophetic voice against the exploitation of women and Mother Earth, Pagans held open the possibility of assimilating their enemies within their matrix of extended kinship between themselves, other beings and the cosmos itself as they drew upon the prophetic power of Whitman and others (Ellwood 1994: 34). In these narratives, the invitation can be extended to a friendly observer, but sometimes the visitor is an "inquisitional" antagonist seeking to harm the community or its deity. The religious praxis of the group then serves to convert opposition into allegiance though a hierophany, or even a hierogamy.

In the early 1970s, P. E. I. (Isaac) Bonewits, founder of Ar nDriaiocht Fein (ADF; 'Our Own Druidry") published "I Fell in Love with the Lady" in the pages of *Green Egg*, and recorded it for his first album in 1988:

> I crept into the woods one night
> To spy upon their dance.
> I saw happy, holy dance –
> I fell into a trance!
> I joined into the dancing then
> And when the Great Rite came,
> The Lady reached out Her hand to me;
> She called me by my name![5]

Bonewits' character is initially a Catholic witch hunter sent to locate and destroy Goddess worshippers during the "Burning Times". But instead of fulfilling his mission of destruction, he is bewitched by the holy and righteous nature of their dancing, and as a final act of magical enticement, the Goddess reveals her power over the potential antagonist by knowing and calling him specifically into a hierogamous sexual encounter. By the end of the song, Bonewits's narrator confesses that his personal identity has changed and his social allegiance switched, telling the listener that the Jesuits know what he has done and will be coming after him. Nonetheless, being properly connected to the Goddess now, he has faith that they too will "come away with none", just as he did.

The role of love – especially the protean power of *eros* – can also illuminate and mediate other theological dimensions in Pagan music, such as the relationship between humans and sacred places (like the Otherworld) or sacred persons (such as the Goddess). An excellent account of the influence of dreams and love relationships involving the Otherworld can be found in Greenwood (2000: 24–5, 166–7). In 1996, a popular Pagan songbook was written by Hugin the Bard and published by Llewellyn Publications. *A Bard's Book of Pagan Songs* was divided into several sections, with the first section adapting stories from the medieval Welsh collection known as the Mabinogion. Other sections focus on specific devotions for the different holy days of the Wiccan and Druidic ritual year and other topics. Two important songs, "Love on the Astral Plane" and "They Call Us Witches", illustrate the role of love in forming bonds between human and "other-than-human" sacred persons. In "They Call Us Witches", Hugin recounts the mythic "Burning Times" narrative in song. He interweaves the survival and rebirth of the Pagan tradition with restatements of the Wiccan Rede ("We swear to ne'er do harm to any living thing") and ascribes to witches the activity of the Goddess as described in the 'Charge of the Goddess" whether as the Great Mother or the Star Goddess ("We are love, we are love … Love is all Our Lady asks in due").[6]

While introducing his ballad "Love on the Astral Plane", Hugin notes that its origin lay in a conversation he had with Carl Weschcke of Llewellyn Publications.[7] The tongue-in-cheek tune is founded on the common conception that there is a superimposed "Otherworld", in which unseen but significant activity can take place, such as contact between human and other-than-human persons. Likewise, actions and activities in the Otherworld can lead to productive events in the material realm. In this case, Hugin as narrator has a romantic encounter in his dreams, but instead of dismissing it as mere fantasy, he sets out to locate the person in the material world that he encountered in the spiritual world. Thus Hugin's theological commitments to multiple realms of possible experience and corresponding mutual influence must be accounted for in attempting to understand his narrative progression.

Much theological discourse within esoteric, occult and Pagan circles is premised on this wider state of consciousness. For Hugin to create music using the Otherworld as a median space for interpersonal relationships, education and romantic love demonstrates multiple embedded spaces of power within Pagan religious discourse without any perceived need for explanation.

In other cases, time rather than space becomes the primary matrix for interacting with the Otherworld. In particular, auspicious times of power such as Samhain (a Celtic fire festival) can become the portal for extended kinship into the Otherworld, especially in the work of Canadian singer-songwriter Loreena McKennitt. McKennitt does not necessarily exclusively self-identify as a Pagan, but has produced a number of works highly regarded in the American Pagan community and often covered by artists at American Pagan festivals. While she seeks inspiration from a variety of religious and mystical traditions (itself a hallmark of contemporary Paganism), she has also used her music to glorify folk traditions explicitly venerated by Goddess worshippers and other Pagans.

In the song "Samhain Night", found on her 1989 album *Parallel Dreams*, she sings in the past tense and subjunctive mood of love, which is "not a simple thing". We learn that all her interactions with her lover are mediated through aspects of the natural world. She likens touching her lover's body and heart to the ever-distant moon exerting its pull on the earthly tides. The song's namesake is for many Pagans the start of the new year, and a time when the "veil" between the material and spiritual dimensions of consciousness are especially thin, suitable for traversing and communication.[8] In McKennitt's song, influences from and journeys to spaces such as the moon and the sun become vehicles for relation (and thus kinship) beyond the material world. Whereas Hugin's Otherworld lover is waiting to be found in the material world, McKennitt's emotive and phenomenological experience of kinship and natural forces binds her within the natural world to her lover in the Otherworld.

NATURE WORSHIP FROM OTHERWORLD TO OCEANWORLD: SACRED SEA, SACRED PERSON

For human beings, oceans occupy a particular ontological space similar to the Otherworld. Both present and distant, long existent in the imago as a space of fecund like and exotic wonder, recently the world of the ocean has come to the attention of academic theologians and other students of religion (Shaw & Francis 2008). As is often the case, Pagan practitioners have been engaged with the element of water more generally and oceans more specifically for far longer.

Pagan and indigenous cultures have long tied themselves to the seas and ocean as a primary way of identifying themselves and their sphere of socio-sacred relationships, especially as articulated in songs of power (J. J. Bradley 2008). Despite much of contemporary American Paganism's common emphasis on seasons and changes in those seasons as theological process, a number of ritual chants and popular devotional songs including water (especially the ocean) have emerged.[9] Alongside this trend, a number of well-known American Pagans have released popular music specifically honouring the seascape as the source of life and power.

In 1972, Gwydion Pendderwen published "Song of Mari" as part of his *Songs for the Old Religion* songbook. Based on a 1970 poem by Victor Anderson (co-founder of the Feri tradition), Pendderwen sung of a Goddess experience to ignite his passion for *eros*, as well as comfort in the face of darkness and death. She arrives to transform him "as sweet as the breath of the sea". Mari's feet are carried on the wave crests, her breath and movement intertwined with the rush of sea waves and the scent of the ocean's brine. She is not explicitly co-identified with the ocean, yet the name of the song reinforces her origin, as "Mari" is the ablative case for the Latin *mar*, or the sea (Pendderwen 1972).

While Pendderwen looked to ocean crests for the coming of Goddess power, Ruth Barrett and Cyntia Smith, in 1993's "Ocean Queen", understand

169

sea-borne waves of power as agents of personal transformation and rebirth. Mari, the ocean, is located as the source of all beginnings, a beginning predicated on an eternal return "… where I was born and to where I'll rest". As teleological and theological mother the nourishment of her "breasts" is the force that moulds and shapes the "islands" (of her human subjects/children. Not only are her children literally surrounded by and existent by means of her royal power, but her ontological positioning affords her of dark secrets given in dreams to her devotees. Barrett and Smith call and call again for Mari to heal them, toss and pull them, thus renewing their life force and purpose via her own (Barrett & Smith 1994).[10]

A different, but no less celebratory, view comes from the worldbeat acoustic folk ensemble KIVA. On its 1994 release *Finding the Balance Within* (and later reprised on a 1997 live album), KIVA's track "Star of the Sea" uses the technique of "recombinant mythology" to weave different cultural names for the divine ocean in a single blessing.[11] The term "Star of the Sea" comes from a Medieval Latin title for Mary, mother of Jesus in the Christian and Islamic religions. Many traditional qualities commonly ascribed to Mary, such as "compassion, forgiveness and grace", are read through the Latin connecting back to "Mother Mari". Most prominently, though, the song calls upon Yemayá, the Yoruba and Afro-Caribbean *orisha* of the sea. Accompanied with a prominent Latinized hand drum beat and tin whistle, "Star of the Sea" connects the performers and audience in an extended filial kinship network as the singers see Yemayá's renowned beauty in themselves, their sisters and kin – all of them Yemayá's children.[12]

The Ocean Mother is named, characterized and called under other aspects as well. Recalling the presence of Metzger's Goddess Chant in Charlie Murphy's music, the phrase "Isis, Mary, Aphrodite, Salmon Woman, Yemayá" forms a theological matrix for Craig Olson in his trance-worship ballad "Ave Stella Maris". Closing his 1999 release, *Beyond the Cedar Moon*, Olson calls his track an "altered-state song of devotion".[13] Olson emphasizes not simply the beautiful aspects of the Ocean Mother, but also her sublime awe as "Lady of the raging storm". Like Pendderwen and Anderson almost three decades earlier, she is not only mother but "Maiden of the Twilight", associated with the liminal boundary between land and sea and the cresting waves that such a boundary creates. Olson sets the devotional hymn as a call/response among dancers "on the shoreline" watching the ocean's transformation of the evening sun into shimmering reflected light. A choir echoes Olson's calls to Stella Maris, even as Olson sings of the courage her worshippers must have to answer her sublime power.

For other Pagan musicians, the importance of the ocean as manifest sacrality is emphasized through artistic, lyrical and instrumental over-determination (or "over-saturation") in the element of water and *orisha* worship. The all-female choral group Libana has produced a number of albums and associated songbooks. In their catalogue, the album *Night Passage* stands out for its association with the moon, the sea and other common emblems of Yemayá. While they display a tender awareness of many different musical and religious traditions, they dedicate a repetitive trance-like "undulating chant" to Yemayá. She is "Yemayá of the Ocean ... the Sea ... of Deep Waters ... of all Tears". Thus Libana connects the human/animal experience of creating salt water through sadness and joy with the protean divine feminine power of the ocean environment. Moreover, the cover art (*Moondrift #1*), along with the album title, suggests a seascape lit only by moonlight. The liner notes again frame the performers as concerned with life, death, renewal, emotional power and the lunar cycle as they sing "at the ocean's edge ... from coast to coast". Other devotional music aimed at the Ocean Mother in an American context also echoes powerful emotional, environmental and healing currents found in the more explicitly popular feminist choirsong.[14]

In other cases, the focus on Yemayá leads back recursively to a cultural saturation of material language expressed as Goddess aspects. In 1993, Robert Gass and On Wings of Song, a noted choral group, released *Ancient Mother*, a collection of songs based on diverse cultural and religious traditions. In his liner notes, Gass explains that his work "invokes the Ancient Mother, honoring and celebrating Her spirit with a wide range of musical styles commensurate with Her multi-faceted, multi-cultural nature". At least three out of the thirteen songs link oceanic aspects and goddesses such as Yemayá with the presence of the Ancient Mother. Yemayá has her own namesake track as the "powerful Mother ... of bottom-most water ... Queen of water ... Yemayá is the owner of rivers".[15] Other songs, including the bookend tracks "Ancient Mother" and "The Circle is Cast", call upon either Yemayá and/or other deities traditionally associated with the ocean. In addition, Gass arranges a track originally written by Goddess musician Lisa Thiel, "Lady of the Flowing Waters". On this track, different environmental regions and biomes, as well as the moons and stars, house the power and presence of the Goddess, literally saturating Nature with vitalistic feminine presence – a feminist restatement of Whitman's paean to the moons and suns as Gods.

The upshot of this recurrent emphasis on the Ocean Mother is twofold. First, these sets of characteristics reflect and transform concerns of contemporary Goddess theology into musical forms, both in terms of basic description (waves, sea) and also in terms of specific ocean goddesses such as Stella Mater and Yemayá.[16] This is especially true with regard to the focus on movement, rhythm, process and change. The human debt to this cosmogyny can in turn be expressed biologically at times of extreme emotion when ocean water is produced through crying, or by celebrating the presence of oceanic beauty/subliminity (or chaos) within her children. Second, this culturally saturated recurrence presents a sacramental identification with biophillic feminism as identified by theologians. In particular, Melissa

Raphael makes the case that uncontained and uncontestable water evokes the *sensus numinous*, especially for both "patriarchal religion and spiritual feminism" (Raphael 1996: 278). Co-identifying sacramental water with sacramentalist feminism, Raphael says it is the *mysterium tremendum et facinans* of "the ontological fluidity of women who will not stay in their place" (*ibid.*).

CONCLUSION: PLAY OF DYAD, PLAY OF KINSHIP

From the beginning of this chapter, I have demonstrated the musical involvement of American Pagans in what Bednarowski calls the "theological imagination" (Bednarowski 1989: 3–5) in American new religious movements. Bednarowski understands two main tasks of this "theological imagination". One, of course, is to draw out the implications of revelations and insights brought forth by the founders of such movements. The other main dimension, she suggests, is to place these insights and their developments within the main discursive model of American theology–dyadic polarities between seemingly exclusive categories (God/World, Sin/Salvation, etc.). The tensions between these polarities, she notes, can be productively stimulating. Contemporary Pagan culture is no exception, as we saw with its dyadic oppositional politics through the early 1970s and 1980s. Then – as now – Pagans often worked socio-historically, theologically and ritually within dyadic polarities such as "past/present" "matter/spirit," "male/female," and "nature/culture" to express various insights and carry out their religious practice.[17] Early British Traditional Wicca (often called BTW for short) took root as a bitheistic tradition framing both a god and goddess as ultimate concerns, and using a sacramental hierogamy as the culmination of their interaction. This reduction of energetic polarity to an apparent essentialized heterosexual fertility has been a difficult point of contention for some Pagans, who understand themselves as marginalized alongside gay, lesbian, bisexual and transgendered communities, rather than in opposition to them.

Yet, at the same time, theologians in contemporary American Paganism have not been completely comfortable working within and between dualistic set of conceptions, especially given that the parameters of such dualisms were originally set by traditions (like Christianity) that many Pagans perceive both as hostile to their own religiosity and as tool of technocratic exploitation. Some, like Isaac Bonewits, have embraced the playful pluralism of Pagan traditions as multiple modes of religious work. In this form of religious play various theological assumptions are valid for the given system being used at any given time. And within these orthopraxic traditions, practitioners embraced as many traditions as called to them, as few Pagans see protean supplies of universal power and energy limited by any single system (Bonewits 2006: 126).

172

Bonewits's own religious organization "Ár nDraíocht Féin: A Druid Fellowship" emphasizes three other-than-human sources of power and influence: "Shining Ones" (gods and goddesses), nature spirits and human ancestors, all of whom form a matrix within which members understand their lives and ritual workings. Other traditions represented by American adherents (like Asatru) tend to emphasize forms of polytheism. Even within Wicca, the model of the triple goddess (embraced especially by eclectic Wiccans) suggests an irreducible theological complexity, a refusal to be bound by the American dyadic tradition. True to form, American Pagans have demonstrated creativity working within and without the dyadic paradigm. In terms of gender, Pagan men have sought to construct spiritual masculinities outside what they see as constricting and oppressive models from the dominant culture.

Earlier I noted the importance of Charlie Murphy's song "Burning Times". No doubt it has made his dominant musical impression in the Pagan community. But his entire album *Catch the Fire* is deeply concerned with patriarchy, Amerindian liberation and a fierce defense of queer liberation. On the track "Under Capricorn" Murphy (and lyricist Jerah Chadwick) boldly reclaim sacramental male power as an ally to female power. Out of the realm of "patterns of male domination and alienation from self, each other, and the natural cycles of the Earth" they seek a veneration of universal masculine form. Male bodies with hands, arms and genitals are all aspects of a single Horned God, but are invoked by specific names as "Pan, Woden, Baphomet, Cernunos and Osiris". Rather than constructing a binary opposition with a "feminine", the co-equal pre-patriarchical male divine is "the god of choice, chance and death in the service of the life force". Lyrically, Chadwick's masculinity is a project seeking to undermine rather than reinforce binary oppositions. It is an agent of transformation through the "god of the crossroads, crossed fingers", climbing and crossing thresholds. Even the distinctions between God and Goddess are playful, protean and shifting, as the Horned God is "represented by ... the crescent moon of the goddess".[18]

It is within this community of poetic play that theological commitments in contemporary American Pagan music find their home. The "Ocean Mother" sacramentally points towards the greater unbounded ocean of existence in which humanity (as child of the mother) finds its ancestral link to all evolutionary life, from plants and animals to Mother Earth and Father Sun and the stars. Theologically speaking, love is the action by which both *eros* and *agape* occurs within this universal matrix, both within the human family and beyond to other-than-human persons. Embodied in flesh through the processes of generative creation and caretaking, Pagan theological imagination seeks to attune human consciousness towards becoming what philosopher Glen A. Mazis calls "earthbodies", or "sensual, perceptual and feeling conductors through which richer meaning flows than we can grasp intellectually" and through which communication with other animals and telluric forces is possible (Mazis 2002: 1). Others, like counter-cultural critic and intellectual historian Theodore Roszak, have come to call this type of consciousness "ecopsychology", an acknowledgment that at the deepest level the human "psyche remains sympathetically bonded to the Earth that mothered us into existence" (Roszak 1995: 4–5). We spoke earlier of commitments to multiple realms of experience and spaces of mutual influence. In different aspects, through Otherworld, Oceanworld and other realms, Pagan sacramental song gives voice to and defends Whitman's, Mazis's and Roszak's consciousness of deep evolutionary and cosmological kinship. To take a cue from Whitman: in the context of moons, suns, and oceans as manifest gods and goddesses, Pagan sacramental song embraces a dialectic of erotic generation and worshipful care towards the cosmos and its myriad inhabitants.

NOTES

1. In invoking these categories, I am of course indebted to the great historian of religion, Joachim Wach, who coined this schema. Wach's matrix tends to emphasize the role of religious experience, an approach I find helpful in discussing this topic. Bedarnowski herself does not use this schema; rather, she is concerned with comparative theology across the spectrum of new religious movements (see Bedarnowski 1989).
2. A fuller discussion of socio-sacrality and its relationship to music in the American context can be found in Chase (2006).
3. In personal communication, Traylor notes that the song was explicitly written as a "teaching tool". "Earth Mother" music and lyrics are © Jack Traylor 1971. All rights reserved. Used by permission.
4. "Burning Times" can be found on Murphy's album *Catch the Fire* (1981). Murphy's original track is widely available on the album *The Best of Pagan Song* (2004). As if a precursor to Murray, 1979 saw the publication of *The Spiral Dance*, one of the landmark texts of American Paganism, especially in its eclectic, environmental and gender-sensitive role. The author, Starhawk, makes the connection between abuse of Native spaces, technocratic exploitation and environmental destruction as a religious call to arms, as well as the claim of Catholic genocide against women (see Starhawk 1999: 22).
5. The melody is taken from folk artist Tim Hardin's 1969 "The Lady Came From Baltimore", later covered by Joan Baez and Johnny Cash. Apart from the fact that Bonewits loved to publish new "Paganized" songs based on existing melodies, his indebtedness to folk and popular music is clear here. Released on Isaac Bonewits and Friends, *Be Pagan Once Again!* cassette, Association for Consciousness Exploration, 1988, CD, 2003. Lyrics © 1974 Issac Bonewits. All rights reserved. Used by permission of the Bonewits estate.
6. There are many versions of the "Charge of the Goddess". Two representative versions for this case can be found in Leek (1971: 189–90); Starhawk (1999: 102–3); Hugin the Bard (2001: 191–2). *A Bard's Book of Pagan Songs: Stories and Music from the Celtic World* by Hugin the Bard © 1998 Llewellyn Worldwide, Ltd., 2143 Wooddale Drive, Woodbury, MN 55125. All rights reserved. Used by permission.
7. For Weschcke's continuing influence and significance, see Weschcke (2009: 14–19); Weschcke (1974: 1, 4).
8. Medieval Irish sagas tend to emphasize the prevalence of other-than-human persons (such as elves) on Samhain, while the nineteenth-century British folklorist James Frazer

wrote of Samhain as a time for deceased human spirits in particular to abound. See Rogers (2002: 19–20).

9. Paradigmatic examples would include Zsuzanna Budapest, "We All Come from the Goddess" (this chant originated in the published work of Budapest's Dianic coven in the late 1970s); Oothoon, "Evocation of the Goddess"; Selena Fox, "Song of the Witch" in Jim Alan and Selena Fox, *Circle Magick Songs*.

10. Barrett and Smith's language echoes a tone remarkably resonant with Theodore Roszak's Gnostic call for a personal and cultural "apocatastasis", a spiritual renewal that embraces the broken, heals and refashions anew. Roszak traditionally has been heralded as a prophetic voice for contemporary Paganism. See Adler (1997: 27–8); Roszak (1973: 421–3).

11. Here I am drawing upon the work of Michael Largey, an ethnomusicologist and scholar of Vodou, who defines "recombinant mythology" as the selective reassembly of culturally saturated mythological figures and historical narratives in order to create a usable past for specific moral and ritual uses. See Largey (2006: 70–73). As will also be seen in the music of Craig Olson, Mary is one of several sacred persons who is claimed within contemporary Paganism as an expression of divine feminine power. KIVA, "Star of the Sea", *Live at the Forest Inn: Volume 1*, self-published, 2006. Lyrics © KIVA 1995. All rights reserved. Used by permission.

12. For an excellent short discussion of Yemayá in an American context, see De La Torre (2004: 36, 45, 54, 72–4). Although it cannot be fully discussed here, the reader is advised that American Pagans have often addressed, interacted with and drawn upon Afro-Caribbean theology as part of the Pagan revival. See Buckland (1971: 123–31); Murray (1996: 23–5).

13. Craig Olson and Joanna Powell Colbert, lyrics for "Ave Stella Maris", found on http://craigolsonband.bandcamp.com/track/ave-stella-maris (accessed January 2011); Craig Olson, "Ave Stella Maris", *Beyond The Cedar Moon*, CD, Mud Bay Records, 1999. Lyrics © 1999 Craig Olson. All rights reserved. Used by permission.

14. For examples, see Arthen (1993: 25); Murphy, "Mother Ocean", *Catch the Fire*. "Yemaya" lyrics are © Marytha Paffrath 2000. All rights reserved. Used by permission.

15. The liner notes of the album *Ancient Mother* are © Spring Hill Music 1993. All rights reserved. Used by permission.

16. There is a growing movement to identify Goddess discourse as "thealogy" rather than "theology", to reflect the ultimate concern with gender and embodiment in the titular language of the discipline. See Reid-Bowen (2007). I am very sympathetic to this trend, but I have used the more conventional term here to minimize confusion.

17. Set to Richard Wagner's overtures, Alex Sanders's infamous 1970 album of ritual initiation, *A Witch is Born*, exemplifies strict attention to gender dyads as a necessary ceremonial component both for him and his prominent students Janet and Stewart Farrar. Dyads have worked across each other as well. In Llewellyn Publishing's short-lived journal *New Dimensions* (1963–4), Gareth Knight explains the significance of "The Empress" in the Tarot as part of a regular column (Knight 1963: 13–14). Knight identifies her "lower" (material) aspects as the female consciousness of the Earth's planetary being, similar to the concept of "Mother Nature". But the terrifying experience of encountering the enormity of this consciousness is tied to masculine elemental forces of the god Pan. Participation with this consciousness is therefore framed along the kinship dyad of "Mother/Father" and its further implication for the worshipper as "Parent/Child". Knight explains the "higher" or spiritual aspects of "The Empress" as the Qabalistic Ain Soph- the "great unmanifest feminine principle". The dyad of "material/spiritual" is thus again interwoven with "female/male".

18. Charlie Murphy and Jerah Chadwick, "Under Capricorn", *Catch the Fire*. Lyrics © Jerah Chadwick 1981. All rights reserved. Used by permission.

12. THE RISE OF THE CELTIC CYBER-DIASPORA: THE INFLUENCE OF THE "NEW AGE" ON INTERNET PAGAN COMMUNITIES AND THE DISSEMINATION OF "CELTIC" MUSIC

Narelle McCoy

The Irish diaspora provides an enormous consumer base for the selling of "Irishness" and nostalgia. However, the appropriation of the word "Celtic" as a marketing tool has expanded this target audience significantly, which has coincided with a renewed interest in "Celtic" mysticism and spirituality. The "New Age" movement is at the forefront of the Celtic renaissance. The plethora of Celtic websites advertising such wide-ranging topics as Druidism, Bardic paths, Celtic Wiccan ritual and Celtic reconstructionism bear testament to a renewed interest in Paganism and nature-based spirituality. The path to Celtic Pagan spirituality appears to centre on several core beliefs, some of which include cultivation of a creative spirit, reverence for the earth and a belief in early Celtic cosmology. The dissemination of Celtic mysticism via New Age websites invites anyone who shares these core beliefs to identify as Celtic, and more particularly as Celtic Pagans. This chapter will examine the various types of Celtic musics promoted on a variety of Celtic Pagan websites under the banner of Celtic popular music, and explore the way in which "Celtic" has become the vehicle for expressions of Paganism in late modern consumer societies.

THE CELTIC/IRISH CONFUSION

The Irish diaspora was exacerbated by the Irish famine that started in 1845. This generated a "sustained and continuous emigration" that saw the exodus of 2.5 million people between 1845 and 1855, a migration that profoundly altered the social and cultural structure of Ireland (Luddy & McLoughlin 2002: 567). Mary Robinson, the former president of Ireland, stated in her address to the Houses of the Oireachtas that the Polish–Irish Society in Cracow and the Mashonaland Irish Society in Zimbabwe bear testament to the notion that "Irishness" is not simply territorial. For impoverished emigrants leaving their homeland, their language, traditional music and dance were often the only cultural inheritance they could take with them.

There are over seventy million people who make up the Irish diaspora (Kenny 2003: 135), scattered as far afield as the Americas, South Africa, Australia and New Zealand (Bielenberg 2000). Their influence cannot be underestimated, so it is hardly surprising that these people would provide a ready market for the packaging and selling of Irish products in their many forms. This may explain the plethora of websites catering to all Irish needs, which include a wide range of products such as shamrocks, Aran Island vests, heraldry, traditional Irish musical instruments, books of children's names, song books, international festivals, holy water from the Shrine of Knock and wake items for mourning the dead. The interchangeable use of the terms "Irish" and "Celtic" on many of these websites may have compounded the confusion about the meaning of "Celtic", so much so that the *Irish Companion to Traditional Music* suggests that the term "Celtic music" is "increasingly used in Britain and the US to denote 'Irish'" (Vallely 1999: 64). This confusion may have been exacerbated further by the British Broadcasting Company's 1986 popular television programme *The Celts*, a six-part documentary that showcased the music of the then-emerging Irish artist Enya. As well as composing the score for the series, she was featured at the start of each episode, and in two episodes that included her video clips. She subsequently released an album of the same name, perhaps cementing in the general public's perception the interchangeability of the words "Irish" and "Celtic".

Hale and Payton suggest that the term "Celtic", as applied to the people and languages of Cornwall, Ireland, Wales, Brittany, the Isle of Man and Scotland, "is in many ways a construction dating from the early modern period and the development of certain academic disciplines" (Hale & Payton 2000: 8). In his book *The Last of the Celts*, Marcus Tanner states that Celtic revivals that have occurred over "many centuries have had little direct connection to the lands or the people they claim as their inspiration" (Tanner 2004: 8). He further opines that the notion of the Celt has been fashioned by others to "act as a counterweight to what they perceived as deficiencies in their own societies; as symbols and representations of otherness, their factual existence has become increasingly unnecessary" (*ibid.*). In *The Celts: The Construction of a Myth*, Malcolm Chapman presents the idea that the Celts, as a recognizable people, are a fantasy. He suggests that modern day "Celts" are only united in their opposition and resistance to the establishment – whether government or mainstream religion (Chapman 1992: 228). The notion of what defines a "Celt" is robustly contested in academic circles and, although there have been a number of definitions, often based on "language or material culture, none seems to provide an adequate description of the variety of 'Celtic' phenomena that are flourishing" (Hale & Payton 2000: 1). Amy Hale and Shannon Thornton examine this conundrum in relation to the Celtic Music and Arts Festival in San Francisco, which is described as a "pan-Celtic event but where 'Irish' served as the ethnic umbrella" (Hale & Thornton 2000: 100). They acknowledge that there was representation by other communities but that the Irish music component was by far the strongest – although this may be due to the fact that the organizer was the Irish Arts Foundation (*ibid*.: 99). The other mitigating factor could be the significant numbers of people who migrated to America during the diaspora, and who still claim Irish heritage – which could explain the proliferation of Irish arts and music organizations and the dominance of Irish music at supposedly "Celtic" events. In her article on religion and the internet, Monica Emerich states that the "great majority of the sites speak to Irish traditions and culture with little mention of the other Celtic territories of Brittany, Cornwall, the Isle of Man, Scotland, and Wales" (Emerich 2003: 23).

Since the advent of *Riverdance,* a pastiche of step dancing, traditional instruments and Irish mythology, which burst on to the world stage as a seven-minute interval "filler" at the 1994 Eurovision Song Contest, the public imagination appears to have been captivated by a craze for Celtic/Irish "culture" and an imagined "Celtic" past. While it may appear that *Riverdance* was an overnight success, it was actually part of the "Irish cultural renaissance" that saw the cultural landscape transformed as international acts toured the world, the film industry flourished, Ireland achieved unprecedented sporting success and the Celtic Tiger roared (Keohane *et al.* 2006). The descendants of the diaspora eagerly embraced this attractively packaged and nostalgic commodity, but the success of *Riverdance* is far more wide-reaching and complex, as it is "invested with the desires and filled out with the fantasies of the consumer/spectator/audience in a mutually fascinated gaze that constitutes the scene of the performance" (*ibid*.). The public thirst for the "authentic" in an increasingly globalized world may go some way towards explaining the desire for many to connect with a simpler time, divorced from the technologically advanced present. Joep Leersen points out that Celtic culture is on the periphery, and therefore has been imbued with a "mystical otherworldliness, exiled from the mainstream of historical progress" (Leersen 1996: 8). Following this train of thought, he opines that, as Ireland is the most peripheral of the Celtic lands, it is no surprise that it is often focused on as the place where there are the most traceable vestiges of culture and tradition. However, he points out that:

> the common-place permeates Irish-related discourse: from the often and enthusiastically repeated truism that Ireland remained outside the sphere of conquest of the Roman Empire ... until the pulp fiction and New Age elucubrations of the present times.
>
> (*Ibid*.: 9)

Norman Davies, in his attempt to define this growing fascination with the "Celtic" legacy, suggests that "Celticity":

combines a romantic attachment to a perceived Celtic heritage with a fascination for mysticism and animist spirituality that are taken to form its essential adjunct. It is linked to reinvigorated nationalist movements, to the ecological movement, which shares a similar empathy for the spirits of nature, and also to the rise of "New Age" neo-paganism.   (Davies 1999: 91)

Marcus Tanner also comments on the romanticism linked with the search for Celtic identity, stating that

revivals tended mainly to reinforce an image of Celtic societies as peripheral. They are quaint, rural, fairy-like, not quite real and something that the inhabitants of the "real" world can escape to when they feel like it, for rest and recreation. (Tanner 2004: 22)

The idea of a pastoral world populated by Noble Savages is examined by George Watson, who asserts that the Celt is unable to change because "change is a non-Celtic quality" and further observes that "tourist boards tell him that he must not change" (G. Watson 1996: 220). This concept of an ongoing connection to an idealized, pastoral idyll is described as "diasporic ethno-nostalgia" or "Celtitude" by Michael Dietler, who asserts that it is "bounded by genealogical connections (or at least purported ones) to a distant homeland of the imagination" (Dietler 2006: 240).

This desire for a lost Celtic Eden and escape from the "ongoing and accelerating process of globalisation" (Keohane *et al.* 2006) may explain the proliferation of websites that offer a cyber place for those who wish to identify as Celtic, despite a lack of genealogy. These websites invite anyone who shares certain core beliefs to claim Celtic ties.

SPIRITUAL CYBERSPACE

Michael Dietler defines the notion of a "global spiritual connection to the idea of the Celtic identity" as "Celticity", and points out that this movement – unlike previous nationalist and regionalist Celtic movements – is "largely decoupled from essentializing notions of race, "blood", genealogy, or even language" (Dietler 2006: 239). He refers to the flourishing Neo-Druid movement, which has a very different idea of the traditional notion of what it is to be "Celtic" and the members of which identify as part of the neo-Pagan or New Age movements (*ibid.*: 240). Though "variously characterized and notoriously difficult to define" (Bowman 2000: 72), the "New Age" movement has been an important factor in the Celtic revival. Adam Possamai argues that the term "New Age" should be redefined to more accurately reflect the beliefs and practices of individuals (Possamai

2005); however, for the purposes of this chapter, the term will be used for websites and music charts that self-identify using this nomenclature. In examining a range of Celtic and New Age websites, it is notable that there is an emphasis on Pagan practices, with sites advertising such wide-ranging topics as Druidism, Bardic paths, Celtic Wiccan ritual and Celtic kitchen witchcraft – all of which bear testament to a renewed interest in nature-based spirituality. With the growing popularity of the internet, a variety of Celtic websites offer a cyber place for people to congregate and explore various Pagan practices in safety and anonymity. Michael York proposes that Paganism is a religion, and points out that it is a "legitimate, albeit different and distinctive, form of belief" (York 2003: 4). York explains that the spirituality for the Pagan is corporeal, thereby allowing for the "perception of the divine in nature, for idolatry, for appreciation of the sacredness of place, for contact with the divine through both local geodynamics and pilgrimage to revered holy centres, and for multiplicity of manifestation" (*ibid.*: 13). He also notes that "Western neopaganism is an important new development and can be considered an aspect of paganism more generally" (*ibid.*).

Hanegraaff posits that the term "Neo-Paganism" in a New Age context "clearly contains a polemical thrust towards institutionalized Christianity, which is held responsible for the decline of western paganism and the subsequent blackening of its image" (Hanegraaff 1998: 77). He avers that the problems of the modern world – particularly the ecological crisis – are a direct result of the loss of wisdom concerning humans' relationship with the natural world; however, it is significant that some Neo-Pagans do not reject Christianity. Hanegraaff gives the example of well-known Neo-Pagan figures Caithlin Matthews and Maxine Saunders, who "consider themselves to be both pagan and Christian" as they believe that the "true esoteric core of Christianity is perfectly compatible with the pagan worldview" and reject a "particular interpretation which happens to have become dominant in some church institutions" (*ibid.*: 77).

The Roman use of the term *Paganus* referred to those whose customs and rituals were intrinsically tied to locality, and hence to land (York 2003: 12); however, Celtic cyber-pagans often have no fixed land to which they pledge allegiance, but rather identify themselves with the notion of the amorphous "Celtic lands". The blurring of these terrestrial boundaries is made evident by Rose Ariadne in her article, "Celtic Wicca" (2007), which refers to a "specific Wiccan path which incorporates several of the elements of the Celtic Tradition into their practices, beliefs and ritual", and stresses the importance of "love for and worship of Celtic Goddesses and Gods". This theme is then expanded as Ariadne discusses the Celtic "Triple Goddess Danu/Anu in Her maiden aspect, Badb in Her mother aspect and Ceridwen in Her crone aspect". The blending of the Irish goddesses Danu, Anu and Badb with the Welsh goddess Ceridwen to form a "Celtic" Mother Goddess is just one example of the way in which "Cyber-Celts" are creating new paradigms for Pagan rituals.

The Celtic Cauldron blog (http://groups.yahoo.com/group/celtic-cauldron), an active list established in 1999, proclaims itself as a "group of individuals seeking the knowledge of the Celtic people, their traditions, beliefs, their way of life, and the Celtic Gods and Goddess [sic]". The moderator explains that the members are "following our own path, whether it be Celtic Wicca/Witta, Celtic Re-constructionist, Druid, Shaman, or Celtic Witch. We gather here to learn from each other". Forums such as The Cauldron: A Pagan Forum (www.ecauldron.com, accessed October 2010) also offer support for members to "foster an interfaith community of Pagans and their friends where all members could learn and grow spiritually and intellectually through discussion and debate – and have a good time doing so". The Celtic Shaman website (www.faeryshaman.org) offers apprenticeships for those who seek enlightenment in the "Celtic Faery Faith", and urges those who enter the website to "tread the paths of Avalon and sail to Tir na nOg". Celtic shamanism is claimed to follow a path that is based on the "Faery Faith of the Celtic peoples of Western Europe and especially of Britain, Scotland, Wales, Ireland, Cornwall, Isle of Man and Brittany". Another organization that was "formed for the study and practice of the goddess-oriented nature-based religion of the ancient Celtic peoples" is the Celtic Witan Church (www.joellessacredgrove.com/Celtic/celtictraditions. html#witan, accessed October 2012).

This is a "fertility religion concerned with all aspects of prosperity, growth, abundance, creativity, and healing. The Church honors the Celtic deities with full moon rituals and sabbat festivals" (*ibid.*). (It should be noted that while these sabbats hark back to the celebration of Celtic fire festivals, such as Beltane and Samhane, the modern interpretation of such festivals may have little in common with the original rituals.) Groups such as the Moon Dance Coven (www.witchvox.com/vn/vn_detail/dt_gr.html?a=usnm&id=35270) have their own websites, though they are a "congregation of the Celtic Witan Church". The array of websites devoted to personal spiritual journeys into Pagan – and particularly Pagan Celtic – practices are staggering, with sites ranging from The Daughters of the Flame (www.obsidianmagazine. com/DaughtersoftheFlame), devoted to Brigit the Irish Fire Goddess, to the Ancient Keltic Church (http://ancientkelticchurch.org, accessed October 2010), dedicated to the "rediscovery and revival of the pagan mystery faith of the ancient Celtic peoples".

Douglas E. Cowan, the author of *Cyberhenge: Modern Pagans on the Internet*, comments that "many modern pagans are using the Internet in sincere attempts to create new forms of community, some of which were unimaginable little more than a decade ago" (Cowan 2005: x). Lisa McSherry observes that: "Where once we were prevented from reaching out, for fear of prosecution, we are now free to worship in the safety and privacy of cyberspace.

No longer are we bound by geography in our search for like-minded Pagans"
(McSherry 2002: 4). This ability to use cyberspace to reshape old traditions
is expounded by M. Macha NightMare, who describes herself as a "Priestess
of the Reclaiming Tradition" and explains that she and her sisters are keep-
ers of the sacred flame of Brigit, the Irish goddess:

> We honour our heritage as we take it into the age of the internet
> ... We construct the ways of our ancestors in our hi-tech, multi-
> cultural postmodern world. We carry Brigit's light of conscious-
> ness through the darkness and into the future.
> (NightMare 2001: 296)

NightMare also has written about the use of the internet in contemporary witchcraft in a book entitled *Witchcraft and the Web: Weaving Pagan
Traditions Online*. She cautions against casting spells in cyberspace unless
the witch has practised the same spells in what she terms "terraspace". This
is because "terraspace" uses traditional Wiccan practices which are linked
to the earth, whereas in cyberspace "everything is connected" and is "truly
magical, since all it is is energy" (NightMare 2002: 66–7).

THE CELTIC PATH

The burgeoning array of websites promoting new versions of Celtic identity are characterized by a "marked hybridity of practices and symbols and
the use of cyberspace to structure and commoditize transnational medias-
capes of identity" (Dietler 2006: 240). Dietler cites the rise of neo-Druid
groups as an example of the very different way in which Celtic identity can
be expressed, as opposed to the more traditional nationalist movements
of the past. For example, The Druid Wisdom Exchange Network (http://
groups.yahoo.com/group/Druid_Wisdom_Exchange) encourages anyone
who is interested in "Druid teachings or Celtic Wisdom" to join, as do a
plethora of other Druidic websites, thus using cyberspace as a virtual link
for this "cyber-diaspora" to access their sacred groves of worship. Another
example of a cyber community that offers a spiritual experience is The
Summerlands (www.summerlands.com), which describes itself as a "Celtic
Pagan Community dedicated to rediscovering, preserving, disseminating,
and when necessary, recreating that which was lost to us ... the magick, history, customs, and religions of our ancestors". This "Otherworldly time and
space" encourages the visitor to "walk the Dreamways through the Dolmen"
and experience the virtual reality of the world. Monica Emerich notes that
nearly all of the Celtic websites make use of some sort of "Celtic symbolism in their design, as a logo, as button designs, or in graphics to reproduce
sacred sites or objects – the means for cyber-rituals" (Emerich 2003).

Erynn Rowan Laurie states: "We can't rely on genealogy or geography to determine who is Celtic" (Laurie 1995). Rather, it is the *desire* to identify as Celtic that is the essential signifier for tribal acceptance. Marion Bowman describes such individuals as "Cardiac Celts" (Bowman 1995) – that is, people who feel in their heart that they are Celtic. This spiritual affiliation is a significant factor in the emergence of an overwhelming, and at times bewildering, number and variety of Celtic websites that offer a cyber place for like-minded people to congregate and explore various Pagan practices. One such site, The Preserving Shrine (www.seanet.com/~inisglas), is mediated by Erynn Rowan Laurie, "poet, *fili* and priestess", who outlines the nine core beliefs for following a Celtic path in an ethical manner. Like the Neo-Druid websites, these beliefs include reverence for the earth, tolerance and polytheism. Laurie is also one of the co-founders of the Celtic Reconstructionist Paganism (also known as Celtic Reconstructionism, or CR) movement, which is a "polytheistic, animistic, religious and cultural movement" (NicDhàna *et al.* 2006: 17). It began in 1985 at the Pagan Spirit Gathering in Wisconsin and continued through internet collaboration, concentrating on the establishment of traditions. Together with Kathryn Price NicDhàna, C. Lee Vermeers and Kym Lambert ní Dhoireann, Laurie has published *The CR FAQ: An Introduction to Celtic Reconstructionist Paganism* (*ibid.*). This group relies on the internet, due to the diasporic nature of its membership. It acknowledges that:

> there are many more CRs whose main sense of community comes from participation in online forums and email lists. Even those who primarily practice with other CRs in person generally join in the online discussions, as that is currently the fastest and easiest way to collaborate with a wide range of people, and can lead to contacts for forming a local community.   (*Ibid.*: 20)

The cultural origin of the members is not relevant, as "although many people of Celtic heritage are drawn to CR, being of 'Celtic descent' is not required" in much the same way as "you don't have to be Asian to be a Buddhist" (*ibid.*: 27). The preferred language is Modern Irish, and words like *Failte* – or "welcome" – are peppered throughout the handbook. The writers are adamant that this is not a Pan-Celtic group, but instead focuses on a "particular Celtic culture (Gaelic, Gaulish, Welsh ...)" (*ibid.*: 84). This is demonstrated by another co-author, Kathryn Price NicDhàna, whose blog spot, "Amhran nam Bandia" (www.blogger.com/profile/10293181815707001620), promotes Gaelic polytheism. In her blog she classifies herself as "one of those Gaelic Polytheist, activist types, with a commitment to preserving traditional languages and cultures, protecting sacred sites, and a deep involvement in the surviving ancestral customs as part of a modern spiritual practice". Marion Bowman states that this "elective affinity" is indicative of the "phenomenon of people regarding themselves as Celts for spiritual purposes" (Bowman 2000: 70). Emerich notes that Celtic spirituality accessed through various websites allows the individual contact with other like-minded people and their sites of traditional worship and ritual, as well as access to the way in which "participants negotiate particular versions of Celtic religion that reflect the age in which they live as well as their social and cultural location" (Emerich 2003).

"CELTIC" MUSIC ON THE INTERNET

The dissemination of Celtic mysticism through a wide range of websites over the last fifteen years has been instrumental in the promotion of the term "Celtic" and its increasing association with Ireland. Websites such as The Celtic and Irish Culture Web Ring (http://hub.webring.org/hub/celtring) promote traditional Celtic music, history, dance and literature. However, the traditional music on this site has a heavy emphasis on Irish music, as does the Celt.net website, which boasts "every Celtic thing on the web", ranging from Celtic ancestry to knot work and tattoos. Surprisingly, the only music listed is Irish music, with sub-categories including Irish Celtic music, Irish country music, Irish traditional music and multiple listings for Irish radio, magazines and performances. As previously discussed, extravaganzas such as *Riverdance* and its subsequent "spin-off" productions *Lord of the Dance* and *Celtic Tiger*, have led to a distortion of the meaning of the word "Celtic" and exacerbated the confusion associated with the terms "Celtic" and "Irish". The significance of this is that the term "Irish" is tied to an actual locality while the term "Celtic", as previously discussed, is a controversial, and for some fantastical, construct that has been used to market the myth of a lost age of enchantment.

In a more commercial vein, record companies have used the generic term "Celtic Music" as a marketing tool to boost album sales. The word "Celtic" may appear on a Chieftains recording of traditional music, such as *Celtic Wedding*, or on albums featuring "mood music" such as *Celtic Circle*. When the words "Celtic music" are placed in the Google search engine, they generate an enormous number of hits, ranging from National Geographic's website to Celtic radio stations. A website such as *Celtic Music Magazine* (http://celticmp3s.com) has a category, "Things Celtic Music Directory" which provides a list of nearly three hundred bands in alphabetical order; however, despite the occasional Scottish and Welsh group, the overwhelming representation is by Irish bands or Irish-inspired bands. Fintan Vallely, in *The Companion to Traditional Irish Music*, describes Celtic music as a "fanciful term which expresses a world-view or record-shelf category rather than actual links between music genres" (Vallely 1999: 64). Michael Dietler claims that there is a new hybrid genre of Celtic music that encompasses "such things as what used to be called traditional Irish music, Scottish bagpipes and a New Age style with high-pitched vocals and synthesizers derived vaguely from Irish ballads" (Dietler 2006: 243). The dominance of Irish music in the contemporary Celtic scene is due to several factors, but it is significant that one of the greatest successes in the categories "New Age" and "Celtic" is the Irish singer, Enya.

In 2001, Willie Dillon of the *Irish Independent* commented that Enya's "lush brush-stroked harmonies give the impression of having been recorded amid towering banks of candlelight" (Dillon 2001). Of course, the reality is much more mundane, with her multi-layered sound comprising up to eighty vocal recordings combined with synthesized symphonic sound and Celtic-inspired pop melodies, meticulously assembled over a period of many months. The imagery in Enya's film clips and on her cover art reinforces the idea of arcane symbolism, which draws on both Christian and Pagan themes. For example, the clip for "Amarantine", from the album of the same name, shows Enya wandering through an empty landscape that appears to be imbued with a magical quality, as evinced by the beams of dancing light and pools of glittering water. The word "amarantine" refers to the immortal, undying flower of Greek mythology, the amaranth. In a newspaper interview with Henna Helne, Enya explained that she found the idea of an eternal flower appealing: "The poets describe an undying flower with that word, and I fell in love with that idea" (Helne 2005). In the film clip for the song, Enya is clad in a trailing, blood-red dress (the colour of amaranth), which ripples like water across the ground. As the dress touches the earth, the colour becomes vibrant, possibly echoing the Pagan idea of spilling blood on the land to renew life. There is a timeless, Eden-like quality to the world portrayed in the clip, and Enya is the only person who inhabits this magical realm, moving through the trees like a Faery spirit or a woman of the *Sidhe*, the immortal people of Irish mythology.

The nostalgic, calming power of Enya's music was made apparent in 2001 after the destruction of the twin towers of the World Trade Center in New York on September 11. CNN used the haunting ballad "Only Time" from the album to accompany its film footage of the tragedy. This counterpointing of shocking images with soothing music reignited public interest in Enya's "dreamy, moon-drenched New Age music ... the antithesis of everything nasty and unpleasant in the world" (Dillon 2001). Her album, which was positioned at number 19 in the charts during the September 11 terrorist attacks, moved swiftly to number 2. Enya's comforting music conjured up notions of a safer, simpler time and pushed her album, *A Day Without Rain*, to the highest position she had ever occupied in the US album charts. With album sales now in excess of 80 million, it is not surprising that Jacques Peretti of *The Telegraph* claimed that her fan base was "getting bigger, growing like some unfathomable geothermal confection of dry ice and Celtic gobbledy-gook that scientists struggle to explain" (Peretti 2008). Her following seems unaffected by harsh reviews from some critics, such as describing her music as "soothing Body Shop Muzak. Elevator New Age balm to light a candle to and soothe the furrowed brow. Uplifting nonsense concealing the most cynically calculated mood music in the history of (Middle) Earth" (*ibid.*). Her popularity shows no sign of diminishing as her latest album, *The Very Best of Enya*, attained number 1 status in *Billboard*'s New Age Chart in 2010.

MARKETING THE SPIRITUAL

Enya's music is meticulously produced, packaged and marketed, which has garnered an enormous fan base and given the artist her title as "the reigning Irish queen of Celtic music". Though Enya is not Pagan, her music is promoted and dispersed on a wide range of Pagan websites – including, for example, the Pagan Pentagram Radio, which describes itself as the "oldest continuous Shoutcast pagan music stream" (http://tunein.com/radio/%C3%81ine-Minogue-m230557), *Pagan Presence* (www.paganpresence.com) and *The Rowan Leaf* (www.summerlands.com/marketplace/Rowanleaf/bookstore.htm) – the "Celtic book, music and video store" attached to The Summerlands Celtic Pagan community which was discussed earlier in this chapter. In its advertisement for the CD *Fairy Lullabies* by Gary Stadler, The Cybermoon Emporium (http://witchcraft-supplies.com/PaganMusic.html), even promotes the artist as having an "Enya-esque" quality to the vocals that will allow the purchaser to "close your eyes and drift away".

A quick browse of Amazon's Celtic New Age section offers the following suggestions for lovers of "Celtic" music: *Windham Hill Classics: Celtic Legacy, Celtic Tranquility, Celtic Spirit, Celtic Treasure, Mystic Irish Rain, Celtic Treasure: The Legacy of Turlough O'Carolan, Celtic Meditation Music, Heart of the Celts: Songs of Love, Celtic Magic: Eleven Irish Instrumentals* and *The Best of Celtic Music*. Reading though the recommendations by the general public, the recurring comments concentrate on the "spirituality", "meditative nature" and "uplifting experience" associated with listening to this type of music. YouTube offers a wide array of film clips when the words "Celtic", "New Age" and "Celtic Pagan" are entered. Enya has been discussed already; however, there are many other examples, including Damh the Bard, a performer who has a great number of clips with titles such as "Cauldron Born", "The Hills They are Hollow", "Noon of the Solstice", "Lugnasad", "The Mabon" and "Samhain Eve". There is live footage, as well as clips that have been compiled by fans. The music is heavily influenced by folk rock, while the footage features images of sacred places such as Stonehenge, as well as beautiful representations of nature. Other artists include Driadas, Celtic New Age, which has an instrumental version of the Irish melody "She Moved Through the Fair" played against a background of images of Dryads or tree spirits; albums include "A Celtic Tale" by Jeff and Mychael Danna which has elements of Irish traditional music and is supported by images of full moons, misty forests and wolves; and "Celtic Lounge II: Song of the Sea" by Sharon Knight, which offers a hypnotic melody line accompanied by acoustic guitar, percussion and flute. Sequoia Records' website states that "Song of the Sea" "evokes the indomitable spirit of the Celts and reminds us we can all view the world through the eyes of enchantment" (www.sequoiarecords. com/x921cd/The+Celtic+Lounge+II). It also suggests that "these spellbinding vocal and instrumental songs weave a mystical spell transporting you to the emerald Isle of dreams; a legendary land of misty green hills draped in morning dew, ancient stone fences along deep green hills and foggy cliffs that stand above the waves". This heavily romanticized description of Ireland offers the nostalgic view that the ancient Celts had a spiritual bond with the land and reinforces Marcus Tanner's idea of escaping to a mythical place for "rest and recreation" via a CD or YouTube clip (Tanner 2004: 22).

While by no means a comprehensive survey, the following results reveal that Celtic Pagan websites often have their own music links or stores to promote music relevant to their members. The British Druid Order, for example, links to the Pig's Whisker Music website (www.pigswhiskermusic.co.uk/ biography.htm), which opens with a solo harp playing an Irish-flavoured melody. This site features the music of Robin and Bina Williamson, whose songs and music are described as "an evocative East–West harmonies [sic] of their voices with harp, percussion and other instruments in a style described recently as Indo-Celtic-Delta". The website for the Order of Bards, Ovates and Druids (www.druidry.org) promotes music by Claire Hamilton, who presents spoken word renditions of Celtic myths accompanied by harp, "inspired by the practice of the ancient bards". Other musicians who are promoted heavily on this site are Damh the Bard; Jules Bitter, a "well known and respected musician in the Celtic folk scene of Holland and Belgium", who is compared with traditional Irish bands Altan, Planxty and the Bothi Band; and Fiona Davidson, a Scottish harpist and singer who performs Scottish, Irish and Welsh tunes. The Wiccan/Pagan Times Music page (www.twpt. com/wpbeat.htm) has a section titled Wiccan/Pagan Beat Music Interviews, which features an interview with Adrienne Piggott of the pagan band Spiral Dance. She discusses the Irish influences in her music, citing the "Irish wonder tales taken from the Mythological and Ulster cycles" as part of her inspiration and describing how performing can become part of the ritual. The owner and programme director of Pagan Radio Network (www.pagan-radio.net) states that he has removed "most of the so-called 'generic' new age music from our playlists and [is] instead focusing on pagan music from around the world". The playlist is comprehensive and includes a number of Irish artists such as Altan and Aine Minogue, as well as many International performers, such as Faun, Sava and Trobar De Morte. The use of the internet in the dissemination of Pagan music is summed nicely on the Pagan Radio Network review page:

> When one thinks of a Bard, one thinks of the Ancient Days when they roamed the country spreading the news of the day and providing entertainment … Only today, he travels the globe via cyberspace, spreading his message through beautiful lyric and song.
>
> (Kelley 2011)

CONCLUSION

The Celtic revival is not a new phenomenon, having occurred in various guises over the centuries; however, instead of appealing to "antiquarians, Romantics, popular folklorists, artists, poets and minority interest groups" (Bowman 2000: 69), the present fascination with all things Celtic has been influenced and intensified by several factors. The sprawling Irish diaspora has provided a marketing springboard for the sales of Irish products – particularly music; however, the interchangeable use of the terms "Celtic" and "Irish" has expanded this target market and provided a ready-made consumer base eager for "Celtic"-branded products. Peter Berresford Ellis notes that there has been "an astonishing upsurge of interest in practically every aspect of Celtic life – in Celtic languages, culture, music and history. Celtic interest groups proliferate and not just in the Celtic countries but throughout the world" (Ellis 1993: 12) The universal success of blockbuster shows such as *Riverdance* and *Lord of the Dance* bears testament to this statement. Another factor in the Celtic revival is that the advent of the internet has facilitated an interest in mysticism and spirituality, which has allowed people to browse in an online "spiritual supermarket" of "mix and match religion" (Bowman 2000: 71). The thirst for the authentic has seen the Celtic culture re-emerge imbued with a mystical glamour and romanticized as a pure tradition untouched by progress. The term "Celtic" has been manipulated as a marketing tool until it "means what I want it to mean, what I feel it means, and no one can tell me what 'Celtic' cannot include" (O'Loughlin 2002: 49). The final factor in the sustained interest in the Celts is the emergence of "New Age" websites, which are integral to the dissemination of "Celtic" Pagan mysticism and the promotion of "Celtic" music across a broad spectrum, appealing to those with Celtic genealogy as well as those cyber Celts who have a spiritual "elective affinity" for Celtic beliefs. Despite the overwhelming and relentless marketing of all things "Celtic", the online Pagan Celtic communities that have emerged from this latest revival bear testament to the human desire to reconnect with the past and establish a sense of shared community and place – even if it is in the realms of cyberspace.

13. ESOTERRORISM AND THE WRECKING OF CIVILIZATION: GENESIS P-ORRIDGE AND THE RISE OF INDUSTRIAL PAGANISM

Christopher Partridge

> I always thought of Paganism as being a form of anti-establish-
> ment activity … My entire life has been about goading, prodding,
> and exposing the pus-filled underbelly of the established social
> status quo.　　　　　(Genesis Breyer P-Orridge 2001: 122)

Several years ago, working with sociological ideas relating to secularization
and sacralization – particularly those related to "the cultic milieu" articulated by Colin Campbell (1972) – I developed a theory about what I had
begun referring to as "occulture" (Partridge 2004, 2005). I had come across
the term in George McKay's excellent *Senseless Acts of Beauty* (McKay 1996:
51–2; see also Partridge 2004: 67–8). I was fairly sure that the term predated
McKay's casual comment, but couldn't quite remember where I had heard
it before. I was aware that it had begun to gain some currency within the
occult community in the late 1980s. I was also aware of a small festival simply
entitled "Occulture" that had been established in Brighton, England in 2000,
in order – so Justin Hankinson, one of the organizers, told me – "to protect
the rights and interests of people working in the esoteric domain". When I
asked Hankinson about the origin of the term, he suggested that it was most
likely to have been coined by Genesis P-Orridge (Neil Andrew Megson), the
founder of the experimental ritual magick network Thee Temple ov Psychick
Youth (TOPY). I immediately realized that this was where I had come across
it before.

P-Orridge, a relatively recent convert to Eshu Eleggua (a principal deity
within the religious system of Santería), is a musician, an artist, an occultist and a self-styled "cultural engineer", whose work with the performance
art group COUM Transmissions, the bands Throbbing Gristle, Psychic
TV and Splinter Test, and the spoken word project Thee Majesty, developed a particular brand of transgressive, experimental sonic and visual art.
A confluence of pornography, violence, death, degradation, the confron-
tation of taboo subjects, noise and Paganism, his work is rarely less than

189

confrontational. As Paul Hegarty comments of Throbbing Gristle's work, it offered "a thoroughgoing critique or even attack on conventional, modern, Christian, artistic, moral, capitalist thought and living", much of which could be understood in terms of "transgression and perversion" (Hegarty 2007: 107). While much of this transgression can perhaps be understood in terms of a juvenile delight gained from extreme behaviour and the offence caused by the challenging of taboos, one also needs to understand that, certainly in the case of P-Orridge, there was – as indicated in the opening quotation – "a deeply rooted desire to expose and challenge the hidden mechanisms of social control" (D. Watson 1999: 30). Needless to say, such "anti-establishment activity" aroused the ire of the government and the right-wing press. Typical of this reaction were the comments of the British Conservative politician Nicholas Fairbairn, who in 1976 declared in the *Daily Mail* that "these people are the wreckers of civilisation",[1] a moniker P-Orridge and his fellow artists happily accepted (see Stubbs 2007: 34). Others, such as the influential DJ John Peel, thought otherwise: "with their performances designed to perplex and involve the audience in something other than traditional responses, some might say that Genesis and COUM were madmen, but constant exposure to mankind forces me to believe that we need more madmen like them" (quoted in P-Orridge 2002a: 6). This involvement of his audience in that which is other than mainstream, in that which forces us to think differently about the Western, largely Christian-informed societies in which we live, is shaped to a large extent by a particular interpretation of the Pagan and the esoteric.

For those unfamiliar with religious traditions, whose understandings are perhaps informed by the short discussions found in textbooks or conveyed in popular culture, it is easy to adopt an essentialist, reductionist view of a tradition, one that assumes all believers have fundamentally the same view of their faith and the world in which they live. This is never true. Faith is always personal and determined by a large number of variables. Paganism is no exception. Indeed, while Pagans are, generally speaking, oriented towards nature and celebrate the natural world, they belong to an enormously broad tradition and their relationship with nature is interpreted in a variety of ways. Hence it is unsurprising that there are a variety of traditions or "paths" within Paganism, from Quaker Pagans/Quagan spirituality[2] to Chaos Magick, from Hedge Witchcraft to the Northern tradition, and from Left Hand Path traditions to Faery Magick (for a helpful short discussion, see Harvey & Hardman 1996). Bearing this in mind, P-Orridge is an interesting figure to analyse in a collection that focuses on the confluence of popular music and Paganism, for while he is clearly a popular musician, he is also a particularly interesting, influential and subversive example of contemporary Paganism.

OCCULTURE

As I'll be making use of the sociological concept of "occulture", this provides a useful theoretical starting point. Western culture is not becoming
less religious, but rather, for a variety of reasons, it is becoming *differently*
religious (see Partridge 2004, 2005; Heelas *et al.* 2005; Heelas 2008). Rather
than becoming secularized, it is witnessing a confluence of secularization
and sacralization, at the heart of which, I have argued (e.g. Partridge 2004),
is a deceptively influential occulture. Even if individuals are not convinced
by all the claims made by particular alternative spiritualities and traditions,
there is nevertheless a conspicuous interest in them and a growing credulity
concerning their plausibility. Indeed, there seems to be a constantly replen-
ished reservoir of ideas and practices associated with esotericism, theosophy, mysticism, Paganism, the paranormal and a range of other theories
from the familiar to the bizarre – a reservoir that is constantly feeding and
being fed by popular culture (Partridge 2004: 65; see also Kripal 2010). It
was while seeking to adequately theorize and organize these processes that
I developed the theory of occulture. Just as, arguably, occult and magical
thought was once a widespread familiar feature of Western societies, in the
sense that their members possessed a consciousness that genuinely participated in an enchanted world (e.g. see Berman 1981; Briggs 1996; Hutton
2009b; Jones & Pennick 1995; K. Thomas 1973; Yates 1983), so today – particularly since the 1960s – we are witnessing the increasing ordinariness of
occulture (see Horowitz 2009; Jenkins 2000: 135–48).

Hence, as a sociological term, occulture refers to the environment within
which, and the social processes by which, particular meanings are disseminated and become influential in the lives of individuals and in the societies
in which they live. These meanings typically relate to spiritual, esoteric, paranormal and conspiratorial ideas. Central to these processes is popular culture, in that it disseminates and remixes occultural ideas, thereby incubating
new spores of occultural thought (see Partridge 2004: 119–88; Jenkins 2000:
139–48). For example, whether one considers the ideas articulated in television series from *The Twilight Zone* and *Dark Skies* to *The X-Files* and
Supernatural, or films such as *Rosemary's Baby* (1968), *The Wicker Man*
(1973), *The Omen* (1976), *Angel Heart* (1987) or *Paranormal Activity* (2007),
or the claims made for the phenomena captured in reality television programmes such as *Ghost Hunters* and *Most Haunted,* or the conspiratorial
ideas developed in books such as *The Da Vinci Code* (see Partridge 2008),
or the ideological themes and styles disseminated within popular music and
acted out within their attendant subcultures (along with the other chapters
in this volume, see Partridge & Christianson 2009: 25–86, Granholm 2011),
popular (oc)culture provides a space within which there is an openness to
the possibility of metaphysical interpretation. For the scholar of religion
and popular music, this is of course important, in that the latter becomes a

significant area of inquiry as an agent of contemporary re-enchantment (see Partridge 2004, 2009). However, it is no easy task to map the flow of ideas and the creation and dissolution of synergies, whether in popular music or elsewhere in popular culture. So rapid is the flow that, once mapped, occultural content quickly becomes passé.

Having said that – although running the risk of reification, and thereby misinterpretation – there is value in the provision of snapshots of occulture in an attempt to understand its processes. This is certainly true of P-Orridge's work, which in its own way has had a significant influence within particular occult and post-punk/industrial/noise subcultures.

INDUSTRIAL CULTURE AND THE HEATHEN EARTH

A cursory examination of P-Orridge's work exposes little that might described as typically "Pagan" – although Paganism's growing plurality and occultural eclecticism make the identification of the *typically Pagan* peculiarly problematic.[3] Having said that, if we follow the popular definition of Paganism as "a religion based on Nature worship and ancient indigenous traditions" (Hardman 1996: ix) – or, more nebulously, as Chas Clifton has thoughtfully argued of American Paganism, a movement which has "rather unconsciously appropriated a particular American discourse about the value of 'being out in nature' and learning from nature" (Clifton 2006: 165, see also 37–70, 73–9; cf. Berger *et al.* 2003; Harvey 2007) – then P-Orridge does appear atypically Pagan. For example, his interview in the RE/Search volume *Modern Pagans* (Vale 2007) is conspicuously distinct from many of the other contributions, in that he rarely mentions Paganism *per se* or discusses his ideas in terms of "being out in nature" and learning from nature. That said, to the extent that the practice of magick, the acquisition of occult knowledge, and the celebration of the bodily and the sexual are Pagan (see Berger *et al.* 2003: 39–40; Clifton 2006: 58–66; Hutton 2003: 193–214; Pearson 2007: 77–93), P-Orridge's Paganism begins to come into focus. Even here, however, things are not quite as straightforward as they initially seem. He clearly has little desire to belong to or to romanticize any particular occult tradition, or to return to an "old religion"; his is not a religious system rooted in romantic notions of place, history and identity; musically, his are not the sacralized bucolic imaginings of the Incredible String Band, of Donovan, of Shirley Collins, of Sandy Denny, of Andy Partridge, of Vashti Bunyan, of Dr Strangely Strange, of Caravan and the Canterbury scene – or even of more recent Pagan troubadours such as Julian Cope and Marillion.[4] P-Orridge's Paganism is urban and decadent; it is more *Rosemary's Baby* than *Wicker Man*;[5] it is what might be described as Crowleyesque "therapeutic blasphemy";[6] it is also an occultism focused on change and the future: it is confrontational, subversive, experimental and, to a large extent, dystopian. A good example of this is the Throbbing Gristle album *Heathen Earth* (1980), recorded live before an invited audience.[7] The music is challenging, disturbing, dark and at times melancholic. The listener is not transported to a pastoral scene, a circle of stones, a wooded copse, an ancient rite; this is not the heathen earth of the "Heathen"; it is not the *Pagan Place* of The Waterboys; it is not Björk's languid, romantic "Pagan Poetry".[8] This is a menacing urban space. Having said that, the affective impact of the album artwork is evocative of a primitive Pagan past. The prospective listener is presented with a frontal image of a dog's skull, focusing on the teeth. While the picture is actually taken from a book on veterinary medicine, it wouldn't look out of place in an archaeological text, in that it evokes a violent, prehistoric, Pagan past. Again, the name of the album and the band are absent from the cover; the only words accompanying the image are those of Charles Manson: "… can the world be as sad as it seems?" The dark affective space is further shaped by the booklet accompanying the CD, which includes a series of evocative photographs: Peter Christopherson, with blood-soaked hands, leaning over a body that is face down in the road; P-Orridge, wearing combat paraphernalia, standing alone in an inner-city setting; Cosey Fanni Tutti portrayed looking more like a glamour model than an industrial musician; and a photograph of an innocuous caravan placed alongside one of a large pile of human skulls gathered from the killing fields being picked at by ravens.[9] This is Throbbing Gristle's heathen earth. The point is that, although P-Orridge is certainly *au fait* with Paganism, it is difficult to avoid the conclusion that it is an ideological tool. That is to say, Paganism, viewed through an "industrial" lens, becomes an approach to the world from below; it is a way of analysing society from its underbelly; an immersion in the dark side; the subversion of Christian hegemony, conservative politics and what nowadays might be described as neoliberalism.

As to Paganism and the occult, it is worth noting that, at least to some extent, P-Orridge began his journey on the heathen earth as a naïve occultist. Although his friend Carl Abrahamsson notes that he "read and studied on occultism all through his youth" (Abrahamsson 2002: 29), at least initially, this was an area in which he tended to follow rather than to lead. While he may have had an early fascination with the occult and the supernatural – as many children and teenagers do – as the work of COUM Transmissions evolved into Throbbing Gristle and eventually into Psychic TV, several friends began to shape his Pagan mind more formatively, notably the late John Balance[10] of Psychic TV and Coil, and particularly David Tibet (David Michael Bunting)[11] of Psychic TV and Current 93. For example, concerning the important influence of the occultist Austin Osman Spare (1886–1956) on P-Orridge's thought – particularly the use of sigils – "it was Balance, alongside Hilmer Örn Hilmarsson, who together thoroughly infused … Spare into the Psychic TV melting pot" (Gavin Semple, quoted in Keenan 2003: 41). Balance had become obsessed with the ideas of Spare:

> I'd go to the Atlantic bookshop ... looking for books and paint-
> ings by him ... But the thing is, I genuinely felt this instant con-
> nection ... It wasn't joking around. Our thing was that we were
> going to try and follow in this guy's footsteps.
>
> (Quoted in Keenan 2003: 104)

He even claimed a form of what he has referred to as "ancestor worship",
during which he communicated with the deceased Spare through a Sparean
method of meditating on his drawings (see Keenan 2003: 104). Again, while
acknowledging the significant influence of David Tibet,[12] P-Orridge notes
that, not only was he "obsessed with Aleister Crowley", but he "wrongly
assumed I was well read and researched in the museum of magick. *I am not*"
(quoted in Keenan 2003: 40; emphasis added). Nevertheless, again viewed
through his very particular ideological lens, Paganism and the occult became
important to him. Along with a fascination with notorious cult leaders,
such as Charles Manson and Jim Jones, the occult, as rejected knowledge,
provided a subversive and challenging lens through which to view society.
Paganism represented the other, and thereby constituted a challenge to
mainstream society and morality. Not only that, but we will see that he came
to believe that occult ideas and methods could be used to change minds
and subvert accepted social mores. As Abrahamsson notes, his interest was
always less in the "the lure and romance of mediaeval magicians, cloaked
in robes and waving wands", and more in "the apparent changing ability the
human mind and activities actually have" (Abrahamsson 2002: 29). Again,
it is unsurprising to learn that P-Orridge is not a follower of occult traditions or particular Pagan paths. His concern was always to challenge tradition, question received ways of thinking, unravel established moralities, and
subvert political and religious hegemonies. This Paganism is free-thinking,
hard-headed esoterrorism. As esoterrorist, P-Orridge offers listeners an
excavation of the heathen earth, an unveiling of a dark hinterland in which
people are manipulated and deceived.

As indicated above, this articulation and celebration of the other is the
concern of post-punk, "industrial" culture. Along with Throbbing Gristle,
generally speaking, several key bands – notably Douglas Pearce's Death in
June and Boyd Rice's NON – explored a similar space defined by decadence,
corruption and occultism.[13] Emerging out of the incendiary punk reaction
to boredom and alienation, industrial musicians inverted received wisdom,
values, ethics, icons and religion: truth is a lie; ugliness is beauty; order is
chaos; noise is music; morality is immorality; religion is manipulation; order
is disorder. As Biba Kopf comments of Throbbing Gristle, they

> sniffed a potential energy source in the gases given off in the
> chemical reactions within the decay of a corpse. Its fumes set
> off their cold rattling laugh in the face of industrialists struggling

to maintain their power base. Elsewhere they transformed the imagery of its decline into a mixed media assault, into which they folded the horror of the Nazi collapse into barbarism … [Throbbing Gristle] always brought real cruelty to their staged representations of inhumanity. They piled horror on horror, matched brutal noise with brutal image. No filters here to reduce them.

(Kopf 1987: 11)

P-Orridge's Paganism, at least initially, needs to be understood within this industrial context, as analysis of the other; as the learning of rejected knowledge; as a path to the dark side. However, this is not simply exploration and analysis. There was a belief in the availability of real occult power. As with Spare's thought, the careful combination of art, sigilization and the occult can bring about cultural change. This is esoterrorism!

ESOTERRORISM AND SIGILIZATION

During the late 1970s, P-Orridge became interested in "how a small number of fanatical individuals could have a disproportionate impact on culture" (Ford 1999: 10.29; see also Vale 2007: 62–77; P-Orridge 2002a). Occultural ideas articulated and developed by film directors, authors, artists and musicians are able to have – through synergies and networks – a disproportionate influence on large numbers of people, and consequently on institutions and societies.[14] From a sociological perspective, because occulture is taken for granted, embedded in the everyday, its viral potential is enormous. This is a significant point. Indeed, although it isn't fully articulated in his work, it would appear that, for P-Orridge, the disproportionate influence of the esoteric ideas of a minority could have, if engineered carefully, "esoterrorist" potential. To understand where this type of thinking is being drawn from, we need to return to the ideas of Spare, who is in many respects a more important influence on P-Orridge's thought than Crowley, with whom he also became fascinated.

Pre-empting the industrial culture, which had largely been shaped by Throbbing Gristle, Spare demonstrated an aversion to moralism and taboos, as well as a fascination with the sexual and the bodily (particularly the significance of combining orgasm with the will and the sigil-focused imagination), and a keen interest in the potential of occult power to manifest desire. A talented artist and draughtsman, at an early age Spare became fascinated with the occult – a fascination that quickly found an outlet in his drawings. Following an early exhibition at London's Bruton Gallery in October 1907, at which the public were introduced to his highly sexualized drawings, which included much occult symbolism, he was contacted by Crowley. By 1910, after contributing four small drawings to Crowley's publication *The Equinox*,

Spare had become a probationer of his Argenteum Astrum order. Although the two parted company, with Crowley referring to Spare as his "black brother", the latter's esoteric explorations continued. Developing a system of magical sigils, he became "probably the first modern occultist to evolve a self-contained working hypothesis about the nature of psychic energy which could be applied without all the paraphernalia of traditional rituals, grimoires, and magical incantations" (Drury 1994: 86). Without unpacking Spare's rather convoluted esoteric thought in detail (see Spare 2001), it is worth noting that he postulated, as Neville Drury comments,

> a primal and universal source of Being, which he termed "Kia" and argued that the human body, "Zos", was an appropriate vehicle through which to manifest the spiritual and the occult energies of the psyche. His technique of arousing these primal energies, an approach he named "atavistic resurgence", involved focusing the will on magical sigils, or individualised symbols, which, in effect, represented instructions to the subconscious.
>
> (Drury 1994: 86)

Inspired by the Kenneth Grant's *Images and Oracles of Austin Osman Spare*[15] (to which he was almost certainly introduced by Tibet),[16] not only did P-Orridge suggest the band name Zos Kia to fellow industrial musician John Gosling (Keenan 2003: 102), but he developed a Sparean understanding of his own visual and musical creations as sigils. Spare's work also encouraged him to theorize and intellectualize the sexual. No longer did he simply indulge a fascination with sex, it was part of an esoteric system, a Pagan path. Just as Spare had employed a technique of ecstasy, central to which was the orgasm, so P-Orridge states that

> thee moment ov orgasm is central to thee process. It is special and all should be done to make it so ... Sex is thee medium for thee magickal act, enacted physically and with direct control ov thee Individual. It generates thee greatest power which, when released, is diverted from its ordinary object and thrust with thee intense force ov will towards thee fulfillment of desire.
>
> (P-Orridge 2002b: 133)

This is pure Spare. The key here is deeply felt desire. Put simplistically, as with much occult thought, any desire deeply felt at the core of the human consciousness is capable of fulfilment. A carefully planned orgasm adds depth to the feeling, thereby increasing the chances of success in manifesting the desire. However, Spare's system also included an added extra: the use of sigils.

Spare's sigilization involved the writing down of a sentence as concisely as possible, which expresses one's desire; letters are then crossed out so that no letter is repeated; the remaining letters are then combined to produce a sigil. Indeed, sometimes the letters are merged to produce an abstract design. The sigil is focused on and mentally absorbed. The sigil is then destroyed and, as far as possible, completely forgotten. The theory is that, at the depths of the subconscious, occulted from the conscious mind, it begins to work. Innate psychic energies manifest the sigilized desire. The point is that such sigilization is central to P-Orridge's understanding of the potential of his own work.[17] Hence P-Orridge's conviction that music is "a platform for propaganda" (Vale 2007: 87, see also 64–5) needs to be understood in this Sparean context.

Of course, at a relatively mundane level, a musician is able to disseminate information that will not only have a significant affective impact on the thinking of fans, but also, by means of that influence, has the potential to subvert mainstream thinking and challenge established authorities. (We will see below that central to his methodology here is the enormous influence of William S. Burroughs, who warned of the "Control Machine", by which he referred to the forces of conformity that would destroy the unique qualities of the individual.) However, when such activities are coupled with the energies made available by sigilization, the potential for esoterrorism is significantly increased.

Hence, following Spare, P-Orridge argued that the occult use of music and performance is enormously powerful; "music is magick", and as such, the key to the creation of a subversive "occult culture":

> We live in limbo and thirst for freedom … Vested interests of every kind want us lazy and atrophied … Man's fall from grace is his fall from inner security. His defeat is his surrender to conditioned boundaries imposed by the strict regime of acceptability instead of the natural honesty of his individual instinct that recognises all things to be in a state of flux …We are trained to not even *want* to think. Decondition the condition. Conditioning is control. Control is stability. Stability is safety for those with a vested interest in control. Let's go out of control. What breaks this cycle is a psychic jolt. Music is magick, a religious phenomena that short circuits control through human response. The moment we forget ourselves and end the limbo-dance we enter a world of struggle, joy and clarity. A tragic, but magickal world where it is possible to accept mortality and thereby deny death. Experience without dogma, anguish without shame or sham. A morality of anti-cult. Occult culture. Its rituals collective, yet private, performed in public, but invisible … The rites of youth. Our alchemical human heritage, encased like a cadaver in a black suit.
>
> (Vale 2007: 87)

Again, this is, of course, a relatively idiosyncratic and convoluted under-standing of magick and the occult. Having said that, it is intended to be a practical, protest esotericism, a popular Paganism for a disillusioned, unem-ployed "blank generation".[18] Rather than

> the magick of the Golden Dawn, designed for the stately Vic-torian manor … it was magick designed for the blank-eyed, TV-flattened, prematurely abyss-dwelling youth of the late Twentieth Century – like the punk kids in Derek Jarman's *Jubilee*, who have never ventured out of the council flats they were born in. Rather than high ceremony, drawing-room intrigue and exalted initiatory ritual, the focus more often than not became simple survival, and defense of individual vision from a malevo-lently dehumanizing culture that the Victorians and Modernists, even in their most racist and reactionary moments, could never have foreseen. (Louv, in P-Orridge 1994)

Similarly, in *Thee Grey Book* – a compendium of techniques written for TOPY and significantly influenced by Tibet and Balance – he states that it

> requires an active individual, dedicated towards thee establish-ment ov a functional system ov magick and a modern pagan philosophy without recourse to mystification, gods or demons; but recognising thee implicit powers ov thee human brain (neu-romancy) linked with guiltless sexuality focused through Will Structure (Sigils). Magick empowers thee individual to embrace and realise their dreams and maximise their natural potential. It is for those with thee courage to touch themselves. It integrates all levels ov thought in thee first steps towards final negation ov control and fear. (TOPY 2010)

As indicated above, to understand this idiosyncratic, Sparean "system ov magick" as an approach to the "negation ov control and fear", and thereby the cultivation of the mastery of the self, reference needs to be made to the influence of William S. Burroughs and Brion Gysin.

OCCULTURE AND CUT-UP

Having known Burroughs since 1971, for several years, P-Orridge had requested an introduction to his friend Brion Gysin, the principal archi-tect of the cut-up method, developed in 1959 and used to great effect by Burroughs. Eventually, Burroughs wrote him a letter of introduction and he met Gysin in Paris, probably in 1980,[19] and quickly established a close master–disciple relationship (see P-Orridge 1988: 34–7). While P-Orridge was enormously influenced by Gysin's ideas (such as his theories regarding the "Dream Machine"),[20] it was the cut-up method, as discussed in *The Third Mind* (a book-length collage manifesto on the method and its uses), that became central to his thought.[21] Put simply, cut-up involves the cutting into pieces of a text, which are then rearranged into a new text. "Whatever you do in your head", insisted Gysin, "bears the prerecorded pattern of your head. Cut through that pattern and all patterns if you want something new ... Cut through the word lines to hear a new voice off the page" (Burroughs & Gysin 1978: 44). For P-Orridge, this method of progressing beyond current patterns of thought and belief was revolutionary. It presented the esoterrorist with a powerful intellectual tool to challenge mainstream thinking, and particularly Christian hegemony. Gysin, he argued,

> understood more than anyone else at that point in culture that, just as we can take apart particles until there's a mystery, so we can do the same with culture, with words, language and image. Everything can be sliced and diced and reassembled, with no limit to the possible combinations.
>   ... If one didn't look at the very nature of how we build and describe our world, [Gysin] thought, we get into very dangerous places. Once you believe things are permanent, you're trapped in a world without doors. Gysin constructed a room with infinite doors for us to walk through. What amazed me about Gysin's work was how it could be applied to behaviour: there were techniques to free oneself through the equivalent of cutting up and reassembling words. If we confound and break up the proposed unfolding the world impresses upon us, we can give ourselves the space to consider what we want to be as a species ... He would take words, break them down into hieroglyphics, then turn the paper and do it again and again until the magical square was filled with words. Gysin worked with the idea of painting as magic, to change the perception of people and to reprogramme the human nervous system ... I made an agreement with Gysin before his death that I would try to champion and vindicate his work and legacy. (P-Orridge 2003)

It is difficult to imagine anyone championing his work and legacy more enthusiastically than P-Orridge. Along with the influence of Spare and Crowley, his approach to the creation of music and occult ritual can be traced back directly to Gysin:

> It can be said, for me at least, that sampling, looping and reassembling both found materials and site specific sounds selected

> for precision ov relevance to thee message implications ov a
> piece ov music or a Transmedia exploration, is an All-Chemical,
> even a Magickal phenomenon.   (P-Orridge 2009a: 297)

Not only did he use the cut-up method to produce new ideas and sounds, but he applied it, quite literally, to his own body in an attempt to recreate himself. He and his late partner, Jacqueline Breyer ("Lady Jaye"), following their marriage in 1993, embarked on what he termed the "Pandrogeny Project",[22] which, informed by the cut-up technique, embraced the aesthetics of body modification as the first step towards becoming a single "pandrogenous" being. Indeed, it is important to understand that, speaking in terms of a "genderless state", for P-Orridge – who now has breast implants and looks feminine – the surgery was not motivated by transsexual concerns. That is to say, he was not struggling to be female while trapped in a male body. The surgery was not even primarily about the construction of a posthuman, post-gendered self, such as Marilyn Manson sought to explore on *Mechanical Animals* (1998).[23] Rather, this was far more of an occult project, in that it was an expression of his belief that the self is pure consciousness trapped in flesh and controlled by DNA. Humans are, he believes, at an early stage in their psychic evolution towards fleshless consciousness; the Pandrogeny Project was a step towards that evolutionary goal; a step away from the "control" of the DNA. He and Lady Jaye therefore sought to become one, in the sense of becoming a "third being",[24] Breyer P-Orridge. That is to say, they referred to themselves *together*, in the singular, as Breyer P-Orridge. The Pandrogeny Project was therefore an empirical reflection of that singularity. However, as with much of P-Orridge's thought, it is typically occultural in that the pandrogeny is a synergy of ideas, the principal thesis drawing on a common stock of esoteric and transpersonal theories of consciousness and "Mind" (e.g. see Capra 1983: 410; Castaneda 1991; M. Ferguson 1982; Hanegraaff 1998: 245–55; Wilber 2000). In other words, in a typically occultural manner, P-Orridge – wittingly or unwittingly – remixes a range of ideas with theories learned from Gysin and Burroughs, as well as his own long-standing interest in body modification.

For the esoterrorist, cut-up and the cultivation of occult culture are central to the subversion of social control, just as pandrogeny is an act of resistance to the control of the DNA. All forms of control must be disrupted and subverted. As indicated in the opening quotation, this agenda lies at the heart of what it means to be Pagan for P-Orridge: "I always thought of Paganism as being a form of anti-establishment activity" (P-Orridge 2001: 122). Again using cut-up as an occult technique, a form of magick, he argues that a small group of esoterrorists could "have a disproportionate impact on culture" (Ford 1999: 81–105; see also Vale 2007: 62–77; P'Orridge 2002a), and thus disrupt social programming and consensus solipsism:

Control. Control needs Time (like a junkie needs junk). Time appears linear. Cut-ups make time arbitrary, non-linear. They reveal, locate and negate Control. Control hides in social structures like Politics, Religion, Education, Mass Media. Control exists like a virus for its own sake. Cut-ups loosen rational order, break preconceptions and expected response. They retrain our perception and acceptance of what we are told is thee nature of reality. They confound and short-circuit Control. All Control ultimately relies upon manipulation of behaviour. In culture thee Cut-up is still a modification of, or alternate, language. It can reveal, describe and measure Control … Magick as a method is a Cut-up Process that goes further than description. It is infused with emotion, intuition, instinct and impulse, and includes emotions and feelings … Control Disintegrates. Magick integrates. Thee idea is to apply thee cut-up principle of behaviour. Thee method is a contemporary, non-mystical interpretation of "Magick." Thee aim is reclamation of self-determination, conscious and unconscious, to the Individual. Thee result is to neutralise and challenge thee essence of social control.　　　(P-Orridge 1988: 18)

It is worth noting that the spelling and grammar are important. Whereas the spelling of "magick" is simply taken from Aleister Crowley's usage to signify high or ritual magic, the other odd spellings and grammatical constructions are intended to challenge thought and ways of reading; they provide a challenge to the ways in which we have learned to think; our angle of vision is bent during the process of reading; words are given, he argues, "added levels of meaning".[25] In short, a belief in sigils, neologisms and idiosyncratic spelling complements cut-up in that it subverts learned behaviours and challenges received worldviews. When communicated through music and the arts, this form of subversive Paganism has significant esoterrorist potential for change.

Finally, a brief comment should be made about "thee splinter test", which is linked both to cut-up and sigilization. In the transition period between Psychic TV and the founding of Thee Majesty, P-Orridge, with Larry Thrasher and other Psychic TV musicians, formed Splinter Test. The name is taken from P-Orridge's essay on sampling – which, as noted above, he understands it in terms of "an All-Chemical, even a Magickal phenomenon".

Sampling is all ways experimental, in that thee potential results are not a given. We are SPLINTERING consensual realities to TEST their substance, utilizing thee tools ov collision, collage, coumposition, decoumposition, progression systems, "random" chance, juxtaposition, cut-ups, hyperdelic vision and any other method available that melts linear conceptions and reveals holographic webs and fresh spaces.   (P-Orridge 2009a: 297)

For P-Orridge, the term "splinter" is a synonym for "sample" and is intended indicate that, as in a hologram, the whole is contained in each of its parts:

> If we shatter, and scatter, a hologram, we will real-eyes that in each fragmeant, no matter how small, large or irregular; we will see thee whole hologram ... It has all ways been my personal contention that if we take, for example, a SPLINTER OV JOHN LENNON; that splinter will in a very real manner, contain within it everything that John Lennon ever said, composed, wrote, drew, expressed; everyone that ever knew John Lennon and thee sum total ov all and any ov those interactions; everyone who ever heard, read, thought ov, saw, reacted to John Lennon or anything remotely connected with John Lennon; every past, present and/ or future combination ov any or all ov thee above.   (*Ibid.*: 298)

For P-Orridge, in magick this means that a sample/splinter of Lennon, or of whatever one desires, formulated as a musical sigil (as understood in the Sparean sense outlined above), can be used to invoke *the whole* of that which has been sampled. Understood in this way, sampling becomes a key magickal technique, which transforms the making and performance of music into an enormously significant occult practice. "Skill full splintering can generate manifestation" (*ibid.*: 299).

PSYCHIC TV AND TOPY

Central to P-Orridge's esoterrorist use of magick was his band Psychic TV (formed with Peter Christopherson and Alex Fergusson, following the break-up of Throbbing Gristle)[26] and the related occult organization, TOPY, which he founded in 1981 with, among others, Balance and Tibet (Keenan 1997, 2003; see also Fava 2012; Moliné 2006) and also, significantly, members of The Process Church of the Final Judgment (on The Process Church of the Final Judgment, see Bainbridge 1978 and Wyllie 2009), which had an influence (via his early interest in Charles Manson) on the development of P-Orridge's occult thought (see P-Orridge 2009b). While TOPY was founded at the same time as Psychic TV, as a parallel occult think-tank, it became both a fan community and an occult organization in its own right that has continued beyond P-Orridge's departure in 1991.[27] Bearing in mind his understanding of popular music as "a platform for propaganda" (Vale 2007: 87, see also 64–5), in many ways Psychic TV initially operated as a mouthpiece for TOPY (see Neal 1987: 21).

The idea of a "psychic television" is significant. Although highly critical of television *per se*, in that he understands it to be a tool of mind control and mass indoctrination, P-Orridge argues that, like popular music, it might also be used by an esoterrorist as a form of magick to combat "control" – "a modern alchemical weapon":

> [Psychic TV] are attempting to knit together thee fine lines ov shamanic initiation and voodoo invocation allegorically coded into western X-tian myth. TV itself becoums thee ceremony, thee language ov thee tribe. It becoums apparent that, cloaked in spurious messianic trivia, are ancient tantric rituals involving small death, limm bo and resurrection that have now been literalised and usurped by a base language system named religion. Just as religion cloaks ancient knowledge and techniques, so Television cloaks its power to invoke thee lowest coumon denominator ov revelation ... We intend to reinstate thee ability ov TV to empower and entrance thee viewer. To remove thee window and passivity, and re-enter thee world ov dreams beyond. We believe TV is a Modern alchemical weapon that can have a positive and cumulative effect upon Intuition.   (P-Orridge 1988: 18–19)

Concerning "thee fine lines ov shamanic initiation and voodoo invocation", not only did Psychic TV's performances include much disturbing imagery and occult sigilization, but there was an attempt to exercise what might be described as shamanic power. This was done, for example, using the Tibetan thighbone trumpet, the *kangling*. Although it was only used on Psychic TV's first album, *Force the Hand of Chance* (1982) and on the track "23 Tibetan Human Thigh Bones" released on *First Transmission* (1982), it attracted the attention they sought, and to some extent served to shape the band's dark occultural image. It was Tibet who introduced the instrument to P-Orridge during discussions about the formation of Psychic TV as a conduit for occult power. "If you talk to people who don't know much about it, they'll say it's a black magical rite for raising demons, which it is in a sense". Tibet continues:

> There's a rite where you sit in a graveyard. You're meant to sit on a corpse cross-legged and blow this thighbone and this summons up the demons. So what it basically means is that you're sitting in a graveyard, you're shit scared and you're blowing something that is made out of a thighbone. It's a way of bringing all your fears to the surface. You're stealing terror that they had and becoming stronger and cleansing yourself. They always had to be made from either the thighbone of a very young virgin who'd been raped or killed, or the murderer. The idea is that you're trying to summon out the worst parts of you. The instrument that you're

actually using had to be the closest you could possibly get to evil, which is the little virgin girl, the purity destroyed, or the murderer ... I first used the instrument when I met [Genesis] and we were formulating the ideas of [Psychic TV]. They were almost impossible to get hold of and we liked the sound and the whole image of it, the mystique and the atmosphere behind them.

(David Tibet, in Neale 1987: 209)

Needless to say, with such ideas in mind, the affective impact created during early Psychic TV performances could be enormously powerful.[28] Bearing in mind that P-Orridge felt that he was addressing a "sleep-ridden and lazy, undisciplined and banal culture" (quoted in Neale 1987: 21), this was a useful tool for direct action, for the esoterrorist assault on contemporary mainstream culture. It was an attempt, through fear – and, it was thought, occult power – to recalibrate received ways of thinking.

TOPY was understood to be the natural successor to the early Ordo Templi Orientis (OTO) – particularly under Crowley's leadership. It was established to be "a secret society created as an access point into the world of magick" (Louv, in P-Orridge 1994: 25). (Indeed, William Breeze, a leading member of the international OTO, has played viola and synthesizer with Psychic TV, as well as Thee Majesty and Splinter Test.)[29] As Jason Louv comments in P-Orridge's *Thee Psychick Bible*:

> Neither the OTO nor TOPY were teaching orders, existing instead to foster socialization around occult ideas – halfway points for those interested in the hidden undercurrents of reality, training wheels that, when eventually discarded, would lead the individual either towards more abstruse orders of robed ritualists or, preferably, onto their own two feet and their own personal apotheosis.
> (Louv, in P-Orridge 1994: 25)

Described by Douglas Rushkoff as "the most severe example of techno-paganism" (Rushkoff 1994: 120), TOPY claimed to be

> a world-wide nett-work ov individuals ... attempting to bring about a radical improvement in the quality of everyday life ... TOPY is a Way of Life ... not a hobby ... The Temple seeks to end personal laziness and engender discipline: Our aim is wakefulness, our enemy is Dreamless Sleep. (TOPY 1991)

These aims are furthered by information and communication technologies, which create "new opportunities for human experience, and raises mankind's limits generally ... From the TOPY point of view magick and technology are compatible" (*ibid*.). More specifically, the organizational "nett-work" consists of:

access points, or stations, which are post office boxes, fax machines, computer modems, or ... phone numbers. Each access point gathers information from places off the web, then distributes it throughout the network, and in turn takes information from the web and makes it available to local members.

(Rushkoff 1994: 120)

Basically, members receive, access and share information with each other. As Kurt, the leader of a TOPY group, insists, "everyone has the right to exchange information. What flows through TOPY is occult-lit, computer tech, shamanistic information and majick – majick as actually a technology, as a tool, or a sort of correlative technology based on intuitive will" (quoted in *ibid.*: 123). As these comments suggest, the basic structure of TOPY is a non-hierarchical network, in which each member of the Temple has equal status and, because of the existence of cyberspace, has access to spiritual/"magickal" power. As an occultural community, TOPY functioned as a conduit for and disseminator of *gnosis*. This is important because, although it emphasized discipline and the ending of personal laziness, it eschewed dogma and regulations:

> We offer no grand solutions to your problems ... We seek no followers and have no gurus ... People have always asked questions like "Where do we come from?", "Why do we die?", and "Why do bad things happen?" Most religions seem to be about selling people easy ... answers to these questions, usually involving the word "GOD" in some form. The Temple encourages people to investigate all answers to these questions and pick their favourites, or make up their own. Or, for those with courage, to face this life which has no reasons ... Again, we offer no quick solutions. People must find their own methods and design their own rituals. We can recommend writers or systems that we've used as a base, but these must be mutated by the individual into a personal, functional system of realizing their desires.

(Quoted in *ibid.*: 123)

CONCLUDING DISCUSSION: INDUSTRIAL PAGANISM AND GROTESQUE REALISM

Paganism for P-Orridge and post-punk industrial occulture took a rather different trajectory to that of the modern Pagan movement, which emerged during the 1960s and 1970s. Again, departing from earlier British, hippie-oriented pop Paganism depicted on the cover of the Incredible String Band's *The Hangman's Beautiful Daughter*, this was not a longing for "ye olde

Albion",[30] a pastoral existence, digging the land, as imagined on the cover of the Albion Country Band's *Battle of the Field*, or a desire to return to some pre-modern, indigenous nature religion. Rather, what I have referred to as "industrial Paganism" sought to invert behavioural codes and the social mores of an oppressive, decadent, urban landscape. Born of disaffected youth, it was the result of a combination of, as Keenan argues,

> the ever increasing feeling of powerlessness and disillusionment with the political process that blossomed under Thatcherism, the narrowing of permissible lifestyle choices, the erosion of social bonds and the widespread use of recreational drugs that high-lighted the infinitely pliable nature of reality. (Keenan 1997: 85)

Empowered by the ideas of key occultists, particularly Crowley and Spare, industrial Paganism sought to recover agency for the disenfranchised who had become peripheral to, and condemned by, conservative political culture and Christian social and moral hegemony. Fusing esoteric ideas with the subversive methods of people like Burroughs and Gysin, P-Orridge and other musicians explored taboo areas and forbidden knowledge in an attempt to create a free-thinking occult culture in which individuals were the resources with which they might be able to carve out their own future. As Balance put it: "We see no difference between our philosophy, our lifestyle and our art. We are what we do. What Spare did in art, we try to do through music ... We try to do with sound what he did with pictures ..." (quoted in Keenan 1997: 104; see also Balance's comments in Neal 1987: 119).

What they tried to do with music was wreck the civilization that had rejected and oppressed them. This was occultural direct action – esoterrorism!

With regard to the wrecking of civilization, those transgressive elements of P-Orridge's performance art that were attacked by Nicholas Fairbairn – such as his use of and involvement in pornography, his displaying of used tampons, and the smearing of urine and excrement in his work with COUM Transmissions, as well as the Pandrogeny Project and industrial noise music – might be understood in terms of Mikhail Bakhtin's grotesque realism. Certainly, at a very literal level, P-Orridge's Pandrogeny Project is a good example of Bakhtin's "grotesque body": "a body in the act of becoming. It is never finished, never completed; it is continually built, created, and builds and creates another body" (Bakhtin 1984a: 317). Bakhtin's understanding of the grotesque body emerged as a result of his observation of, as Peter Stallybrass and Allon White comment, "the compelling difference between the human body as represented in popular festivity and the body as represented in classical statuary in the Renaissance" (Stallybrass & White 1986: 21). Usually elevated on a pedestal, viewed from below, closed, "with no openings or orifices", affectively detached from its viewer, static and disengaged, the classical body can be understood as distant and, in this sense, "disembodied" (see *ibid*.: 21–2). This articulation of the human form is a manifestation of a "bodily canon", which has been shaped and maintained by a culture determined by particular ideas of politeness, taste, manners and rational, institutional values. The point is that this received bodily canon has obscured an earlier, pre-modern – arguably "Pagan" (e.g. see Hutton 2003: 193–214) – fascination with the "grotesque body". However, Bakhtin argues, this earlier embrace of the "earthy" still exists, particularly in folkloric imagination and humour – and, we might add nowadays, in film, contemporary art and, of course, popular music. According to Bakhtin, images of the grotesque body

> predominate in extra-official life of the people. For example, the theme of mockery and abuse is almost entirely bodily and grotesque. The body that figures in all the expressions of the unofficial speech of the people is the body that fecundates and is fecundated, that gives birth and is born, devours and is devoured, drinks, defecates, is sick and dying. In all languages there is a great number of expressions related to genital organs, the anus and buttocks, the belly, the mouth and nose.
>
> (Bakhtin 1984a: 319)

While there isn't the space in this chapter for a detailed exploration of articulations of the bodily within industrial culture, it is not difficult to interpret P-Orridge's work in terms of a critique of the bodily canon, a questioning of the politics of politeness and respectability, as well as a Pagan celebration of the bodily, the sexual and the earthy (e.g. Starhawk 1997: 135–53), and thereby a challenge to Christian hegemony.

The bodily canon, argues Bakhtin (1984a), asserts that human beings exist outside the hierarchy of the cosmos, stressing that we are finished products, defined characters. This reductionism, moreover, as represented in Renaissance statuary, seeks to seal off the bodily processes of organic life from any interchange with the external world and other bodies. In particular, it attempts to: close bodily orifices; stop the engagement of the body with the external world; hide all signs of inner life processes and bodily functions (hence, for example, the cultural taboos of farting in public or displaying signs of menstruation); ignore all evidence of fecundation and pregnancy; eliminate bodily protrusions; and obscure evidence of death and decay. The aim is to present an image of a completed, rational, individual body. Again, the point for us to note is that both Paganism and industrial culture challenge this resistance to and flight from the bodily and the earthy. (Because of this challenge, both have, of course, been attacked – not only as the corrupting "wreckers of civilization", but even as demonic.)[31] In other words, the rise of industrial Paganism can be interpreted as a challenge to the "the modern image of the individual body", for which "sexual life, eating, drinking, and defecation have radically changed their meaning" (Bakhtin 1984a: 322). P-Orridge questions their transfer "to the private and psychological level where their connotation becomes narrow and specific, torn away from the direct relation to the life of society and to the cosmic whole" (*ibid*.: 322).

Particularly explicit within Paganism and industrial culture is the embrace of death and decay as part of the cosmic whole:

> The first death (according to the Bible, Abel was the first man to die) renewed the earth's fertility. Here we have the combination of killing and birth ... Death, the dead body, blood and seed buried in the earth, rising for another life – this is one of the oldest and most widespread themes. A variant is death inseminating mother earth and making her bear fruit once more. This variant often produces a flowering of erotic images ...   (*Ibid*.: 327)

Birth, sex and death are core industrial Pagan themes, which are ritualized throughout P-Orridge's work. Typical is the COUM Transmissions performance "Stations Ov Thee Cross". Not only is this an inversion of the Christian "Stations of the Cross" (the pictures used to represent certain scenes at the Passion of Christ) but, hooded and in darkness, P-Orridge interprets it in terms of birth, death and resurrection:

> Within the ritual circumstances of Stations ov Thee Cross the hood translates into the hood of the condemned, the darkness before execution, the veil of darkness before birth ... P-Orridge uses ritual in order to access deeper states of altered consciousness and to gain access to the fundamental workings of the mind. He is generally initiated into these states by ... the process of cutting and "blood-letting" ... The cut is also viewed as a Yoni, a slit in the skin which has significant feminine overtones, used to induce a periodic flow of blood which marks the decay of the old body in order to facilitate renewal.   (J. Wilson 2002: 76, 77–8)

Again, Throbbing Gristle openly exploited the themes of death and extreme violence: reading transcripts from, and producing photographs of, serial killers; naming its studio "the Death Factory"; and using photographs of Auschwitz and canisters of the poison gas Zyklon B – the band's bestselling single was "Zyklon B Zombie" (1978).[32] The aim, P-Orridge has always claimed, is to expose a society that has, as Hegarty comments, "rationalized its production to the point where death is industrialized ... As Baudrillard put it ... 'society as a whole takes on the appearance of a factory'" (Hegarty 2007: 108–9). Whether such an intellectual justification stands up to scrutiny is questioned by Hegarty. Nevertheless, from the perspective of this discussion, there is something here that is conspicuously (industrial) Pagan and, in Bakhtin's terms, both grotesque and carnivalesque.

Concerning the carnivalesque, Bakhtin argues that the carnival embodies popular, folk-based activity, defined by its suspension of social and behavioural codes, manifested in an irreverent antipathy to the official and hierarchical structures of everyday life: "a boundless world of humorous forms and manifestations opposed the official and serious tone of medieval ecclesiastical and feudal culture" (Bakhtin 1984a: 4) (compare, for example, "Stations ov Thee Cross"). The imposed hierarchical barriers in society are breached and oppressive norms are challenged. The carnivalesque frees people "completely from all religious and ecclesiastical dogmatism" (*ibid.*: 7), thereby occasioning a "temporary liberation from the prevailing truth and from the established order" (*ibid.*: 10); "laws, prohibitions and restrictions that determine the structure and order of ordinary, that is non-carnival, life are suspended during carnival ... what is suspended first of all is hierarchical structure and all the forms of terror, reverence, piety and etiquette connected with it – that is, everything resulting from socio-hierarchical inequality or any other form of inequality among people (including age)" (Bakhtin 1984b: 122–3). Eccentricity is key here, in that the exercise of eccentricity "exaggerates and caricatures the negative, the inappropriate" (*ibid.*: 306). Again, in many ways this is a good description of P-Orridge and the rise of industrial Paganism.

Whatever we may think of P-Orridge, it is difficult to ignore the subversive significance of his work, which he explicitly locates within an esoteric sphere. While there were, of course, other industrial and post-industrial bands that were as interesting musically as Throbbing Gristle, such as Test Department and particularly Berlin's Einstürzende Neubauten,[33] and while, we have seen, there were musicians who were particularly formative figures in the rise of industrial Paganism and important for the development of P-Orridge's own thought – notably Tibet and Balance – and certainly others who were as shocking in their portrayals of sex, violence and death, such as William Bennett's Whitehouse (the material of which was even attacked by P-Orridge because of the unreflective, uncritical and therefore unethical way in which it was treated),[34] P-Orridge himself has been catalytic, the principal creative force in the shaping a particular occulture. The confluence of several streams of thought (notably those flowing from Burroughs, Gysin, Crowley and Spare, as well as several minor tributaries), P-Orridge's work is genuinely original, Pagan and constructively disturbing.

NOTES

1. P-Orridge has provided copies of the newspaper articles reporting Fairbairn's comments and illustrating the media outrage at the time (P-Orridge 2002a: 163).

2. On Quagans and Goddess worship in the United Kingdom, see Vincett (2008).

3. Barbara Jane Davy makes this point in her *Introduction to Pagan Studies*: "In discussing the forms and types of Paganism, it is necessary to use a flexible typology, because practitioners do not necessarily fall into distinct categories. There are identifiable denominations in Paganism, named groups or traditions of Pagan practice, but there are also forms of practice that run across the denominations, such as eclectic and solitary practice. There are also overlapping religious movements and types of religious practice that generate cross-denominational forms of Pagan practice, such as shamanism, feminist spirituality, and New Age practices ... The generally diverse and flexible structure of Paganism makes Pagan traditions difficult to categorize" (Davy 2007: 145).

4. For example, listen to Julian Cope's *Jehovahkill* and, with Donald Ross Skinner, *Rite*; Incredible String Band, *The Hangman's Beautiful Daughter*; Dr Strangely Strange, *Kip of the Serenes*. Also see Boswell (2001: 20–22) and Cope (1998, 1998–99).

5. Unlike Roman Polanski, who was influenced by the urban occult revival of 1960s America when making *Rosemary's Baby*, Robin Hardy's *The Wicker Man* highlighted continuities between the new folk music, British folklore and contemporary rural Paganism.

6. The term is taken from Hutton (2009b: 45).

7. Recorded in London between 8.10 p.m. and 9.00 p.m. on Saturday, 16 February 1980 at the studios of Industrial Records (their own label).

8. "Pagan Poetry" is the second single from Björk's album *Vespertine*. Interestingly, Nick Knight's video for 'Pagan Poetry" can be usefully compared with P-Orridge's work. Not only does Björk appear topless, but there are scenes included that she has recorded from her love life, some of which are relatively explicit – although the film is treated to obscure some material. More particularly, there is explicit use of body piercing. Unsurprisingly, it was banned by MTV in the United States.

9. Her artistic explorations into the bodily and the erotic took her into the sex industry for a time: "I'm using that process to learn something about myself, the sex industry and the people in it. You can't do a film in the sex industry without being naked at some point. My nakedness there was basically part of the job description, rather than me in the gallery using my body as an art object." (Sprott 2010: 70).

10. He was born Geoffrey Burton, but later, following the remarriage of his mother, changed his name to Geoffrey Rushton, and finally to John Balance (also spelt Jhonn and Jhon).

11. P-Orridge, in order to distinguish between him and another David he knew, taking into account his spiritual interests, gave him the name David Tibet.

12. A good interview with Tibet, exploring his beliefs, can be found in Neal (1987: 205–11).

13. For example, Boyd Rice's interests led him to a friendship with Anton LaVey and eventually to priesthood within the Church of Satan. Similarly, Douglas Pearce (also known as Douglas P), largely through his relationship with David Tibet and the Pagan writer and speaker Freya Answyn (now an Elder in the Ring of Troth), became increasingly interested in the Northern Tradition/Heathenism and runic divination. Indeed, he has recently stated that he views "Death in June as part of a European cultural revival. I'm pleased that the Old Gods are being resurrected ... Old symbols. I feel very pleased that I am a part of that process and that I have had influence." (Powell 2005).

14. Of particular interest is *In the Shadow of the Sun*, an occult film by Derek Jarman for which Throbbing Gristle produced a particularly menacing soundtrack.

15. Grant's volume is recommended in a typically occultural and eclectic reading list, which includes: John Michel, *The View Over Atlantis*; Michael Baigent, Richard Leigh and Henry Lincoln, *Holy Blood, Holy Grail*; John Keel, *UFOs: Operation Trojan Horse*; Colin Wilson, *The Occult*; Robert Anton Wilson, *The Illuminatus! Trilogy*;

Louis Pauwels and Jacques Bergier, *The Morning of the Magicians*; Marilyn Ferguson, *The Aquarian Conspiracy*; Dion Fortune, *Psychic Self-Defense*; William Shakespeare, *The Tempest*; John Symonds *The Great Beast*. See www.genesisbreyerporridge.com/reading-list.html (accessed February 2011).

16. David Tibet was a member of Grant's occult order, Typhonian Ordo Templi Orientis.

17. Spare's thought has also been very influential within contemporary Chaos Magick. Indeed, if one were to seek a natural home for much of P-Orridge's thought, Chaos Magick would be a good place to begin.

18. *Blank Generation* is the title of the 1977 debut album from Richard Hell and the Voidoids. The title song reflects the despair and nihilism of the generation (see McNeil & McCain 1996: 282–3). It is this despair and nihilism that provides the background to P-Orridge's analysis of society in the 1970s and 1980s.

19. The year of his meeting with Gysin isn't entirely clear. In one early interview he couldn't remember when he first met Gysin (Vale 2007: 71), but later – in 2000 – he seems to have reached the conclusion that it was 1980 (Geiger 2005: 292).

20. The Dream Machine, developed with the British electrical engineer Ian Sommerville, was essentially a rather basic stroboscope, consisting of a tube with slits cut into it, through which the light from a bulb would shine. Inside the tubes, calligraphic symbols were painted. The construction was then placed on a record turntable and rotated at 78 rpm. By focusing on the flashes of light produced, "visions start with a kaleidoscope of colours on a plane in front of the eyes and gradually become more complex and beautiful, breaking like a surf on a shore until whole patterns of colour are pounding to get in. After a while the visions were permanently behind my eyes and I was in the middle of the whole scene with limitless patterns being generated around me. There was an almost unbearable feeling of spatial movement for a while but it was well worth getting through for I found that when it stopped I was high above the earth in a universal blaze of glory. Afterwards I found that my perception of the world around me had increased very notably" (quoted in Geiger 2005: 161–2).

21. The cut-up method was also used by other artists, notably David Bowie and Patti Smith. "'I use Burroughs' cut up technique,' Bowie explained in the BBC documentary, *Cracked Actor*. The camera panned in to show Bowie tearing sheets of lyrics down the middle and moving the edges against each other to find new lines created in the process" (Sandford 1998: 120).

22. He was able to do this when, in 1998, he was awarded $1.5 million after he sued the producer Rick Rubin following serious injuries – including nearly losing his left arm – when escaping a fire at his Los Angeles home.

23. For a good discussion of the post-human in relation to Marilyn Manson, see Toffoletti (2007: 81–105).

24. "Third being" is a reference to the "third mind", created by cut-up, as discussed by Gysin and Burroughs in *The Third Mind*.

25. This, of course, is similar to the use of "I" words in Rastafarianism and reggae (see Johnson-Hill 1995: 143–99).

26. It is interesting to compile a list of those musicians and artists that have collaborated with Psychic TV, which includes a range of counter-cultural icons from Timothy Leary to Derek Jarman. As well as the usual suspects from Coil and Current 93 (and related musicians such as Larry Thrasher, The Hafler Trio and Nurse With Wound), other bands and musicians include The Cult, The Master Musicians of Jajouka, Soft Cell and Andrew Weatherall.

27. It should be noted that, at the end of January 2008, its US website reported that "the Temple Ov Psychick Youth North America will be directing all of its attention at the launch of the new phase in our communal growth, the Autonomous Individuals' Network". See www.ain23.com/topy.net/news.html (accessed January 2011).

28. As is common in occulture, this Western occult understanding of the *Kangling* is a little sensational and misleading. While it is interesting because it tells us something about Psychic TV's interests and motivations, when used within tantric Buddhism in the Chöel ritual, the sound is understood to be "terrifying to evil spirits. Tibetan shamans ... employ the thighbone trumpet in many rituals of exorcism and weather control. Here the instrument's threatening drone is said to unhinge the powers of malignant spirits ... In the tantric tradition the left femur of a sixteen-year-old Brahmin girl was considered to be the most effective ... The femur of a 'twice-born' Brahmin was the next best kind of bone, followed by the thighbone of a murder victim, then a person who died from a sudden accidental death, then one who died from a virulent or contagious disease. The bone of a person who died from old age or 'natural causes' was considered virtually powerless in its efficacy against the powers of evil spirits" (Beer 2004: 259).

29. Splinter Test, *Thee Fractured Garden* (see also Thee Majesty, *Thee Fractured Garden*); Genesis P-Orridge and Splinter Test, *Spatial Memory*; Psychic TV, *Cold Blue Torch*; Psychic TV, *Trip Reset*; Psychic TV, *Spatial Memory*.

30. A fascinating recent overview of folk and rock in Britain, which covers much of this neo-Romantic culture – including, to some extent, the turn to Paganism and the occult – can be found in R. Young (2010).

31. Accusations of Satanism and human sacrifice, as well as other forms of persecution that demonize the "other" in society, have always been a concern for Pagans (see Davy 2007: 185–7; Harvey 2007: 217–19). It is not surprising, therefore, that P-Orridge and TOPY have likewise been accused Satanism and human sacrifice by Evangelical Christians and the media, the most notable example being an episode of *Dispatches*, the British television current affairs documentary series on Channel 4. Entitled "Beyond Belief", it was aired on 19 February 1992 and claimed to expose devil worship and the ritual human sacrifice of a baby (see Keenan 2003: 224–7).

32. For example, Throbbing Gristle, *Music From the Death Factory* (1991); this box set includes "Zyklon B Zombie", which also appears on the re-issue of *The Second Annual Report* (1991); see particularly the cover of the 7-inch single "United/Zyklon B Zombie" (1978).

33. As well as guitar, bass and vocals, Einstürzende Neubauten created a violent and destructive percussive sound using cement mixers, pneumatic drills, industrial cutting equipment, pieces of metal, large springs and hammers.

34. "... it's not anything to do with what we were saying ... It's very misguided. We were ethical. We always were ethical. We were very thoughtful about what we chose to talk about" (P-Orridge, in Stubbs 2007: 34).

BIBLIOGRAPHY

Abrahamsson, C. 2002. "Changing Compositions". In *Painful but Fabulous: The Lives and Art of Genesis P-Orridge*, G. P-Orridge (ed.), 29–39. New York: Soft Skull Shortwave.

Ackerman, Robert 1987. *J. G. Frazer: His Life and Work*. Cambridge: Cambridge University Press.

Adler, Margot 1997. *Drawing Down the Moon: Witches, Druids, Goddess-Worshippers and Other Pagans in America*, 3rd edn. New York: Penguin.

Ahmed, Sara 2004. *The Cultural Politics of Emotion*. New York: Routledge.

Albanese, Catherine 1990. *Nature Religion in America: From the Algonkian Indians to the New Age*. Chicago, IL: University of Chicago Press.

Albanese, Catherine 1996. "Religion and American Popular Culture: An Introductory Essay". *Journal of the American Academy of Religion* **64**(4): 733–42.

Alderman, Derek H. & Steven Hoelscher 2004. "Memory and Place: Geographies of a Critical Relationship". *Social and Cultural Geography* **5**(3): 347–55.

Allen, M. L. & M. Sabini 1997. "Renewal of the World Tree: Direct Experience of the Sacred as a Fundamental Source of Healing in Shamanism, Psychology and Religion". In *The Sacred Heritage: The Influence of Shamanism on Analytical Psychology*, Donald F. Sandner & Steven H. Wong (eds), 63–9. New York: Routledge.

Anderson, Benedict 1983. *Imagined Communities: Reflections on the Origins and Spread of Nationalism*. New York: Verso.

AngryMetalguy 2010. "Skyforger – Kurbads Review". www.angryMetalguy.com/skyforger-kurbads-review (accessed September 2010).

Ariadne, Rose 2007. "Celtic Wicca – A Unique and Intricate Path". www.articlesbase.com/religion-articles/celtic-wicca-a-unique-and-intricate-path-237617.html (accessed October 2010).

Arvidsson, Stefan 1999. "Aryan Mythology as Science and Ideology". *Journal of the American Academy of Religion* **67**(2): 327–54.

Assmann, Jan 2006. *Religion and Cultural Memory: Ten Studies*, Rodney Livingstone (trans.). Stanford, CA: Stanford University Press.

Assmann, Jan & John Czaplicka 1995. "Collective Memory and Cultural Identity". *New German Critique* **65**: 125–33.

Ataraxia undated. "Biography". www.sing365.com/music/lyric.nsf/Ataraxia-Biography/0235D889401975BA48256CE200185CC7.

Bader-Saye, S 2006. "Improvising Church: An Introduction to the Emerging Church Conversation". *IJSCC* **6**(1): 18–19.

Bado-Fralick, Nikki 2005. *Coming to the Edge of the Circle: A Wiccan Initiation Ritual*. New York: Oxford University Press.

Bailey, E. 1997. *Implicit Religion in Contemporary Society*. Kampen: Kok Pharos.

Bailey, E. 2001. *The Secular Faith Controversy: Religion in Three Dimensions*. London: Continuum.

Bainbridge, W. S. 1978. *Satan's Power: A Deviant Psychotherapy Cult*. Berkeley, CA: University of California Press.

Baker, P. 2010. *Austin Osman Spare: The Life and Legend of London's Lost Artist*. London: Strange Attractor.

Bakhtin, M. 1984a. *Rabelais and His World*, H. Iswolsky (trans.). Bloomington, IN: Indiana University Press.

Bakhtin, M. 1984b. *Problems of Dostoevsky's Poetics*, C. Emerson (ed. and trans.). Manchester: Manchester University Press.

Baldini, Chiara 2010. "Dionysus Returns: Tuscan Trancers and Euripides' *The Bacchae*". In *The Local Scenes and Global Culture of Psytrance*, Graham St John (ed.), 170–85. New York: Routledge.

Bardenstein, Carol B. 1999, "Trees, Forests, and the Shaping of Palestinian and Israeli Collective Memory." In *Acts of Memory: Cultural Recall in the Present*, Mieke Bal, Jonathon Crewe & Leo Spitzer (eds), 148–68. Hanover, NH: UPNE.

Barnard, F. M. 1965. *Herder's Social and Political Thought*. Oxford: Clarendon Press.

Bauerle-Willert, Dorothée 2003. "Culture, Place and Location". In *Place and Location: Studies in Environmental Aesthetics and Semiotics III*, Virve Sarapik & Kadri Tüür (eds), 149–53. Tallinn: Estonian Academy of Arts.

Bauman, Z. 1993. *Postmodern Ethics*. Oxford: Blackwell.

Bedlam, B. 2008. "The Roof". www.stonehenge.tv/roof.html (accessed November 2012).

Bednarowski, Mary Ferrell 1989. *New Religions and the Theological Imagination in America*. Indianapolis, IN: Indiana University Press.

Beer, R. 2004. *The Encyclopedia of Tibetan Symbols and Motifs*. Chicago, IL: Serindia.

Bell, D. (ed.) 1999. *Woodstock: An Inside Look at the Movie That Shook Up the World and Defined a Generation*. Studio City, CA: Michael Wiese Productions.

Benjamin, Jessica 1998. *Shadow of the Other: Intersubjectivity and Gender in Psychoanalysis*. New York: Routledge.

Bennett, Andy 2001. *Cultures of Popular Music*. Milton Keynes: Open University Press.

Bennett, Andy (ed.) 2004. *Remembering Woodstock*. Aldershot: Ashgate.

Bennett, Andy 2005. *Culture and Everyday Life*. London: Sage.

Bennett, Andy 2008. "'Things They Do Look Awful Cool': Ageing Rock Icons and Contemporary Youth Audiences". *Leisure/Loisir* **32**(1): 259–78.

Bennett, Andy 2013. *Music, Aging and Lifestyle: Growing Old Disgracefully?* Philadelphia, PA: Temple University Press.

Bennett, Andy & Richard A. Peterson (eds) 2004. *Music Scenes: Local, Translocal, and Virtual*. Nashville, TN: Vanderbilt University Press.

Bennett, Gillian 1994. "Geologists and Folklorists: Cultural Evolution and 'the Science of Folklore'". *Folklore* **105**: 25–37.

Berger, Helen & Douglas Ezzy 2007. *Teenage Witches*. New Brunswick, NJ: Rutgers University Press.

Berger, H., E. A. Leach & L. S. Shaffer 2003. *Voices from the Pagan Census: A National Survey of Witches and Neo-Pagans in the United States*. Columbia, SC: University of South Carolina Press.

Berman, M. 1981. *The Re-enchantment of the World*. Ithaca, NY: Cornell University Press.

Bielenberg, Andy (ed.) 2000. *The Irish Diaspora*. London: Longman.

Bithell, Caroline 2006. "The Past in Music: Introduction". *Ethnomusicology Forum* **15**(1): 3–16.

Blabbermouth 2008. "Moonsorrow: We Are Not Nazis". www.roadrunnerrecords.com/blabbermouth.net (accessed June 2010).

Blain, Jenny & Robert J. Wallis 2003. "Sites, Sacredness, and Stories: Interactions of Archaelogy and Contemporary Paganism". *Folklore* 114: 307–21.

Blain, Jenny, Douglas Ezzy & Graham Harvey 2004. *Researching Paganisms*. Walnut Creek, CA: AltaMira Press.

Blake, Andrew 1997. *The Land Without Music: Music, Culture and Society in Twentieth-Century Britain*. Manchester: Manchester University Press.

Bleyer, J. 2004. "An Anarchist in the Hudson Valley: Peter Lamborn Wilson with Jennifer Bleyer". *The Brooklyn Rail*. www.brooklynrail.org/2004/07/express/an-anarchist-in-the-hudson-valley-br-pet (accessed November 2011).

Bonewits, Isaac. 1974. "I Fell In Love With the Lady". *Green Egg* **6**(60): 12.

Bonewits, Isaac 2006. *Bonewits's Essential Guide to Druidism*. New York: Citadel Press.

Boswell, K. 2001. "Marillion: Latter Day Druidic Bards". *Pagan Dawn* **140**: 20–22.

Bourdieu, P. 1971. "Une interprétation de la théorie de la religion selon Max Weber". *Archives Européennes de sociologie* **XII**: 3–21.

Bourdieu, P. 1993. *The Field of Cultural Production: Essays on Art and Literature*. Cambridge: Polity Press.

Bowman, Marion 1995. "Cardiac Celts: Images of the Celts in Contemporary British Paganism". In *Paganism Today*, Graham Harvey & Charlotte Hardman (eds), 242–51. London: Thorsons.

Bowman, Marion 2000. "Contemporary Celtic Spirituality". In *New Directions in Celtic Studies*, Amy Hale & Philip Payton (eds), 69–94. Exeter: University of Exeter Press.

Boyes, Georgina 1993. *The Imagined Village: Culture, Ideology and the English Folk Revival*. Manchester: Manchester University Press.

Bradley, John J. 2008. "Singing Through the Sea: Song, Sea and Emotion". In *Deep Blue: Critical Reflections on Nature, Religion, and Water*, Sylvia Shaw & Andrew Francis (eds), 28–38. London: Equinox.

Bradley, Richard 1992. *Understanding Rock'n'roll: Popular Music in Britain, 1955–1964*. Milton Keynes: Open University Press.

Briggs, R. 1996. *Witches and Neighbours: The Social and Cultural Context of European Witchcraft*. London: Fontana.

Brown, Allan 2000. *Inside the Wicker Man: The Morbid Ingenuities*. Basingstoke: Sidgwick & Jackson.

Browning, Barbara 1995. *Samba: Resistance in Motion*. Bloomington, IN: Indiana University Press.

Buckland, Raymond 1971. *Witchcraft from the Inside*. St Paul, MN: Llewellyn.

Bullivant, S. 2008. "Introducing Irreligious Experiences". *Implicit Religion* **11**(1): 7–24.

Burroughs, W. S. & B. Gysin 1978. *The Third Mind*. New York: Viking.

Campbell, C. 1972. "The Cult, the Cultic Milieu and Secularization". In *Sociological Yearbook of Religion in Britain* 5, M. Hill (ed.), 119–36. London: SCM. Also published in J. Kaplan & H. Lööw (eds) 2002. *The Cultic Milieu: Oppositional Subcultures in an Age of Globalization*, 12–25. Walnut Creek, CA: AltaMira Press.

Campbell, Joseph 2008. *The Hero with a Thousand Faces*. Novato, CA: New World Library.

Capra, F. 1983. *The Turning Point: Science, Society and the Rising Culture*. London: Flamingo.

Casey, Edward S. 1993. *Getting Back into Place*. Indianapolis, IN: Indiana University Press.

Casey, Edward S. 1998. *The Fate of Place: A Philosophical History*. Berkeley, CA: University of California Press.

Castaneda, Carlos 1991. *Tales of Power*. New York: Washington Square Press.

Catchlove, L. 2002. "Redefining the Ancient Tribal Ritual for the 21st Century". *Remix Magazine*, www.goagil.com/remix.html (accessed November 2011).

Chapman, Malcolm 1992. *The Celts: The Construction of a Myth*. London: Palgrave Macmillan.

Chase, Christopher W. 2006. "Be Pagan Once Again: Folk Music, Heritage, and Socio-sacred Networks in Contemporary American Paganism." *The Pomegranate: The International Journal of Pagan Studies* **8**(2): 146–60.

Chris D. 2009. "Tomi Joutsen (Amorphis) interviewed". *Decibel Magazine*, June. http://decibelmagazine.com/Content.aspx?ncid=309291 (accessed January 2010).

Clayton, M., R. Sager & U. Will 2005. "In Time with the Music: The Concept of Entrainment and Its Significance for Ethnomusicology". *European Meetings in Ethnomusicology* **11** (ESEM Counterpoint 1): 3–75.

Cleal, R. M. J., K. E. Walker & R. Montague 1995. *Stonehenge in Its Landscape: Twentieth Century Excavations*, English Heritage Archaeological Report 10. Swindon: English Heritage.

Clecak, P. 1983. *America's Quest for the Ideal Self: Dissent and Fulfilment in the 60s and 70s*. Oxford: Oxford University Press.

Clifton, C. 2006. *Her Hidden Children: The Rise of Wicca and Paganism in America*. Walnut Creek, CA: AltaMira Press.

Clifton, Chas S. & Graham Harvey 2004. *The Paganism Reader*. New York: Routledge.

Cohen, Erik 1992. "Pilgrimage and Tourism: Convergence and Divergence". In *Sacred Journeys: The Anthropology of Pilgrimage*, Alan Morinis (ed.), 47–64. Westport, CN: Greenwood Press.

Cohn, N. 1995. *Cosmos, Chaos and the World to Come: The Ancient Roots of Apocalyptic Faith*. London: Yale University Press.

Cold Spring 2010a. "Cold Spring: What We Are". www.coldspring.co.uk/what_we_are.php (accessed 13 January 2011).

Collins, Helen 2010. "At the Edges: A Place and a Space for Tears: Exploring the Framing of Depression in Contemporary Western Culture". Unpublished PhD thesis, University of Tasmania.

Collins, T. 1995. *Rock Mr. Blues: The Life and Music of Wynonie Harris*. Milford, NH: Big Nickel.

Connell, John & Chris Gibson 2003. *Sound Tracks: Popular Music, Identity and Place*. New York: Routledge.

Cope, J. 1998. *The Modern Antiquarian: A Pre-millennial Odyssey Through Megalithic Britain*. London: Thorsons.

Cope, J. 1998–99. "From Punk to Pre-history". *Kindred Spirit* **45**: 25–8.

Coughlin, J. 2002. *Reclaiming Darkness in Paganism: A Call to Balance*. www.waningmoon.com/jcoughlin/writing/reclaimdark.shtml (accessed July 2011).

Cowan, Douglas E. 2005. *Cyberhenge: Modern Pagans on the Internet*. New York: Routledge.

Cowan, D. E. & D. G. Bromley 2008. *Cults and New Religions: A Brief History*. Oxford: Blackwell.

Cresswell, Tim 2004. *Place: A Short Introduction*. Oxford: Wiley-Blackwell.

Csikszentmihalyi, Mihaly 1990. *Flow: The Psychology of Optimal Experience*. New York: Harper & Row.

D'Andrea, Anthony 2004. "Global Nomads: Techno and the New Age as Transnational Countercultures in Ibiza and Goa". In *Rave Culture and Religion*, Graham St John (ed.), 236–55. London: Routledge.

D'Andrea, Anthony 2007. *Global Nomads: Techno and New Age as Transnational Countercultures in Ibiza and Goa*. New York: Routledge.

Daniel, Yvonne 2005. *Dancing Wisdom: Embodied Knowledge in Haitian Vodou, Cuban Yoruba, and Bahian Candomble*. Urbana, IL: University of Illinois Press.

D'Aquili, Eugene G. & Andrew B. Newberg 1999. *The Mystical Mind: Probing the Biology of Religious Experience*. Minneapolis, MN: Fortress Press.

Darvill, T. 2009. "Stonehenge in Rock". In *The Sounds of Stonehenge*, S. Banfield (ed.), 66–73. Oxford: Archaeopress.

Darvill, T. & G. Wainwright 2011. "The Stones of Stonehenge". *Current Archaeology* **21**(12): 28–35.

Davies, Norman 1999. *The Isles: A History*. London: Macmillan.

Davis, E. 1999. *Techgnosis: Myth, Magic and Mysticism in the Age of Information*. London: Serpent's Tail.

Davis, E. 2004. "Golden Goa's Trance Transmission". In *Rave Culture and Religion*, Graham St John (ed.), 256–72. London: Routledge.

Davy, B. J. 2007. *Introduction to Pagan Studies*. Walnut Creek, CA: AltaMira Press.

De Groot, K. 2006. "The Church in Liquid Modernity: A Sociological and Theological Exploration of a Liquid Church". *International Journal for the Study of the Christian Church* **6**(1): 91–103.

De Klepper, Stefan, Sophia Molpheta, Simon Pille & Reem Saouma 2007. "Cultural Heritage and History in the Metal Scene". October. http://webdocs.alterra.wur.nl/internet/corporate/nieuws/blackMetal.pdf (accessed December 2009).

De La Torre, Miguel, A. 2004. *Santería: The Beliefs and Rituals of a Growing Religion in America*. Grand Rapids, MI: Eerdmans.

Deutscher, Guy 2006. *The Unfolding of Language: The Evolution of Mankind's Greatest Invention*. London: Arrow Books.

Deverell, Garry 2008a. "The Liturgy of the Dance". www.southcom.com.au/~gjd/liturgy_of_the_dance.html (accessed June 2008).

Deverell, Garry 2008b. *The Bonds of Freedom: Vows, Sacraments and the Formation of the Christian Self*. Milton Keynes: Paternoster Press.

Devereux, P. 2001. *Stone Age Soundtracks: The Acoustic Archaeology of Ancient Sites*. London: Vega.

Dianteill, E. 2003. "Pierre Bourdieu and the Sociology of Religion: A Central and Peripheral Concern". *Theory and Society* **32**: 529–49.

Dietler, Michael 2006. "Celticism, Celtitude, and Celticity: The Consumption of the Past in the Age of Globalization". In *Celtes et Gaulois dans l'histoire, l'historiographie et l'idéologie moderne. Actes de la table ronde de Leipzig, 16–17 juin 2005*, S. Rieckhoff (ed.), 237–48. Glux-en-Glenne: Bibracte, Centre Archéologique Européen.

Digitalis, Raven 2007. *Goth Craft: The Magickal Side of Dark Culture*. Woodbury, MN: Llewellyn.

Dillon, Willie 2001. "Why the US Turned to Enya for Comfort". *Irish Independent*, 20 October. www.independent.ie/lifestyle/independent-woman/celebrity-news-gossip/why-us-turned-to-enya-for-comfort-330150.html (accessed November 2010).

DJ Tundra 2007. "The History of Goa/PsyTrance by DJ Tundra". http://tribes.tribe.net/d7ecdbcd-5ff2-4f62-99ac-5699148dc91b/thread/7c05363a-7f14-4b0b-8dcf-0a739c725815 (accessed 20 September 2011).

Dowden, Ken 2000. *European Paganism: The Realities of Cult from Antiquity to the Middle Ages*. London: Routledge.

Drane, J. 2006. "What is the Emerging Church?". http://2churchmice.files.wordpress.com/2008/12/what-is-emerging-church.pdf (accessed 20 September 2011).

Drengson, Alan R. 1991. "Coming Full Place: Personal Reflections on *The Trumpeter*". *The Trumpeter: Journal of Ecosophy* **8**(4): 159–60.

Drury, N. 1994. *Echoes from the Void: Writings on Magic, Visionary Art and the New Consciousness*. Bridport: Prism Press.

Dundes, Alan (ed.) 2005. *Folklore: Critical Concepts in Literary and Cultural Studies. Volumes 1 and 2*. London: Routledge.

Durkheim, Émile [1912] 1976. *The Elementary Forms of the Religious Life*. London: Allen & Unwin.

Ehrenreich, B. 2006. *Dancing in the Streets: A History of Collective Joy*. New York: Metropolitan.

Ehrlich, D. 1997. *Inside the Music: Conversations with Contemporary Musicians About Spirituality, Creativity, and Consciousness*. Boston, MA: Shambhala.

Eliade, M. 1964. *Shamanism: Archaic Techniques of Ecstasy*. Princeton, NJ: Princeton University Press.

Eliade, M. 1976. *Occultism, Witchcraft, and Cultural Fashions: Essays in Comparative Religions*. Chicago, IL: University of Chicago Press.
Ellis, Peter Berresford 1993. *The Celtic Dawn: A History of Pan Celticism*. London: Constable.
Ellwood, Robert 1994. *The 60s Spiritual Awakening: American Religion Moving from Modern to Postmodern*. New Brunswick, NJ: Rutgers University Press.
Emerich, Monica 2003. "Constructing 'Celticity': How Pagans Define Celtic Spirituality Through Popular Discourse on the World Wide Web". Paper presented at Celtic Representations conference, University of Colorado, Boulder, CO, 23–25 October.
Encyclopedia Metallicum. www.metal-archives.com/index.php (accessed May 10, 2010).
English, P. 2002. "Disputing Stonehenge: Law and Access to a National Symbol". *Entertainment Law* **1**(2): 1–22.
Ezzy, Douglas 2001. "The Commodification of Witchcraft". *Australian Religion Studies Review* **14**(1): 31–44.
Ezzy, Douglas 2011. "An Underworld Rite: A Pagan Re-enactment of Persephone's Descent into the Underworld". *Journal of Contemporary Religion* **26**(2): 245–59.
Farley, H. 2009. "Demons, Devils and Witches: The Occult in Heavy Metal Music". In *Heavy Metal Music in Britain*, G. Bayer (ed.), 73–88. Farnham: Ashgate.
Fava, S. 2012. "'When Rome Falls, Falls the World': Current 93 and Apocalyptic Folk". In *Anthems of Apocalypse: Popular Music and Apocalyptic Thought*, C. Partridge (ed.), 72–89. Sheffield: Phoenix Press.
Fazenda, B. 2010. "Measuring the Acoustics of Stonehenge". www.acoustics.salford.ac.uk/res/fazenda/acoustics-of-stonehenge (accessed April 2012).
Ferguson, James & Akhil Gupta 1992. "Beyond 'Culture': Space, Identity, and the Politics of Difference". *Cultural Anthropology* **7**(1): 6–23.
Ferguson, Marilyn 1982. *The Aquarian Conspiracy: Personal and Social Transformation in Our Times*. London: Paladin.
Fjordi 2005. "Interview with Rihards Skudrītis of Skyforger". From Below (blog), 24 February. http://web.archive.org/web/20050224041207/http://frombelow.dk/metal_skyforger_interview.htm (accessed September 2009).
Flood, Gavin 1999. *Beyond Phenomenology: Rethinking the Study of Religion*. London: Cassell.
Ford, S. 1999. *Wreckers of Civilization: The Story of Coum Transmissions and Throbbing Gristle*. London: Black Dog Publishing.
François, Stéphane 2008. "The Euro-Pagan Scene: Between Paganism and Radical Right", Ariel Godwin (trans.). *Journal for the Study of Radicalism* **1**(2): 35–54.
Frazer, James G. 1913. *The Golden Bough: A Study in Magic and Religion, Volume 11. Balder the Beautiful: The Fire-Festivals of Europe and the Doctrine of the External Soul, Part 1*, 3rd edn. London: Macmillan.
Freeman, W. 2000. "A Neurobiological Role of Music in Social Bonding". In *The Origins of Music*, N. L. Wallin, B. Merker & S. Brown (eds). Cambridge, MA: MIT Press.
Freud, Sigmund [1913] 2001. *Totem and Taboo: Some Points of Agreement Between the Mental Lives of Savages and Neurotics*. London: Routledge.
Freud, Sigmund [1919] 2003. *The Uncanny*. London: Penguin.
Frith, Simon 1981. "The Magic That Can Set You Free: The Ideology of Folk and the Myth of Rock". *Popular Music* **1**: 159–68.
Frith, Simon 2007. *Taking Popular Music Seriously: Selected Essays*. Burlington, VT: Ashgate.
Fritz, J. 1999. *Rave Culture: An Insider's Overview*. Toronto: Small Fry Press.
Fuller, Charles H. 2001. *Spiritual But Not Religious: Understanding Unchurched America*. New York: Oxford University Press.
Gardner, Gerald [1954] 2004. *Witchcraft Today*. New York: Citadel.
Gaus212 2009. "StoneHenge or Water Tank War Against Academia at WaterHenge". www.youtube.com/watch?v=gXdGwqSEhEQ&list=UUvPEw8G9_0OysM_Y0VtAqbA (accessed January 2013).

218

Gauthier, François 2004. "Rapturous Ruptures: the 'Instituant' Religious Experience of Rave". In *Rave Culture and Religion*, Graham St John (ed.), 65–84. London: Routledge.

Gavanas, A. 2008. "Grasping Communitas". *Ethnos* **73**(1): 127–33.

Geiger, J. 2005. *Nothing is True, Everything is Permitted: The Life of Brion Gysin*. New York: Disinformation Company.

Gibson, C. & R. Pagan 2006. "Rave Culture in Sydney, Australia: Mapping Youth Spaces in Media Discourse". *Youth-Sound-Space*, www.cia.com.au/peril/youth (accessed October 2010).

Gibson, W. 1984. *Neuromancer*. New York: Ace.

Giddens, Anthony 1991. *Modernity and Self-Identity*. Stanford, CA: Stanford University Press.

Goodlad, L. & M. Bibby (eds) 2007. *Goth: Undead Subculture*, Durham, NC: Duke University Press.

Goodrick-Clarke, Nicholas 1992. *The Occult Roots of Nazism. Secret Aryan Cults and their Influence on Nazi Ideology*. New York: New York University Press.

Gordon, Mary-Jo 1999. "Designing for Spirituality in the Lanscape: An Exploration". Masters dissertation, University of Guelph.

Granholm, K. 2011. "'Sons of Northern Darkness': Heathen Influences in Black Metal and Neofolk Music". *Numen* **58**(4): 514–44.

Grant, K. 1975. *Images and Oracles of Austin Osman Spare*. London: Muller.

Graves, Robert 1961. *The White Goddess: A Historical Grammar of Poetic Myth*. London: Faber & Faber.

Green, D. 2010. "Trance-gression: Technoshamanism, Conservatism and Pagan Politics". *Politics and Religion* **2**(4): 201–20.

Greenwood, Susan 2000. *Magic, Witchcraft and the Otherworld: An Anthropology*. Oxford: Berg.

Grimes, Ronald 2000. *Deeply into the Bone: Re-inventing Rites of Passage*. Berkeley, CA: University of California Press.

Grimm, Jacob [1880] 1999. *Teutonic Mythology*. Translated from the fourth edition by James Steven Stallybrass. London: Routledge/Thoemmes Press.

Halbwachs, Maurice 1939. "Individual Consciousness and the Collective Mind". *The American Journal of Sociology* **44**(6): 812–22.

Hale, Amy & Philip Payton 2000. *New Directions in Celtic*. Exeter: University of Exeter Press.

Hale, Amy & Shannon Thornton 2000. "Pagans, Pipers and Politicos". In *New Directions in Celtic Studies*, Amy Hale & Philip Payton (eds), 97–107. Exeter: University of Exeter Press.

Hall, Stuart & Tony Jefferson 2007. *Resistance Through Rituals: Youth Subcultures in Post-War Britain*. London: Routledge.

Hanegraaff, Wouter J. 1998. *New Age Religion and Western Culture: Esotericism in the Mirror of Secular Thought*. Albany, NY: SUNY Press.

Hardman, C. 1996. "Introduction". In *Paganism Today*, G. Harvey & C. Hardman (eds), ix–xix. London: Thorsons.

Hardy, T. 1891. *Tess of the D'Urbervilles*. London: Macmillan.

Harner, Michael [1980] 1990. *The Way of the Shaman*. San Francisco, CA: Harper & Row.

Harrison, T. 1992. *Elvis People: The Cult of the King*. London: HarperCollins.

Harrod, Howard 2000. *The Animals Came Dancing: Native American Sacred Ecology and Animal Kinship*. Tucson, AZ: University of Arizona Press.

Harvey, Graham 1996. "Heathenism: a North European Pagan Tradition". In *Paganism Today*, G. Harvey & C. Hardman (eds), 49–64. London: Thorsons.

Harvey, Graham 1997. *Contemporary Paganism: Listening People, Speaking Earth*. New York: New York University Press.

Harvey, Graham 2000. *Indigenous Religions: A Companion*. London: Cassell.

Harvey, Graham 2005. *Animism: Respective the Living World*. Adelaide: Wakefield Press.

Harvey, Graham 2007. *Listening People, Speaking Earth: Contemporary Paganism*, rev. edn. London: C. Hurst.

Harvey, Graham & C. Hardman (eds). 1996. *Paganism Today*, London: Thorsons.

Hay, D. 1990. *Religious Experience Today: Studying the Facts*, London: Cassell.

Hay, D. 2007. *Why Spirituality is Difficult for Westerners*. London: Societas.

Heelas, P. 2008. *Spiritualities of Life: New Age Romanticism and Consumptive Capitalism*. Oxford: Blackwell.

Heelas, P. & L. Woodhead 2001. "Homeless Minds Today?" In *Peter Berger and the Study of Religion*, P. L. Berger, L. Woodhead, P. Heelas & D. Martin (eds). New York: Routledge.

Heelas, P., L. Woodhead, B. Seel, K. Tusting & B. Szerszynski 2005. *The Spiritual Revolution: Why Religion is Giving Way to Spirituality*, Religion and Spirituality in the Modern World. Oxford: Wiley Blackwell.

Hegarty, P. 2007. *Noise/Music: A History*. London: Continuum.

Helne, Henna 2005. "A Rare Interview with Enya", Suvi Kaikkonen (trans.). http://enya.sk/articles/rare-meeting-with-enya.htm (accessed November 2010).

Henry, Holly & Amanda Taylor 2009. "Re-thinking Apollo: Envisioning Environmentalism in Space". *Sociological Review* **57**(1): 190–203.

Hetherington, Kevin 2000. *New Age Travellers: Vanloads of Uproarious Humanity*. New York: Continuum.

Hodkinson, P. 2002. *Goth: Identity, Style and Subculture*. Oxford: Berg.

Horowitz, M. 2009. *Occult America: The Secret History of How Mysticism Shaped Our Nation*. New York: Bantam.

Hugin the Bard 2001. *A Bard's Book of Pagan Songs: Stories and Music from the Celtic World*. St Paul, MN: Llewellyn.

Hume, Lynne 1997. *Witchcraft and Paganism in Australia*. Melbourne: Melbourne University Press.

Hume, Lynne & Kathleen McPhillips (eds) 1996. *Popular Spiritualities: The Politics of Contemporary Enchantment*. Aldershot: Ashgate.

Huneidi, S. 2006. "Sacred Stonehenge: A Spiritual Tour". www.merrynjose.com/artman/publish/article_639.shtml (accessed April 2012).

Hutton, Ronald 1991. *The Pagan Religions of the Ancient British Isles*. Oxford: Blackwell.

Hutton, Ronald 1996. *The Stations of the Sun: A History of the Ritual Year in Britain*. Oxford: Oxford University Press.

Hutton, Ronald 1999. *The Triumph of the Moon: A History of Modern Pagan Witchcraft*. Oxford: Oxford University Press.

Hutton, Ronald 2003. *Witches, Druids and King Arthur*. London: Hambledon.

Hutton, Ronald 2009a. *Blood and Mistletoe: The History of the Druids in Britain*. New Haven, CT: Yale University Press.

Hutton, Ronald 2009b. "The Roots of Modern Paganism". In *Paganism: History and Development, Vol. 1*, B. J. Davey (ed.), 43–53. London: Routledge.

Iannaccone, L. 1990. "Religious Practice: A Human Capital Approach". *Journal for the Scientific Study of Religion* **29**: 297–314.

Ingold, Tim 2011. *Being Alive: Essays on Movement, Knowledge and Description*. London: Routledge.

Insane Events 2009. "Insane Events Australia – Dance Music, Events and Nightlife". *Insane Events Forum*. www.insanevents.com.au/forums (accessed June 2009).

Irigaray, Luce 2001. *Two Be Two*, M. Rhodes & M. Concito-Monoc (trans.). New York: Routledge.

Ivakhiv, Adrian 2001. *Claiming Sacred Ground: Pilgrims and Politics at Glastonbury and Sedona*. Bloomington, IN: Indiana University Press.

Ivakhiv, Adrian 2003. "Nature and Self in New Age Pilgrimage". *Culture and Religion* **4**(1): 93–118.

Ivakhiv, Adrian 2005. "Nature and Ethnicity in Eastern European Paganism: An Environmental Ethic of the Religious Right?" *The Pomegranate* 7(2): 194–225.

Jackson, Phil 2004. *Inside Clubbing*. New York: Berg.

Jenkins, P. 2000. *Mystics and Messiahs: Cults and New Religions in American History*. New York: Oxford University Press.

Jennings, M. 2010. "'I've Got a Spirit Coming Through Me': Music as Heirophany and Musicians as Shamans". *Australian Religion Studies Review* 23(2): 208–26.

John-Krol, Louisa 2006. *Gothtronic* interview (January). www.gothtronic.com/?page=23& interviews=907 (accessed January 2007).

Johnson-Hill, J. A. 1995. *I-sight: The World of Rastafari: An Interpretative Sociological Account.* Lanham, MD: Scarecrow Press.

Jones, P. & N. Pennick 1995. *A History of Pagan Europe*. London: Routledge.

Jordan, T. 1995. "Collective Bodies: Raving and the Politics of Gilles Deleuze and Felix Guattari". *Body & Society* 1(1): 125–44.

Jung, Carl 1964. *Man and His Symbols*. New York: Doubleday.

Jung, Carl 1970. *The Structure and Dynamics of the Psyche: The Collected Works of C. G. Jung, Vol. 8*. Princeton, NJ: Princeton University Press.

Jung, Carl 1976. *The Collected Works of C.G. Jung, Vol. 9*. Princeton, NJ: Princeton University Press.

Jung, Carl 1996. *The Archetypes and the Collective Unconscious*. Princeton, NJ: Princeton University Press.

Kahn-Harris, Keith 2007. *Extreme Metal: Music and Culture on the Edge*. New York: Berg.

Kavanaugh, P. R. & T. L. Anderson 2008. "Solidarity and Drug Use in Electronic Dance Music Scene". *The Sociological Quarterly* 49: 181–208.

Keenan, D. 1997. "Childhood's End: Current 93". *The Wire* 163: 34–7.

Keenan, D. 2003. *England's Hidden Reverse: A Secret History of the Esoteric Underground*. London: SAF Publishing.

Kelley, Beth Wytchskate 2011. "Wild Soul: Cernunnos Rising". www.paganradio.net/2011/05/wild-soul-cernunnos-rising (accessed September 2010).

Kenny, Kevin 2003. "Diaspora and Comparison: The Global Irish as a Case Study". *The Journal of American History* 190(1): 34–162. www.jstor.org/stable/3659794 (accessed November 2010).

Keohane, Kieran, Donncha Kavanagh & Carmen Kuhling 2006. "The Creative Scene of *Riverdance*: Artrepreneurship and the Celtic Tiger". Working paper for Department of Management and Marketing, University College, Cork.

Kilpatrick, N. 2004a. *The Goth Bible*. New York: St Martin's Griffin.

Knight, Gareth 1963. "The Empress of Nature". *New Dimensions* 1(4): 13–16.

Kopf, B. 1987. "Bacillus Culture". In *Tape Delay*, C. Neal (ed.), 10–15. London: SAF Publishing.

Kripal, J. J. 2010. *Authors of the Impossible: The Paranormal and the Sacred*. Chicago, IL: Chicago University Press.

Landau, James 2004. "The Flesh of Raving: Merleau-Ponty and the 'Experience' of 'Ecstasy'". In *Rave Culture and Religion*, Graham St John (ed.) 107–24. London: Routledge.

Largey, Michael 2006. *Vodou Nation: Haitian Art Music and Cultural Nationalism*. Chicago, IL: University of Chicago Press.

Larkey, Edward 2000. "Just for Fun? Language Choice in German Popular Music". *Popular Music and Society* 24(3): 1–20.

Larkin, C. (ed.) 2006. "Graveland". In *Encyclopedia of Popular Music: Oxford Music Online*. www.oxfordmusiconline.com/subscriber/article/epm/93028 (accessed December 2009).

Lau, Stella Sai-Chun 2006. "Churched Ibiza: Evangelical Christianity and Club Culture". *Culture and Religion* 7(1): 77–92.

Laurie, Erynn Rowan 1995. "Following a Celtic Path". www.imbas.org/articles/following_a_celtic_path (accessed September 2010).

Leek, Sybil 1971. *The Complete Art of Witchcraft*. New York: Harper & Row.

Leersen, Joep 1996. "Celticism". In *Celticism, Vol. 8: Studia Imagologica*, Terrence Brown (ed.), 1–21. Amsterdam: Rodopi.

Letcher, Andy 2001. "The Role of the Bard in Contemporary Pagan Movements". Unpublished PhD thesis, King Alfred's College, Winchester.

Letcher, Andy 2003. "'Gaia Told Me to Do It': Resistance and the Idea of Nature Within Contemporary British Eco-Paganism". *EcoTheology* 8: 61–84.

Letcher, Andy 2004. "Raising the Dragon: Folklore and the Development of Contemporary British Eco-Paganism". *The Pomegranate* **6**(2): 175–98.

Letcher, Andy 2005. "'There's Bulldozers in the Fairy Garden': Re-Enchantment Narratives in British Eco-Paganism". In *Popular Spiritualities: The Politics of Contemporary Enchantment*, Lynne Hume & Kathleen Phillips (eds), 175–86. Aldershot: Ashgate.

Letcher, Andy 2006. *Shroom: A Cultural History of the Magic Mushroom*. London: Faber & Faber.

Letcher, Andy 2012. "What is a Bard?". In *The 2012 Mount Haemus Awards*. Lewes: The Order of Bards, Ovates and Druids.

Lipsitz, George 2001. *Time Passages: Collective Memory and American Popular Culture*. Minneapolis, MN: University of Minnesota Press.

Littmann, Mark, Fred Espenak & Ken Willcox 2008. *Totality: Eclipses of the Sun*. Oxford: Oxford University Press.

Llewellyn, Meic 2000. "Popular Music in the Welsh Language and the Affirmation of Youth Identities". *Popular Music* **19**(3): 319–39.

Lobo, K. 2007. "Trance Guru". *Mumbai Times*, 25 March, www.goagil.com/MMIR_2007_3_25_11.pdf (accessed November 2011).

Lovelock, J. 1995. *The Ages of Gaia: A Biography of Our Living Earth*. New York: Norton.

Luddy, Maria & Dympna McLoughlin 2002. "Women and Emigration from Ireland from the Seventeenth Century". In *The Field Day Anthology of Irish Writing: Irish Women's Writing and Traditions*, Angela Bourke (ed.), 567–608. New York: New York University Press.

Lynch, Gordon 2005. *Understanding Theology and Popular Culture*. Oxford: Blackwell.

Lynch, Gordon 2006. "The Role of Popular Music in the Construction of Alternative Spiritual Identities and Ideologies". *Journal for the Scientific Study of Religion* **45**(4): 481–8.

Lynch, G. & E. Badger 2006. "The Mainstream Post Rave Club Scene as a Secondary Institution: A British Perspective". *Culture and Religion* **7**(1): 27–40.

Lyng, Stephen 2005. "Edgework and the Risk-Taking Experience". In *Edgework: The Sociology of Risk-Taking*, Stephen Lyng (ed.), 3–16. London: Routledge.

MacKinnon, Niall 1994. *The British Folk Scene: Musical Performance and Social Identity*. Buckingham: Open University Press.

Maffesoli, M. 1996. *The Time of Tribes: The Decline of Individualism in Mass Society*. London: Sage.

Magliocco, Sabina 2004. *Witching Culture: Folklore and Neo-Paganism in America*. Philadelphia, PA: University of Pennsylvania Press.

Malbon, B. 1999. *Clubbing: Dancing, Ecstasy and Vitality*. London: Routledge.

Mallay, J. D. & W. Vaughn 1993. *Elvis: The Messiah?* Chicago, IL: TCB Publishing.

Mannhardt, Wilhelm 1875–77. *Wald und Feldkulte*, 2 vols. Berlin: Gebrüder Borntraeger.

Manwaring, Kevan 2006. *The Bardic Handbook: The Complete Manual for the Twenty-First Century Bard*. Glastonbury: Gothic Image Publications.

Mareš, Miroslav 2008. "Environmental Radicalism and Extremism in Postcommunist Europe". *Journal for the Study of Radicalism* **2**(1): 91–107.

Marini, Stephen 2003. *Sacred Song in America: Religion, Music and Public Culture*. Urbana, IL: University of Illinois Press.

Marrou, H. 1957. *Saint Augustine and His Influence Through the Ages*. New York: Longman.

Martin, D. 1999. "Power, Play and Party Politics: The Significance of Raving". *Journal of Popular Culture* **31**(4): 77–99.

Mazis, Glen A. 2002. *Earthbodies: Rediscovering Our Planetary Senses.* Albany, NY: SUNY Press.

McGlynn, Cindy 1998. "Weekend of the Living Dead". *Eye Weekly.*

McGuire, William & R. F. C. Hull (eds) 1977. *C. G. Jung Speaking: Interviews and Encounters.* Princeton, NJ: Princeton University Press.

McIver, Joel 2006. *Sabbath Bloody Sabbath.* London: Omnibus.

McKay, George 1996. *Senseless Acts of Beauty: Cultures of Resistance.* New York: Verso.

McKay, George (ed.) 1998. *DIY Culture: Party & Protest in Nineties Britain.* London: Verso.

McKay, George 2000. *Glastonbury: A Very English Affair.* London: Victor Gollancz.

McKenna, Terence 1991. *The Archaic Revival: Speculations on Psychedelic Mushrooms, the Amazon, Virtual Reality, UFOs, Evolution, Shamanism, the Rebirth of the Goddess, and the End of History.* San Francisco, CA: Harper.

McNeil, L. & G. McCain 1996. *Please Kill Me: The Uncensored Oral History of Punk.* New York: Grove Press.

McSherry, Lisa 2002. *The Virtual Pagan: Exploring Wicca and Paganism Through the Internet.* York Beach: Red Wheel/Weiser.

Mendoza, Zoila 2000. *Shaping Society Through Dance: Meztizo Ritual Performance in the Peruvian Andes.* Chicago, IL: University of Chicago Press.

Mercer, M. 1997. *Hex Files: The Goth Bible.* London: Overlook.

Mithen, S. 2005. *The Singing Neanderthals: The Origins of Music, Language, Mind and Body.* London: Weidenfeld & Nicolson.

Moberg, Marcus 2007. "The Transnational Christian Metal Scene Expressing Alternative Christian Identity through a Form of Popular Music." Paper presented at INTER: A European Cultural Studies Conference, Norrköping, Sweden, June 2007. www.ep.liu.se/ecp/025/045/ecp072545.pdf (accessed December 2009).

Moliné, K. 2006. "The Road to Salvation: Current 93". *The Wire* **269**: 28–33.

Moynihan, Michael & Didrik Søderlind 1998. *Lords of Chaos: The Bloody Rise of the Satanic Metal Underground.* Venice, CA: Feral House.

Murray, Judy C. 1996. "Voodoo is Nigger Spelled Backwards". *Green Egg* **29**(114): 23–5.

Murray, Margaret Alice [1921] 2007. *The Witch Cult in Western Europe.* Minneapolis, MN: Filiquarian Publishing.

Murray, Margaret Alice [1931] 2004. *The God of the Witches.* Sioux Falls, SD: NuVision.

Neal, C. 1987. *Tape Delay.* London: SAF Publishing.

Nettl, B. 2000. "An Ethnomusicologist Contemplates Musical Universals". In *The Origins of Music*, N. L. Wallin, B. Merker & S. Brown (eds), 463–72. Cambridge, MA: MIT Press.

NicDhàna, Kathryn Price (moderator) 2010. "Home Page, Amhran nam Bandia" blog, www.blogger.com/profile/10293181815707001620 (accessed October 2010).

NicDhàna, Kathryn Price, Erynn Rowan Laurie, C. Lee Vermeers & Kym Lambert ní Dhoireann 2006. *The CR FAQ: An Introduction to Celtic Reconstructionist Paganism.* Memphis, TN: River House Publishing.

NightMare, M. Macha 2001. "Bridey in Cyberspace". In *Irish Spirit*, Patricia Monaghan (ed.), 292–6. Dublin: Irish Wolfhound Press.

NightMare, M. Macha 2002. *Witchcraft and the Web: Weaving Pagan Traditions Online.* Toronto: ECW Press.

Niman, Michael I. 1997. *People of the Rainbow: A Nomadic Utopia.* Knoxville, TN: University of Tennessee Press.

Nixon, A. 2009. "Adaptation from the 'Edge of Chaos': The Mechanisms of Meaning Construction Within the Mainstream Electronic Dance Music (EDM) Scene in Sydney Australia". Unpublished Honours thesis, University of Western Sydney.

Nussbaum, Martha 1906. *The Fragility of Goodness.* Cambridge: Cambridge University Press.

Nussbaum, Martha 2001. *Upheavals of Thought: The Intelligence of Emotions.* Cambridge: Cambridge University Press.

Olaveson, T. 2004. "'Connectedness' and the Rave Experience: Rave as a New Religious Movement?". In *Rave Culture and Religion*, Graham St John (ed.), 85–106. London: Routledge.

O'Loughlin, Thomas 2002. "A Celtic Theology: Some Awkward Questions and Observations". In *Identifying the Celtic: CSANA Yearbook 2*, Joseph Falaky Nagy (ed.), 49–65. Dublin: Four Courts Press.

Oothoon 1975. "Evocation of the Goddess". *Green Egg* **8**(69): 24.

Orion 2003. "The Surrounding Moat of Stonehenge 1". *The Megalithic Portal*, www.megalithic.co.uk/article.php?sid=2146410949 (accessed November 2011).

Pan, David 2001. *Primitive Renaissance: Rethinking German Expressionism.* Lincoln, NE: University of Nebraska Press.

Paper, Jordan 2005. *The Deities are Many: A Polytheistic Theology.* Albany, NY: SUNY Press.

Parker Pearson, M., J. Pollard, C. Richards, J. Thomas, C. Tilley, K. Welham & U. Albarella 2006. "Materializing Stonehenge: The Stonehenge Riverside Project and New Discoveries". *Journal of Material Culture* 11: 227–61.

Partridge, Christopher H. 2004. *The Re-Enchantment of the West: Alternative Spiritualities, Sacralization, Popular Culture, and Occulture, Vol. 1.* London: T. & T. Clark International.

Partridge, Christopher H. 2005. *The Re-Enchantment of the West: Alternative Spiritualities, Sacralization, Popular Culture, and Occulture, Vol. 2.* London: T. & T. Clark International.

Partridge, Christopher H. 2006. "The Spiritual and the Revolutionary: Alternative Spirituality, British Free Festivals, and the Emergence of *Rave* Culture". *Culture and Religion* **7**(1): 41–60.

Partridge, C. 2008. "The Occultural Significance of *The Da Vinci Code*". In *Northern Lights: Film and Media Studies Yearbook Vol. 6*, S. Hjarvard (ed.), 107–26. Bristol: Intellect.

Partridge, C. 2009. "Religion and Popular Culture". In *Religions in the Modern World: Traditions and Transformations*, L. Woodhead, H. Kawanami & C. Partridge (eds), 489–521. London: Routledge.

Partridge, Christopher H. forthcoming. "Popular Music, Affective Space, and Meaning". In *Religion, Popular Culture and Everyday Life*, G. Lynch (ed.). London: Routledge.

Partridge, C. & E. Christanson (eds) 2009. *The Lure of the Dark Side: Satan and Western Demonology in Popular Culture.* London: Equinox.

Pattison, Robert 1987. *The Triumph of Vulgarity: Rock Music in the Mirror of Romanticism.* New York: Oxford University Press.

Pearson, J. 2007. *Wicca and the Christian Heritage: Ritual, Sex and Magic.* London: Routledge.

Pendderwen, Gwydion 1972. *Songs for the Old Religion.* Oakland, CA: Nemeton.

Pendragon, A. U. & C. J. Stone 2003. *The Trials of Arthur: The Life and Times of a Modern-day King.* London: Thorsons.

Peretti, Jacques 2008. "Enya Talks About Her New Album *And Winter Came*". *The Telegraph*, 12 October, www.telegraph.co.uk/culture/music/3562058/Enya-talks-about-her-new-album-And-Winter-Came.html (accessed November 2010).

Perry, Brendan 1984. "Dead-Can-Dance.Com". www.dead-can-dance.com/disco/dcd/dcd/deadcandance.htm (accessed January 2013).

Piggot, S. 1985. *William Stukeley: An Eighteenth-Century Antiquary.* New York: Thames & Hudson.

Pike, Sarah 2001. *Earthly Bodies, Magical Selves: Contemporary Pagans and the Search for Community.* Berkeley, CA: University of California Press.

Pike, Sarah 2004. *New Age and NeoPagan Religions in America.* New York: Columbia University Press.

Pitzl-Waters, Jason & Jacqueline Enstrom-Waters 2003. "A Darker Shade of Pagan". *newWitch* **4** (summer): 27–9.

Pizek, Jeff 2000. "Scandinavian Metal Attack." *Daily Herald* (January 28), Time Out section: 32.

Plumwood, Val 2002. *Environmental Culture: The Ecological Crises of Reason.* London: Routledge.

P-Orridge, Genesis 1988. *Esoterrorist: Selected Essays 1980–1988*. London: OV Press. www.scribd.com/doc/21064820/Genesis-P-Orridge-Esoterrorist (accessed August 2010).

P-Orridge, Genesis 1994. *Thee Psychick Bible: Thee Apocryphal Scriptures of Genesis P-Orridge and Thee Third MIND ov Psychic TV*, J. Louv (ed.). Port Townsend: Feral House.

P-Orridge, Genesis 2001. "Genesis P-Orridge". In *Modern Pagans: An Investigation of Contemporary Paganism*, V. Vale (ed.), 122–7. San Francisco: RE/Search.

P-Orridge, Genesis (ed.) 2002a. *Painful But Fabulous: The Lives and Art of Genesis P-Orridge*. New York: Soft Skull Shortwave.

P-Orridge, Genesis 2002b. "'Sigils' – An Alphabet of Desire". In *Painful But Fabulous: The Lives and Art of Genesis P-Orridge*, G. P-Orridge (ed.), 133–5. New York: Soft Skull Shortwave.

P-Orridge, Genesis 2003. "Eyes Wide Shut". *The Guardian*, 15 November.

P-Orridge, Genesis 2009a. "Thee Splinter Test". http://genesisporridgearchive.blogspot.com.au/2009/10/splinter-test-essay.html (accessed November 2010).

P-Orridge, Genesis 2009b. "The Process is the Product: The Processean Influence on Thee Temple Ov Psychick Youth". In *Love, Sex, Fear, Death: The Inside Story of the Process Church of the Final Judgment*, T. Wyllie, 173–84. Port Townsend, WA: Feral House.

Possamai, A. 2005. *In Search of New Age Spiritualities*. Farnham: Ashgate.

Possamai, A. 2007. *Religion and Popular Culture: A Hyper-Real Testament*. New York: Peter Lang.

Powell, A. 2007. "God's Own Medicine: Religion and Parareligion in UK Goth Culture". In *Goth: Undead Subculture*, L. Goodlad and M. Bibby (eds), 357–74. Durham, NC: Duke University Press.

Powell, E. 2005. "Death in June Interview: 2005 – Heathen Harvest". www.deathinjune.org/modules/mediawiki/index.php/Interview:2005-Heathen_Harvest (accessed February 2011).

Raphael, Melissa 1996. *Thealogy and Embodiment: The Post-Patriarchal Reconstruction of Female Sacrality*. Sheffield: Sheffield Academic Press.

Reece, G. L. 2006. *Elvis Religion: The Cult of the King*. London: I. B. Tauris.

Reich, C.A. 1971. *The Greening of America*. Harmondsworth: Allen Lane.

Reid-Bowen, Paul 2007. *Goddess as Nature: Towards a Philosophical Thealogy*. Burlington, VT: Ashgate.

Reynolds, S. 2006. *Rip It Up and Start Again: Postpunk 1978–1984*. Harmondsworth: Penguin.

Rich & Dawn (Solarworld) 1997. "An Evolving Ecology of Intuitive Signals". http://music.hyperreal.org/artists/metanet/meld2.html (accessed March 2011).

Richards, Julian 2007. *Stonehenge: The Story So Far*. Swindon: English Heritage.

Rietveld, H. C. 2004. "Ephemeral Spirit: Sacrificial Cyborg and Communal Soul". In *Rave Culture and Religion*, Graham St John (ed.), 46–62. London: Routledge.

Robinson, Mary 1995. "Cherishing the Diaspora". Address by Uachtarán na hÉireann Mary Robinson to the Houses of the Oireachtas, 2 February, www.oireachtas.ie/viewdoc.asp?fn=/documents/addresses/2Feb1995.htm (accessed September 2011).

Rogers, Nicholas 2002. *Halloween: From Pagan Ritual to Party Night*. New York: Oxford University Press.

Rom, Tom & Pascal Querner 2010. *Goa: 20 Years of Psychedelic Trance*. Solothurn: Nachtschatten.

Rose, Tricia 2008. *What We Talk About When We Talk About Hip Hop and Why It Matters*. New York: BasicCivitas.

Roszak, Theodore 1969. *The Making of a Counter Culture: Reflections on the Technocratic Society and its Youthful Opposition*. London: Faber & Faber.

Roszak, Theodore 1973. *Where the Wasteland Ends: Politics and Transcedence in Post-Industrial Society*. New York: Anchor Books.

Roszak, Theodore 1995. "Where Psyche Meets Gaia". In *Ecopsychology: Restoring the Earth, Healing the Mind*, T. Roszak, M. E. Gomes & A. D. Kanner (eds), 1–20. New York: Sierra Club Books.

Roth, Gabrielle 1997. *Sweat Your Prayers*. Dublin: Newleaf.

Rouget, G. 1985. *Music and Trance: A Theory of the Relations Between Music and Possession*. Chicago, IL: University of Chicago Press.

Rushkoff, Douglas 1994. *Cyberia: Life in the Trenches of Hyperspace*. San Francisco: Harper.

Sabini, Meredith 2002. *The Earth Has a Soul: C. G. Jung on Nature, Technology and Modern Life*. Berkeley, CA: North Atlantic Books.

Sage, Vanessa 2009. "Encountering the Wilderness, Encountering the Mist: Nature, Romanticism, and Contemporary Paganism". *Anthropology of Consciousness* **20**(1): 27–52.

Saïd, Edward 2000. "Invention, Memory and Place". *Critical Enquiry* **26**(2): 175–92.

Saldanha, A. 2004. "Goa Trance and Trance in Goa: Smooth Striations". In *Rave Culture and Religion*, Graham St John (ed.), 256–72. London: Routledge.

Salomonsen, Jone 2002. *Enchanted Feminism*. New York: Routledge.

Saltanaviciute, Jurgita 2002. "Death Metal Music: A Socio-Cultural Perspective". Paper presented at the American Popular Culture Association, Albuquerque, NM.

Sams, Greg 2009. *Sun of gOd: Discover the Self-Organizing Consciousness that Underlies Everything*. Newburyport, MA: Weiser Books.

Sandford, C. 1998. *Bowie: Loving the Alien*. New York: Da Capo Press.

Sanneh, Kelefa 2007. "On the Road to Spread the Word of Good, Old-Fashioned Evil". *The New York Times*, November 8, www.nytimes.com/2007/11/08/arts/music/08ens.html (accessed January 2010).

Scarre, C. & G. Lawson (eds) 2006. *Archaeoacoustics*. Cambridge: McDonald Institute for Archaeological Research.

Seamon, David 1991. "Phenomenology and Vernacular Lifeworlds". *The Trumpeter: Journal of Ecosophy* **8**(4): 201–6.

Sharp, Cecil 1907. *English Folk Song: Some Conclusions*. London: Simkin & Co.

Shaw, Sylvie & Andrew Francis (eds) 2008. *Deep Blue: Critical Reflections on Nature, Religion and Water*. London: Equinox.

Sheldrake, Rupert 2009. *Morphic Resonance: The Nature of Formative Causation*. Rochester, VT: Park Street Press.

Shnirelman, Victor A. 2002. "'Christians! Go Home': A Revival of Neo-Paganism between the Baltic Sea and Transcaucasia (An Overview)". *Journal of Contemporary Religion* **17**(2): 197–211.

Slobin, Mark 2008. *Global Soundtracks: Worlds of Film Music*. Middletown, CT: Wesleyan University Press.

Small, Christopher. 1998. *Musicking: The Meanings of Performing and Listening*. Hanover, NH: Wesleyan University Press.

Smith, Anthony D. 1990. "Towards a Global Culture?". *Theory, Culture and Society* **7**: 171–91.

Spare, A. O. 2001. *Ethos: The Magical Writings of Austin Osman Spare*. Thame: I-H-O Books.

Sprott, S. 2010. "Cosy Fanni Tutti: Interview", *Vice* **8**(11): 66–70.

Stallybrass, P. & A. White 1986. *The Politics and Poetics of Transgression*. London: Methuen.

Starhawk 1997. *Dreaming the Dark: Magic, Sex and Politics*, 15th anniversary edition. Boston, MA: Beacon Press.

Starhawk 1999. *The Spiral Dance: A Rebirth of the Ancient Religion of the Great Goddess*, 20th anniversary edition. New York: HarperCollins.

Stefanovic, Ingrid Leman 1991. "Evolving Sustainability: A Re-Thinking of Ontological Foundations". *The Trumpeter: Journal of Ecosophy* **8**(4): 194–200.

Stein, Murry 1995. *Jung on Evil*. Princeton, NJ: Princeton University Press.

St John, Graham 2004a. "The Difference Engine: Liberation and the Rave Imaginary". In *Rave Culture and Religion*, Graham St John (ed.), 19–45. London: Routledge.

St John, Graham 2004b. "Techno Millennium: Dance, Ecology and Future Primitives". In *Rave Culture and Religion*, Graham St John (ed.), 213–35. London: Routledge.

St John, Graham (ed.) 2004c. *Rave Culture and Religion*. London: Routledge.

St John, Graham 2006. "Electronic Dance Music Culture and Religion: An Overview". *Culture and Religion* **7**(1): 1–24.

St John, Graham 2009a. "Neotrance and the Psychedelic Festival". *Dancecult* **1**(1): 35–64.

St John, Graham 2009b. *Technomad: Global Raving Countercultures*. London: Equinox.

St John, Graham 2010a. "Liminal Culture and Global Movement: The Transitional World of Psytrance". In *The Local Scenes and Global Culture of Psytrance*, Graham St John (ed.), 220–46. New York: Routledge.

St John, Graham (ed.) 2010b. *The Local Scenes and Global Culture of Psytrance*. New York: Routledge.

St John, Graham 2011a. "The 2012 Movement, Visionary Arts and Psytrance Culture". In *2012: Decoding the Countercultural Apocalypse*, Joseph Gelfer (ed.), 123–43. London: Equinox.

St John, Graham 2011b. "DJ Goa Gil: Kalifornian Exile, Dark Yogi and Dreaded Anomaly". *Dancecult: Journal of Electronic Dance Music Culture* **3**(1): 97–128.

St John, Graham 2012. *Global Tribe: Technology, Spirituality and Psytrance*. London: Equinox.

St John, Graham forthcoming. "Aliens Are Us: Space Travel, Neo-Mysticism and Cosmic Trance". *Journal of Religion and Popular Culture* (under review).

St John, Graham & Chiara Baldini 2012. "Dancing at the Crossroads of Consciousness: Techno-Mysticism, Visionary Arts and Portugal's Boom Festival". In *Handbook of New Religions and Cultural Production*, Carole M. Cusack & Alex Norman (eds), 521–52. Leiden: Brill.

Stokes, Martin (ed.) 1994. *Ethnicity, Identity and Music: The Musical Construction of Place*. Oxford: Berg.

Stowe, David W. 2004. *How Sweet the Sound: Music in the Spiritual Lives of Americans*. Cambridge, MA: Harvard University Press.

Strmiska, Michael F. 2005. *Modern Paganism In World Cultures: Comparative Perspectives*, Santa Barbara, CA: ABC-CLIO.

Stubbs, D. 2007. "Clearing the Wreckage: Throbbing Gristle". *The Wire* **281**: 30–37.

Stump, P. 1997. *The Music's All That Matters: A History of Progressive Rock*. London: Quartet Books.

Sutcliffe, Steven 2000. "'Wandering Stars': Seekers and Gurus in the Modern World". In *Beyond New Age: Exploring Alternative Spirituality*, Steven Sutcliffe & Marion Bowman (eds), 220–36. Edinburgh: Edinburgh University Press.

Sutcliffe Steven 2007. "The Origins of 'New Age' Religion Between the Two World Wars". In *Handbook of New Age*, Daren Kemp & James R. Lewis (eds), 51–76. Leiden: Brill.

Sylvan, R. 2005. *Trance Formation: The Spiritual and Religious Dimensions of Global Rave Culture*. New York: Routledge.

Takahashi, M. 2004. "The 'Natural High': Altered States, Flashbacks and Neural Tuning at Raves". In *Rave Culture and Religion*, Graham St John (ed.), 145–64. New York: Routledge.

Tanner, Marcus 2004. *The Last of the Celts*. London: Yale University Press.

Taylor, Bron 2000. "Bioregionalism: An Ethics of Loyalty to Place". *Landscape Journal* **19**: 50–72.

Taylor, Bron 2001a. "Earth and Nature-Based Spirituality (Part I): From Earth First! And Bioregionalism to Scientific Paganism and the New Age". *Religion* **31**: 225–45.

Taylor, Bron 2001b. "Earth and Nature-Based Spirituality (Part II): From Deep Ecology to Radical Environmentalism". *Religion* **31**: 175–93.

Taylor, Bron 2010. *Dark Green Religion: Nature, Spirituality, and the Planetary Future*. Berkeley, CA: University of California Press.

Terry, Nick 1998. "Letters reply page". *Terrorizer* **58** (September): 66.

Thomas, Helen 2003. *The Body, Dance, and Cultural Theory*. London: Palgrave Macmillan.

Thomas, K. 1973. *Religion and the Decline of Magic: Studies in Popular Beliefs in Sixteenth and Seventeenth Century England*. Harmondsworth: Penguin.

Thompson, T. R. 2010. "Stonehenge as a Landing Pad". http://ufo-news-club.ning.com/forum/topics/stonehenge-as-a-landing-pad?xg_source=activity (accessed April 2012).

Till, R. 2006. "The Nine O'Clock Service: Mixing Club Culture and Postmodern Christianity". *Culture and Religion* 7(1): 93–110.

Till, R. 2009. "Possession Trance Ritual in Electronic Dance Music Culture: A Popular Ritual Technology for Reenchantment, Addressing the Crisis of the Homeless Self, and Reinserting the Individual into the Community". In *Exploring Religion and the Sacred in a Media Age*, Chris Deacy (ed.), 169–89. Aldershot: Ashgate.

Till, R. 2010a. *Pop Cult: Religion and Popular Music*. London: Continuum.

Till R. 2010b. "Songs of the Stones: The Acoustics of Stonehenge". In *BAR 504 2009: The Sounds of Stonehenge*, Stephen Banfield (ed.). CHOMBEC Working Papers No. 1. Oxford: Archaeopress.

Till, R. 2011. "Songs of the Stones: An Investigation into the Acoustic Culture of Stonehenge". *Journal@IASPM, Journal of the International Association for the Study of Popular Music* 1(2). www.iaspmjournal.net (accessed November 2011).

Toffoletti, K. 2007. *Cyborgs and Barbie Dolls: Feminism, Popular Culture and the Posthuman Body*. London: I. B. Tauris.

Tolvanen, Hannu 2007. "The Quiet Past and the Loud Present: The Kalevala and Heavy Metal". *Volume! La Revue des musiques populaires* 5(2): 75–89.

Tomasi, L. (ed.) 1999. *Alternative Religions Among European Youth*. Aldershot: Ashgate.

TOPY 1991. "TOPY London Interviewed by *AntiClockwise Magazine* 1991", www.uncarved.org/23texts/clockwise.html (accessed 31 August 2003).

TOPY 2010. "Thee Grey Book". www.kondole.com/theegreybook/greycover.htm (accessed October 2010).

Tramacchi, Des 2000 "Field Tripping: Psychedelic Communitas and Ritual in the Australian Bush". *Journal of Contemporary Religion* 15: 201–13.

Tramacchi, Des 2004. "Ethneogenic Dance Ecstasis: Cross Cultural Contexts". In *Rave Culture and Religion*, Graham St John (ed.), 125–44. London: Routledge.

Trull, D. 1998. "Druids Go Home to Stonehenge". http://dagmar.lunarpages.com/~parasc2/articles/slips/fs27_2.htm (accessed April 2012).

Tuan, Yi-Fu 1977. *Space and Place: The Perspective of Experience*. Minneapolis, MN: University of Minnesota Press.

Turner, Bryan S. 2008. Religious Speech: The Ineffable Nature of Religious Communication in the Information Age. *Theory Culture Society*. 25: 219

Turner, Edith 1992. *Experiencing Ritual: A New Interpretation of African Healing*. Philadelphia, PA: University of Pennsylvania Press.

Turner, Victor 1969. *The Ritual Process: Structure and Anti-structure*. Chicago, IL: Aldine.

Turner, Victor 1973. "The Center Out There: Pilgrim's Goal". *History of Religions* 12(1): 191–230.

Twilightheart & OhLi 2007. "Interview:Týr". *Sheol Magazine* (March 31). www.sheol-magazine.com/index2.htm (accessed January 2010).

Tybjerg, Tove 2005. "Wilhelm Mannhardt – A Pioneer in the Study of Rituals". In *Folklore: Critical Concepts in Literary and Cultural Studies*, volume 2, Alan Dundes (ed.), 111–20. London: Routledge.

Vale, V. (ed.) 2007. *RE/Search 4/5: William S. Burroughs, Brion Gysin and Throbbing Gristle*. San Francisco, CA: RE/Search Publications.

Vallely, Fintan (ed.) 1999. *The Companion to Irish Traditional Music*. New York: New York University Press.

Verter, B. 2003. "Spiritual Capital: Theorizing Religion with Bourdieu against Bourdieu". *Sociological Theory* 21(2): 150–74.

Vincett, Giselle 2008. *Feminism and Religion: A Study of Christian Feminists and Goddess Feminists in the UK*. Lancaster: Lancaster University.

von Sydow, C. W. 1934. "The Mannhardtian Theories About the Last Sheaf and the Fertility Demons from a Modern Critical Point of View". *Folklore* 45(4): 291–309.

Wallach, Jeremy 2004. "'Goodbye My Blind Majesty': Music, Language, and Politics in the Indonesian Underground". In *Global Pop, Local Language*, Harris M. Berger & Michael Thomas Carroll (eds), 53–86. Jackson, MS: University Press of Mississippi.

Watson, A. & D. Keating 1999. "Architecture and Sound: An Acoustic Analysis of Megalithic Monuments in Prehistoric Britain". *Antiquity* **73**: 325–6.

Watson, D. 1999. "Beyond Evil: Genesis P-Orridge". *The Wire* **182**: 30–35.

Watson, George 1996. "Celticism and the Annulment of History". In *Celticism, Vol. 8: Studia Imagologica*, Terrence Brown (ed.), 207–21. Amsterdam: Rodopi.

Webster, C. 1976. "Communes: A Thematic Typology". In *Resistance Through Rituals: Youth Subcultures in Post-War Britain*, S. Hall & T. Jefferson (eds), 127–34. London: Hutchinson.

Weil, Andrew 1980. *Marriage of the Sun and Moon: A Quest for Unity in Consciousness*. Boston, MA: Houghton Mifflin.

Weinstein, Deena 1991. *Heavy Metal: A Cultural Sociology*. New York: Macmillan.

Weschcke, Carl 1974. "Witchcraft in Service to Man, Planet and God/dess". *Gnostica: News of the Aquarian Frontier* **3**(11): 1, 4.

Weschcke, Carl 2009. "Carl Llewellyn Weschcke: Bringing Magick to the Masses". *PanGaia* **50** (Spring): 14–19.

Weston, Donna 2010. "Basque Pagan Metal: View to a Primordial Past". *European Journal of Cultural Studies* **14**(1): 103–22.

Weston, Jessie L. 1973. *Where The Wasteland Ends: Politics and Transcendence in Post-Industrial Society*. New York: Anchor Books.

Weston, Jessie L. [1919] 1993. *From Ritual to Romance*. Princeton, NJ: Princeton University Press.

Wheatley, D. [1934] 2007. *The Devil Rides Out*. London: Wordsworth Editions.

Whitman, Walt 1904. *Leaves of Grass*, rev. edn. Boston, MA: Small, Maynard & Company.

Whitman, Walt 1921. *Leaves of Grass*. New York: Modern Library.

Wiederhorn, Jon 2009. "Stairway to Heathen". *Revolver*, April: 60–61.

Wilber, K. 2000. "The Atman-Project". In *Holistic Revolution: The Essential New Age Reader*, W. Bloom (ed.). Harmondsworth: Allen Lane.

Will, U. & E. Berg 2007. "Brain Wave Synchronization and Entrainment to Periodic Acoustic Stimuli". *Neuroscience Letters* **424**: 55–60.

Williams, Raymond 1985. *Keywords: A Vocabulary of Culture and Society*. New York: Oxford University Press.

Willis, P. 1978. *Profane Culture*. London: Routledge & Kegan Paul.

Wilson, Julie 2002. "As It Is". In *Painful but Fabulous: The Lives and Art of Genesis P-Orridge*, G. P-Orridge (ed.), 51–110. New York: Soft Skull Shortwave.

Wilson, William A. 2005. "Herder, Folklore and Romantic Nationalism". In *Folklore: Critical Concepts in Literary and Cultural Studies, Volume 2*, Alan Dundes (ed.), 4–21. London: Routledge.

Wood, Peter. 2004. "John Barleycorn: The Evolution of a Folk-Song Family". *Folk Music Journal* **8**(4): 438–55.

Worthington, Andy 2004. *Stonehenge: Celebration and Subversion*. Borehamwood: Alternative Publications.

Worthington, Andy 2005. *The Battle of the Beanfield*. Eyemouth: Enabler Publications.

Wozencroft, J. & P. Devereux 2012. *The Landscape and Perception Project*. www.landscape-perception.com (accessed December 2012).

Wyatt, Simon 2008. "The Classification of the Clay Drums of the Southern Trichterbecher Culture (TRB)". www.jungsteinsite.unikiel.de/2000_wyatt/2008_Wyatt_high.pdf (accessed July 2011).

Wyllie, T. 2009. *Love, Sex, Fear, Death: The Inside Story of the Process Church of the Final Judgment*, A. Parfray (ed.). Port Townsend, WA: Feral House.

Yates, F. 1983. *The Occult Philosophy in the Elizabethan Age*. London: Ark.

York, Michael 1995. *The Emerging Network: Sociology of the New Age and Neo-Pagan Movement*. Lanham, MD: Rowman & Littlefield.

York, Michael 2000. "Defining Paganism". *Proteus*, www.draknet.com/proteus/Pagndef.htm (accessed January 2011).

York, Michael 2003. *Pagan Theology: Paganism as a World Religion*. New York: New York University Press.

York, Michael 2005. "Sun Worship". In *The Encyclopedia of Religion and Nature*, 1606–7. London: Thoemmes Continuum.

Young, A. 1997. *Woke Me Up This Morning: Black Gospel Singers and the Gospel Life*. Jackson, MS: University of Mississippi Press.

Young, R. 2010. *Electric Eden: Unearthing Britain's Visionary Music*. London: Faber & Faber.

Zebub, Bill 2009. *Pagan Metal: A Documentary*. www.paganroots.net/forum/index.php/topic,498.0.html (accessed August 2010).

DISCOGRAPHY AND FILMOGRAPHY

ALBUMS

Albion Country Band 1976. *Battle for the Field*. UK: Island Records.

Amon Amarth 2006. *With Oden On Our Side*. Los Angeles, CA: Metal Blade.

Arthen, Inanna 1993. *"Ocean Mother" in The Wheel of the Year: A Magical Journey Through the Seasons*. As performed by MotherTongue, the Ritual Chorus of the Earthspirit Community. Chester, MA: Abyss Distribution.

Bathory 1990. *Hammerheart*. Berlin: Noise.

The Beatles 1966. *Revolver*. UK: Parlophone.

The Beatles 1967. *Sergeant Pepper's Lonely Hearts Club Band*. UK: Parlophone.

The Beatles 1968. *The White Album*. UK: Apple.

The Best of Pagan Song. 2004. Bodega Bay, CA: Serpentine Music.

Björk 2001. *Vespertine*. London: One Little Indian.

Black Sabbath 1970. *Black Sabbath*. UK: Vertigo.

Black Sabbath 1970. *Paranoid*. UK: Vertigo.

Black Sabbath 1983. *Born Again*. UK: Vertigo.

Bonewits, Isaac and Friends 1988 (cassette), 2003 (CD). *Be Pagan Once Again!* Cleveland, OH: Association for Consciousness Exploration.

Brighteyes 2007. *Cassadaga*. Omaha, NE: Saddle Creek.

Cold Spring 2007. *John Barleycorn Reborn: Dark Britannica*. Northants, UK: Cold Spring.

Cold Spring 2010b. *We Bring You a King with a Head of Gold: Dark Britannica II*. Northants, UK: Cold Spring.

Cope, Julian 1992. *Jehovahkill*. UK: Island Records.

Cope, Julian & Donald Ross Skinner 1992. *Rite*. UK: K.A.K.

Damh the Bard 2006. *The Spirit of Albion*. Available from www.paganmusic.co.uk (accessed December 2012).

Dr Strangely Strange 1969. *Kip of the Serenes*. UK: Island Records.

The Dreamside 2002. *Faery Child*. USA: Dancing Ferret Discs.

Electric Universe 1994. *Solar Energy*. Hamburg: Spirit Zone (EP).

Enslaved 1994. *Frost*. Beaurainville, France: Osmose Productions.

Enya 2000. *A Day Without Rain*, New York: Reprise/WEA

Filteria 2009. *Daze Of Our Lives*. Ghent: Suntrip Records.

Gass, Robert & On Wings of Song 1993. *Ancient Mother*. Boulder, CO: Spring Hill Music.

Genesis 1971. *Nursery Cryme*. UK: Chrysalis.

Graveland 1995. *Thousand Swords*. Vienna: Lethal Records.

Havens, Richie 1970. *Stonehenge*. USA: Stormy Forest.

Hawkwind 1976. *Astounding Sounds, Amazing Music*. London: Atomhenge.

Hawkwind 1983. *Zones*. UK: Flicknife Records.

Hell, Richard and the Voidoids 1977. *Blank Generation*. USA: Sire Records.

Incredible String Band 1968. *The Hangman's Beautiful Daughter*. USA: Elektra.

Inkubus Sukkubus 1993. *Belladonna and Aconite*. UK: Nightbreed Recordings.

Jethro Tull 1977. *Songs from the Wood*. UK: Chrysalis.

Jethro Tull 1978. *Heavy Horses*. UK: Island Records.

Jethro Tull 1979. *Stormwatch*. UK: Island Records.

Kantner, Paul & Grace Slick 1971. *Sunfighter*. USA: Grunt Records.

KIVA 1994. *Finding the Balance Within*. USA: KIVA.

Kraus, Sharron 2006. *Right Wantonly a-Mumming: A Collection of Seasonal Songs and Cele-brations by Sharron Kraus*. London: Bo'Weavil Recordings.

Led Zeppelin 1971. *Led Zeppelin III*. New York: Atlantic.

Led Zeppelin 1973. *Houses of the Holy*. New York: Atlantic.

Libana, 'Yemayá 2000. *Night Passage: Invocations for the Journey*. Glasgow: Spinning Records.

Marilyn Manson 1998. *Mechanical Animals*. Santa Monica, CA: Interscope.

McKennitt, Loreena 1989. *Parallel Dreams*. Stratford, Ontario: Quinlan Road.

Murphy, Charlie 1981. *Catch the Fire*. USA: Good Fairy Productions.

Obtest 1997. *Tukstantmetis* (Millenium). Lithuania: V.M.V.

Olson, Craig 1999. *Beyond the Cedar Moon*. Washington, DC: Mud Bay Records.

Pink Floyd 1969. *Ummagumma*. London: Harvest, EMI.

Pink Floyd 1973. *The Dark Side of the Moon*. London: Harvest, EMI.

P-Orridge, Genesis & Astrid Monroe 2004. *When I Was Young*. Groveland, MA: Important Records.

P-Orridge, Genesis & Splinter Test 1996a. *Thee Fractured Garden*. USA: Invisible.

P-Orridge, Genesis & Splinter Test 1996b. *Spatial Memory*. Berlin: Dossier.

Psychic TV 1982a. *Force the Hand of Chance*. UK: WEA, Some Bizarre.

Psychic TV 1982b. *First Transmission*. Self-released.

Psychic TV 1996a. *Cold Blue Torch*. Los Angeles, CA: Cleopatra.

Psychic TV 1996b. *Trip Reset*. Los Angeles, CA: Cleopatra.

Psychic TV 1996c. *Spatial Memory*. Los Angeles, CA: Cleopatra.

Richards, Monica 2006. *InfraWarrior*. Hesse, Germany: Alice In …

Sanders, Alex 1970. *A Witch is Born*. London: A&M Records.

Sequoia Records 2008. *The Celtic Lounge II*, www.sequoiarecords.com/x921cd/The+Celtic+Lounge+II.html (accessed November 2010).

Shakta 1997. *Silicon Trip*. London: Dragonfly Records.

Shpongle 1998. *Are You Shpongled?* London: Twisted Records.

Skyclad 1991. *The Wayward Songs of Mother Earth*. Berlin: Noise.

Skyforger 1998. *Kauja Pie Saules*. Middle Island, NY: Paragon Records.

Skyforger 2005. *Thunderforge (Perkonkalve)*. Berlin: Folter Records.

Space Goats 1993. *Inamorata and Other Tales*. Self-released cassette, available from www.pondlifestudios.com.

Spiral Dance 2010. www.spiraldance.com.au/?Song_Lyrics#songA8.

Ten Years After 1969. *Stonedhenge*. London: Deram.

Thee Majesty 2004. *Thee Fractured Garden*. UK: Temple Records/Voiceprint.

Throbbing Gristle 1980. *Heathen Earth*. London: Industrial Records.

Throbbing Gristle 1984. *In the Shadow of the Sun*. London, Illuminate Records.

Throbbing Gristle 1979. *20 Jazz Funk Greats*. London, Industrial Records.

Throbbing Gristle 1991a. *Music From The Death Factory*. London: The Grey Area.

Throbbing Gristle 1991b. *The Second Annual Report*. London: The Grey Area.

Total Eclipse 1996a. *Violent Relaxation*. London: Blue Room.

Traffic 1970. *John Barleycorn Must Die*. UK: Island Records.

Thistletown 2007. *Rosemarie*. London: Big Bertha.

Waterson: Carthy 2006. *Holy Heathens and the Old Green Man*. Uppingham: Topic Records.

Various Artists 1993. *Project II Trance*. London: Dragonfly Records.

Various Artists 1994. *Order Odonata Vol. 1*. London: Dragonfly Records.

Various Artists 1995. *Return to the Source: Deep Trance and Ritual Beats*. London: RTTS.

Various Artists 1996. *Trust in Trance*. 1996. London: TIP.

Various Artists n.d. *Black Sun – Eclipse in Japan*. Japan: Rockdenashi Productionz.

Various Artists 1998a. *Eclipse – A Journey Of Permanence & Impermanence*. London: Twisted Records.

Various Artists 1998b. *Strong Sun Moon*. Berlin: Equinox.

Various Artists 1998c. *Trip to Cyberspace (Vol. 2)*. Hameln: Clubware.

Various Artists 2002. *First Impression*. Colorado Sprigs, CO: A.P. Records.

Various Artists 2004. *Gather in the Mushrooms: The British Acid Folk Underground 1968–1974*. UK: Sanctuary Records.

Various Artists 2006a. *Early Morning Hush: Notes From the UK Folk Underground 1969–1976*. UK: Sanctuary Records.

Various Artists 2006b. *Folk Off: New Folk and Psychedelia From the British Isles and North America – Compiled by Rob da Bank*. London: Sunday Best.

Various Artists 2006c. *Fuzzy-Felt Folk. A Small Collection of Rare, Delightful Folk Oddities for Strange Adults and Maybe Their Children Too*. UK: Trunk Records.

Various Artists 2006d. *Strange Folk*. London: Albion Records.

Various Artists 2010. *Lucas Presents Tales of Heads*. London: TIP Records.

The Waterboys 1984. *A Pagan Place*. UK: Island Records/Virgin Records.

The Watersons 1965. *Frost and Fire: A Calendar of Ritual and Magical Songs*. Uppingham: Topic Records.

The Wicker Man 2002. *The Wicker Man: The Original Soundtrack Album*. London: Silva Screen Records.

Wood, Chris 2005. *The Lark Descending*. Lindewerra, Germany: Ruf Records.

Wood, Chris 2007. *Trespasser*. Lindewerra, Germany: Ruf Records.

SONGS

Barrett, Ruth & Cyntia Smith 1994. "Ocean Queen". Korschenbroich, Germany: Aeolus Music.

Bathory 1990. "Shores in Flames" & "One Rode to Asa Bay". *Hammerheart*. Berlin, Noise.

The Beatles 1966. "Tomorrow Never Knows". UK: Parlophone.

The Beatles 1968. "Mother Nature's Son". UK: Apple.

The Beatles 1968. "Blackbird". UK: Apple.

Black Sabbath 1970. "Black Sabbath". UK: Vertigo.

Black Sabbath 1970. "NIB". UK: Vertigo.

Black Sabbath 1970. "The Wizard". UK: Vertigo.

Black Sabbath 1970. "Sleeping Village". UK: Vertigo.

Black Sabbath 1970. "Planet Caravan". UK: Vertigo.

Brighteyes 2007. "I Must Belong Somewhere". Omaha, NE: Saddle Creek.

Budapest, Zsuzanna 1994. "We All Come from the Goddess". *Chants: Ritual Music from Reclaiming and Friends*. Bodega Bay, CA: Serpentine Music.

Canned Heat 1968. "Going Up the Country". USA; Liberty.

Desert Wind 1992. "Return to the Goddess". *Return to the Goddess*. Self-published.

Faithless 2010. "God is a DJ Live". www.youtube.com/watch?v=MiczMZmyOnQ (accessed December 2012).

Fox, Selena 1977. "Song of the Witch", written by Jim Alan & Selena Fox. *Circle Magick Songs.* Mt Horeb, WI: Circle Sanctuary.
Gabriel, Peter 1982. "Rhythm of the Heat". UK: Charisma.
Gabriel, Peter 1977. "Solsbury Hill". UK: Charisma.
Gass, Robert 1993. "Ancient Mother". Boulder, CO: Spring Hill Music.
Gass, Robert 1993. "The Circle is Cast". Boulder, CO: Spring Hill Music.
Genesis 1971. "Harlequin". UK: Chrysalis.
Goanna 1982. "Solid Rock". Australia: WEA.
Icehouse 1989. "Great Southern Land". UK: Chrysalis.
Hugin the Bard nd. "Love on the Astral Plane". UK: Raven's Eye.
Hugin the Bard nd. "They Call us Witches". UK: Raven's Eye.
Jethro Tull 1977. "Jack-in-the-Green". UK: Chrysalis.
Kantner, Paul & Grace Slick 1971. "Earth Mother". USA: Grunt Records.
KIVA 1994. "Star of the Sea". USA: KIVA.
Led Zeppelin 1970. "The Immigrant Song". USA: Atlantic.
Led Zeppelin 1970. "Bron-Yr-Stomp". USA: Atlantic.
Led Zeppelin 1970. "Gallows Pole". USA: Atlantic.
Led Zeppelin 1971. "The Battle of Evermore". USA: Atlantic.
Led Zeppelin 1973. "No Quarter". USA: Atlantic.
McKennitt, Loreena 1989. "Samhain Night". Stratford, Ontario: Quinlan Road.
Mitchell, Joni 1969. "Woodstock". USA: MCA.
Murphy, Charlie 1968. "Burning Times", "Mother Ocean" and "Under Capricorn". *Catch the Fire.* USA: Good Fairy Productions.
Olson, Craig 1999. "Ave Stella Maris". *Beyond The Cedar Moon.* Lummi Island, WA: Mud Bay Records.
Olson, Craig & Joanna Powell Colbert 2011. "Ave Stella Maris" (lyrics). http://craigolsonband.bandcamp.com/track/ave-stella-maris (accessed January 2011).
Pink Floyd 1969. "Greatchester Meadows". UK: Harvest, EMI.
Pink Floyd 1973. "Eclipse". UK: Harvest, EMI.
Skyclad 1991. "Pagan Man". Berlin: Noise.
Spiral Dance 1996. "Woman of the Earth". Australia: Greenman Music.
Spiral Dance 2002. "Boys of Bedlam". Australia: Greenman Music.
Spiral Dance 2002. "The Rape of Maude Bowen". Australia: Greenman Music.
Throbbing Gristle 1978. "United/Zyklon B Zombie". London: Industrial Records.
Traffic 1970. "John Barleycorn Must Die". UK: Island Records.
XTC 1999. "Greenman". UK: Cooking Vinyl.

FILMS AND DVDS

Angel Heart. 1987. Alan Parker (dir.). USA: TriStar Pictures.
Classic Albums: Paranoid. 2010. London: Eagle Rock Entertainment.
Contact. 1997. Robert Zemeckis (dir.). USA: Warner Brothers.
The Da Vinci Code. 2006. Ron Howard (dir.). USA: Colombia Pictures.
The Devil Rides Out. 1968. Terence Fisher (dir.). UK: EMI Films.
Easy Rider. 1969. Dennis Hopper (dir.). USA: Columbia Pictures.
Hawkwind – The Solstice at Stonehenge. 2004. UK: Hawkwind.
Help! 1965. R. Lester (dir.). UK: United Artists.
In the Shadow of the Sun. 1980. Derek Jarman (dir.). UK: Dark Pictures.
The Matrix. 1999. Andy Wachowski & Lana Wachowski (dirs). USA: Warner Brothers.

The Ninth Gate. 1999. Roman Polanski (dir.). France: Bac Films; Spain: Araba Films; USA: Artisan Entertainment.

The Omen. 1976. Richard Donner (dir.). USA: 20th Century Fox.

The Outback Eclipse Story. 2003. NZ: Lastlight Films.

Paranormal Activity. 2007. Oren Peli (dir.). USA: Paramount Pictures.

Rosemary's Baby. 1968. Roman Polanski (dir.). USA, Paramount Pictures.

The Sixth Sense. 1999. M. Night Shyamalan (dir.). USA: Hollywood Pictures.

The Song Remains the Same. 1976. Peter Clifton & Joe Massot (dirs). USA: Warner Bros.

This is Spinal Tap. 1984. R. Reiner (dir.). Spinal Tap Productions. USA: Embassy Pictures.

The Wicker Man. 1973. Robin Hardy (dir.). UK: British Lion Films.

Woodstock: The Movie. 1970. Michael Wadleigh (dir.). USA: Warner Brothers.

INDEX

236

Printed in Great Britain
by Amazon

77366761R00147